Employment Relations

A.J. Geare & F.J. Edgar

OTAGO

Published by Otago University Press
PO Box 56/Level 1, 398 Cumberland Street
Dunedin, New Zealand
Fax: 64 3 479 8385, Email: university.press@.otago.ac.nz
www.otago.ac.nz/press
First published in this edition in 2007

ISBN 978 1 877372 43 8

Cover image: *Rolling In* by Wallace Crossman, 1984 (private collection).
Crossman is a New Zealand abstract artist.

Printed in New Zealand by Astra Print Ltd, Wellington.

Contents

List of Figures

List of Tables

ACKNOWLEDGEMENTS

Our sincere thanks to Lee-Mor Reichman, Kelly Honey and Brian Casey for their research assistance, editing, proof-reading and word processing. Any remaining errors are unfortunately our fault.

A.J. Geare and F.J. Edgar

Common Abbreviations

AFL–CIO	American Federation of Labour – Congress of Industrial Organisations (US)
CEA	Collective Employment Contract
CSU	Combined State Unions
CTU	Council of Trade Unions
EC Act	Employment Contracts Act
EE Act	Employment Equity Act
EEO	Equal Employment Opportunity
EI	Employee Involvement
ESOPs	Employee Stock Ownership Plans
FOA	Final Offer Arbitration
FOL	Federation of Labour
GWO	General Wage Order
HRM	Human Resource Management
ICA Act	Industrial Conciliation and Arbitration Act
IEA	Industrial Employment Agreement
IEC	Individual Employment Contract
ILO	International Labour Organisation
IR Act	Industrial Relations Act
LR Act	Labour Relations Act
M-H Theory	Motivation-Hygiene Theory
NIR	New Industrial Relations
NZBR	New Zealand Business Roundtable
NZEF	New Zealand Employers' Federation
PSA	Public Service Association
QC	Quality Circles
QWL	Quality of Work Life
SOE Act	State Owned Enterprises Act
SS Act	State Services Act, State Sector Act
SSC	State Services Commission
SSCE Act	State Services Conditions of Employment Act
SSRCE Act	State Services Remuneration and Conditions of Employment Act
TQM	Total Quality Management
UFL	United Federation of Labour

Foreword

It is an honour to be asked to write this foreword to Professor Alan Geare and Dr Fiona Edgar's work. I still have my second (revised) edition of Alan Geare's work purchased (in 1988 for $72 plus GST at ten per cent) as a barrister moving from a firm to sole practice at the independent bar. I thought then it was an essential part of a limited professional library and subsequent editions have re-proved the strength of that conviction.

The cover of my second edition is a dramatic black and white photograph of striking seamen in 1931. Events from that time are now recalled by only a few, although no doubt vividly, among them my father who still recalls clearly his fear as a child upon emerging from a cinema, in Queen Street, Auckland, to the 1932 unemployment riots. The link between these times and current legislative provisions and practices for employment security is tangible. Those who practise in the field of 'employment relations' (itself a term examined critically in the opening pages) need the context of, and links with, such history to understand the present and plan for the future. This text makes those links.

But this work does much more than provide an historical context to present-day employment relations. In an era with a plethora of employment law texts, a work that deals with more than the law alone and integrates it with history and employment relations practice is still refreshingly relevant and welcome. It is timely that the book addresses the distinct environment under the Employment Relations Act 2000. Knowledge, however comprehensive, of current legal provisions alone may win points or even cases, but it is unlikely to advance the study of employment relations, permit the best advice to a client, or advocate the wisest solution to an apparently intractable problem.

The now predictable and regular swing of the legislative pendulum of employment legislation not only makes work for lawyers (and judges), but provides a wealth of fresh material for academic writers. Employment law and practice under the Employment Relations Act 2000 is now sufficiently clear and settled to enable this book to present its contents confidently and authoritatively, even if the consequences of the December 2004 amendments to the legislation are only now, a year after their enactment, revealing themselves in judgements and employment practices. If we can rely on history and the present regime lasts the same nine years as did its predecessor (the Employment Contracts Act

1991), this work by Geare and Edgar may provide its authors with a few years' respite.

In writing the foreword to the second (revised) edition of Geare's work in 1988, the Honorable Stan Rodger, then Minister of Labour, noted: 'I am very pleased to see commentaries such as Professor Geare's appearing which look at New Zealand industrial relations in the context of recent developments. Informed debate is essential to healthy labour relations and Professor Geare's contribution is invaluable'. While the adjectives may have changed, the sentiment remains as strong as it was at the dawning of the Labour Relations Act 1987 and the State Sector Act 1988 when that foreword was written.

This is an enduring work for students, employment relations practitioners, academics, and employment lawyers alike. I congratulate the authors and their publisher on its publication in this revised edition and commend it to all pracititioners of the art.

GRAEME COLGAN
Chief Judge of the Employment Court

Part One

Employment Relations

A General Introduction

[A] The Framework

Chapter One

Introduction to Employment Relations

A. The Field of Study of Employment Relations

[101] 'Employment Relations' and 'Industrial Relations'

Until relatively recently what is now referred to as either employment relations or industrial relations was referred to only by the latter label. However, over the last ten to fifteen years there has been a growing trend to prefer 'employment relations' as a more accurate and expressive term. Kaufman (1993:161) observed that 'industrial relations', as a label, faced a bleak future in that it was perceived by most people as associated (only) with 'unionism, collective bargaining and with the blue collar factory economy' and he predicted the label would 'gradually fade (not always quietly) from the academic scene.'

Somewhat ironically, his latest major projects (Kaufman, 2004(a), 2004(b)) are an edited book using the new label 'employment relations' and a massive tome using the old label, 'industrial relations'. However, his position remains the same as it was in 1993, where he claims (2004:629) the problem with the name of the field is the fact that 'industrial relations' sounds increasingly old-fashioned and alludes to a blue-collar economy, and asks whether 'some new term, such as employment relations, can serve as a popular and effective substitute.'

So far, leading academic industrial relations journals in the USA, UK and Australia have retained the old label, but not without some apparent reluctance. For example, the *British Journal of Industrial Relations* claims on its cover that it is an 'International Journal of Employment Relations.'

One significant change is that the very prestigious Industrial Relations Research Association which (although based in the USA, it is truly international) proposed in 2003 to change its name to Labor and Employment Relations Association (Industrial Relations Research Association 2003:1-4). The reasons were similar to those cited above by Kaufman.

Closer to home, although clearly of little international significance, the Department of Labour in 2000 renamed its Industrial Relations Service the Employment Relations Service and the *New Zealand Journal of Industrial Relations* in 2004 was also relabelled the *New Zealand Journal of Employment Relations.*

From the 1990s to the present day the term 'industrial relations' (IR) has increasingly been replaced by 'employment relations' (ER). The terms can be considered synonymous. This book will try to be consistent and use ER, except when discussing historical contributions to the subject and theory.

[102] What is meant by 'employment relations'?

As a description of social activity, employment relations is as old as work and employment. As a Western academic *field of study* however, it has a much shorter history. The first major writings in the area were those by the Webbs (1896, 1902) in the UK, and by Commons (1911, 1934) and Perlman (1928) in the USA. However, it is really only in the last sixty years that the subject has really established itself. Laflamme (1994) claims the Canadian journal *Relations Industrielles/Industrial Relations* is the oldest university journal specialising in the subject, and it was not founded until 1945.

Through the 1960s and 1970s, countless articles, books and theses were written on the subject. Many companies appointed industrial relations managers and an increasing number of universities provided industrial relations courses. In Western countries, the subject attained sufficient standing for there to be professors of industrial relations and ministers of industrial relations in some cabinets. According to public opinion polls, the topic was often seen as one of the major issues facing society. Hence, one would imagine, the *meaning* of the term 'industrial/employment relations' would be widely understood. In fact, almost everyone knew what the term meant – at least to their own satisfaction. The problem was that views on the actual meaning rarely coincided.

[103] The need to have a definition

The need for an acceptable and accepted definition of employment relations (ER) is greater for academics and authors than for practitioners.

Practitioners have their roles as ER managers, consultants or union secretaries defined by their organisation and constituents. To an extent, ER is a combination of what they make it and what they are told it is. However, even if it is only to reduce role ambiguity, practitioners will also benefit from a better understanding of precisely what is involved in the subject. Walker (1977) observes that theory can help practitioners understand the present situation, forecast trends and bring about desired changes now or in the future – as well as avoid undesired events.

[104] John Dunlop's concept of industrial relations

One of the first, and possibly most important, explicitly theoretical industrial relations works is that by John Dunlop (1958): *Industrial Relations Systems*. Although published nearly fifty years ago, it is still very influential and in a recent collection of articles (Barbash and Meltz, 1997) half of the contributors made reference to Dunlop's 1958 work. In 1993, it was published as a revised edition. The work still provokes theoretical modification (e.g. Bellemare (2000)). As Kaufman (2004c:48) observes:

> The *sine qua non* of a theory is specification of one or more cause-and-effect relationships. Dunlop's model does not specify any such relationships. Rather, he provided a useful conceptual framework that helps identify key features and processes of the industrial relations system.

Such a system (Dunlop, 1958: viii) may:

> vary in scope from an enterprise to a sector or to a country as a whole ... Every industrial relations system involves three groups of actors: (1) workers and their organisations, (2) managers and their organisations, and (3) governmental agencies concerned with the workplace and the work community. Every industrial relations system creates a complex set of rules to govern the workplace and the work community. The environment is comprised of three interrelated contexts: the technology, the market or budgetary constraints, and the power relations and statuses of the actors. The system is bound together by an ideology or understanding shared by all the actors.

[105] The definition of employment relations

It is a truism that a definition 'cannot by its very nature be right or wrong. It can only be more or less useful for purposes of analysis' (Bain and Clegg, 1974:96). A useful definition of employment relations may be considered to be one which has the following characteristics:

a. it should be narrow enough for the boundaries of the subject to be discernible;
b. it should be broad enough not to exclude relevant topics;
c. it should help provide some understanding of what is involved in the subject by indicating the independent and dependent variables – that is, the inputs and outputs. Thus there must be objectives built into the definition;
d. it should not presuppose any particular ideology.

The following definition is based on one for industrial relations (Geare, 1977) which has been explicitly utilised by others (Plowman, Deery, Fisher, 1980) and, according to Barbash and Meltz (1997:247), influenced a series of later theoretical works:

> the interaction both among and between the three major parties and is concerned with obtaining, regulating and adapting the formal and informal rules that govern the work environment for the purpose of enabling the parties to obtain one or more of their principal industrial relations objectives.

The three major parties in this definition may be considered to be:

1. managers and employers and their organisations;
2. the State;
3. employees and their organisations.

The principal employment relations objectives that the parties are trying to attain may be considered to be one or more of:

1. to retain, and possibly increase one's existing power within the work environment;
2. to maintain, and possibly improve, labour-related productivity;
3. to maintain, and possibly improve, personal satisfaction with the factors that make up the job.

The subject is concerned with how the interaction among and between the major parties may be affected by external variables (that is, they become relevant only when they affect the interaction) such as technology, technological change, market conditions, economic conditions, power in society, personalities and personality differences. The study of employment relations can be taken at a variety of levels: a particular works, company-wide, industry-wide, or at national or international levels.

It must be emphasised the definition refers to interaction *among* the major parties as well as *between* the parties. The significance of this is to reinforce the fact that the parties represent loose groupings of participants in employment relations, not a homogenous whole. The reason the definition groups participants into three major parties is that a totally desegregated definition would be too confusing.

The definition refers to *employment relations* objectives, rather than overriding objectives the groups are pursuing. Employers' and managers' overriding objectives may be seen as profit and survival and/or growth. To achieve this, they must provide goods and/or services which satisfy a demand. Clearly the success with which they achieve these objectives may or may not relate to employer-employee-State interactions. Likewise, the overriding objective of most members of government is their personal re-election followed by their political party's re-election. Employees, as workers, probably have an overriding objective of achieving satisfaction from their job. Employees, managers and members of government, as people, probably have an overriding objective of getting maximum satisfaction and happiness out of life. In order to focus on *employment relations*, however, specific employment relations objectives are defined. These are discussed in more detail in Chapter Five.

Earlier definitions have been criticised for 'defining out' of the subject such areas as, for example, motivation, job regulation imposed by work groups alone, or the effects of taxation on strike activity. The definition submitted above clearly covers all those topics – and hopefully all other topics generally considered to be employment relations. On the other hand, the definition is not so broad as to include all, or nearly all, human activity. In addition, it provides a model of clearly defined inputs and outputs. The objectives defined are both necessary and sufficient, in that an overall objective cannot be used to substitute for any two or all three objectives and virtually all interaction in employment relations can be interpreted as being for the purpose of achieving one of the objectives.

The above definition also does not presuppose an unrealistically conservative ideology, or indeed any particular ideology. No common set of beliefs is postulated. The study of employment relations therefore can be seen to include a study of the major parties, the rules, and how they are obtained, legal constraints and their effectiveness, manifestations of conflict and finally the principal objectives of the parties manifested in various ways. As an example, redundancy is an issue which relates to all three objectives – productivity, job security (aspect of job satisfaction), and power.

B. Ideology and Employment Relations

[106] Ideology

The concept that embodies value and beliefs in employment has come to be termed ideology and it originated from the domain of industrial relations with the work of Fox in the 1960s.

[107] Defining ideology

Ideology can be defined as (Geare, 1994:125):

> A connected set of beliefs, attitudes and values held by an identifiable social group which refer to a specific aspect of social reality, which comprise normative, empirical and prescriptive elements and which may be at a general or particular level of abstraction.

This definition of ideology can be seen to comprise three elements:

1. Empirical – outlining beliefs as to 'what is', i.e. the actual situation;
2. Normative – outlining values as to 'what should be', i.e. the ideal situation;
3. Prescriptive – outlining beliefs and values as to 'what should be done', i.e. what should be done to achieve the ideal situation.

Distinguishing between these elements is important because empirical studies on employment ideology reveal that responses from employees can be quite different, depending upon whether the concept is applied abstractly or concretely. For example, Ramsay (1975) found that whilst seventy-nine per cent of employee respondents agreed with the analogy that in general 'a firm is like a football team', only fifty-four per cent agreed with this statement as it applied to their workplace.

Managerial ideology has long been considered important in organisational research because it is the values and beliefs, i.e. the ideology, of key decision-makers within an organisation that is purportedly central to explaining their choices about employment relations and human resource management policy and practice. Indeed, according to Godard (1997:207), the highly influential 'strategic choice' model posits

> employer decisions to adopt particular strategies, policies, practices, and, ultimately, outcomes are explained as much or more by their ideologies than

> by rational (or boundedly rational) choice processes attributable to contextual considerations … Thus, policymakers should focus as much or more on the encouragement of desired IR ideologies and the strategies and policies associated with them as on major structural or legal reforms.

Furthermore, Dunlop in his seminal work, *Industrial Relations Systems* (1958:16), suggested it is the

> ideology or set of beliefs commonly held by the actors that helps to bind or integrate the system together as an entity.

[108] Employment relations ideologies – unitarism, pluralism and the radical view

(1) The Unitarist Ideology

Fox (1966b) identified two main managerial ideologies or views – unitarism and pluralism. The essence of unitary theory is that 'every work organization is an integrated and harmonious whole existing for a common purpose' (Farnham and Pilmott, 1986:4). The unitarist ideology reflects the view that the organisation is a team; management have legitimate control over their employees; congruent interests exist between managers and employees; and conflict is an aberration, and if it arises, its source is attributed to external sources (such as an agitator). Thus the validity of conflict is denied, it being considered to be either:

a. merely frictional, e.g., due to incompatible personalities or 'things going wrong'; and/or
b. having been caused by faulty 'communications', e.g., 'misunderstandings' about aims or methods; and/or
c. to be the result of stupidity in the form of failure to grasp the community interest; and/or
d. the work of agitators inciting the supine majority who would otherwise be content.

Unitary theory, according to Farnham and Pilmott (1986:15),

> provides an image of the ideal world … its interpretation of society with its emphasis on an orderly and stable community, imbued with common purpose and a value consensus, bears little relation to the reality of everyday social relations.

(2) The Pluralist Ideology

Pluralism, on the other hand, sees the organisation as comprising different sectional groups with 'common and competing interests' (Horwitz, 1991:4-5). The degree of common purpose which can exist is only of a limited nature and conflict is endemic to an industrial organisation.

The pluralist ideology is clearly in tune with the definition of employment relations outlined above. There are different interest groups in employment relations, they have different objectives, and conflicts of interest must arise. Usually these conflicts are settled by compromise, insofar as all the parties consider the objectives of the other parties to some extent and modify their own positions. Clearly the power held by the various parties is an important determinant of the end result. A totalitarian government can totally impose wages and conditions of work on the workforce. Powerful organisations in the absence of reasonably strong trade unions can impose conditions on their employees which take into account nothing except the views of the organisation and external market forces. However it is submitted that in Western society no party has total, or anything near total, domination and there *is* interaction not imposition. In reality, very few people will be 'pure' ideologues, with most holding both unitary and pluralist inclinations.

(3) The Radical Ideology

A third ideology – the radical ideology – has been put forward, but as opposed to representing a new view of employment relationships it offers a critique of unitarism and pluralism. This view suggests a disparity of power exists in employment relationships, with capital holding all power. Furthermore, social reality is dominated by pressures for change, nothing is immutable, and everything, including the capitalist system, is a changing phenomenon and hence all power relations are transitory. This view receives little support and no evidence exists to suggest it realistically reflects the views of managers or employees.

In fact, pluralism appears to offer the most realistic view of employment relationships. Farnham and Pilmott (1986:15) agree:

> It is empirically obvious, for example, that diverse pressure groups, pursuing their own self interest through intergroup negotiation and compromise, are a basic feature of our society.

Similarly, Payne and Wayland (1999:6) claim pluralism is the reality in the workplace:

> Employee cynicism and a lack of solidarity among employees to 'pull together' to reach certain organisational goals seems the result in many organisations.

The functional purpose of ideologies is that they help 'define and to advance the core interests of a group, mobilising and uniting members to protect and defend their interests against opposing groups' (Horwitz, 1991:4). Thus, as Horwitz (1991) suggests, ideologies can be used as instruments of persuasion.

The ideological orientation of the organisation in which people work can have a major impact on their ideology. While some organisations may select individuals whose basic ideology fits with that of the organisation, it is also probable that the organisation moulds individuals (Fox, 1971:32). Allen has emphasised the important effect the ideology of the organisation can have on the individual's ideology and hence behaviour (1971:20):

> How a person behaves in a situation depends not simply on individual perception but also on the ideological orientation of the institution through which that person works … By and large, then, a person behaves not simply as he or she thinks, but as institutions stipulate.

Thus the ideology a person holds and works under will affect that person's:

1. perception of situations;
2. expectations of others' behaviour;
3. reactions to others' behaviour; and
4. own choice of behaviour.

[109] Extent to which ideologies are held

Until research was undertaken in the mid 1980s into the employment relations ideologies of Australian and New Zealand managers, there was no data on which to base assertions as to whether managers were unitary or pluralist in their ideologies. This has hardly restricted the body of HRM knowledge being developed around the assumption that managers, and indeed employees, hold unitary views towards the employment relationship (Delaney & Godard, 2001).

Actual data on managerial views obtained in 1986 revealed that, contrary to the commonplace opinion that unitary ideology is the dominant and widely held view by managers (see for example the works of Hill & Brosnan, 1983 and Deeks, 1976), significant support for pluralism exists.

Using a bank of questions to test managers' ideologies, the 1986 study identified a quite different scenario. As shown in Table 1.1, the vast majority of managers reported moderate support for the pluralist ideology. As can be

Table 1.1. Percentage expressing moderate support for ideology

	Australia N = 280	New Zealand N = 461
Unitarist Ideology		
Empirical	55.0	55.5
Normative	52.5	54.4
Prescriptive	41.8	30.1
Pluralist Ideology		
Empirical	85.4	81.8
Normative	85.7	82.9
Prescriptive	82.5	76.7
Radical Ideology		
Empirical	2.5	0.8
Normative	0.0	0.0
Prescriptive	1.4	0.0

Table 1.2. Percentage expressing strong support for ideology

	Australia N = 280	New Zealand N = 461
Unitarist Ideology		
Empirical	19.3	13.0
Normative	21.1	15.4
Prescriptive	26.1	15.8
Pluralist Ideology		
Empirical	42.5	36.0
Normative	39.6	35.8
Prescriptive	53.6	51.8
Radical Ideology		
Empirical	0.0	0.4
Normative	0.0	0.0
Prescriptive	0.0	0.0

Table 1.3. Ideological orientation of New Zealand managers and employees

	Unitarist %	Mixed %	Pluralist %
Managers			
Societal Level (n=759)	36	37	27
Workplace (n=673)	61	30	9
Employees			
Societal Level (n=405)	17	33	50
Workplace (n=366)	30	35	35

seen, many managers clearly had moderate support for *both* the pluralist and unitarist ideologies – but the support for the pluralist clearly predominates. Not surprisingly, Table 1.2 shows there are considerably fewer managers who *strongly* supported any of the ideologies – but again comparatively there was considerably more support for the pluralist ideology. It must be emphasised that this research took place in the mid 1980s.

More recent employment-relations ideologies data, collected in 2005 (shown in Table 1.3), which looked at both managers and employees, found that managers were significantly more unitarist than employees, but also more unitarist than the sample of managers shown in Tables 1.1 and 1.2. In this latest research, respondents indicated from questions whether they agreed with a more unitarist or more pluralistic view. They responded on two levels of abstraction: society as a whole and relative to their specific workplace.

One of the more recent classics in industrial relations is the work by Kochan, Katz and McKersie (1989:15). Statistics-reinforced observations made in their text explain the importance of accepting and understanding the definition of ideology, proposed in [107]:

> while American management remained hostile to unionization in their own firms, there also has been a long tradition of leading executives of large corporations supporting the legitimacy or even the desirability of a free labor movement as a part of our democratic society ... there has been a curious inconsistency in the dominant management belief or value system: unions are an essential part of the democratic fabric of society, but they are not necessarily desirable or acceptable 'in my firm or on my property.'

This paradox is clearly either evidence of differing ideologies at different levels of abstraction or simply evidence that leading executives are pathological liars. If the latter, it begs the question: why do they perceive the need to apparently pander to public opinion by lying? It is clearly more probable that they actually hold a different ideology at the particular level of abstraction of their own firm, than they do 'in general'.

What is likely to have occurred is that when unions are perceived as powerful, empirical pluralism becomes permanent. Poole and Mansfield (1993), building on the earlier work by Poole *et al* (1981, 1982), produce evidence in the UK that in 1980 82.1 per cent of managers felt unions had too much power and 52.1 per cent felt they had more power than management. In 1990, the respective percentage had fallen dramatically to 31.7 per cent and 14.1 per cent respectively. Earlier, Purcell and Sissons (1983:117) saw that in the UK 'the pragmatic basis for the adoption of pluralist policies had been weakened.' This supported Kochan *et al* (1989:14) on the other side of the Atlantic, whose view was that 'the conclusion that management had adopted and accepted unions as legitimate partners misinterpreted as a change in managerial *preferences* or *ideology* what was actually a *pragmatic* or *strategic* adaption to the high costs of avoiding or dislodging established unions.'

While a change in one's empirical (or descriptive) ideology will probably influence one's true normative ideology, it is probable that what has occurred between the 1970s and the present is not so much a change in the *normative* ideology of managers as a change to their *empirical* ideology. Deep down, as a description of the ideal world, the unitarist concept of managerial prerogatives, common objectives, accepted authority and irrelevant or non-existent unions has probably always been significant. Once managers perceive that it is a realistic possibility to at least have compliance with, if not commitment to, the normative unitarist ideology, then they will probably pursue it with increasing vigour.

CHAPTER TWO

THE STATE

A. Introduction

[201] What is 'the State'?

Miliband (1973:46) points out that a major problem in understanding the concept of the State is the fact that

> 'the state' is not a thing, that it does not, as such, exist. What 'the state' stands for is a number of particular institutions which, together, constitute its reality, and which interact as parts of what may be called the state system.

Miliband (1973:50) defines the State as 'the institutions – the government, the administration, the military and the police, the judicial branch, sub-central government and parliamentary assemblies'.

The State is also an employer, but when for example one considers public sector bargaining, the State should be considered as an *employer* rather than *the State*, unless particular State powers are wielded (such as specific legislation). There are, of course, differences between public sector and private sector employment relations. As suggested, a major difference is that the State, if it wishes, can quickly and directly introduce legislation to suit the purpose of another branch of the State which is a public sector employer.

There are a variety of conceptions of the State:

a. it is a neutral conduit, through which interest groups exert pressure;
b. it serves the public interest;
c. it serves the dominant class;
d. it is an independent party with its own interests.

[202] The State as a neutral conduit

Somewhat ironically, this view tends to be argued by those who disagree with it, so that later they can demolish it. Thus Giles (1989:135) claims that pluralists view the State as

> an inherently neutral set of institutions and rules with no will of its own ... far from taking decisions, it is merely the vehicle through which decisions are made.

[203] The State and the public interest

The concept that the State serves the public interest has normative and empirical overtones. These include whether the State *should* (or *should not*) serve the public interest, and whether it *does* (or *does not*) achieve this. Hyman (1978) states that while it is very easy to refer to the public interest, it is very difficult to actually define what *is* the public interest. Frequently the 'public interest', as expressed by pressure groups, coincides with their own interests.

Even if the public interest is defined as the wishes of the public as expressed by public opinion polls, this is also highly problematic. Giles (1989:138) points out that the use of opinion polls

> evades the critical issue of opinion formation. How is it that the public at certain points in time suddenly becomes concerned over a particular issue? How is this opinion translated into public policy?

It also ignores the problem that, while 'public opinion' may be a function of what the public thinks, it is to a greater extent a function of what questions were put, how the questions were framed, and how they were analysed.

A further difficulty arises when people profess to be acting in the 'true' public interest – although the public does not yet realise that this is its 'true' interests. Marxists have no difficulty with this, as they have defined a very useful concept: 'false consciousness.' This is any view expressed by, for example, employees which contradicts Marxist dogma. Mulgan (1993:142) points out that such concepts

> make the questionable assumption that there is a potentially true consciousness, based upon some independent, supposedly objective view of human needs and potentialities, which is available to the social analyst but not to the people being analysed.

Notwithstanding these difficulties, it is probably true that governments, since they are *elected* by the public, at least assume they are acting to a degree in line with the public interests, and would certainly wish to do so to the extent necessary to gain re-election.

Other institutions in the State, are not directly concerned with re-election, but will still usually consider their actions to be in the public interest. As argued earlier, there is the difficulty in anyone defining what *is* the public interest, and a further difficulty arises if an institution, such as the judiciary, attempts to do it when they are predominantly from a particular stratum in society. Griffith (1981:240) writes:

> the judges define the public interest, inevitably, from the viewpoint of their own class. And the public interest, so defined, is by a natural, not an artificial, coincidence, the interest of others in authority, whether in government, in the City or in the church. It includes the maintenance of order, the protection of private property, the promotion of certain general economic aims, the containment of the

> trade union movement, and the continuance of governments which conduct their business largely in private and on the advice of other members of what I have called the governing group.

This leads to the third possibility, that the State serves the dominant class.

[204] The State and the dominant class

This viewpoint of the State is strongly endorsed by radical or Marxist theorists and assumes that the State operates simply to serve the interests of the dominant class, or indeed is simply a puppet of the dominant class which are the Capitalists, or at least 'Business.'

While there is some intuitive appeal to this viewpoint (in that if there is a truly dominant class, surely it would ensure that the State was concerned with its interests?), it begs a number of questions.

The first is whether it is in fact useful to think of business as being a *class* – with connotations both of homogeneity and of a mentality of their class versus the rest of society. As mentioned in [105], considerable differences occur *within* parties in employment relations because they are *not* homogeneous. Certainly there will be issues on which there will be general agreement by most major employers, but equally there will be issues on which there are major disagreements.

The second question this viewpoint begs is why, if a class is so dominant and has the State so under its control, does it give away any power at all? Why extend political franchise? With the army and police force ready and waiting to do the dominant class's bidding, why worry about employee unrest? Adams (1992:491) points out that

> early in the course of industrialization, the state, in essentially all of the countries that are now classified as industrialized, market-orientated democracies, chose to intervene in order to outlaw combinations in restraint of trade.

This effectively prevented the creation of viable unions. Why then did the different States, if they were/are simply puppets of capitalists, cease this oppression, effectively allowing unions to develop?

A third question to consider is how capitalists find time, energy and motivation to ensure the State is always serving their interests while at the same time, presumably, they are busy exploiting the working class?

As with the three previous viewpoints, there is an *element* of truth in the dominant class hypothesis. 'Capital' or 'Business' clearly has significant power. This power is used to ensure that a comfortable level of profitability is maintained. If the State appears to be moving to attack that position, then business does come together – to a degree – to contest the State. But so do other pressure groups in society. It thus appears that the most realistic concept of the State is the fourth alternative – that the State is an independent party with its own interests.

[205] The State as an independent party

The problem faced in conceptualising the State either as a neutral conduit, or as the servant of public interest, or as the puppet of capitalists, is considerably lessened if the State is seen as an independent party, comprising a number of agencies, which have their own objectives and agendas which they try to achieve in the face of interactions with other pressure groups. Some expert political analysts also agree this is the most realistic view. For example, Mulgan (1993:130-131) writes that now it is

> generally agreed by theorists of almost every ideological bent, that the State has its own interests and objectives which it exerts against those of the rest of society … the State itself must be examined as a collection of agencies which can exert independent pressure on their own interests.

Zeitlin (1985:34) considers that there are many cases of States as independent parties pursuing economic policies which cannot be considered to relate either to 'the maximization of general economic welfare (or) to the promotion of the collective interest of the capitalist class.'

Thus 'the State' – the government, the administration, the judiciary, government agencies – pursue policies and objectives which further:

a. their own self interest;
b. what they perceive as being in the 'public interest'; and
c. what they perceive as assisting other interest groups in society able to exert pressure on the State.

A combination of factors can result in significant changes in State behaviour. Adams (1992:492, 496) observes that

> after World War II public policy changed significantly. The depression of the 1930s had demonstrated serious failings of a largely unregulated market and, thus, governments began to take responsibility for active economic management … a consensus was reached among the liberal democratic nations that, in the public interests, the state should take responsibility for the achievement of a list of goals including all of the following: economic growth, full employment, economic and social security, price stability, industrial peace, and industrial democracy in the sense of participation of working people in the making of decisions that impact their conditions of work.

He points out that in the 1980s, as a result of the recession in 1981–2, increased competition from low-wage Third World countries, and argument by employers that they required more flexibility and freedom from union- and government-imposed restrictions, state policy changed to deregulation of the economy in ways congenial to business.

B. The State and Employment Relations

[206] Objectives of the State

The overriding objectives of the individuals who comprise the State are to maintain or possibly increase their personal satisfaction with the factors that affect their jobs, re-election for elected members, and increase their personal power and importance and that of their institution. In addition, partly as a means to those earlier objectives, and partly as an end in itself, they wish to satisfy the public interest and pressure groups.

The *employment relations* objectives of the State are, as discussed in [105], to maintain and possibly improve labour-related productivity and the level of power and influence held by the State in the work environment. In order to help achieve those objectives, the State hopes the environment will allow employees to maintain or even improve their satisfaction with the work environment. Clearly if these employment relations objectives are achieved, the probability is that the overriding objectives will also be attained.

[207] The State as a party in employment relations

Adams (1992:516) observes:

> it will be necessary to focus more specifically on the role of the State; not only on the impact of public policy, but also on its generation and real function. We should no longer implicitly accept the proposition that the State acts in the public interest or its interpretation of the public interest. Instead we should question, analyse and investigate its motives.

It is certainly true that there is comparatively little research done by employment relations scholars into the role of the State, as such, in employment relations. There is, however, a significant amount of research into employment relations law, and legislation and the agencies created to enforce that legislation are certainly not ignored in the literature.

The degree of legislative involvement in employment relations varies significantly between different countries, and within countries over time. This is well illustrated by considering the UK and New Zealand in three periods: up to 1971, 1971–91 and from 1991.

Up to 1971, the British system was described with reasonable accuracy by Roberts and Rothwell (1972:543) as being 'less regulated by law than that of any other industrialised country.' Wedderburn (1971:13) wrote that British workers wanted 'nothing more of the law than it should leave them alone.' In direct contrast, the New Zealand system of employment relations from 1895 to 1991 was probably *more* regulated by law than that of any other Western democracy (see Chapters Seventeen and Eighteen). Overall, the regulation, although frequently criticised by unions and employees, was of net benefit to them.

From 1971 to 1991, the UK's employment relations system experienced a dramatic increase in government involvement. Although the British Industrial

Relations Act 1971 was repealed following strong union opposition, this was only temporary and by the 1980s new policies were in place. The regulation during this period was intensive and fundamentally anti-union. During the same period, New Zealand also had a high degree of regulation – but it remained supportive of unions and collective bargaining.

From 1991, the two countries have had a great degree of similarity with comparable intensity of state regulation. In both cases the underlying philosophy has been anti-union in the garb of 'pro-individual' (see Chapter Nineteen). In both countries this abated, but only to a degree, with the return to power of Labour governments.

[208] The power of the State

As already noted, employment relations theorists originally concentrated on unions and collective bargaining. From the late 1980s much more emphasis has been put on managers and employers (see [305]). There is a considerable degree of worry in all this, given that the State is the most powerful party. As Adams (1992:517) observes:

> Government is the dominant actor in industrial relations systems. It has power resources that considerably outweigh those of either labour or business. Because of that power the state, more so than the other two actors, must be held accountable for good or bad industrial relations.

This power could be illustrated by examining any of the following areas of State influence in the Section below. As an example, the effect of legislation on unions in the USA, UK and New Zealand will be briefly considered.

C. Areas of State Influence

[209] Unions

Kochan, Katz and McKersie (1989) discuss the traditional hostility towards unions felt by American managers. Notwithstanding this (and counter to the dominant class hypothesis) the National Labour Relations Act 1935 (Wagner Act) was passed.

Just prior to the passing of the Act, the president of the American Economic Associations, George Barnett, made his presidential address stating (Kaufman, 2002: 330):

> I see no reason to believe that American trade unionism will now revolutionise itself within a short period of time as to become in the next decade a more potent social influence ... We may take it as probable that trade unionism is likely to be a declining influence in determining conditions of labor.

The Wagner Act had an immediate and major impact on unionisation. St Antoine (1981:159) observes that

> sparked by this government endorsement, the labor movement went on to enjoy the most spectacular decade of growth in its history.

Later the Labour Management Relations Act 1947 (Taft-Hartley Act) was passed. This Act, again according to St Antoine (1981:160)

> did signal a major shift in the predominant American attitudes toward organized labor, from sympathy and support to neutrality at best and increasing distrust or hostility at worst ... (and) coincided with an abrupt halt in the forward progress of unionization throughout the country.

The results are illustrated in Figure 2.1 below.

In the British context, legislation has had specific targets. Mitchnick (1993:456) points out that after taking office in 1979, the Conservative Government 'moved to eliminate in stages the legal means whereby closed shop claims ... can be enforced.' The closed shop (see [421]) is a situation in which union membership is a requirement for employment in a particular workplace. The anti-union legislation culminating in s.11 of the UK Employment Act 1988 (which rendered all dismissals on the grounds of non-membership – or membership – to be legally 'unfair') has certainly had an impact. Gilbert (1993:245) discusses how the major Workplace Industrial Relations Surveys undertaken in the UK have demonstrated

> how far altering the law governing closed shops through the 1980s has induced dramatic change in behaviour. Closed shops were recorded in 1 in every 5 workplaces at the time of the 1984 survey; by 1990 the figure was down to 1 in every 25 establishments.

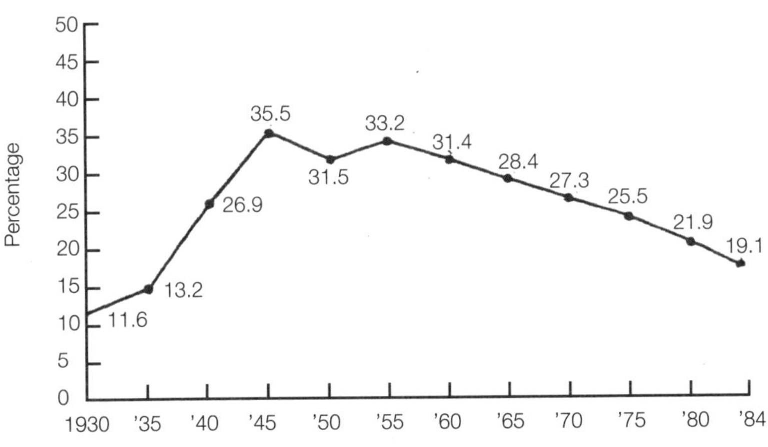

Figure 2.1. Union membership as a percentage of the non-agricultural United States labour force 1930–85. Source: *Kochan, Katz and McKersie (1989:151)*

Table 2.1. Union membership in New Zealand

Year	Membership
1934	74,391
1935	80,929
1936	185,527
1937	232,986
1989	648,825
1991	603,118
1992	428,160
1998	306,687
1999	302,405
2000	318,519
2001	329,919
2002	334,783
2003	341,631

Source: Various New Zealand Yearbooks.

In the New Zealand context, union membership has been affected dramatically by the introduction of compulsory union membership by law in 1936 and by the change in law in 1991 which made any form of compulsion illegal. Table 2.1 shows that increasing unemployment caused some drop in union membership between 1989 and 1991, but nothing like the dramatic drop between 1991 and 1992 resulting predominantly from the New Zealand Employment Contracts Act 1991 (see Chapter Nineteen), and the licence it gave employers to be anti-union, if they so desired.

[210] Further areas

Every significant area in employment relations is as dependent on legislation – either directly or indirectly – as is the strength of the union movement.

The State may decide to *withdraw* from the employment relations arena. This withdrawal may well be as significant as is its intervention. When it intervenes it affects the balance of power, usually in favour of the less powerful. When it withdraws it allows free rein to the *more* powerful party or parties.

Adams (1992:508) considers that

> unless checked by the government or a very powerful labour movement, employers will always attempt to escape from the fetters imposed by collective bargaining. A considerable amount of evidence from many countries supports this theory.

As suggested in [209] above, there will not be a powerful labour movement unless this has the support and approval of the State. Adams (1992:495, 508) goes on to indicate that influence of the State goes further than its direct legislation. Its own actions and attitudes form powerful signals as to what managerial behaviour and attitudes will be tolerated or even encouraged. Thus when the Reagan administration in the USA destroyed the Air Traffic Controllers Union, this 'established a symbolic precedent that was not lost on private sector employees' and even was seen to encourage 'aggressive anti-union employer behaviour.'

In summary, it can be claimed that either indirectly by its own behaviour, or directly through legislation, the State has a significant influence on, amongst others:

a. managers, employers and their behaviour;
b. employees and their behaviour;
c. unions and their behaviour;
d. bargaining scope and nature;
e. the resolution of industrial conflict;
f. the resolution of personal grievances;
g. the extent of industrial democracy;
h. the extent of Equal Employment Opportunities (EEO);
i. the extent of personal, racial and sexual discrimination in the workplace; and
j. the level and rate of change of wages.

Chapter Three

Managers and Employers

A. Introduction

[301] What is a manager?

There are numerous basic texts on management, with many different definitions of 'a manager' or of 'management.' One definition by Hodgett (1975:5) is that management is 'getting things done through people'. This is probably a generally accepted definition, but is incomplete in that it omits any reference to the *purpose* for getting things done through other people. Possibly the best-read management writer in the Western world, Peter Drucker (1968:30), defines management as 'a multi-purpose organ that manages a business *and* manages managers *and* manages workers and work.'

The two definitions taken together are illuminating. First, they emphasise that the purpose of management is the business or organisation and its furtherance. Thus managers, in general, see the *organisation's* objectives as being at least close to *their* objectives. Second, they emphasise that managers are themselves employees, and are managed by other managers. Thus, notwithstanding the first fact, under *certain* circumstances lower-level managers can align themselves with the employee-union party in employment relations and hence may unionise.

[302] Employers and managers

An employer may be defined as a person who owns or has a significant ownership share in a business or organisation and who employs labour.

Fifty to one hundred years ago, many managers owned the business and were the 'complete boss.' Today in small operations, many owner-managers or employer-managers still exist. However, in larger organisations, most managers are *not* owners of the organisation. Those responsible for employment are not employers in their own right, but simply act as agents for the organisation, and the concept of managers being employers and owners of businesses is outdated.

[303] Managers, employers and their organisations

In employment relations, while employee 'organisations', namely unions, are often more significant than 'employees' or informal workgroups, when considering the manager/employer party it is individual managers or employers who are of greater significance. Occasionally, as in New Zealand in the late 1980s and early 1990s, *organisations* of employers (in this case the New Zealand Business Roundtable (NZBR) and to a lesser extent the New Zealand Employers Federation (NZEF – now Business New Zealand)) can play a major role. Usually, however, they play only a secondary role. The reason is obvious – employers are in competition with each other and are prepared to make concessions for the 'common good' only to a limited extent. Nonetheless, some two and a quarter centuries ago Adam Smith (1976 ed:84) observed:

> we rarely hear, it has been said, of the combination of masters, though frequently of those of workmen. But whoever imagines upon this account that masters rarely combine, is as ignorant of the world as of the subject. Masters are always and everywhere in a sort of tacit but constant and uniform combination not to raise the wages of labour above their actual rate. To violate this combination is everywhere a most unpopular act, and a sort of reproach to a master among his neighbours and equals.

However, as Smith suggests, early employer organisations operated more on tacit understandings than formal structure. It has been suggested, both in New Zealand (Rudman, 1974) and in the UK (Clegg, 1970), that formal employer federations were formed as a reaction to the growth of employee organisations. The general employment relations trend towards enterprise bargaining that has occurred in recent years will reduce the influence of employer associations working as such. Gilbert (1993:237) points out that in the UK 'where over a quarter of establishments were members of employers' associations in 1980, by 1990 the figure had halved.' In New Zealand, provincial employer associations provide consultancy-type services, which maintains their significance.

As stated, managers and employers normally involve themselves directly in employment relations. Employer organisations provide information services, liaison between employers and negotiation services when employers do not have the required expertise. Thus, it is not an 'anti-employer organisation' bias that results in *employee* organisations getting more emphasis in employment relations texts and courses than employer organisations – but a reflection of reality. In employment relations, *managers and employers themselves* are the most significant factor.

B. Managers and Employers

[304] The objectives of managers and employers

Just as individuals employed by the State have personal objectives, so too do managers. In that respect, they may be likened to non-managerial employees. As agents for the organisation that employs them, managers have similar overall objectives to employers. While the overall objectives may vary, in most cases they will be:

a. profits and/or
b. growth and/or
c. survival.

In order to achieve these overall objectives, managers and employers have more specific employment relations objectives, as outlined in [105]. There it was suggested that managers and employers try to at least maintain, and possibly improve or increase:

a. labour-related productivity and/or
b. the employees' level of satisfaction with job factors and/or
c. power within the work environment.

[305] Managerial prerogatives

The phrase 'managerial prerogative' refers to what is considered by many in the management/employer party as the *inalienable right* of managers to operate without restriction in certain areas. Prerogatives can be defined as rights, authority or power. Amongst managers themselves there is no agreed list of prerogatives but the right to set policy, prices, profits, wage margins, employment levels and production levels: to hire and to fire. All these have been strongly claimed as managerial prerogatives. Today managers have lost the right to operate in these areas without restriction, through the activities of unions and work groups, and through legislation.

Since these *unrestricted* rights have been lost, they clearly cannot be 'inalienable'. However a large proportion of managers still feel that even if they have lost or are losing managerial prerogatives, they *should* be entitled to them.

This section will not discuss the prerogatives themselves (but see, for example Chapter Nine on The Right to Fire) but rather will discuss the extent, not so much that they *do* exist, as the extent they *should* exist.

A view that managers *should* have prerogative is closely tied to the unitarist ideology. Kaufman (2004b: 83) cites a railway magnate in the early part of the twentieth century who declared without fear of ridicule:

> The rights and interests of the labouring man will be protected and cared for, not by the labour association, but by the Christian men to whom God in his infinite wisdom has given control of the property interests of the country

The classic book on managerial prerogatives is that by Chamberlain (1948). In this book he postulates two justifications for prerogatives: the legal and the functional arguments. To these may be added an ethical argument.

The *legal* argument put forward by Chamberlain (1948:18) is that management has a legally imposed responsibility to the owners (i.e. the shareholders) of the organisation to manage the business in the shareholders' interests. Of course, this legal justification is weakened by the fact that management has given up some of its prerogatives, although it can be assumed that

> insofar as management has consented to any dilution of its authority not required by law, it has presumably done so only because it believes that course of action to be in the best interests of the owners – perhaps by improving the morale of the workers, stimulating greater cooperation by the union, or by forestalling or settling a strike …

The significance is that management is not legally *compelled* to retain all, or indeed any, managerial prerogatives. Of course, for their own ends, managers may claim there is a legal requirement for doing so.

The *functional* argument, simply put, is that in order to perform the functions of management effectively, management must have the opportunity to manage without restriction. That is, according to Chamberlain (1948:51),

> protection of management rights is not a matter of defending technical legal rights alone: it is simply and fundamentally a matter of protecting the freedom and authority that management must have, if it is to discharge its responsibility of managing the business.

The *ethical* argument for managerial prerogatives is simply that since employers have risked their money or capital in the organisation, then everyone's value system should accept that employers and their agents (i.e. managers) *should* have the right to set policy and act in any way that suits them, without let or hindrance.

The above gives a succinct account of the three arguments pertaining to managerial prerogative. It is generally accepted that there can be legal rights (both managerial or union). It is absurd to discuss ethical rights, however, as if a universal value system exists. Clearly one does not. To owners of capital, or the average manager, the ethical argument may seem sound. To an employee, the counter-ethical argument – that because employees have agreed to spend part of their working lives in an organisation *they* should have rights and be able to at least influence policy – may seem vastly more justifiable, hence ethical. Thus the ethical 'argument' for managerial prerogatives (and, for that matter, for 'union rights') is not an argument, it is simply an expression of a value judgement.

The legal argument has already been rebutted above. This leaves the functional argument. This can in fact be restated in terms of the objectives of the parties in employment relations, outlined in [105], which illustrates the absence of logic in the case. Managers are stating that they *should* be allowed to retain managerial prerogatives, a euphemism for power (employment relations objective one), in order to make it easier for them to be efficient, that is productive and profitable (employment relations objective two). It would be equally as valid (or non-valid) for unions to state that managers *should* give up all their prerogatives and allow unions and employees to gain power (objective one) as this will give employees more job security, better conditions and more satisfaction (employment relations objective three).

In brief, there is no fundamental, logical or ethical argument for managerial prerogatives. The issue is simply one of power. Managers try to maintain and increase their power in the work situation – as does the government, and as do employees and unions. It would undoubtedly, however, make life *easier* for managers if they could regain and hold all the so-called prerogatives. Reality dictates that, under current conditions, this is not possible. Whether one believes they *should* be able to depends on one's value system.

[306] Increasing emphasis on management in employment relations

In its infancy as an academic subject, 'industrial relations' concentrated in particular on unions, strikes by employees and collective bargaining (predominantly from a union perspective). This reflected the ideologies and values of the early writers (such as the Webbs) who were sympathetic to employees and unions and also the concerns of the State and industrialists who wanted solutions to the 'labour problem.' Thus Jacoby (1993:401) points out that, in the 1950s,

> when post-war strikes resurrected the labor question, government again turned to academia to stabilize the new labor-relations system. Yet, universities were more than agencies for social control; historically they also were pork barrels for powerful groups – initially farmers and businessmen, and now organized labor, which showed every sign of becoming a vested interest. From the universities, unions received not only labor education programs but social respectability, although these were a pittance compared to the recognition and support given to other groups. Moreover, the chief beneficiaries of the new IR programs were the academics. For them, it literally was a 'golden age' for IR. It paid to narrowly concentrate one's research on unions.

However, the academics of this era were not simply pragmatists, pursuing research into unions because that was how one received funding. Most were committed pluralists in the normative sense.

As outlined in Chapter One, Dunlop (1958) in his model gave 'management and employers' equal status with 'government' and 'workers and unions'. However, after doing so he too tended to regard management predominantly as reacting to union pressures and has been criticised by Laffer (1968:22) for 'his almost complete neglect of one half of the story – personnel management.' This lack of balance was further exacerbated by the fact that academic study is to a great degree determined by existing published material. If most of the literature is concerned with unions, most courses and much future research will have a similar emphasis. (It is also probably true to say that union activity, strikes and collective bargaining were considered much more interesting by relevant employment relations academics than, for example, job descriptions, interviewing and training.)

Interestingly, HRM is now critiqued for neglecting the role of employees (Marchington, 2000).

However, by the 1980s matters had begun to change. In the UK, Wood (1982) called for more research into the role of management, and in the USA, Kochan, McKersie and Cappelli (1984:20) stated that 'a more realistic model of industrial relations should recognise the active role played by management in shaping industrial relations as opposed to the traditional view which sees management as reactive, responding to union pressures.'

Guest (1991:149, 150) claims that in the 1980s, 'management'

> has been *the* topic of fastest growing research and teaching interest within the broad subject area of industrial relations ... probably the dominant research issue in industrial relations during the 1980s has been the exploration of what is broadly termed the 'new industrial relations'.

[307] NIR and HRM

The 'New Industrial Relations' (NIR) is closely associated with Human Resource Management (HRM). Indeed NIR and HRM are at times used virtually synonymously. Kelly and Kelly (1991) outline NIR techniques as including: rewards (e.g., share ownership, profit-related pay); work organisation (e.g., autonomous work groups, quality circles) and decision-making (e.g., joint consultative committees and employee communication programmes).

Beaumont (1991:300) considers the components of an HRM package as being very similar, namely:

i. relatively well-developed internal labour market arrangements (in matters of promotion, training and individual career development);
ii. flexible work organisation systems;
iii. contingent compensation practices and/or skills or knowledge-based pay structures;
iv. relatively high levels of individual employee and work-group participation in task-related decisions;
v. extensive internal communications arrangements.

As Beaumont also points out, the key message is that HRM has a *strategic focus*. The purpose of both NIR and HRM is ostensibly to effect organisational changes which (Kelly and Kelly, 1991:26) will

> lead not only to changes in worker behaviour, but more importantly to enduring changes in underlying attitudes, and that these in turn will result in gains to the company, such as productivity or quality improvements ...

Both NIR and HRM are clearly unitarist in the normative sense. Dunn (1990:5) points out that

> the new paradigm, by contrast, blurs the distinction between industrial relations and business. The problems, techniques and strategies of management are far more prominent. Workers are of research interest mainly as a resource to be developed. In short, they become the objects of managerial expertise, the assumption being

> that only management has sufficient information, particularly about markets, to reconcile the interests of employees with the success of the enterprise.

It is also very clear that NIR and HRM techniques are seen as part of an anti-union strategy. As Boxall (1993:658) puts it, one of the two broad strands of meaning of HRM in the literature is that HRM is 'a particular management strategy emphasising employee commitment and rendering unions unnecessary.'

While most companies employing NIR and HRM are attempting to reduce union influence, and increase employee commitment and involvement in order to achieve their objectives of productivity and power (see Storey (1995) in which the introductory section examines the rhetoric, reality and hidden agendas), some may also be trying simply to increase employee job satisfaction. For some, indeed, this may be a 'terminal' objective, but others will be well aware 'that job satisfaction is significantly negatively related to employee support for unions and to employees' voting for unions in representation elections' (Lewin, 1987:11), and will be doing it as part of an anti-union strategy. As Beaumont (1991:305) observes, the view that

> HRM is in essence the development of a set of policies, practices and arrangements designed essentially to 'individualise' industrial relations, and thus circumvent the unions and weaken individual membership commitment and loyalty to the union, is one that is probably widely accepted throughout the British union movement.

This emphasises the normative commitment to the unitarist ideology.

[308] Management and ideology

In [109] it was pointed out that HRM is fundamentally unitarist. In [108] the concept of an ideology comprising different *elements* was discussed. Managers may have a different normative ideology (relating to what *should be*) to their empirical or descriptive ideology (relating to what *is*). However, even this elaboration is insufficient. As Purcell (1987:535) points out:

> wide variations can be found within the unitary frame between those firms which are essentially exploitive of labor and those which emphasize the value of loyalty and commitment. Similarly, pluralism needs to be sub-divided between those maintaining highly structured, often antagonistic, formal relations with employees through their trade unions and those which emphasize dialogue, understanding and co-operation between management and organized labor.

It is suggested that the unitarist ideology, in terms of each element, can also be considered on a continuum:

Unitarist: Exploitive → Paternalistic → Developmental

The reality is that most organisations are probably in the first two categories.

Thus organisations and their management may believe that managerial power is theirs as of right and is generally accepted; and that the objectives of the organisation, of management and of the employees are the same. Thus they are unitarist. However, in some cases employees are seen as little different to raw material, to be used or discarded as management sees fit. Just as it is in the 'interest' of raw materials to be exploited and processed, it is in the 'interests' of employees to be exploited. This is exploitive unitarism. In other cases, employees are seen more as children, to be looked after as well as utilised, and here the unitarism is paternalistic. In some cases there may be genuine efforts to develop employees to their full potential – developmental unitarism.

Similarly, the pluralist ideology may be considered:

Pluralist: Confrontational → Tolerant → Cooperative

This scenario suggests that again there may be differences in approach, although in every case there is acceptance that employees have objectives which do not wholly or always coincide with that of management or the organisation. The approach however, may be highly confrontational and aggressive, reasonably well settled or highly co-operative. The concept of collective bargaining normally encompasses the first two variations, productivity bargaining the third.

C. Managerial Techniques

[309] Managerial techniques and employment relations

As mentioned above, since the 1980s NIR and HRM practices have been much discussed. Certainly there have been a number of well-publicised cases in which 'new' techniques have apparently been introduced. What is actually 'new' is not so much the technique – strategic thinking, team building, employee involvement or whatever – so much as the labelling and the *degree* of apparent enthusiasm for the practice. However, it must be stressed that *nothing* is really *new* when it comes to human interactions. Every technique introduced in the 1980s and 1990s reflects similar practices of twenty, fifty or a hundred years ago. As Lewin (1987:30) states:

> it should be kept in mind that union avoidance and opposition to unions are hardly new phenomena. In a nutshell, US employers have always been opposed to unionism – indeed, union win rates in NLRB-conducted representation elections have declined consistently since the early 1940s – and employers have often tried to provide substitutes for unionism. These have included the American Plan, company unions, industrial psychologists, counselling and human relations programs, and other devices.

These anti-union behaviours and attitudes remain. Lawler (1980) points out that firms in the US spend more than two hundred million dollars each year on consultants and lawyers – specifically so as to attempt to prevent organising drives by unions.

The so-called new practices are very similar to the Human Relations Movement, which reached its zenith in the 1930s and 1940s. Kochan (1980:11) claims:

> the best interpretation of the human relations movement is that it rejected the assumption of the institutionalists that goals of workers and employers were incompatible, viewed conflict in the organization as pathological, and accepted the supremacy of the goals of management and the need to induce cooperation from workers through acceptance of management's policies and actions. The strategy for gaining acceptance was the consideration of the workers' social needs and desires on the job.

HRM in theory is somewhat different to the old personnel management. However it has been pointed out (Guest, 1987, 1990a, 1991) that when the two are compared, HRM is described normatively (what writers believe it *should be* like), while personnel management is described empirically or descriptively (what writers consider it actually *is* like). Many people do not believe that HRM has resulted in a significant change in practice. In the USA, Strauss (1989:249) points out that 'regardless of its broader pretensions, HRM's heart, at least as it is taught in most schools and covered in most textbooks, is still what used to be called Personnel.' Indeed Ferner and Hyman (1992:xxii) found in their study of HRM departments across seventeen European countries that 'in many cases, the adoption of HRM seems confined to changing the name of the personnel departments whose essential functions remain unaltered.'

Thus the techniques discussed very briefly below (for detailed description see any personnel or HRM text) and in later chapters have all been practised with varying degrees of expertise and success by organisations over the years. Their use *may* have been more widespread in the 1990s than it was in the 1970s, although assessments of the real impact of NIR and HRM are not impressive (see [319] below).

The techniques include:

a. job analysis, job descriptions and person descriptions;
b. human resource planning;
c. selection;
d. work study;
e. training;
f. performance appraisal;
g. job evaluation;
h. incentive schemes;
i. productivity bargaining;
j. participation;
k. flexibility.

The last three techniques will be considered in more detail in Chapters Seven, Thirteen and Fourteen.

[310] Job analysis, job descriptions and person descriptions

Job analysis is the process of collecting information about a job and analysing the data in order to determine the title, function, objectives and key tasks of the job

(job description) and the sort of person needed to do the job (person description). This information is necessary before recruitment, selection, appraisal, training, development, wage and salary administration, job evaluation and, to a great extent, any effective motivation can take place. If the information is inaccurate, incomplete or purely subjective, only luck will prevent poor decision-making.

The job description should include the *major* objectives, not an exhaustive wish-list. Likewise, the tasks should include only the *key* tasks: those which make a substantial contribution to achieving the major objective(s) of the job.

It is possible to look at each key task in turn and consider what knowledge and skills are required for the job, both before selection and after on-the-job training. They may be categorised as those that are 'necessary' and those that are 'desirable.' This information gives a person description.

[311] Human resource planning

The objective of human resource planning is to help the organisation ensure that it has 'the right number of people, and the right kind of people, in the right places, at the right time, doing things for which they are economically most useful' (Patten, 1971:14). The planning should reduce staffing problems by forecasting demands for, and supply of, both employees and skills.

Two policy decisions are closely related to human resource planning. The first is whether someone appointed to a job has to be competent at the job almost immediately or whether they need only be of a standard whereby they could be competent after training. The second policy decision is whether, as a general rule, appointments should be made from within the organisation or from outside, or from either, depending on circumstances.

[312] Selection

The selection process should perform *two* functions. It should select the person:

a. who is the best of the applicants on a cost-benefit basis; and
b. who has all the necessary attributes and is able to perform to the standard deemed *necessary*.

If a person is selected who does not meet those two criteria, then the selection is illogical. While few managers would openly admit to not appointing the best available on a cost-benefit basis, a small group appoint only 'the best' regardless of cost, while a larger group appoint only 'the cheapest', regardless of benefit. Both groups are inept. Far more frequently, managers appoint someone who is possibly the best available, on a cost-benefit basis, but does not have those attributes previously identified as *necessary*. Clearly, either those attributes are *not* in fact necessary or the selection process is flawed.

Although some use is made in large organisations of assessment centres, most selection takes place using some or all of:

a. analysis of the application form;
b. checking references and claims;
c. tests (intelligence, aptitude, psychological, work-related);
d. interviews.

[313] Work study

Work study comprises two techniques – method study and work measurement.

Method study is employed to improve methods of production. Because of practical considerations, it is desirable that these improvements be made with the minimum of modification and expense. Hence, the existing method should be improved if possible, rather than having a new method substituted for it.

The process of method study has three stages:

a. the job is selected and the problem identified;
b. the facts about the job are recorded and examined;
c. the improved method is developed, installed and used.

In the ideal situation, method study should come *before* work measurement, which in turn should come before any type of incentive scheme is introduced. In practice, this may not be possible as the company may already have in place an incentive scheme, which may already be 'demoralised', and may wish to introduce method study, or the company may have already undertaken method study, etc., but later wishes to do method study again. Under these situations, the company must be very careful to prevent conflict, particularly if the employee's pay is based on output. If an employee is paid proportional to output and an improved method is introduced (by management) which results in, for example, a fifty per cent increase in output for *less* effort, the 'right' payment will almost certainly cause employment relations problems. If the employee is granted the fifty per cent increase, that will upset the relativities with other employees. They will be upset, particularly if the employee is seen to be working less hard than previously. If, on the other hand, management does not give the increase, management appears dishonest and the employee will feel robbed.

As stated, work measurement is often used in payment systems, with the assumption commonly being made that a particular rate of work is associated with, for example, minimum rates of pay. However, a clear distinction should be drawn between the measurement of work and the methods by which payment is made for work. The aim of work measurement is to find the amount of work in a job, that is, the time in which it should be completed at a stated level of performance. It is equally applicable where there is no question of incentive payment.

To understand the use of work measurement, assume that a job is being performed by an employee at a particular rate (86 widgets per hour) or alternatively, by a number of employees at different rates (68–103 widgets per hour). It is impossible to state arbitrarily whether 68 is very slow or 103 is very fast. Possibly 68 is fast and 103 is exceptionally fast. Work measurement is used to evaluate a qualified employee, rating his/her performance so that management can decide what is slow, reasonable and fast.

Work measurement is designed to provide a standard time for a job. This is the time in which a task should be carried out by a qualified employee, working at the benchmark performance level. The procedure for a direct time study is for a task to be broken down into 'elements'. These elements are then separately timed repeatedly in order to obtain an accurate timing (usually expressed in decimalised minutes). The operator's work performance is then 'rated' so that the time can later be standardised. Allowances (for breaks, etc.) are then made and the standard time calculated.

Without rating (either objective or subjective), work measurement would become farcical. A trained and able work-measurement practitioner attempts to rate the performance of an operator and give the performance a numerical value based on a rating scale. Four factors are usually taken as the object of the rating: speed of movement, physical and mental effort, dexterity and consistency. Speed is the factor easiest to rate, mental effort the most difficult. While those involved in work study emphasise the skill and accuracy of the process, Guest (1990b:299) points out that

> all the evidence reinforces the view that work measurement, far from being 'scientific management', is better considered as an art ... it is almost inevitable that, in making judgements about highly ambiguous issues like fairness and effort, work measurement officers will engage in social information processing and will allow the norms and expectations of those around them to influence their judgement.

[314] Training

In its broadest sense, training is designed to achieve one or more of the following objectives:

a. fitting a person into a new position;
b. improving performance in the present job;
c. preparing the individual for transfer or promotion.

Training to achieve the first objective is often referred to as 'induction', the second as 'training' and the third as 'development'.

The analytical approach to the second objective, 'training' goes through a number of stages:

a. job analysis giving a job description;
b. analysis of training needs and determination of training objectives;
c. design of a training programme;
d. implementation of the training programme;
e. evaluation of the training programme.

This completes the process which may then start again if the individual is ready to take on a new aspect of the job, or indeed a new job.

[315] Performance appraisal

Performance appraisal can, in theory, be either formal or informal, but in practice usually refers to a *formal* system in which the performance of an individual is appraised or evaluated. Formal performance appraisal should, however, complement, and certainly not replace, informal day-to-day assessment and feedback on a subordinate's performance by a manager. Indeed, informal ongoing appraisal is crucial if the formal system intends to achieve the common objective of improving performance.

Performance appraisal is one example of a management control system; it is designed to control individual performance. Like most control techniques, performance appraisal can be highly effective or an expensive failure producing negative results. The effectiveness of an organisation's performance-appraisal system depends on how well the objectives are thought out, how well the system is designed and how well it is put into practice. Some appraisal systems can help meet certain objectives but are ineffective or counter-productive in achieving other objectives. Managers who are reluctant to do performance appraisals, possibly because, as McGregor (1957) claims, they resent 'playing God', or who are poorly trained at appraisal interviewing, may ensure that a well-designed system does *not* work.

The basic objective of performance appraisal is to measure the performance of an individual, usually as a means to a further objective. Typical organisational objectives for performance appraisal include one or more of the following:

a. to compare performance against standards;
b. to motivate improved performance;
c. to determine, and get accepted, training and development needs;
d. to determine merit pay;
e. to assess if discipline is needed;
f. to select for promotion;
g. to validate selection criteria – by checking that the selection process predictions are accurate;
h. to provide a 'human resource audit', or general picture of the organisation.

For a performance appraisal system to work, it is crucial that management have determined which is the single most important objective, and that the system will achieve that objective. All too often management hope that their system will achieve multiple objectives when in fact they achieve none.

A number of basic choices have to be made which determine the overall type of system, and then further decisions as to detail are required. The first choice is whether employees should be appraised against absolute standards (against criteria) or relative standards (against their peers). The second choice is whether the system should be a feedback or non-feedback one (i.e. the appraisal undertaken in secret).

The major difficulty management faces in developing a useful performance appraisal system is ensuring that the system, and those using it, are working towards specific objectives for the scheme. A scheme which simply creates strain and negative reactions is unlikely to 'improve performance'.

One of the simplest and most effective approaches to performance appraisal is for the manager and the subordinate to simply discuss their job and roles and identify one to four areas where things are going well and one to four areas where things could be improved. (These may be the *same* areas. If people cannot rectify weaknesses, they should be helped to build on strengths).

[316] Job evaluation

Job evaluation can be considered a systematic procedure to determine the relative worth of jobs to each other, so that a hierarchy of jobs can be created for a rational wage system. A job can be considered to be a position or group of positions which are identical or nearly identical with respect to their major or significant tasks. Job evaluation is concerned with the job, not the job holder. That is, a number of people in different positions may perform fundamentally the same tasks – hence there is only one 'job'. The first stage of job evaluation structures jobs into a hierarchy with some methods also assigning proportionate 'worths' to the job. The second stage converts the 'worths' into wage or salary levels.

There are four basic methods: points rating, factor comparisons, job ranking and job classification. Points rating is used in the vast majority of cases. This system involves selecting factors to be used to differentiate jobs. Common factors include: education, experience, initiative and ingenuity, mental or visual demands, physical demands, responsibility for equipment or process, responsibility for material or product, responsibility for safety of others, responsibility for work of others, unavoidable hazards, and working conditions. The factors must be defined in varying degrees and values assigned to each degree.

Clearly the initial choice of factors, and then the assigning of values, are both subjective. There are no factors which 'must' be included, and there is no logical basis for deciding that one factor has a maximum value of X points and another Y or Z points. The important detail is that there is general agreement that the factors chosen are fair and reasonable and the values assigned to them also fair and reasonable. Even if there is overall agreement by the workforce, individual employees may disagree, and feel aggrieved.

The jobs have to be evaluated factor-by-factor giving a hierarchy of jobs with numerical differences. This hierarchy must then either be imposed on the employees, or mutually accepted. If the employees and/or their unions were involved in the evaluation, acceptance is more probable.

Assuming points rating has been employed, and that all jobs are in a hierarchy with relative points given, a job with 750 points should have a wage higher by fifty per cent than a job given 500 points. However it is not known if the job with 500 points should be paid $8 per hour (or if a salary, say $20,000 per year) or $7.80 or $9.15, and so forth. To set benchmarks, a wage survey is conducted using a few benchmark jobs to create a 'community wage profile'.

This indicates the organisation's position in the community and a value can be set on the benchmark jobs.

Although job evaluation is normally introduced because there is dissatisfaction amongst both management and the workforce about unfairness between basic wages, and is designed to rectify this, it can still create new conflicts.

Obviously if relativities are going to be altered, even if it is to make them better accepted, some individuals will suffer in relative if not absolute terms. Although points rating can give a different value to each job, practical consideration results in most cases in the jobs finally being grouped into classes. In some cases the difference in original points between the job at the top of one class and the job at the bottom of another may have been slight – but the difference in wages once the jobs have been grouped into classes may be significant.

A major difficulty is deciding how to deal with an individual currently being paid more than the evaluated rate. If inequities were solved by allowing the lowest ranked job to keep its current salary and adjust every other job upwards, it would be enormously expensive. The possible actions are:

a. to do nothing until the current job holder leaves, then alter the rate;
b. keep paying the old rate but specify there is an evaluated rate and a 'personal supplement';
c. reduce the personal supplement over a period to zero.

The choice of action will depend on the relative importance given to the individual's self-esteem and the need for equity in pay rates.

[317] Incentive schemes

The popularity of incentive schemes waxes and wanes. In the 1970s and 1980s they appeared to be losing favour, but by the 1990s 'payment for performance' had regained popularity. Employers and managers, employees and unions are frequently very self-assured about the impact of incentive schemes (both individual and team-based). Ehrenberg and Milkovich (1987:92) are not so sure, pointing out that very few studies 'actually provide convincing evidence that compensation policy *affects* firm performance.'

Notwithstanding, there is a general belief by employers that individual incentive schemes will motivate increased performance from employees and likewise, there is a strong belief among employees that a good incentive scheme will give them more money than any other type of payment system. Thus both the manager/employer party and the employee/union party may achieve their objectives of increased productivity and increased satisfaction. Unfortunately, there are also strong points against incentives.

The introduction (or existence) of these schemes is very likely to cause dissatisfaction among employees not included in the incentive scheme, particularly when long standing differentials disappear (e.g. skilled tradesmen earning less than unskilled or semi-skilled operatives). This problem should be anticipated and possible solutions devised (e.g. by putting these employees on to a measured daywork scheme).

Schemes which are poorly designed (without work study) or are allowed to keep running without frequent review usually become 'demoralised'. As Flanders (1973) pointed out, demoralised schemes can result in:

a. manifest and growing inequities in pay and effort between different groups and, probably, individuals;
b. the fluctuating incentive yield or bonus becoming an ever greater proportion of total pay;
c. an increase in special allowances and non-standard times and payments;
d. a growth of 'in lieu bonuses' or other compensatory payments for 'indirect' employees.

'In lieu' bonuses obviously reduce the productivity benefits of the incentive scheme, although they do provide one method of reducing the dissatisfaction of non-production employees. The danger, from a company's point of view, is that bonuses (and special allowances) can increase at a faster rate than production.

Employees on individual incentive schemes are often believed to deliberately restrict their output. The reasons for the restriction are varied, but include:

a. a fear that excessive production will lead to either rate cutting or rate readjustment. Managerial actions in both the past and the present have created and nurtured this fear. Companies wishing to remove this fear need to demonstrate their integrity, not merely protest their innocence;
b. a desire to gain social acceptance – or avoid social pressures – by conforming to group norms. This is related to the first point since group norms are usually created to avoid rate cutting. There may also be a desire to stop able employees 'showing up' those who are less competent. When rates have been negotiated rather than imposed, the possibility that group norms will be closer to established rates is greater;
c. a desire to 'beat the system' and secure bonuses by cunning rather than input.

As mentioned in [105] an objective of all parties in employment relations is to maintain at least the level of power held in the work environment. Power is of particular relevance with incentive schemes: employees, work groups and unions on the one hand, and managers on the other, are in conflict over who should control, or have power over, the incentive scheme. Thus what Flanders (and managers) refer to as a 'demoralised' scheme may be considered very satisfactory from a work group's point of view.

With *group incentives*, the group (team, department, plant or company) is paid an incentive bonus whenever a particular output standard is achieved. Group schemes may be used instead of individual schemes either because individual output cannot be differentiated in the work operation, or from choice. Group schemes can involve all employees, direct and indirect. A feature of these is that there is a less direct relationship between an individual's effort and output and reward. A well known example is the Scanlon Plan (Geare, 1976). This plan has been around since the 1940s, but is plagiarised in the present by consultants who sell it as 'gainsharing.' The similarity between gainsharing and the Scanlon Plan is explained in a recent work (Collins, 1998), entitled *Gainsharing and Power* and subtitled *Lessons from six Scanlon Plans*.

[318] The Scanlon Plan

The Scanlon Plan has two main parts:

a. a base productivity 'norm' which, if bettered, gives rise to a productivity bonus. This norm is usually based on performance over a period – often a year. The choice of the base year is crucial. To avoid suspicion, the year chosen must be as recent as possible, but must also be an average year with regards to profitability and performance. If the year chosen as a 'base' happened to be a 'boom' year then it would be most unlikely that bonuses would ever be obtained, leading to disillusionment in the plan and its inevitable failure. If the year chosen was a 'bust' year, the company would be paying out large bonuses – as it slowly, or not so slowly, went bankrupt;
b. a system of works committees, usually on a departmental basis with an overall 'screening' committee, to consider employee and managerial suggestions to improve efficiency and productivity, to save costs and to ensure that suitable suggestions are implemented.

Evidence strongly suggests that to bring about the required attitudinal change someone must act as a catalyst and stimulant. This person usually needs to be outside the management and union teams – however able the individuals in those teams may be. Scanlon himself was a vital part of many early Scanlon Plans, and Scanlon disciples, such as Lesieur, later continued in Scanlon's role.

Difficulties can arise with the plan in industries or situations where increased efficiency basically necessitates a reduction in manpower. In the Linwood plant of the Pressed Steel Company, employees 'demanded a separate union committee to screen suggestions and eliminate those likely to be detrimental to worker interests' (Gray, 1971:303).

The ideology behind the Scanlon Plan involves a move away from working on people's selfish motives. Unfortunately these still exist and there can be problems where employees consider others are not contributing their share to the productivity improvement and hence the bonus. Notwithstanding the difficulties, remarkable success has been claimed from Scanlon Plans (Lesieur, 1968). Where they work, it is because the basic objectives of the parties can all be achieved if effort is made to ensure this and power conflicts are not crucial. Ehrenberg and Milkovich (1987:109) report that in the USA a 'renewed interest in, and even popularity of gain-sharing and other productivity-sharing schemes is evident in industrial relations.'

[319] Assessment of NIR and HRM

Ferner and Hyman (1992:xxix) point out that a 'notable common feature of the past decade is the considerable decline in strike activity in almost the whole of western Europe' and they go on to ask how this general decline can be explained. They ask:

> have the realities of a tougher competitive environment, and the policies of conservative governments, encouraged a 'culture shift' towards cooperation and productivism? Or have circumstances in the 1980s merely caused a pragmatic (and reversible) adaptation to a shift in the balance of power and in the calculus of the costs and benefits of militant action?

The second explanation seems more likely. From the 1980s, economic conditions and conservative legislation worldwide has reduced union power significantly. In the UK, for example, Poole and Mansfield (1993:17) point out that

> in 1980 82.1% of managers considered that trade unions had too much power; this figure had fallen to 31.7% in 1990 (t = -25.2;p<0.001). In 1980 the majority of respondents (52.9%) agreed with the statement that `all in all, trade unions have more power than management'; this figure declined to 14.1% in 1990.

It is submitted that it is this decrease in union power which has brought about a decrease in strike activity – not successful NIR and HRM policies. Indeed, many researchers are somewhat scathing about the significance of NIR and HRM in practice.

Conversely there are strong supporters of NIR. For example Kochan, Katz and McKersie (1989:249, 250) claim

> Human-resource practices have demonstrated their durability through ups and downs in a large number of firms precisely because they are not solely or primarily motivated by the goals of avoiding unions. Instead, many of these practices fit the economic needs of their firm and the expectations of employees.

Notwithstanding the eminence of these three American academics, case studies used to justify NIR and HRM should be viewed with caution. Certainly they reflect *goals* for management to *aim for*. It is highly debatable whether these practices are widespread. (Indeed, even Kochan *et al* (1989:224) state that 'the benefits ... have diffused to only a limited number (at the most twenty-five per cent) of employees.' They were not prepared to give an 'at the least' estimate.) There are also questions as to whether these practices even occur in isolated incidents. As Guest (1990a:393) points out:

> the contemporary stories of organizations like General Motors are of the HRM or QWL (Quality of Work Life) achievements and not of the downsizing and closure programs occurring simultaneously in other parts of the organization. The HRM cases can therefore help to obscure the rather less pleasant reality.

On the other side of the Atlantic, Godard (1991:380-1) observes:

> there have been numerous case studies reporting positive effects for progressive HRM practices, but these studies are more often than not impressionistic and may reflect the preconceptions and biases of their authors, who are typically advocates of progressive IR/HRM policies and often rely primarily upon information provided by management. Moreover, follow-ups to these studies, when conducted, often find that the original program has either been scaled down or discontinued altogether. Thus, the incidence of highly successful cases may be far lower than these analyses suggest.

To conclude, the optimism that NIR and HRM have affected cultural changes and long-term improvement in attitude and behaviour is unfounded. Attitude and culture change and employment relations improvement for all parties *can* be achieved – but only after considerable effort and work. Changes brought about by weakened unions through high unemployment and conservative legislation are very different. They will be short-term only. Kelly and Kelly (1991:43-44) sound pessimistic but probably are accurate when they claim:

> there is little or no evidence to suggest that a variety of NIR practices has altered workers' largely negative views of management in general and of union-management relations. The ways in which NIR schemes have been designed, implemented and managed – by employers in the face of economic crisis – have worked against such attitude change.

Chapter Four

Employees and Their Organisations

A. Introduction

[401] What is a worker?

A 'worker' (also referred to as an employee) may be defined according to *common law,* that is, case law or judge-made law, or by *statute law,* that is by Acts of Parliament, or by employment relations definitions.

Common law differentiates between *employees* who are considered to be under a *contract of service*, and *independent contractors* who are deemed to be under a *contract for services*. Employees are further differentiated into managers and workers. While strong unitarists may suggest that all employees are similar (whether or not they are chief executives or unskilled labourers) for realistic understanding of employment-relations situations such suggestions are unhelpful.

[402] Statute law

The concept of a worker, or employee, may be further defined by statute law. Thus, for example, New Zealand statute law over many years has *deemed* to be workers or employees some people who, according to common law would, or could, be considered to be independent contractors. Under the Industrial Conciliation and Arbitration Act 1954 a worker was defined as

> any person of any age of either sex employed by any employer to do any work for hire or reward

But the Act went on to state:

> for the purposes of this Act every person who is wholly or mainly engaged in procuring proposals or contracts of industrial life assurance or in collecting industrial life assurance premiums for any person carrying on industrial life assurance business, and is remunerated wholly or partly by fees or commission, shall be deemed to be a worker employed by the last-mentioned person, whether or not the relation between them is that of master and servant.

While 'master and servant' terminology may now seem quaint and archaic, it was part of New Zealand statute law until 1973. Under the Labour Relations Act 1987 (LRAct), the term 'worker':

a. means any person of any age employed by an employer to do any work for hire or reward; and
b. includes –
   (i) a homeworker; or
   (ii) a person intending to work.

A 'homeworker' in turn

> means a person who is engaged, employed, or contracted by any other person (in the course of that other person's trade or business) to do work for that other person in a dwellinghouse (not being work on that dwellinghouse or on fixtures, fittings, or furniture in it); and includes a person who is in substance so engaged, employed, or contracted notwithstanding that the form of the contract between the parties is technically that of vendor and purchaser

The tests outlined in [404] to [410] below would suggest that in the absence of this statute's definition, most Courts would consider a homeworker to be a *contractor* – not a worker or employee. Thus in effect the law is saying that homeworkers – who are contractors – shall be treated as if they were workers, and people who are about to be employed, but are not yet employed, shall be assumed to be employed and hence to be workers or employees.

For many years statutes did not define the meaning of 'a person intending to work'. However, under common law, (*Canterbury Hotel v The Elms* at 959) the Court deemed it to mean a person who had been offered, and who had accepted the position, but who was yet to commence work. Eventually, the Employment Relations Act 2000 (ER Act) incorporated this definition within the statute.

The Employment Relations Act 2000 defines 'employee' in a similar fashion to 'worker' in the LR Act.

[403] Objectives in employment relations

The *overall* objectives of employees is to gain satisfaction (achievement, contentment, happiness) from their lives. Their major employment relations objectives – satisfaction from the factors that make up their job, and power and possibly increased productivity – are a *means* to those overall objectives. For union objectives see [420].

B. Employees and Contractors

[404] Differentiating employees from contractors

When an employer hires an employee, the employee is always an individual person. However, when an employer hires a contractor, the contractor could be an organisation which itself employs thousands of employees. The relationship, from any employment relations perspective, is one between two employer bodies. However, the contractor could also be an individual human being and from an industrial relations perspective the situation is much closer to that of employer-employee than that of two employers. Notwithstanding, because of the law they are differentiated.

Under New Zealand law, in contrast to employees, contractors have certain advantages:

a. they do not pay PAYE income tax;
b. they may make deductions for expenses.

And also certain disadvantages:

a. they do not have entitlement to holiday or sick pay provisions;
b. they do not have access to personal grievance procedures.

Some contracts are clearly ones of service and the employed person is 'obviously' a worker. In other cases, the employed person is clearly accepting a contract for services and is 'obviously' an independent contractor. The crucial point is: what makes it obviously one, and not the other? There are many 'grey' areas where there are elements of both types of contract. In *Stevenson v MacDonald,* Denning L.J. observed at 111, that 'it is often easy to recognise a contract of service when you see it, but difficult to say wherein the difference lies.' With the utmost respect, that observation is trite and reflects judicial laziness. If it actually is easy to recognise a contract of service, and the judge does not simply have a 'gut feeling', then it should be straightforward to articulate the reason. Further, a person employed under a contract of service may also be employed under a contract for services by the same employer.

The common law tests which Courts have used over time to differentiate have been summarised by Justice Holland in *Challenge Realty v Inland Revenue.* (His decision was later upheld by the Court of Appeal.)

[405] Control test

This was for many years virtually the sole test used. The 'control' refers to the employer's right to control *how* the work is done by an employee – as the employer can tell an independent contractor as well as an employee *what* is to be done. It must be noted that the employer does not have to be shown to *be* exercising the right of control, but only to have the right to do so, should he/she so desire. This test is still of paramount importance, but with the complexities of industrial work has been found inadequate in some circumstances. Occasionally employers provide such rigid specifications to independent contractors that they would appear to be controlling how the work is done. The situation is more complex when the employee is so skilled or specialised that the employer is not able or would not wish to tell the employee how to do the work. Examples are ship's masters or surgeons employed by a hospital board. However, the employer still has the *right* to exercise control.

In *NZEI v Director General* it was pointed out that the control test 'was once thought ... the decisive test ... (but) the evolution of a more sophisticated society has in many cases left that test behind' (p. 539).

[406] The integration test

This test was popularised by Denning L.J. in the *Stevenson* case, who stated:

> under a contract of service, a man is employed as part of the business, and his work is done as an integral part of the business; whereas, under a contract for services, his work, although done for the business, is not integrated into it but is only accessory to it.

As examples he used the fact that a ship's master, a chauffeur, and a reporter on the staff of a newspaper are all employed under a contract of service; but a ship's pilot, a taxi-man (*sic*), and a newspaper contributor are employed under a contract for services.

[407] The 'stated intentions' test

This is a significant test where there is an element of ambiguity. As the often quoted Lord Denning from *Massey v Crown Life* (at 579) put it:

> The law, as I see it, is this: if the true relationship of the parties is that of master and servant under a contract of service, the parties cannot alter the truth of that relationship by putting a different label upon it ... On the other hand, if their relationship is ambiguous and capable of being one or the other (i.e., either service or agency) then the parties can remove that ambiguity, by the very agreement itself which they make with one another. The agreement itself then becomes the best material from which to gather the true legal relationship between them.

The stated intentions must not be a sham. As discussed in *Calder v Kitson*, if an employee's description as self-employed is simply a device to evade tax, then it is a mere label and should be disregarded.

[408] The fundamental test

This test was defined by Holland who quoted Cooke J. from the *Market Investigations* (1968) case:

> the fundamental test to be applied is this: 'is the person who has engaged himself to perform these services performing them as a person in business on his own account'?

If 'yes' – contract for services; if 'no' – contract of service.

[409] The 'right to hire and fire' test

Justice Holland states that this test

> (does) not appear to me, in this case, to be particularly helpful one way or the other. A principal almost always has the right to select his agent and likewise has the right to terminate the agency either on notice or instantly. The relationship between an employer and employee does not appear to me to be materially different.

For all Holland's acumen, it may be this is a misinterpretation of the test. It is not whether or not the employer can choose or dismiss the person who is either an employee or contractor, but rather whether that *person* is in turn able to choose and dismiss an employee in his or her own right. If the answer is yes, the person is a contractor, if no the person is an employee. (Note that senior managers who are employees and who have the right to hire and fire do not do so *in their own right*, but as agents of their employer.)

[410] The ordinary person test

In 1910 Buckley L.J. proposed that the test was really 'what an ordinary person would consider the relationship to be', (*Simmons v Heath Laundry Co* (at 553)). It was never seriously proposed as a test on its own but was more of a rhetorical question: 'Given these facts what would an ordinary person think?'

This approach, utilising the mythical ordinary person, is fraught with difficulties, and should always be qualified with reasons as to why the ordinary person should think in such a way. Without this qualification, the test is incomplete and virtually valueless. In reality of course this approach is used to support a subjective view. One side feels the contract is of service, the other for services. The Judge agrees with one side – and says it was the view of an ordinary person. The implication is that anyone who disagrees is 'extraordinary', used in a pejorative sense.

[411] Consistency test and broad view test

Although sometimes cited separately, these two tests are in effect identical. The approach is to take a broad view of all the relevant factors and see if they are consistent with being a contract of service, or for services. By themselves, both tests have the same defect as the 'Ordinary Person' test: they are incomplete and need justification to show *why* a broad view would come to the conclusion actually reached. In effect, this necessitates use of the multiple test.

[412] Industry context

Brought into prominence by the 2:1 majority Court of Appeal decision in *Threefoot Six Ltd v. Bryson*, this case stressed that industry practice and the impact on the industry should be given significant weight, notwithstanding the failure of the statute to specify this.

[413] The multiple test

In the *Market Investigations* case, it was proposed that the following be considered:

1. control;
2. ownership of equipment;
3. whether the employed hires helpers;
4. degree of financial risk;

5. responsibility for investment and management, and
6. opportunity of profit.

However, Cook J. went on to point out:

> no exhaustive list has been compiled and perhaps no exhaustive list can be compiled of considerations which are relevant in determining that question, nor can strict rules be laid down as to the relative weight which the various considerations should carry in particular cases.

This observation is very true. It is also necessary to stress that any factor by itself can indicate one type of contract is actually the other. Notwithstanding both problems, the following examples are suggested as significant indicators of a contract *of* service (the opposite would suggest one *for* services):

1. control: employer has right to control how work is done;
2. integration: work part and parcel of organisation;
3. hours of work: controlled by employer;
4. tools: supplied by employer;
5. equipment: supplied by employer;
6. sick pay: provision made for sick pay;
7. holiday pay: provision made for holiday pay;
8. PAYE: If PAYE tax deducted;
9. method of payment: if regular weekly, fortnightly, or monthly payment (lump sum payment indicates contract for services);
10. hiring of other labour: if employed has *no* independent rights to hire;
11. firing of other labour: if employed has *no* independent rights to dismiss;
12. management: if employed has *no* independent management responsibilities;
13. profit: if employed has *no* opportunity to make profits;
14. loss: if employed has *no* risk of making loss.

[414] Employing the tests in practice

In practice some tests, or parts of the multiple test, will suggest a contract *for* services, other tests, that it is a contract *of* service. In the *Challenge* case, Holland J. observed:

> Pointing to an independent contractual relationship are the following facts:
> (1) the lack of fixed working times of any nature;
> (2) the lack of provision for holiday pay, sick leave, superannuation and the like;
> (3) the lack of close supervision and the relative lack of control of the manner in which the salesmen carry out their work;
> (4) the responsibility of the salesmen to provide their own cars, telephones and to some extent places of work;
> (5) the absence of any trade union;
> (6) the fact that one salesman employed his wife and paid her from his commission;
> (7) the expressed intention of the parties.

Pointing to an employee relationship are:

(a) the salesmen by their contract and by law are carrying out sales on behalf of one licensed real estate agent, and no other;

(b) each contract that is negotiated by a salesman is in fact and in law the contract of the licensed real estate agent;

(c) the fact that the immediate effect of termination of the contract between the licensed real estate agent and the salesman would be that the salesman had no 'business' at all;

(d) the requirement to pay a deposit received by the salesman forthwith to the licensed real estate agent;

(e) the office systems of allocation of properties for sale to salesmen and the general briefing systems as to properties for sale and related matters conducted by the licensed real estate agents;

(f) the general provisions in the Real Estate Agents Act 1976 relating to salesmen and their status notwithstanding the use of the word 'engaged' as well as 'employed'.

[415] Changing emphasis

As stated in [405], at one stage the *control test* was considered decisive and while it could still be considered the single most important test over the years it has assumed less significance. Now it is simply one of a large number of tests. However, every new case can put a different emphasis on different factors. The case of *Cunningham v TNT Worldwide Express* is a prime example. In this case both the Employment Tribunal, and on appeal the Employment Court, found that Cunningham was an employee. Following the common law as generally understood, the Court stated that the correct test is the totality of the picture. The control test and the fundamental test were most appropriate. Although Cunningham had to provide his own car, could claim expenses, and paid ACC levies and GST levies, the control exercised was very stringent. The contract was poorly worded and he was required to work exclusively for TNT and had little independence. The Court of Appeal however, possibly with the handicap of less experience in such cases, came to the surprising conclusion that Cunningham was a contractor. Left unchecked, this decision would have dramatically reduced the significance of the control test and put much more weight on the written words of the contract – and much less weight on how the contract was put into effect. However, the significance of Cunningham was substantially reduced by the Employment Relations Act 2000 in s.5.6 which states that in determining if the contract is of service or for services:

The Court or the Authority:

(d) must consider all relevant matters, in deciding any matters that indicate the intention of the parties; and

(d) is not to treat as a determining matter any statement by the persons that describes the nature of the their relationship.

C. Employees and their Organisations

[416] Unions role in the worker/union party

Individual workers/employees and informal groups operate in employment relations. However, formal employee organisations (i.e. unions) play the major role in employment relations for the 'employee/union' party.

Unions, certainly in a form similar to that seen today, did not really appear until the nineteenth century and there is little evidence of the existence of any unions prior to the eighteenth century. Pelling (1976:17) observes:

> the concept of a separate organisation of employed workers to determine wages and conditions by negotiation with their employers, had no place in the medieval system of industry. The recognised crafts were catered for by the guilds.

[417] Guilds

Guilds were three-tiered. At the top was the master craftsman. He combined the functions of not only employer, supervisor and worker, but also merchant – he bought the raw materials, designed, made and sold the finished product. At the next level was the journeyman – a proficient worker who was paid by the day. He had every prospect of becoming a master craftsman eventually. At the bottom level was the apprentice who was learning the trade from scratch, learning to become a journeyman. The number of apprentices was restricted to ensure that journeymen and masters retained a scarcity value.

These institutions date back for centuries. There were guilds in Ancient Babylon, Greece and Rome, written records of Korean guilds from the ninth century (which refer to contemporary Chinese guilds), and evidence of guilds in London from the tenth century. Phelps Brown (1962:30) considers that this widespread appearance of guilds suggests they met

> needs common to the self-employed worker in very different societies. One of those needs was for the preservation of his art … for a way to transmit (it) to the young entrant … Another need was for security … to regulate entry into the trade, to keep interlopers and 'foreign' wares out of the local market, and to maintain agreed prices for the product and wages for journeymen.

Eventually, however, guilds failed to meet the needs, particularly of the journeyman. The failure rose from the increased scale of industrial organisation. As markets grew larger and the population expanded, it became impossible for the master craftsman to retain all his traditional roles and so middlemen – merchants, shopkeepers and employers – appeared. An additional factor was that the number of journeymen increased rapidly and this, together with the breakdown of the master craftsman position, resulted in there being a large number of people with every likelihood of remaining *wage earners* for the whole of their working lives. These permanent wage earners felt the need for an organisation designed to assist them rather than the guilds which primarily catered for the master craftsman.

[418] Emergence of unions

Once wage earners (employees) lost confidence in guilds, they would create *ad hoc* bodies to meet particular emergencies. Many would exist only for a short time, but others would survive. Thus developed the union, described by the Webbs (1896:1) as 'a continuous association of wage-earners for the purpose of maintaining or improving the conditions of their working lives.'

An important aspect of the Webbs' description is their observation that the union was created to maintain as well as improve conditions. In fact, many more unions grew out of action groups formed to protest what they considered attacks on their conditions (wage cuts, dismissals or changed work practices), than from groups formed to improve conditions. Indeed, French unions were called *'Resistances'* – indicating the idea of resisting attacks rather than initiating them.

Phelps Brown (1962:40-41) has pointed out that certain conditions are necessary before unions will develop:

a. there must be a class of permanent wage earners sufficiently numerous and concentrated to be able to keep in touch with one another and to get together in some force;
b. efforts at combination must not be repressed by the authorities absolutely;
c. wages of their members must already be high enough to be able to pay their dues regularly; and
d. some among the members (must be) educated enough to … administer the business of the branch.

In addition, there needs to be a breakdown in customary practices which in the past protected employees, and an absence of particular economic factors (either labour scarcity which results in good conditions, or abundant land to which the employee can revert).

There also needs to be a catalyst – some action by the employer which triggers sufficient dissatisfaction to overcome inertia and tolerance of bad conditions. Budd, Gomez and Meltz (2004:198) point out the shocking work accident statistics in the USA in the early part of the twentieth century:

> According to one estimate, industrial accidents resulted in 25,000 deaths, 25,000 permanent disabilities cases and 2,000,000 temporary disability cases per year, which implies that during World War I, US casualties were greater in the workforce than on the battlefield. Workers seem quite willing to tolerate, what appears to outsiders to be totally unacceptable conditions.

Charness and Levine (2000:393) observe that 'many studies find that people tend to perceive what is usual as reasonably fair.' So it was usually not bad conditions *per se* which resulted in a demand for unions, but a *worsening* of conditions: a pay cut, a speed-up of work or a lay-off of employees. Not surprisingly, there is a strong relationship between employee dissatisfaction and their desire for union representation (Farber, 1990). The necessary conditions discussed above create the ironical situation, however, that the most downtrodden employees are often the last to unionise, while the 'aristocrats' of the working class are more able to meet the conditions of sufficiently high wages and educational standards and unionise first. Pelling (1976:15) points out that:

> unionism up to the middle of the nineteenth century was largely confined to artisans. The scarcity value of their skill enabled them to extract concessions from their employers; their regular earnings allowed something to spare for union contributions; and their ranks included a sufficient proportion of persons able to read and write and thus see to the union accounts and organising.

Thus the earliest unions were in general *craft unions* – unions of skilled employees of a particular calling: carpenters, painters, and so forth. The employees usually had to complete an apprenticeship, and, like the guilds, craft unions utilise apprenticeships as a means not only of preserving the craft but also of restricting the entry of workers into the craft. Later unions were also in the form of *industrial unions*, where all employees in a particular industry – skilled, semi-skilled and unskilled – were recruited into the one union; *general unions* which are open to employees of all skill levels and industrial occupations; and *occupational unions* which are of employees of one particular occupation (but unlike craft unions they do not require apprenticeships).

In Western society today, there are few unions which fit exactly into the above categories. Unions which are 'craft' often include elements of an industrial union, and include semi-skilled and unskilled employees. Industrial and occupational unions rarely, and probably never, recruit *all* employees in the industry or occupation, and general unions usually have their membership from particular areas.

[419] Union structure

There is a wide range of union structures. There are small, local, totally autonomous unions, some catering only for employees in a particular firm. There are also national unions catering for many thousands and, in the UK and the USA, indeed millions of employees. These unions often break down into branch unions (or 'locals', as they are known in the USA) which cover employees in a particular area or organisation.

Most district or national unions are run by full-time union officials, the most powerful being, usually, the union secretary. At branch level there are union delegates, also known as shop stewards, representing work groups or departments, usually with an executive run by the branch officials. Moving in the other direction, unions also combine into central organisations such as, in New Zealand, the Council of Trade Unions (CTU).

[420] Union objectives

As outlined in [105] and to be discussed more fully in Chapter Five, the objectives of employees are in general to maintain, and possibly improve, the level of satisfaction with the factors that make up the job. For many, wages and conditions are the major factors. In times of high unemployment, job security becomes paramount. Particularly in these times there is greater concern for increasing the level of productivity which is seen, not only as desirable, but also a means of helping the organisation to survive, thus giving job security.

To the extent that a union is seen simply as a group of employees, the objectives of the union could be seen simply as objectives sought by its members. However, as noted by Fiorito and Hendricks (1987:569), 'unions may differ considerably in their objectives.' The reason is that although 'the union' may be a legal entity it comprises:

- membership;
- rank and file union leaders ('delegates' or 'shop stewards');
- full-time union officials.

The 'union' of course, cannot speak. Full-time union officials may have the right to speak *for* 'the union'. Rank and file leaders may speak for 'their members'. All these individuals have their own values, beliefs, personal objectives and ambitions. Just as some managers, politicians, and church leaders may act out of self-interest rather than work for the interests of their organisation or constituents, so too can some union officials. So, when considering the objectives of the union, one needs to be clear if the focus is the legal entity, the membership or the leaders.

D. Features and Characteristics of Unions

[421] Compulsory union membership

This topic encapsulates many of the issues and problems of employment relations overall. Views abound on this topic, with varying ideological standpoints. Value judgements are often expressed as facts, and motives frequently concealed behind high-sounding platitudes. Before discussing the various ethical arguments, different types of compulsory membership arrangements need to be defined:

a. a 'closed shop' is where prior membership in the union is a pre-requisite for employment (sometimes referred to as pre-entry closed shop);
b. a 'union shop' is where a worker must become a member of the union within a short and stated space of time and must remain a member (sometimes referred to as post-entry closed shop);
c. an 'agency shop' is where workers must either join the union, or pay a fee in lieu of the membership dues.

Often considered closely related to closed/union shop agreements is an agreement for union membership fees to be automatically deducted from employees' pay packets on a weekly/monthly basis and paid to the union. Clearly, this arrangement does not require compulsory membership but equally clearly it is a major benefit to the union, at little cost to the employer. Consequently it can be a powerful negotiating item for the employer to offer or withdraw. Reid and Kurth (1984:396) quote an American union official who claimed that 'without voluntary dues deduction, what we call "checkoff", a blue-collar organisation cannot exist.'

While most of the arguments for and against compulsory union membership are couched in high-flown appeals for 'union rights', 'democracy in action', 'freedom of the individual' and 'right to work', it is submitted that, in most cases, the real motives behind support or opposition for compulsory membership are simple calculations about costs and benefits to the party concerned. This can result in some surprising situations.

Before the New Zealand Labour Government introduced compulsory membership by law in 1936, both the central union organisation and the New Zealand Employers' Federation opposed the proposal. The central organisation opposed the proposal because they thought that the influx of reluctant members who had been compelled to join would reduce the militancy of all unions, and also would result in 'weaker' unions who would gain the most new members, having an undue say in the central organisation. The NZEF thought the increase in membership, and hence union fees, would be an unwarranted benefit to unions, and would in general strengthen the union movement. By 1951, when the National Government proposed to repeal the law, both these organisations had changed their stance and were in favour. The central union organisation found the benefits of increased income outweighed the problem of 'weaker' unions dominating the central organisation. Those in leadership positions found the block votes of large but 'uninvolved' unions essential for their personal power bases. The NZEF on the other hand found the system reduced worker-worker conflict, and ensured better employment relations. The parties were more honest in those days, and less inclined to hide their real interests. In recent times arguments are better packaged, to appear less self-serving.

[422] Arguments against compulsory union membership

The most common arguments put openly against compulsory membership are that it is an infringement on individual freedom, it attacks the individual's right to work, and it results in unions not being concerned about giving good service, as they have monopoly control.

The 'freedom' argument is not only socially acceptable, but also difficult to attack without appearing to be a fascist of the left or right, unconcerned with individual freedom. However, one does not have to be very cynical to question the sincerity of governments and employers who impose a myriad of restrictions on individual freedom – but profess to be genuinely so concerned about this one aspect of individual freedom. The same champions of individual freedom were apparently unconcerned about attacking the freedom of unionists to elect not to work alongside non-unionists. It is purely a value judgement which, of a number of freedoms, is more important.

The 'right to work' argument, which is associated mainly with the USA, implies that compulsory membership is an attack on an employee's right to work. If a union was able to *refuse* an employee membership, then a closed or union shop situation *could* be seen in this light. An agency shop situation creates no problems. However, the terminology 'right to work' is dishonest as anti-compulsory membership laws do not give anyone a 'right to work.' If there was such a 'right to work', unemployment figures would be dramatically affected. In countries where closed or union shops existed there have been remarkably few accusations that unions arbitrarily and/or unjustly refused membership. Obviously legislation could require unions to justify any refusal of membership before a Tribunal or Court as a *quid pro quo* for a closed or union shop.

The third argument against compulsory membership is that it results in unions not providing good service. With voluntary membership, it is argued unions will have to provide better services in order to *attract* members. The counter to this is that many services are 'general' rather than individual-specific and employees can enjoy the services and benefits (wage increases, improved conditions) while remaining non-members and saving on union fees.

[423] Arguments for compulsory union membership

The most common arguments for compulsory membership are that it is a reflection of normal democratic principles, that it prevents 'free-riders', that it improves union service, and that it results in better work relations.

Mitchnick (1993:466) quotes Madam Justice Wilson:

> to my mind, there is no distinction in principle between our overall system of government and the role of taxation within it and the mini-democracy of the workplace. Under our labour relations regime all members of the bargaining unit have an equal opportunity to participate in choosing who is to represent them and to join the ranks of the union or not as they see fit. Further, as in our system of representative democracy, members of a bargaining unit may also decide to oust their bargaining agent if dissatisfied with its performance.

This very neatly encapsulates the democracy argument.

The free-rider argument is virtually self-explanatory. If all employees are going to benefit from union activity resulting in higher wages and better conditions, then there should be no free-riders, and all who benefit should share the cost.

The 'service' argument is somewhat confusing as it is used as an argument both for and against compulsory membership. Those who claim compulsory membership improves service argue that the increased membership results in increased revenue allowing the union to provide better service, and also that unions are able to concentrate on providing better service rather than competing against each other for members, or simply concentrating on gaining members. Certainly, as illustrated in [209], the introduction of compulsory membership by law dramatically increases union membership levels. There is a degree of plausibility to the arguments on both sides, and no clear-cut answers.

The final argument for compulsory membership is that it results in better employment relations, first by reducing conflict within the workforce between members and non-members and second by giving the workforce a more cohesive voice where employers need to negotiate with the union knowing it represents all employees in that category and area. With voluntary membership, the union will represent only a proportion of the workforce.

[424] Changing attitudes to compulsory unionism

New Zealand is a classic example of how employer attitudes change dramatically. In 1983 when the National Government (which has remained consistent in its policy *statements*, if not actions) moved once more to abolish compulsory unions (after an abortive effort in 1951 and a token effort in 1961) employers in general again opposed the move. By the late 1980s, however, the NZEF was pushing for the legislative changes which resulted in the Employment Contracts Act 1991 and the outlawing of compulsory membership.

This attitudinal change is not restricted to New Zealand and is repeated in the UK. The USA was less liberal for many years and only accepted union or agency shops, but the common law there has been less supportive of both in recent years.

The attack by governments and employers on the concept of compulsory union membership in recent years is in part due to acceptance of the New Right ideology, in part due to a perceived need for increased flexibility resulting from increased competition from emerging nations in Asia, and in part due to the recession and increased levels of unemployment which have weakened unions.

[425] Growth in white-collar unions

From the 1850s to the 1950s, there was a generally steady increase in union membership throughout the industrialised world. Consideration of the conditions necessary for union development makes this growth unsurprising. Industry has increased in size, resulting in greater concentration of workers; in general, repressive legislation has been reduced or removed and in some cases, like New Zealand in 1894, Australia a few years later and the USA in 1935, legislation encouraging union growth was passed; increased productivity raised wages above subsistence levels and the general levels of education were improved.

Except for the USA (see [209]) where the decline began in 1955, union growth basically continued into the 1980s. Since then, the majority of industrialised countries have witnessed a decrease in union density and even raw union membership.

A major growth area in unions since the Second World War has been in 'white-collar' unions: clerical, technical, and more recently in lower managerial areas. The growth in white-collar union membership is due to two reasons. The first is the tremendous growth in the number of white-collar jobs and the increased proportion of these jobs to the total number of jobs. This is illustrated by the dramatic change from labour markets being predominantly manufacturing to predominantly service, as illustrated in Table 4.1.

The second reason for the growth in white-collar union membership is the increased density of membership, i.e., the proportion of people in white-collar jobs who now join unions.

Smith (1987:101) pointed out that in the New Zealand context:

> in the decade 1971–81, the rate of unionisation of white-collar workers outstripped the rate of growth of the white-collar workforce.

The development of white-collar unions has some close similarities with the development of the more traditional unions – although there are some differences. White-collar employees in past years were often better paid and educated than most of their manual counterparts and could have unionised much earlier. They, in fact, were in a position where the *need* for unionism was not apparent as their wages and conditions were much better; getting sickness benefits, paid holidays and pensions. In addition, as instanced by Table 4.2 below, their job security was greater. Also, management worked very hard to create a class consciousness. White-collar workers were called staff (not hands), paid a salary (not a wage), and given separate facilities. This created a feeling of superiority, or snobbishness – they were 'above' unions.

Table 4.1. Market structure percentage service

	US	Canada	Netherlands	UK	Sweden
1975	62	58	53	50	50
1985	67	64	61	59	58
	Norway	Italy	France	Switzerland	Germany
1975	47	46	45	44	41
1985	56	50	54	50	47

Source: Troy (1990)

Table 4.2. 1931 UK unemployment – by work category

Work Category	% Unemployed
Unskilled Manual	30.5
Skilled and Semi-skilled	14.4
Shop Assistants	7.9
Clerks and Typists	5.5

Source: Clark (1938:46)

In recent years, many of the advantages white-collar employees had over manual workers have disappeared. Manual workers now have sickness benefits, pension schemes, holidays and pay rates which nearly match and often do match those of white-collar employees. In New Zealand between 1973 and 1991, protection against unjustifiable dismissal was much better for unionised empoyees than for lower-level managers. Managers used to 'joke' in those days that the way to get rid of troublesome employees was to promote them to supervisory positions, make them unpopular – and fire them. Thus white-collar employees witnessed an *attack* on their comparative standards. This has been sufficient in many cases to overcome the basic anti-union feeling.

In addition, there has been increased concentration of employment – bureaucratisation – so that more white-collar employees are being treated as part of a group (a Grade IV secretary) rather than as individuals. This also results in fewer promotion opportunities, less identity with management and less opportunity for the worker to make an individual deal.

However, while white-collar employees over the last thirty or so years have not had legislation preventing unionisation, there has been strong managerial opposition. Both Bain (1970) and Lumley (1973) agree that management attitudes, together with bureaucratisation, are important factors in the extent of white-collar unionism. Particularly with management or supervisory-level unions, there are implicit signals or explicit threats that to join a union indicates a lack of loyalty to the organisation and will affect promotion chances and job security. Smith (1987:115) felt that white-collar employees in New Zealand who wished to unionise were 'subject to considerable dissuasion by employers.' As discussed in Chapter Nineteen, the intensity of anti-unionism in New Zealand increased dramatically from the late 1980s.

[426] Public sector unionisation

Ozaki (1987a) points out that

> the massive unionisation of public servants has been a relatively recent phenomenon in comparison with the long tradition of trade unionism in the private sector, at least in most industrialised countries ... in a large majority of industrialised countries and many developing countries, the density of unionisation in the public service today considerably exceeds that in the private sector.

This rapid growth in the relative importance of public as opposed to private sector unionism can be attributed to a number of factors.

The first is that there was a major shift in employment from the private to the public sector occurring over the 1970s and 1980s, as shown in Table 4.3 below, but this trend reversed in the 1990s, with 'restructuring' and privatisation.

The above-mentioned 'restructuring', however, is also an impetus to unionise as one of the major benefits of working in the public sector used to be job security. Job security has been attacked in a number of countries, and theory suggests this would encourage unionisation. (See Table 4.3). A further factor

Table 4.3. Public employment as a percentage of total employment

	1975	1985	1997
France	18.7	27.9	18.1
Germany	21.9	23.3	11.6
Italy	20.4	23.1	13.4
Netherlands	15.5	19.9	10.5
Sweden	33.2	33.1	
Great Britain	29	27	
Canada	29.8	29.9	16.7
USA	18.3	16.3	13.8

Source: OECD Surveys

has been the general relaxation in legislation regarding public sector employees. This has occurred at different times. Thus in the USA it took place in 1962, in New Zealand not until the State Sector Act 1988.

In 1984, in the New Zealand public sector, a new style of management sometimes referred to as 'New Public Management' (NPM) was introduced (Boston, Martin, Pallot & Walsh, 1996; Hood, 1991). NPM promotes competition, supposedly encourages 'efficiency and effectiveness' and was seen as the best possible solution to removing perceived inefficiencies in the public sector (Ironside & Siefert, 2002).

In contrast to other countries, the public sector workforce in New Zealand does not make up a high proportion of the total workforce. A high level of variation between estimates of government employment as a percentage of total employment has been found and Whitehouse (1992) found the range varied

Table 4.4. Union membership by occupational group and public/private sector in the USA

	White-collar workers/employees							
	Executive, administrative and managerial		Professionals		Technical, sales and clerical		White-collar total	
	Public	Private	Public	Private	Public	Private	Public	Private
Member	25	2	34	8	39	8	39	6
Non Member	75	98	66	92	61	92	61	93
Total	100	100	100	100	100	100	100	100
N	22	111	127	152	68	234	217	498

Table 4.4. Cont'd.

	Blue-collar workers/employees							
	Precision, production, craft and repair		Operators, fabricators, and labourers		Blue-collar, total		Service occupations	
	Public	Private	Public	Private	Public	Private	Public	Private
Member	43	32	32	27	38	29	31	9
Non Member	57	68	68	73	62	71	68	91
Total	100	100	100	100	100	100	100	100
N	10	59	27	144	37	203	51	108

Source: Lipset and Katchanovski (2002:1)

from 6.3 per cent (Japan, 1974) to 33.1 per cent (Sweden, 1985). More recently the WERS reported that the UK public sector comprised around 32 per cent of the total workforce (Cully *et al*, 1999). In New Zealand, only 18 per cent of the total workforce is employed by the State. During the 1990s, when employment in New Zealand grew by 16–17 per cent, public sector employment decreased by nearly 20 per cent. This decrease was mainly in response to the NPM reforms aimed at making the public sector more efficient and accountable.

Economic objectives became a priority for public sector employers. This threatened the former objectives of social justice and equity, as well as the public sector's status as a model employer. Possibly to lessen this threat, but more likely as a means to appease union opposition, the State legislated for 'good' employment practice in the public sector, in Section 56, subsections (1) and (2), of the State Sector Act 1988, titled the 'Good Employer Obligation'. Effectively this obligation provides a mandate for 'good' or 'desirable' employment practice in the public sector. The introduction of the State Sector Act 1988 was viewed by the State, at the time of its inception, as an instrumental vehicle for implementing change (Walsh, 1989). Prior to this, Boston reports employment relations were (1996:206)

> organised around principles of centralised and uniform bureaucratic control … Rules were prescribed and their application monitored from the centre. In departments, superiors apply these rules so as to control the behaviour of subordinates. These rules limited the discretion and constrained the behaviour of managers and employers at an individual level and union and management at a collective level … the flexible deployment of staff, the harnessing of the creative

potential of employees, the use of initiative and lateral thinking were, as in all bureaucratic control systems, assigned less priority than the certainties of clear-cut responsibilities, the advantages of known and methodical procedures, and the commitment engendered by employment security and the existence of diverse and well-understood opportunities for promotion.

[427] Women in unions

The traditional view of women in unions is illustrated by Paul (1939:26) in his history of the Dunedin Tailoresses Union. He quotes a Royal Commission report which stated that

> women cannot combine together as workmen do in their trades union to protect themselves …

And also a woman worker who stated

> it's no use speaking of trade organisation amongst women. They never will combine. They would submit to anything rather than do that …

Although more recently women by their actions have demonstrated that both statements are false, the view that women make poor unionists and that women would not be prepared to strike and make the sacrifices necessary to create a strong union still exists in some quarters. The traditional explanation used to be that it was in women's *nature* to be poor unionists, that women are not serious workers in that they are frequently secondary income earners and go to work primarily for social reasons or to earn 'pin' money. These arguments are clearly flawed. Many women, both now and in the past, have been the primary income-earners for their households. Second, the fact that an income is the second in a household very rarely means it is perceived as insignificant (or for 'pin' money only).

A further possibility is that women have too many home and/or childcare commitments to be able to be serious unionists. This view is put by both traditionalists who denigrate women and by apologists for women. While few would dispute that most home and childcare is undertaken by women, as discussed later, research shows that there are few, if any, differences in attitude to unionism, or behaviour with respect to unions, between women and men who work full-time.

Since the overall trend for union membership is downwards, and the overall picture for unions is bleak, it would be incorrect to suggest that women in union movements can expect significant gains. However, it is reasonable to predict that women in unions and female-dominated unions in the union movement will become relatively more significant in the future. As Lynn and Brister (1989:111) point out, 'predominantly female industries have experienced employment growth in recent years while predominantly male industries have been shrinking.'

E. Challenge of the New Millennium

[428] The challenge for unions

Nearly forty years ago J.K. Galbraith (1967:262, 282) predicted that unions in the future would have 'a drastically reduced function' and will 'retreat more or less permanently into the shadows.' On the other hand Deeks *et al* (1994:299) suggest:

> the union movement is a recognised institution, part of 'the establishment', closely integrated with the economic and political life of the capitalist system ...

Most would agree that Galbraith was remarkably prescient with respect to the present. Over the last decade, unions have become increasingly marginalised in many countries. There may of course be a revival, even in the face of what Smith and Morton (1994) describe as a dynamic process of union exclusion. Certainly it is too early to forecast the total demise of unions. As Kirkland (1986:393) has observed with respect to the union movement in the USA, 'Labour's obituary has been written at least once in every one of the 105 years of our existence.' However, it is certainly true that since the early 1990s unions have faced a major challenge to retain their former status, relevance and viability.

Indeed for many countries, the drop in union density is quite dramatic even over a short time-span. This is illustrated in Table 4.5.

Table 4.5. Union density in developed countries, 1960–95

	1960	1970	1980	1990	1995
Sweden	70.7	66.6	78.2	82.4	87.5
Denmark	60.2	62.1	77.5	74.5	78.1
Finland	29.3	51.4	70.0	72.5	78.8
Norway	51.6	50.0	54.1	53.1	52.5
Belgium	40.7	42.3	56.6	56.7	59.8
New Zealand	54.0	46.1	56.0	45.0	24.3
Australia	49.1	44.4	48.0	41.0	35.2
Austria	57.8	55.4	50.8	45.2	38.9
Ireland	45.8	54.2	57.4	48.2	44.4
United Kingdom	44.3	48.6	52.8	40.1	32.2
Italy	22.4	34.0	44.4	33.6	32.4
Germany	34.2	31.8	33.6	29.9	26.5
Canada	28.3	29.8	36.0	36.0	37.4
Switzerland	-	29.9	30.7	26.3	22.7
Japan	32.2	34.5	31.0	25.0	24.0
Netherlands	41.0	36.0	32.4	22.3	22.9
United States	28.9	25.9	22.0	16.0	14.2
France	19.2	21.0	17.1	9.2	8.6

Source: Lipset and Katchanovski (2002:16)

[429] Causes of the crisis

As discussed in [209], the attitude of the State towards unions is a critical factor. In a number of industrialised countries there have been legislative changes designed directly or indirectly to weaken and hinder unions. Thus Freeman and Pelletier (1990:156) claim that 'the vast bulk of the observed 1980s decline in union density in the UK is due to the changed legal environment for industrial relations.' Towers (1989:167) considers the main reason for this change in attitude by government in the UK to be that

> the trade unions with their traditional role in wage bargaining and their collectivist pursuit of their goals, were seen as seriously impeding individualism and the working of free labour markets. The outcome was an interventionist strategy that sought to subordinate labour law and the trade unions to the governments economic and ideological goals ...

Also in [209], the dramatic drop in union membership in New Zealand following the Employment Contracts Act 1991 was noted. While the impact of legislation is generally accepted, there are some dissenters. In contrast to the view of Freeman and Pelletier (1990), Disney (1990:173) considers that for the UK in the 1980s 'the industrial relations legislation of the period also seems to have had no direct effect', and he suggests that 'it is macro-economic factors' which give the best explanation. On the other hand, Bridgford (1990:130) points out that in France

> in contradistinction to the British case, there was no government-led campaign during the 1980s to reduce trade union power by the introduction of restrictive labour law ... overall, French labour legislation introduced between 1981 and 1986 tended to reinforce the position of the trade unions.

Legislation is, and has been, clearly of great significance, but certainly it is not the only factor causing problems for unions. Unemployment and increasing competition, particularly from Asia, are also highly significant.

Individual unions can be significantly affected by particular events. For example, terrorism has a major impact on the travel industry and hospitality industry – consequently with a much greater effect on unions involved in those industries. Clark, Delaney and Frost (2002:6) point out that 'the hotel employees and restaurant employees suffered approximately eleven per cent (88,000 of 800,000) of the layoffs occurring in the USA' as a result of the September 11th 2001 terrorist attacks on New York.

[430] Strategy and tactics

For unions to successfully meet these challenges they will need to carefully select the correct strategy or strategies to meet their particular needs. In this context, the terms have been defined by Lipsig-Mumme (1989:231) as:

> *union strategy* means a focussed response to a defined problem or series of problems arising in, or in interaction with, the environment in which unions operate. *Tactics* refer to a short-term response to a defined problem or problems arising in, or in interaction with, the environment within which unions operate.

In some cases it is difficult to discern from particular *actions*, whether that action was part of a strategy or simply a reflex reaction and better described as a tactic.

[431] Merger

One strategy to overcome declining membership is for two or more unions to merge. Conant and Kaserman 1989:245) point out that a

> merger may allow unions to economize on management services ... the result may not only be lower average costs but also greater effectiveness in the negotiation process due to the division of labor. Merger may also improve administration of economic sanctions due to increased financial resources.

On the downside from union officials' point of view, is the fact that a merger halves the number of top jobs. While some officials increase their power and status, others will lose. Some members of small unions which merge with large unions may well feel dominated in the new, much larger unions, and may feel that the union's financial concern is for the majority and that their concerns will be overlooked. Indeed the lack of merger activity, except when unions are under serious threat, shows there must be perceived costs which previously were considered to outweigh the benefits.

[432] Increased subscription rates

Decreasing membership, all things being equal, will create a vicious spiral in that decreasing union funds will mean the union can afford fewer officials and will provide poorer services. This in turn will discourage membership, causing a further drop – and the spiral continues. Research in both the USA (Bennett, 1991) and the UK (Willman, 1989) shows that some unions which faced dropping membership levels substantially increased their subscription rates to the extent that real income levels remained unaffected. This strategy, of course, cannot be pursued indefinitely. It clearly suggests that in the past unions underpriced themselves but at current subscription levels demand will be very much more elastic.

[433] Public relations

Craft (1990:148) points out that in the USA striking unions 'were shocked at the lack of community support when they resisted employer concession demands and members of the community crossed their picket lines to take the strikers' jobs.' Some unions then worked to form coalitions with community groups to get public support and use community pressure more effectively. Increasing public support for unions is highly dependent on their image. Unions in the past have not put much effort or resources into public relations, and this is one strategy which could be considered. More recently, as Schmidt (1993) points out, public opinion is influenced by media coverage which is biased against strike activity, and reports on strike behaviour have a negative effect on public opinion. There is still considerable scope for improvement in the public relations activity of unions.

[434] Political involvement

A fourth strategy some unions and union movements are working on is increased political involvement: both lobbying governments and trying to influence the election of a government more sympathetic to unions and employees.

In some cases, the obvious union-oriented political party may have economic strategies which belie that fact. Thus New Zealand elected a Labour Government in both 1984 and 1987 and while that government introduced supportive employment relations legislation – the Labour Relations Act 1987 was described as 'more pluralist' than any of its predecessors (Geare, 1989:227) – in its economic policies it appeared bewilderingly right wing. (See [1946] for a discussion of the Labour-Alliance coalition's legislation for 2000.)

A second problem with this strategy is the major difficulty union movements seem to have in persuading union members to vote for the 'labour' or union-sympathetic party. Until recently New Zealand has returned a Labour Government fairly infrequently. In the UK, even when it was clear that Mrs Thatcher was going to introduce increasingly anti-union legislation, her government (and her successor's) kept being returned. Towers (1989:185) points out that 'only a slightly higher percentage of trade unionists voted Labour in the 1987 election than four years previously – 43% up from 39%.' Similarly, with respect to the USA, Lipsig-Mumme (1989:246) writes of the AFL-CIO's 'slide into marginalization … underscored by its repeated failure to both reinforce the Democratic Party and make the party more responsive to labor's needs'. A further difficulty in the US is the lack of real 'democracy' in that country, with respect to both the House of Representatives and Senate. Bennett (1991:67) claims that re-election of incumbents for the House of Representatives since 1986

> has been 98 per cent or higher. A similar pattern is apparent in election to the Senate … the advantages of incumbency are so powerful that even the taint of scandal or moral turpitude may not be sufficient to oust an entrenched and determined member of the House or Senate. Retirement, death, and disability are almost the only avenues of entry into Congress … because of the advantages of incumbency, votes are not the lifeblood of politics – money is.

Hence there appears to be little to be gained by unions exhorting their members to vote in a particular way. The result is almost a foregone conclusion.

[435] Accommodating the 'new' management

Some unions have employed a strategy of cooperation with new management styles – Japanese-type management, TQM and employee involvement. There is a basic problem in that frequently these techniques are employed by management to marginalise unions and make them either truly redundant or at least seemingly redundant. Consequently, as Smith (1989:305) has found:

> unions have also been lukewarm towards participation programs such as quality of working life, quality circles, team concepts and related employee involvement initiatives. They have taken the position that such participation is rarely a genuine attempt to enhance the quality of working life and tends to undermine the representative role of the union in the workplace.

Other unions have tried to negate this problem by negotiating 'single union' deals. This has been a strategy particularly employed in the UK by unions dealing with Japanese firms. Although initially it appeared attractive, interest is waning. Gall (1993:73-74) claims:

> many unions have found that such great deals do not guarantee high membership levels because the employer selects the union, undermining employee choice, and the structures of bargaining are often restrictive rendering the unions ineffectual. Indeed at Nissan, where the AEU has a single union deal, membership has never risen above 40% and a recent AEU recruitment campaign was launched to prevent other unions entering the plant. The result of this dissatisfaction has led the GMB and TGWU to refuse to compete for future single union deals. This will lead to fewer unions offering such deals to the employers.

[436] Return to basics

Towers (1989:183) reports that some unions have a strategic approach which is to return to the basics, and a concern for pay and conditions:

> they argue that the primary, even exclusive, purpose of trade unions is to improve the pay and conditions of individual members. Wider social, community and political goals are seen as an irrelevance at best and, at worst, a threat to the primary purpose of trade unions – and even their existence – should the political climate become hostile.

This strategy will not be seen as progressive – or politically correct – but could be successful and attractive, particularly to unions of skilled employees.

[437] Organisational/recruitment activity

Union membership is related to the ability of unions to organise, recruit and present a united collective front to employers (Cully, Woodland, O'Reilly and Dix, 2000:85).

So although it is far from exotic, the evidence would suggest that the best strategy unions could employ to meet the challenges ahead is a commitment to straight work, and organisational and recruitment activity. A number of significant factors have been cited which work against unions. However, Dickens and Leonard (1985) point out that while the economy worked against unions in the 1970s, in the early 1960s economic factors were worse, but more organising activity took place – and it was more successful. Beaumont and Harris (1990) on the other hand observe that a number of studies show that many individuals, and whole worksites, in the UK that are non-union remain so because unions have just not bothered to organise them. Mason and Bain (1993:349) believe that

> trade union activity plays a key role in motivating workers to join unions, and that the large-scale union membership growth during the 1970s was related to union activity over a wide range of issues …

In an earlier paper, those two authors point out (1991:44) that such lip service is paid to the need to recruit. They quote a union official:

> the topic of recruitment is very high on the agenda … in terms of what is said at conferences … and in our journal. But the reality is that in terms of clerical and administrative resources given to it, it has a very low priority. Indeed it is the poor relation of our centralised system ...

If unions wish to regain the status and significance they enjoyed a few decades past, they will have to accept that a considerable amount of effort and activity is required.

Chapter Five

The Objectives of the Parties

A. Introduction

[501] Significance of objectives

As outlined in [105], the objectives of the parties are a crucial part of the definition of employment relations. However, the importance of objectives is not simply in academic theorising. Proper understanding of the role of objectives in employment relations by any party significantly increases the probability that that party's objectives will be achieved. First, understanding assists the party to make a more rational selection from various actions and to focus on end results rather than on intermediary results. A second benefit is that it enables the party to analyse *others'* actions and to better understand them. In cases where others in fact appear not to be acting 'rationally' with respect to their objectives, knowledge and understanding of this may allow for a more effective strategy.

[502] Employment relations objectives

In earlier chapters and specifically in [206], [304] and [403], the relationship between employment relations objectives and the overall objectives of the parties was discussed. While accepting that the overall objective of a parliamentarian may be re-election and of an organisation may be survival, growth and profits, the emphasis in this work is on the *employment relations* objectives which help ensure the overall objective will be achieved.

As already defined, the *principal* employment relations objectives of the three major parties will in general be one or more of:

a. retaining and possibly increasing one's existing power within the work environment;
b. maintaining and possibly improving labour-related productivity;
c. maintaining and possibly improving satisfaction with the factors that make up the job.

As a broad generalisation, power is a major objective of all three parties, both as an end in itself, and also as a means to the other objectives. (Thus Pfeffer (1992) argues that managers use power to achieve their *other* goals.) Labour-related productivity is a major objective of employers and of the State and an intermediary objective of employees and unions, since it is seen as a means to increased security and wages and hence satisfaction. Satisfaction with work factors is a major objective of employees and unions and an intermediary objective of employers and the State, who at times would see increased satisfaction as a precursor to productivity.

There are a number of issues that need to be explored about the above objectives:

a. the inter-relationship between objectives and the extent to which they coincide or clash;
b. the extent to which parties try to maximise objectives or merely 'comfortise'; and
c. the extent to which parties are proactive in their pursuit of objectives or reactive to external changes.

These will be considered below in [526] to [528].

B. Power

[503] Definition of power

Kirkbride (1985:265-6) has observed that

> power forms part of our everyday commonsense language ... yet despite obvious centrality and importance of power to the study of industrial relations ... the concept represents a major lacuna in the theoretical development of the discipline.

He rightly points out that major texts and authors often provide no clear definition when referring to power. However, when authors *do* define power, the definitions are frequently idiosyncratic and not always enlightening. In one of the earlier theoretical papers on power and industrial relations, Dubin (1957:60) wrote that 'power may be defined as the importance that consequences of actions have in a social relationship.' Brass (1984:518), on the other hand, observes that power 'is often defined from a dependency framework such that the power of A over B is equal to the extent to which B is dependent on A.' This latter definition purports to define power, but actually fails to say what it *is*.

Approaches to power tend to fall into one of four categories, depending on whether the primary concern of the writer is with preceding conditions, decision-making, situational outcomes or behavioural outcomes. It would appear that, as with so many concepts, the comment made by a learned Judge about a dog is apposite. In effect the Judge observed that 'people find it very easy to recognise a dog if they see one. They find it very difficult to *define* a dog.' Similarly, many people can recognise that in a particular situation one party has relatively more power than another party – yet defining power escapes them.

Given the lack of a generally accepted definition, clearly no particular definition will satisfy all critics. Notwithstanding, this book adopts a definition of power derived from the work of Weber (1947) and Dahl (1957). Power is defined as:

> the ability to act as one wishes even if opposed by others; and/or the ability to make other parties act as you wish, even against their preference.

Thus employers have power if they are able to act as they want, regardless of the wishes of the State as expressed by policy or legislation. A union has power if it is able to force an employer to make concessions and agree to bargaining demands. Individual employees have power if they can work and behave according to their wishes and contrary to their supervisor's wishes.

The definition above raises a number of issues, including:

a. how parties come to gain power;
b. the importance of perception in power situations;
c. how power can be lessened or increased.

[504] Sources of power

Handy (1976) has listed five sources of power, namely physical, resource, position, expert and personal power. These were derived from the work of French and Raven (1959) who submitted a similar list, namely coercion, reward, legitimacy, expert and referent power. Later Raven and Kruglanski (1970) added information as a sixth source of power. These two versions of the sources of power can be considered together as there are large areas of similarity.

If the source is physical (coercion), this implies that power is derived from the threatened or actual use of physical force, or the use of sanctions, or the threatened reduction in another's outcomes. Strikes, suspensions, sabotage and personal violence are examples of physical sources of power.

Resource sources (rewards) is in effect the opposite to physical sources, in that power is derived from the ability to positively increase outcomes for other parties. An obvious use of resource power is providing financial incentives to alter behaviour.

Position source (legitimacy) refers to power that is derived from the position held by the person. It is sometimes referred to as 'legitimate power' or 'authority' because it is generally accepted that people in that position *should have* the power they hold. Managerial prerogatives – where they are accepted – are examples of position power. Where the prerogative of, for example, the right to fire is generally accepted, then managers have power derived from their position. They can fire employees without recourse to other sources of power because it is accepted that they should have the ability to act in that way, if they so choose.

Expertise is also a source of power. As the expertise is often knowledge, this clearly overlaps with that source, as well as frequently overlapping with position source. Expertise only exists as a power source if it is recognised and accepted by the parties on whom the influence or force is to be applied. An illustration of expert power is the situation that arises when a union secretary or employment relations manager is recognised as being able to interpret union-management agreements consistently and accurately, in terms of Court decisions. If a dispute arises over a matter of interpretation, then the expert's view may be accepted by the other party because the expert was recognised as such.

Power derived from the person (sometimes referred to as 'referent' power) is by virtue of his or her personality alone. In reality, the source of personal power is usually bolstered by one or more of: position-related, physical, resource-related, or expert sources. As Handy (1976:119-120) states:

> many a manager will attribute his degree of influence to his charisma rather than to his position, only to be disillusioned when, having been removed from his position, he finds that no-one invites him to meetings, consults him or seeks him out.

The final source of power is information or knowledge about what occurs or has occurred, how and why it takes place. There is an obvious overlap between this source of power and expertise as a source of power, but also differences in that information and knowledge can also be used to apply sanctions and give rewards.

Thus, these theorists suggest that people have power, or the ability to act or cause others to act, if they can:

a. apply sanctions;
b. give inducements;
c. have accepted positions of authority;
d. have expertise;
e. have charisma;
f. have knowledge and information.

People can increase their power by building on these sources. However other theorists point out that the above so-called 'sources' of power provide a dissatisfying analysis of power. As indicated, some sources overlap, some indicate *what* is used by the party in power (resources or sanctions), while others indicate *why* the party is in a powerful position (expertise).

Bacharach and Lawler (1981:34) claim that

> ambiguity in the French and Raven scheme results from their confusion of the bases of power with the sources of power. A distinction must be made between bases of power and sources of power. This distinction has important implications for the authority-influence contrast. In dealing with the bases of power we are interested in what parties control that enables them to manipulate the behaviour of others; in referring to the sources of power we are speaking of how parties come to control the bases of power.

They go on to identify four primary 'power bases', and state that it is from the *sources* of power that people come to control these *bases*. The following discussion is based on their ideas, with minor changes in terminology.

[505] *Power bases*

Rather than Handy's and French and Raven's concept of power coming from a power source, power can be more accurately considered as coming from a base. The various parties in employment relations have differing degrees of control over various power bases. The major power bases are:

a. coercive – indicating control of sanctions;
b. remunerative – indicating control of rewards;
c. normative – indicating control of values;
d. knowledge – indicating control of information.

With these power bases defined, the power source must clearly differ to an extent from those given in [504]. The sources of power – which enable one to control one or more of the power bases – are defined as position, personal characteristics and expertise.

This differentiation between sources and bases may not appear very significant, but it is helpful in understanding power relationships. Thus, the position held will affect one's ability to control all four power bases. Personal characteristics will affect, in particular, one's ability to control the operant value system. Expertise will affect the ability to control information, values and to a lesser extent rewards and sanctions. Control of sanctions and information will depend to a degree on chance, as well as conscious effort.

The coercive and remunerative power bases may be effective, but suffer by being blatant and overt. If a party threatens sanctions or uses rewards, it is obvious that power is being used to achieve particular objectives. (However, attempts to undermine others' coercive power bases may be more subtle.) Notwithstanding, emphasis is frequently put on these two bases. For instance, a fairly common view, as expressed by Mabry (1966:317) with relation to bargaining power, is that 'in the final analysis, the ability to obtain one's goals in bargaining usually rests on the rewards and punishments the bargainers are capable of generating.'

However, this overlooks the normative power base which gives control of the system of values and hence may be of greater significance since this control can actually determine what is open to dispute. That is, if one can at least influence the system of values one can make a subject 'non-negotiable'. Other parties accept that it is one's right to arbitrarily determine the matter. Making a matter non-negotiable is in fact a more significant use of power than achieving the same result by use of overt power. Bachrach and Baratz (1962:948) emphasise this by observing that

> of course power is exercised when A participates in the making of decisions that affect B. But power is also exercised when A devotes his energies to creating or reinforcing social and political values and institutional practices that limit the scope of the political process to public consideration of only those issues which are comparatively innocuous to A. To the extent that A succeeds in doing this, B

> is prevented, for all practical purposes, from bringing to the fore any issue that might in their resolution be seriously detrimental to A's set of preferences.

Hyman (1975:26) argues that, by influencing ideology, one increases power – another way to describe gaining control of the normative power base. He writes:

> the ability to overcome opposition is one sign of power: but a more subtle yet perhaps even more significant form of power is the ability to preclude opposition from even arising – simply because, for example, those subject to a particular type of control do not question its legitimacy or can see no alternative.

Once the system of values is at least partly controlled, power is hidden as 'authority' or 'prerogatives' or 'rights'. Authority may be 'legitimised power' – but it is still power. Parsons was partly responsible for perpetuating the myth that authority is somehow different to power in his translation of Weber (1947). Gouldner (1971:294) points out that Parsons treats power and authority in two ways:

> either as two different stages in development, in which, for instance, power is viewed as the degenerate or the immature form of authority; or as two alternative ways in which one person or group can structure the behaviour of others. In both cases they are viewed as mutually exclusive, as if, when one exists, the other does not ...

The normative power base also allows the party in control to condition views as to what is in the 'national interest', or is for the 'good of society'. Not surprisingly, parties generally advocate for the 'good of society' what is also 'good for them'. As Lockwood (1958:209) observes, 'a dominant class has never existed which did not seek to make its position legitimate by placing the highest value on those qualities and activities which came closest to its own.'

This raises the question as to the extent to which true 'free will' actually exists. For example, during the nineteenth century in the UK, the Protestant ethic which emphasised the virtue of hard work for its own reward received considerable support. The more it was accepted, the greater the influence it would have on people's views as to their behaviour, and consequently the less 'free will'. It is not surprising that Spillane (1973:199) considers that

> the assertion of the Protestant Ethic that the divine right of property and power meant that God intended the poor to heed the voice of wealth was greatly accepted by industrial chiefs.

What is surprising is the extent to which the ethic was accepted by those it tended to hurt rather than help.

Similarly, the concept of *Bushido*, originally discussed by Musashi (1982 edition) over four centuries ago, has now permeated all levels of Japanese society. Bushido, or the way of the samurai, stresses patience, frugality, intense effort and constant self-improvement. It has become part of the social ethos of all Japan. In recent years it is perceived in 'Toyotism', and constant self-improvement is part of 'the Japanese way'.

Control of the knowledge power base implies the control of information. By controlling information, a party can obviously both inform and mislead, which can also influence norms and values. In addition, by controlling information a party can influence the other party's objectives and behaviour. Thus, in a collective bargaining situation one party, by feeding selected information to the other party, may alter their targets and resistance points to the first party's advantage.

Interestingly, consideration of this power base emphasises that 'disclosure of information' – for example from companies to unions – is not necessarily an advantage to the unions. Because the companies can adjust the information that goes to the unions, they therefore strengthen their power base. Hence unions that refuse to listen to financial data from companies may be indicating a sophisticated knowledge of how power works, rather than being 'foolish' or 'uninterested in vital affairs'.

[506] Relative power

A party increases its power by developing one or more of its power bases. However, power can be considered to be relative, and hence, if opponents or targets are also building up *their* power bases, this will have an adverse effect on the party's power. Thus, *reducing* opponents' power bases is as significant as increasing one's own. To know to build up one's own power bases or to attack opponents' bases requires *perception*.

[507] Perception of power

It is possible for a party to have, in fact, a significant power base but be unaware of the fact. Thus, for example, a work group could be in a position to inflict considerable cost on their employer should they take strike action, but not be *aware* of this fact. They have a strong coercive power base, but lack the self-perception or knowledge. Without this knowledge, they will never make the threats or take the action which enables them to influence the employer's behaviour.

On the other hand, the employer may not realise the costs the work group could inflict, while the work group itself is aware. In this case a threat of strike action would not be effective, but *actual* strike action may well be effective. As Kirkbride (1987:6) states:

> your opponent needs to be made aware of the costs that possibly could be inflicted upon him should he fail to submit to your demands.

[508] Overt and covert power bases

To an extent the first two power bases (coercive and remunerative) defined in [505] above can be considered overt, the second two (normative and knowledge) can be considered covert. That is, the use of sanctions and rewards is an open use of power, while controlling information and the system of values is a hidden, or at any rate, much less obvious use of power. Indeed, it is *so* much less obvious, that people with such power can often quite successfully appear not to have power. Thus the paradox exists that persons with the greatest power often may appear to have little or no power.

Given that opponents will both build up their own power bases in response to a party's actions and try to reduce that party's own power base, it clearly pays to have *covert* power bases. If a party is relying on overt power bases, then it again pays to ensure that they are used only to the extent that they influence opponents, and not to the extent that the opponents either:

a. discover the power bases are *less* significant than they feared; and/or
b. take action to reduce them.

Bachrach and Baratz (1963:636) point out that power may be lessened if the threatened sanctions are applied, since the 'invocation of sanctions often causes a radical reordering of values within the coerced person' and the invocation of sanctions 'may prove in retrospect far less severe than it appeared in prospect as a result of which future noncompliance is not discouraged and may even be encouraged.'

This re-emphasises the vital significance in being able to influence norms and values. If a party has control of the normative power base, then targets may actually *want* to act in a way that suits the party – without realising that they have been manipulated into such a situation. Gaski (1986:63) refers to a 'manipulative power source' or 'ecological control'. However, this can be subsumed under the normative power base.

C. Labour-related Productivity

[509] Introduction

In [306] mention was made of the increasing emphasis on management in employment relations in the 1980s and 1990s. It must be stressed however that this recent surge in interest followed decades of considerable neglect so that as late as 1979 S. Clegg (1979:164) concluded that 'the truth of the matter is that the study of management in industrial relations is in a primitive state.'

There has also been a lack of concern for the objectives of employers and managers. To a great extent it has been assumed in the literature that employers have objectives of efficiency or productivity or profits – to which end the matter is ignored.

[510] Productivity defined

Productivity is normally expressed as a ratio: units of output divided by units of input. Output may be any of a number of things, but commonly would be gross production, standardised units of production or dollar value of production. Similarly, there are many possibilities of input, including number of employees, number of employee-hours or shifts, or the wage bill.

Specifically, it is suggested that the objective be considered 'labour-related productivity', rather than productivity or labour productivity. This is to emphasise that productivity, which has nothing to do with labour, is outside the employment relations system, but equally there will be cases where machine productivity will change, which *affects* labour.

It must be stressed that the term productivity does not in itself determine the particular output and inputs. Managers may wish to focus on quality and to increase productivity by increasing the percentage of output that is of top quality per dollar wage bill. Unfortunately some statements seem to indicate otherwise. Lever-Tracy (1990:186) makes reference to employment relations at Ford (Australia). She states:

> Ford had chosen to identify the Japanese threat as posed primarily by improved quality and reduced inventory costs and interruptions to the line, rather than by increasing labour productivity and line speeds.

A better description would be that Ford has chosen to increase productivity through improved quality and reduced inventory costs per employee shift, rather than by increased production per employee shift.

However it is defined, it needs to be clear, and the definition employed capable of measurement. Proxies for productivity – such as 'employee morale', 'good relationships', 'low strike activity' – are notoriously subjective and inaccurate. Indeed, recent research on the effects of strike activity on labour productivity in manufacturing produced results totally contrary to conventional wisdom. Knight (1989:370) claims his research

> clearly rejects the popular view of strike activity and especially the frequency dimension – that it indicates a poor state of industrial relations, which lowers labour productivity and impairs economic performance. Some of the results actually imply instead that high strike frequency is associated with high labour productivity, and this effect is not, in general, offset by the adverse effects of strike duration. Strikes appear, in part, to have played a therapeutic role as a vent for frustration, or as a mechanism for resolving otherwise unresolvable conflicts in the majority of manufacturing industries in the sample.

[511] Productivity as an objective

In [304] the employment relations objective of increased labour-related productivity was related to the overall organisational objective of profits and/or survival and/or growth. It should be noted that ideally *all* managers should have concern for overall organisational objectives and most, if not all, should have regard for the employment relations objectives.

[512] Lack of proactivity

As a generalisation, managers and employers are not proactive in pursuing this objective. There is a tendency to accept the *status quo* and become concerned about productivity levels only when there is a severe threat from external sources. Time and time again it is clear that managers wait to *react* to increasing competition or decreasing demand. The description of the coal industry by Smith (1990:23) is typical:

> deteriorating market conditions in the coal industry led producers to formulate an industry strategy. The central feature of this strategy was the call for the continued introduction of new technology, and increased flexibility in its use, with the aim of achieving significant reductions in mine site production costs.

[513] Achieving productivity gains

This objective can be pursued by a variety of methods – productivity bargaining, discussed in Chapter Seven, HRM techniques discussed in Chapter Three, and generally by increased efforts to reduce costs, and increase quality and output. Frequently managers find that greater gains in productivity can be achieved if employees clearly benefit as well, although paying for productivity has its critics. Walsh (1993:418) cites a manager who complained:

> initially there is a lot to go at but … if you educate everybody into the idea [that] … money is only coming when you do something to improve productivity/efficiency, people will start hoarding it or … [will] look for bogus improvements.

The approach of management to productivity gains will clearly have a major effect on the attitude and co-operation of the workforce. If the approach is to increase quality and production, but at a faster rate than the increase in wage bill, co-operation is quite probable. If the approach is to slash labour costs by removing penal rates or lowering basic wages, or by wide-scale redundancies, co-operation is much less probable. It would appear that the trend for productivity increases is primarily through redundancies.

D. Satisfaction with Job Factors

[514] The meaning of 'satisfaction with job factors'

The phrase 'job satisfaction' has become hackneyed, particularly in the last few decades. It has reached the stage where the phrase is often used in a totally circular and hence meaningless fashion. Thus people will say that what they like about their jobs is the job satisfaction. Literally translated, they are saying that what they like about their jobs is liking their jobs – an observation that is not particularly enlightening. The reason for such statements is that in many circles 'job satisfaction' no longer means 'satisfaction with the job', but usually means something like 'interesting work.'

In this discussion, the objective of maintaining and possibly increasing general satisfaction refers to *all* factors which make up the job. These factors include wages or salary, working conditions, job security, the work itself, supervision, fellow employees, prospects for promotion, and so on. It must be emphasised that 'the work to be done' is only one of the many factors, albeit an important one, that make up a job.

Maintaining and possibly improving these factors, in particular of course those of importance, is a major objective of employees and their unions. Managers will obviously be concerned about their *own* job satisfaction, but usually will be concerned with the job satisfaction of the general workforce only in a secondary sense in that some managers consider that if employees had increased their job satisfaction this would lead on to increased productivity.

The relationship between satisfaction and performance is unclear. Two reviews performed at almost the same time produced conflicting results. Petty *et al* (1984:719) report a meta-analysis (a method of statistically combining a large number of previous studies) which they claim

> indicate[s] that individual job satisfaction and job performance are positively correlated ... the size of the mean correlation that is reported in the present study between overall satisfaction and job performance is impressive.

However, Podsakoff and Williams (1986:242) claim:

> it would be misguided, for example, to conclude from the data provided ... that any inherent relationship exists between satisfaction and performance. Indeed, based on the results of our review, such a conclusion is questionable at best ...

Even if there is positive correlation, this does not prove a causal relationship. Employees may perform well because they are satisfied, or they could be satisfied because they perform well, *or* a third factor (such as high pay) could cause both satisfaction and high performance which need not be directly related.

[515] Levels of satisfaction in the workforce

It has become increasingly fashionable to point out that employees are alienated, that 'blue-collar blues' and 'white-collar woes' exist. Horner (1974:16) states categorically that

> no discussion on industrial democracy will mean anything to trade unionists unless all the participants recognize that millions of people hate their work with a deep, abiding hatred. Work for these people is preferred only as an alternative to the worse condition of poverty through unemployment.

However, such writers basically assume that it is accepted that employees are alienated and hate their jobs. They never, ever, produce evidence of even fairly widespread job dissatisfaction. As Kristol (1973:11) points out:

> about 85 percent of American workers, when asked if they are satisfied with their jobs, answer in the affirmative. 'Work in America' tries to show that they don't mean what they say. Thus, if an employee tells an interviewer that he finds his work satisfying, but also says he would like to change his job for something better, 'Work in America' promptly concludes that he is not 'really' satisfied with, but is rather 'alienated' from his work. Similarly, if factory workers or file clerks indicate that they are not as fascinated with their daily tasks as are doctors and professors, this too is taken as an unmistakable sign of 'alienation.'

In the New Zealand context, a recent large-scale study of manager and employee attitudes towards their jobs (see Tables 5.1 and 5.2) supports Kristol's view; albeit the level of dissatisfaction is slightly higher in this recent study compared with the data obtained in the 1970s.

Table 5.1. Levels of job satisfaction by gender

	Males		Females		Total	
	No.	%	No.	%	No.	%
Extremely dissatisfied	6	1.9	5	2.0	11	2.0
Dissatisfied	29	9.4	19	7.5	48	8.6
Neither satisfied nor dissatisfied	56	18.2	59	23.3	115	20.5
Satisfied	152	49.4	107	42.3	259	46.2
Extremely satisfied	65	21.1	63	24.9	128	22.8
Total	308	100.0	253	100.0	561	100.0

Table 5.2. Levels of job satisfaction by role

	Role in Organisation					
	Managers		Workers/ Employees		Total	
	No.	%	No.	%	No.	%
Extremely dissatisfied	1	0.6	10	2.6	11	2.0
Dissatisfied	6	3.4	42	10.9	48	8.6
Neither satisfied nor dissatisfied	34	19.5	80	20.8	114	20.4
Satisfied	93	53.4	165	43.0	258	46.2
Extremely satisfied	40	23.0	87	22.7	127	22.8
Total	174	100.0	384	100.0	558	100.0

Source: Geare and Edgar (2005)

[516] Important factors as currently perceived by employees

Although opinions as to what should be, or what might be, are very varied, it is clear from their behaviour that what most employees see as being important to their overall job satisfaction are wages, and, in times of high unemployment, job security and to a lesser degree working conditions.

[517] Psychological theories of job satisfaction

To a great extent current views downplaying the role of money, security and conditions, as factors relevant to employees' job satisfaction, stem from popular theories developed mainly by psychologists in the 1930s, 1950s and 1960s. These theories are basically those of the 'human relations' and 'self-actualisation' movements. Also relevant however is the scientific management movement of the turn of the century, for it was through its loss of popularity that the other movements gained momentum.

The major theorists through this century have been:

a. Taylor and Scientific Management;
b. Mayo and Human Relations;
c. Maslow and the Hierarchy of Needs;
d. McGregor and Theory X and Theory Y;
e. Herzberg and the Two-Factor Theory.

These theories, sometimes portrayed as truths, are recounted *ad nauseam* in industrial psychology, personnel and HRM texts. A brief summary will be given here because no matter how much criticism is levelled against them people still turn to them as panaceas. Indeed, much of the current HRM movement is founded on these theories – which does not bode well for the success of HRM. Guest (1990a:391) observes that

> HRM takes as its starting point the view that organizations should be designed on the basis of the assumptions inherent in McGregor's (1960) Theory Y ... assumptions about the nature of human potential and the ability to tap that potential by providing opportunities for growth at work are based on the ideas of writers such as Herzberg (1966) and Maslow (1943), as well as McGregor. In the United Kingdom these writers have never been taken seriously. Their ideas are treated as naive, overly value-laden and unsupported by empirical evidence.

However, Guest also recognises the 'stubborn hold on the American mind' taken by them.

[518] Taylor and scientific management

The theory of scientific management, developed by F.W. Taylor, rests on four principles:

1. develop a science for each job element to replace the old rule-of-thumb method;

2. scientifically select, train, teach and develop workers, instead of letting workers choose their own work and train themselves as best they could;
3. heartily co-operate with workers to ensure they perform the work in accordance with the scientific principles which have been developed (and reward them when they do so);
4. divide the responsibility for the work equally between management and workers. Management takes over all work for which they are better fitted than the workers, while in the past, almost all the work and the greater part of the responsibility were thrown upon the workers.

Although the principles of scientific management were taken up with enthusiasm by Japanese industry from the 1920s, the movement certainly lost popularity in the West, although it has had numerous revivals.

Later theorists claimed that scientific management lost popularity, because it ignored either 'human relations' or opportunities for 'self-actualisation'. Thus Livy (1975:20) claims that

> the reason why the so-called 'principles of scientific management' do not work, on the whole, when applied to the individual, group or team activities in modern organisations is that they are based on traditional, but ill-founded, assumptions about the motive of human needs and behaviour. The assumptions are that people only try to satisfy economic needs at work ... emotional needs do not enter the picture.

However, there are alternative explanations. The so-called failure of scientific management can be attributed to two employment relations issues: job security and fairness. One of Taylor's 'successes' was at Bethlehem Steel Works. In one experiment he is reported to have reduced the number of employees required from 500 to 140. As observed by Brown (1954), scientific management was hardly likely to gain the approval from employees made redundant. In another experiment at Bethlehem Steel, Taylor (1960) reported an increase in output of 256.2 per cent for a wage increase of 63.5 per cent. Those employees may have been satisfied then, but over a period of time it is unlikely that workers would continue considering it fair to receive an increase in wages that amounted to one fourth their increase in output. To exacerbate the problem, there were reports of managers cheating and refusing to pay even the fractional amount that had been agreed.

The decline in the popularity of scientific management has been taken to 'prove' that money does not have significant motivational power. As indicated above, the 'failure' of scientific management cannot be said to indicate the lack of relevance of money as a major source of job satisfaction. Scientific management lost favour through its inability – because of the way it was utilised – to satisfy normal workforce objectives of secure employment and perceived equitable payment.

[519] Mayo and human relations

The Human Relations Movement stems from the so-called Hawthorne Studies which were conducted at the Hawthorne Plant of the Western Electric Company, which supplied the telephone companies of the Bell System. Mayo and others from Harvard University were involved in the major phase of the studies from 1927 to 1932. This phase involved studies of experimental groups of workers involved in 'relay assembly', 'mica splitting' and 'bank wiring', and large-scale interviews.

The research was reported in two major forms. The first was a thorough, long, turgid book by Roethlisberger and Dickson (1939). The second form was two reasonably short, easily readable monographs by Elton Mayo (1933 and 1947). For decades it would appear that those writing industrial psychology, management and personnel texts took the easy option and read only Mayo (or, indeed, read only someone who had read Mayo). The sad fact is that while Mayo is to some a heroic figure, he was at best, as described by Landsberger (1958:31), a man with a tendency to 'override existing facts in his enthusiasm for his own approach and solutions'. Indeed he could simply be deemed a charlatan.

The Hawthorne Studies were originally designed to measure the effects on production of different conditions of work and different payment systems. After the studies had been under way for some time, Mayo and his researchers came to the conclusion (Carey, 1967:404) that

> social satisfactions arising out of human association in work were more important determinants of work behaviour in general and output in particular than were any of the physical and economic aspects of the work situation in which their attention had originally been limited.

It is not clear whether Mayo came to these conclusions out of a driving desire to prove something in which he deeply believed, or out of analytical ineptitude, or out of a cunning awareness that the impact of these 'conclusions' would have and the subsequent fame he would acquire.

The 'Relay Assembly' room experiment is the most famous aspect of the Human Relations theory. Unfortunately as a piece of *research* the experiment was abysmal. Landsberger (1958) highlights some of the inadequacies:

a. it used a test group of *five* workers out of 29,000;
b. there was no control group;
c. changes were introduced cumulatively;
d. reporting was totally unreliable, with different researchers detailing different results from the same exercise.

In addition to this, the extreme management bias of the studies should be noted, illustrated by the fact that unions were not given a mention. Admittedly there *were* no unions actually allowed at the plant at the time – but this fact itself was worthy of mention. Pressure for the establishment of unions must have been present since Landsberger (1958) observed that between 1933 and 1936

Western Electric paid out more than $28,000 for spies (who would report on pro-union workers who would then be sacked and probably blacklisted).

However, the major criticism of the Human Relations Movement came from Sykes (1965) and Carey (1967), who expose the biased and dishonest analyses of what went on in the Hawthorne Plant. In brief, Roethlisberger and Dickson (1939) provide honest *reporting* of the experiment – but come up with the conclusions (possibly in deference to Mayo) that bear little relationship to the facts they report.

[520] The relay assembly experiment

There were five women (referred to as 'girls') in the test group which lasted two years. After six months two operators were sacked from the group and replaced. After numerous changes in payment systems, rest periods and a forty per cent change in staff, it was considered that at the end of the two years, output had increased by roughly thirty per cent. Mayo (1947:72) claims the output increase was not due to wages or personnel changes, but that 'what actually happened was that six individuals [the five girls plus their supervisor] became a team and the team gave itself wholeheartedly and spontaneously to co-operation in the experiment'. This piece of fantasy has become folklore. Roethlisberger and Dickson (1939:33-55) report that the women had been told to work as hard or otherwise as they felt inclined and that 'no attempt would be made to force up production'. However, when they stopped working hard, they were 'called into the office by the foreman and given a talk to regarding their behaviour.' Stricter supervision seemed to get results, and it was noted that 'a marked difference in attitudes was noticeable today after yesterday's reprimand for talking.' Two women in particular were considered to be failing to display

> that wholehearted co-operation desired by the investigators … any effort to reprimand them would bring the reply, 'we thought you wanted us to work as we feel' … (one of the two) was told of her offenses of being moody, inattentive and not co-operative.

The two women were then sacked from the test group, and replaced. Mayo (1933:56) first claimed they had 'dropped out' of the test groups. Later (1947:71), the lie had grown to the extent that reference was made to their 'retirement'.

The two replacements *immediately* (before they became part of the 'team', or any human relations aspects could have had effect) produced at a higher rate than either of the two who were sacked. It appears one was the principal breadwinner of her family. When she joined the test group they were on an incentive scheme based on the output of all five. Roethlisberger and Dickson (1939:63) acknowledge she immediately urged 'the other girls to increase their pace' to boost earnings.

Since a major objective of Mayo was to attack the idea of financial motivation, it was not surprising that the 'conclusions' from the experiment bore no relationship to what happened. Roethlisberger and Dickson (1939:132-3) report that when the women were put on a small group incentive scheme so that their individual performance had a visible effect on their earnings, the group's average output rose '12.6% above the base period', but presumably because this did not suit the researchers, they considered it was 'difficult to conclude whether the increase in output was an immediate response to the change in work incentive.' The bonuses the women in the test group were earning made the remaining one hundred workers in the department jealous and they wanted to be put on a similar scheme. The company would not do this and instead the five in the test group were put back on the old scheme. Immediately their output dropped markedly (by 16 per cent). Amazingly, the Human Relations theorists did not, or would not, see any significance in financial motivation.

Sykes (1965:262) also examined a second major experiment, the 'Bank Wiring' study and he showed the conclusions reached by the human relationists were totally unsubstantiated. He stated:

> possibly the most surprising feature of all is not the weakness of the case presented by Roethlisberger and Dickson but in fact that, in spite of much criticism of the study, so many people have assumed for so long that they had produced clear proof of their assertions.

Indeed this is true for all aspects of the Hawthorne Studies. The so-called 'Hawthorne Effect' (the idea that workers perform *better* because they are under observation) did not occur. At times they performed better, at times worse. The concept of teamworking never eventuated. If the Hawthorne Studies are able to suggest *anything*, it is that financial incentives and strict supervision produce results (see Gottfredson (1996)).

[521] Maslow's hierarchy of needs

Maslow's theory of hierarchy of needs was introduced as a general theory of human motivation and did not originally refer to the work environment. Maslow (1943) suggests that there are five basic needs:

1. physiological needs (the need for food, water, sleep, etc.);
2. safety needs (the need for security as well as the absence of danger);
3. love needs (the need to give, and receive love, affection and friendship);
4. esteem needs (the need for self-respect, and esteem of others);
5. self-actualisation needs (the need for self-fulfilment).

These needs may be considered to be in a hierarchy, with physiological needs at the bottom and self-actualisation needs at the top. As the lower, prepotent needs become at least partially satisfied, higher order needs gradually emerge.

Maslow (1943:386) does point out that

> we have spoken so far as if this hierarchy were a fixed order but actually it is not nearly so rigid as we may have implied. It is true that most of the people with whom we have worked have seemed to have basic needs in about the order that has been indicated. However, there has been a number of exceptions.

Maslow (1954:105) considers that whichever need is more prepotent is the one which has motivational power. If we are interested in what actually motivates us, and not in what has, will, or might motivate us, then a satisfied need is not a motivator. Hence the theory suggests that once the physiological needs are reasonably satisfied they cease to motivate.

As stated earlier, the hierarchy-of-needs theory was first put forward to explain human motivation in general terms. However, the theory was soon assumed to be relevant to the work environment, and it was adopted by many 'self-actualisation' proponents (including McGregor and Herzberg) to help support their view. Later Maslow (1965) himself used his theory to apply it to organisational settings.

Research by Goodman (1968), Hall and Nougaim (1968), and by Lawler and Suttle (1972), all failed to produce any support for the concept of a hierarchy of needs. In the face of such discouraging evidence, Maslow has produced the not very impressive defence that there can be a long time period between the emergence of various need levels. The theory can be considered of some value, however, if it makes people realise that motivational factors may differ for different people, and may differ for the same people over time. A *theory* should make people think, not be blindly followed as a *fact*.

[522] McGregor's Theory X and Theory Y

In simple terms, Theory X is put as the traditional (incorrect) management view, while Theory Y is put as the correct management view. Table 5.3 below summarises McGregor's opinions on the two different views on the nature of man and managerial responsibility.

McGregor (1960:40-1) makes the claim that motivation comes from higher order needs alone since:

> under today's conditions management has provided relatively well for the satisfaction of physiological and safety needs. The standard of living in our country is high; people do not suffer major deprivation of their physiological needs except during periods of severe unemployment. The fact that management has provided for these physiological and safety needs has shifted the motivational emphasis to the social and egotistical needs. Unless there are opportunities at work to satisfy these higher level needs, people will be deprived and their behaviour will reflect this deprivation. The 'carrot and stick' theory does not work at all once man has reached an adequate subsistence level and is motivated primarily by higher needs.

The Theory X – Theory Y thesis depends on a hierarchy of needs existing in the work environment, operating in the manner suggested by Maslow. As stated in [521], efforts to test this assumption have had negative results. The second assumption is that the two lowest needs – physiological and safety – have already been satisfied and hence the higher-order needs are now the motivators. That is, the average employee cannot be motivated by money or conditions but

Table 5.3. Theory X and Theory Y

The Nature of Man	
Theory X	**Theory Y**
1. Work is inherently distasteful to most people. 2. Most people are not ambitious, have little desire for responsibility, and prefer to be directed. 3. Most people have little capacity for creativity in solving organisational problems. 4. Most people must be closely controlled and often coerced to achieve organisational objectives.	1. Work is as natural as play, if the conditions are favourable. 2. Self control is often indispensable in achieving organisational goals. 3. The capacity for creativity in solving organisational problems is widely distributed in the population. 4. Motivation occurs at the social, esteem, and self-actualisation levels, as well as the physiological and security levels. 5. People can be self-directed and creative at work if properly motivated.

Managerial Responsibility	
Theory X	**Theory Y**
1. Management is responsible for organising the elements of productive enterprise – money, materials, equipment, people – in the interest of economic ends. 2. With respect to people, this is a process of directing their effort, motivating them, controlling their actions, modifying their behaviour to fit the needs of the organisation. 3. Without this active intervention by management, people would be passive – even resistant – to organisational needs. They must therefore be persuaded, rewarded, punished, controlled – their activities must be directed. This is management's task. We often sum it up by saying that management consists of getting things done through people.	1. Management is responsible for organising the element of productive enterprise – money, materials, equipment, people – in the interest of economic ends. 2. People are not by nature passive or resistant to organisational needs. They have become so as a result of experience in organisations. 3. The motivation, the potential for development, the capacity for assuming responsibility, the readiness to direct behaviour toward organisational goals are all present in people. Management does not put them there. It is a responsibility of management to make it possible for people to recognise and develop these human characteristics for themselves. 4. The essential task of management is to arrange organisational conditions and methods of operation so that people can achieve their own goals best by directing their own efforts toward organisation activities.

instead is motivated by the opportunities to gain friends, boost self-esteem, or enable self-actualisation – and cannot do this through increased wages or better conditions.

This second assumption is far from being substantiated. Theory Y is not really a testable theory; however, companies can experiment by operating 'as a Theory Y company' to see if this results in higher productivity by motivating the employee to a greater level. Kuriloff (1963), Chief Executive of Non-Linear Systems Inc., claimed that three years after the company put Theory Y into practice, productivity was 30 per cent higher than ever before. However, he admitted that they also established a minimum wage that was 32.4 per cent above comparable rates paid in the community. It is thus impossible to determine what actually motivated the employees.

[523] Herzberg's two-factor theory

The two-factor theory was put forward as a general theory of job 'motivation.' It suggests that only job factors which are content or intrinsic (achievement, recognition, the work itself, responsibility and opportunity for advancement) can produce satisfaction. If those factors are sub-standard, or non-existent, the result is not dissatisfaction, but rather a neutral, or 'no satisfaction' state. Job factors which are context or extrinsic (e.g., company policy and administration, supervision, salary, interpersonal relations and working conditions) can only produce job dissatisfaction if they are sub-standard. If they are considered in a very positive sense they will result only in a move to the neutral or 'no dissatisfaction' state.

This theory contradicts the usual assumption that the opposite of job satisfaction is job dissatisfaction. Instead, it states the opposite of job satisfaction is no satisfaction; the opposite of job dissatisfaction is no dissatisfaction. The intrinsic factors are termed 'motivators' to indicate that they have potential for satisfaction, the extrinsic factors 'hygienes' to indicate that they have potential only to reduce job dissatisfaction. (Thus the two-factor theory is often referred to as the Motivation-Hygiene or M-H Theory.)

Supporters of the M-H Theory are touchy on the question of overall job satisfaction. Whitsett and Winslow (1967:395-7), two of Herzberg's colleagues at Western Reserve University and among his strongest supporters, state the 'theory does not, and purposely does not, make statements about overall job satisfaction.' However, they do acknowledge that

> man lives his life as a unity and consequently combines his feeling of satisfaction and dissatisfaction. He thus may 'feel' neutral. However M-H Theory contends that this neutral feeling is made up of some amount of satisfaction (derived from motivators) and some amount of dissatisfaction (derived from hygiene).

Thus it would appear that improving hygienes is as vital as improving motivators in boosting the overall feeling of satisfaction and dissatisfaction. This, of course, means overall job satisfaction to most people. However Herzberg *et al* (1959:114) state that

> it should be understood that both kinds of factors meet the needs of the employee; but it is primarily the 'motivators' that serve to bring about the kind of job satisfaction and … the kind of improvement in performance that industry is seeking from its workforce.

The implication is clear. If you accept the M-H Theory, then you accept that wages cannot really motivate: rather it is the opportunity for self-actualisation that counts, and wages are not a significant component of job satisfaction. There is, however, a strong body of opinion that the M-H Theory has no basis in reality. Moreover, even if the theory is accepted, this does not deny the impact of money as a motivator. Whitsett and Winslow (1967:405) for example state that if a pay increase is a merit increase then 'since it serves as a recognition, [it] should be interpreted as a motivator.' Herzberg *et al* (1959) also point out that money earned as a reward for performance is a reinforcement of the motivators of recognition and achievement.

[524] Goal Setting

In more recent times, goal-setting theory (Locke & Latham, 1990) has been one of the most convincing and satisfactory theories of motivation. When employees are set challenging but attainable goals, their motivation to try to achieve that standard seems to increase, even without the added incentive of monetary reward. Fried and Slowik (2004: 404) claim that 'goal setting theory has arguably become one of the dominant motivational theories'.

[525] Deficiencies in psychological theories of job satisfaction

The above sections have shown serious deficiencies in the theories, predominantly of psychologists, which have denied or at least played down the significance of money. These theories may have resulted from strong beliefs and a desire to prove them, come what may; or possibly Opsahl and Dunnette (1966:115) are correct and it is because they 'have depended heavily on rats and psychology sophomores (university students) to build a psychology of motivation.' It is interesting that Herzberg (1964) has prefaced an article with an admission that he lacks competence in the field of manpower.

Practitioners, and observers of employment relations in practice, accept that for most employees money in the form of wages, salaries and bonuses is *a* major job factor, and often *the* major factor, and is of prime importance in job satisfaction. Its importance lies in the many needs money can satisfy.

E. Conclusion

[526] The interrelationship between objectives

For any one party, and between parties, there is a tie-in between objectives. If management increases its power, then it has a greater probability of implementing changes which will lead to increased productivity. Likewise if the workforce increases its power, then it should have a greater probability of inducing changes leading to greater satisfaction, with the factors making up the job. Ironically, however, increased power may also make it more *difficult* for employees to gain satisfaction. This is because satisfaction is a subjective measure related to one's expectations.

For example, employees with little power may have low expectations – a one per cent wage increase may be granted and the employees be reasonably satisfied. Employees with considerably more power may have much greater expectations – say an eight per cent wage increase – employees finally achieve only four per cent and may in fact be *less* satisfied with the result.

[527] The interrelationship between parties

The above sections have outlined what is meant by the three major objectives of the parties in employment relations. A significant issue is whether two or more parties can each achieve their objectives or whether one party can only achieve its objectives at the expense of another.

As a generalisation, the answer appears to depend both on *what* objective is being pursued and *how* it is pursued. If two parties are both trying to increase their relative power in the work environment, then if one achieves success it will be at the expense of the other.

However, if management is attempting to increase productivity and the workforce is attempting to increase satisfaction with the factors that make up the job, then, depending on how the objectives are pursued, there will be a number of outcomes: neither, only one, or possibly both parties may succeed. If, for example, management attempts to increase productivity by increasing workloads and removing penal rates for weekend and overtime work this may result in increased productivity provided that output is maintained, or may result in a significant drop in work standards giving a decrease in productivity. If the changes are introduced with no compensatory changes, the workforce will clearly have a decrease in satisfaction with the job.

On the other hand, if management attempts to increase productivity by improving work methods, increasing morale and efficiency and decreasing the need for overtime work but compensating by a better base payment, both management and the workforce may achieve their objectives.

[528] Possibility of achieving objectives

A major theme of this book is the importance of considering objectives. Effective practitioners in employment relations are those who achieve their objectives both in the short-term and long-term. While it is theoretically possible to do so without thought or consideration of other parties' objectives, a strategy for achieving one's own objective has a much greater chance of success if it is designed, where possible, so as not to prevent other parties achieving their own objectives.

One factor which contributes significantly to the probability that two or three parties may be able to achieve objectives is that most parties are not maximisers but rather 'comfortisers' and, as has been discussed earlier, most are reactive rather than proactive. In as much as the majority are attempting to reach a comfortable degree of productivity or satisfaction rather than the maximum, clearly this increases the probability that others may also be able to achieve their objectives in the employment relations system.

Also, while to be successful parties should be more proactive, the fact that so many are reactive and will reasonably happily tolerate the *status quo* also means that clashes of objectives occur less often and are less severe.

[B] INTERACTIONS

Chapter Six

Interpretation Skills

A. Introduction

[601] Rules in employment relations

The definition of employment relations given in [104] illustrated the importance of rules as the vital intermediate phase between interactions and objectives. As stated, employment relations is concerned with obtaining, regulating and adapting the rules – and clearly this cannot be achieved without a thorough understanding of what the rules actually mean.

The rules with which we are concerned include:

a. legislative rules: statutes and regulations imposed by the State influenced to some degree by lobbying and power of other parties;
b. formal management-employee documents. These include individual employment agreements and collective employment agreements. They may be imposed by management or the result of bargaining or arbitration/adjudication;
c. less formal agreements. These may be written, or may be 'custom and practice.'

This chapter is concerned with the *interpretation* of rules.

[602] Objectives of interpretation

The primary objective of interpretation is to discover the intent of the parties to the document – whether agreement, contract or statute – from the words used in the document. It is not to try to predict the intentions of the parties, other than from the words used. It has been noted (*Simpson v Foxton* at 57) that

> what a man intends and the expression of his intention are two different things. He is bound, and those who take after him are bound, by his expressed intention.

For that reason Lord Halsbury stated 'the worst person to construe a statute is the person who is responsible for its drafting, for he is much disposed to confuse what he intended to do, with the effect of the language which in fact he has employed' (*Hilder v Dexter*). Thus, in the case of statute interpretation in the UK, it was not considered permissible to use Hansard (verbatim transcripts of Parliament speeches and debates) in order to interpret the statute. It has been said that if the language of an Act was different to the declared intention of its framers, then it would be inferred that the difference was intentional – not accidental (*Salkeld v Johnston*). However, in a 1994 case in New Zealand, the full Employment Court not only made reference to Hansard, but also referred to a propaganda pamphlet sent out to householders by the Minister of Labour in its effort to interpret what is meant by a 'lockout' (*Witehira v Presbyterian Support Services*).

Many employment relations practitioners benefit from having interpretation skills by being able to predict with accuracy how the Court will rule on disputes going for interpretation. They can thus plan strategies with greater certainty of alternatives. Also, as their skill becomes recognised and accepted, it is likely that more disputes will be conceded. As discussed in Chapter Five, these practitioners have increased their power by increasing their expertise.

[603] Need for interpretation

The simple reason why there is a need for interpretation is that documents do not always express the unanimous, agreed intent of those responsible for them in clear, precise and unambiguous language. This results from a number of factors, some of which apply to documents in general, others which are more applicable to statutes, yet others which concern union-management agreements. Factors included are outlined in [604] to [609] below.

[604] Imprecise use of language

Language is fundamentally imprecise and cannot always accurately express intentions. Words often have different meanings, and the meaning that is relevant is apparent only from the context. Thus the phrase 'in any year', could mean:

a. in any calendar year (e.g., 2007);
b. in any twelve calendar months (e.g., 1 June 2007 to 31 May 2008);
c. in a financial year (e.g., 1 April 2007 to 31 March 2008); or
d. in any 365 (or 366) day period (e.g., 7 May 2007 to 6 May 2008).

[605] Unclear thinking

Unfortunately people responsible for both statutes and agreements (the principals and the drafters) frequently have not properly clarified their intentions. If those responsible for the document have not ensured their intentions are clear and finalised, certainly the document will not express the intentions accurately, clearly and unambiguously.

This muddled thinking can be well illustrated by the Employment Contracts Act 1991, in the sections concerning the Employment Tribunal. The Act states that a member of the Tribunal may provide mediation and/or adjudication (that is, arbitration) services (see Chapter Eight). S.88(2) of the Act states:

> where a member of the Tribunal provides mediation services within the adjudication jurisdiction of the Tribunal, and as a result the parties conclude a settlement or agree to the member making a decision, the parties may request the member to sign the terms of settlement and in any such case those terms of settlement shall be final and binding on the parties.

The first half of this section appears to allow a member who is providing mediation to 'make a decision' – which would seem to imply that the member is able, on request, to adjudicate. Yet if so, this would appear to contradict or be contradicted by s.81(5), which states:

> where the Tribunal is called upon in relation to any particular matter both to provide mediation services and to adjudicate, the same member of the Tribunal shall not perform both mediation services and adjudication services.

The second half of s.88(2) above appears to suggest that the terms of settlement 'shall be final and binding' – and hence not open to appeal. Yet this would appear to contradict or be contradicted by s.95(1), which states:

> any party to any proceedings before the Tribunal who is dissatisfied with any decision of the Tribunal in the proceedings may appeal to the Court against that decision.

When legislation is drafted as badly as this, interpretation must obviously be somewhat haphazard and it is virtually impossible for any Court rulings on contradictions to be other than unconvincing. Probably the best approach, although a difficult one in their position, would be for the Judges to honestly state that

> the law is confused and contradictory. There are two (or more) possible interpretations. We choose, for the following reasons, to favour this one.

[606] Deliberately confusing language

This should be differentiated from [604] and [605] in that it probably results from deliberately ambiguous and/or confused language. Thus, for example, the Employment Contracts Act 1991 states in its title that it is an Act

> (c) To enable each employee to choose either –
> (i) to negotiate an individual employment contract with his or her employer or
> (ii) to be bound by a collective employment contract to which his or her employer is a party:
> (d) To enable each employer to choose –
> (i) to negotiate an individual employment contract with any employee:
> (ii) to negotiate or to elect to be bound by a collective employment contract that binds 2 or more employees.

Employees have a choice. If they want to be under an individual contract, they can so choose. If they want to be under a collective contract, they can choose that. (With a little thought, a problem arises, how can *one* employee in isolation choose to be under a collective contract?). When (d) is considered alongside (c), it is clear that the Act is deliberately confusing. Unless, by chance, *all* employees and their employer want the same thing, it is impossible for them all to be able to choose what they will get. The parties can choose to try to negotiate the number and mix of contracts they want, but they certainly cannot all choose what they will get.

Later in the Act (s.18) it is made explicit that the number and mix of employment contracts is a matter for negotiation. The more powerful party will get what it wants. Hence the confusing nature of (c) and (d) in the Act is almost certainly deliberate to create the false impression that the Act is designed to give maximum freedom and choice and allow *all* to get what they want.

Clearly if those responsible for statutes make parts of them deliberately confusing and ambiguous, interpretation skills are very necessary.

[607] Bad drafting

In some cases the principals may have clarified their intentions, but the persons drafting the document may be weak in grammar or weak in interpretation skills. Hence they may be unaware that by convention in interpretation certain phrases have acquired meanings which create traps for the unwary. For example, one discretionary rule of interpretation, *expressio unius est exclusio alterius* (see [626] below) provides that where *some* conditions are explicitly *included*, *other* conditions – which could otherwise have been included – are in fact explicitly *excluded*. In effect, a rule of interpretation is that 'including' means 'including only'. Thus, for example, a company rule book could state: 'employees guilty of serious misconduct may be summarily dismissed.' This leaves open whether particular actions by employees are to be deemed serious misconduct. A person drafting the rule book may decide to give examples to clarify serious misconduct and add:

> Serious misconduct includes:
> (1) fighting;
> (2) theft from company;
> (3) falsifying work sheets;
> (4) drinking on the job;
> . . .
> (26) vandalism.

However, if an employee commits an action *missing* from the list (for example, theft from a fellow employee), that action by the *expressio unius* rule can be argued to be *not* serious misconduct since 'includes' means 'includes only'. Knowledge of the rule allows the person doing the drafting either to refrain from giving examples or to word it in a non-exclusionary way:

> the following are examples of serious misconduct. The list is not exhaustive and other actions may be deemed serious misconduct.

[608] Inability to cover all eventualities

Particularly with regard to statutes, pragmatically it is impossible for documents to cover all eventualities. Hence a Judge must interpret what the statute means when applied to a particular situation. This judgement becomes case law which is then added to the statute law.

Thus, for example, a statute can provide remedies and procedures if employees consider they have been unjustifiably dismissed. The Employment Relations Act 2000 in s.103A goes on to say the test is whether the actions were what 'a fair and reasonable employer would have done', but without clear elaboration. Certainly the statute could go further and make explicit that a dismissal could be unjustified on substantive and/or procedural grounds. This has been left for Judges to make explicit. However, even if the statute was expanded, it still leaves open the issue of what actions by employees make dismissals substantively fair, and what procedural actions by the employer are required to make the dismissal procedurally fair. To try to cover all future possibilities would convert the two words 'unjustifiably dismissed' into hundreds, if not thousands, of words.

[609] Incomplete agreements

This final factor relates in particular to management-workforce or management-union agreements. In some cases, a point is reached in negotiations when it is clear that total agreement is unlikely to be reached in the near future. Both negotiating sides may be willing to work under a position of 'near agreement' and realise the only workable compromise is to deliberately leave matters somewhat vague and ambiguous. This may work for a while, until personalities change or one or other party tries to take advantage of the situation. In these situations, the need for interpretation may in fact reflect a need for settlement.

[610] The use of rules in interpretation

The rules of interpretation should be considered as tools to be used by the practitioner, aiding but not dictating to them. If the rules are followed blindly then confusion will result as some are contradictory. Indeed, many judgements concerning interpretation have had the counterview expressed – as illustrated in Table 6.1 below.

The rules of interpretation are far from all being equal. Some are dominant – indeed one is all-pervading – while others are rarely employed. In the paragraphs below, rules have been divided into two classes: (1) the major underlying principles or rules which should always be dominant, and (2) the second class of rules, the discretionary rules. As the term suggests, these rules must be used with discretion, bearing in mind at all times the major underlying principles outlined in [612] to [617]. If the use of a discretionary rule conflicts with a major principle, then *in general* the rule must be considered subordinate to the major principle. This highlights the fact that interpretation is an art, to be acquired by practice rather than the straight-forward application of rules.

Both classes have been developed from the standard published works of Maxwell (1953) and Burrows (1946), an unpublished paper (Duncan, 1972), and discussions with many practitioners.

[611] Preparatory work

Before interpretation begins, some very important preparatory work should be done. The most important preparation is to ensure that the document has been read thoroughly and carefully. Secondly, relevant Court interpretations and pronouncements should be collected and considered. Court decisions on clauses of *similar*, but not identical, wording need to be used with great care as slight differences can be crucial. Identically worded sections will *in general* be interpreted in the same way, although this is not certain. As illustrated by points 7 and 8 in Table 6.1, different Judges can produce totally contradictory rulings within a short space of time. Fortunately, this is rare. The reasoning behind earlier decisions should be studied as that should help develop interpretation skills. Court decisions that are most likely to be followed rigidly in future are clearly those of a general nature, less dependent on the context. Examples are given in [617] below. Finally, whenever applicable, the history of clauses and sections need to be traced. If the wording of the section has changed at any stage, this fact could be of significance as it is assumed the change would only have been made for a reason.

B. Major Underlying Principles

[612] If plain and unambiguous, give effect

The major underlying principle of interpretation is that if words are plain and unambiguous then they must be given effect to, no matter what the consequences, and no matter how unjust or arbitrary. This principle has been described by O'Keefe and Farands (1980:10) as 'one of the cardinal rules of statutory interpretation.'

Indeed, the principle is so fundamental that it is also said *not* to be a rule of interpretation at all. Maxwell (1953:4) claims:

> when the language is not only plain but admits of but one meaning, the task of interpretation can hardly be said to arise. It is not allowable, says Vattel, to interpret what has no need of interpretation.

This principle is well accepted by New Zealand Courts, and has been for many years. Judge Blair has been frequently cited:

> a Court is not entitled to speculate as to the purpose of a document if the meaning is otherwise plain. In other words, when the parties to an agreement have expressed their meaning in words that are plain, a Court has no right to alter that meaning *(Inspector of Awards v ARA* [1969] BA 2316).

Table 6.1. Views and counterviews in law

View	Counterview
1. The meaning of a statutory rule may be governed by the other sections of the Act. (*Minister for Housing and Local Government v. Lambert* [1969] 2 W.L.R. 447)	There may be good reason for not constructing the rule according to the meaning of other sections (*Ching Garage v. Chingfield Corp.* [1961] 1 W.L.R. 470)
2. The history of the prior legislation may indicate how the present Act is to be interpreted (*Brown v. Dyerson* [1969] 1 Q.B.45)	The history of the prior legislation must not displace the plain wording of the present Act. (*Clixby v. Pountnoy* [1968] ch. 719)
3. The interpretation of statutory rules should not result in artificial or anomalous results (*Becke v. Smith* [1836] 2 M. & W. 191; *Thomas v. Rose* [1960] A.C. 748)	Unambiguous wording in a statute must be applied as it stands, even if the result is unreasonable or anomalous (*I.R.C v. Hinchy* [1968] 1 W.R. 840)
4. Effect must be given to clear and unambiguous language in the statute (*Heaney v. Smith* [1964] 1 W.L.R. 789)	In interpreting even clear and unambiguous rules, consideration must be given to the mischief which Parliament intended to neutralise. (*Smith v. Hughes* [1960] 1 W.L.R. 890; *Gill v. Humberstone* [1963] 1 W.L.R. 292)
5. All statutory criminal offences are presumed, irrespective of their wording, to include a *mens rea* requirement. (*Sweet v. Parsley* [1970] A.C. 132)	The presumption that all statutory offences includes a *mens rea* requirement may be rebutted by the seriousness of the conduct to be prohibited (*R. v. St Margaret's Trust* [1958] 1 W.L.R. 522)
6. It is presumed that statutes are not intended to change the law beyond that which is necessarily implied by this Act. (*N.C.B v. Wilkinson* [1952] 2 Q.B. 648)	Where the language of an Act plainly indicates that the law is to be altered it must be implemented as such. (*C.E.B. v. Halifax Corp.* [1963] A.C. 785)
7. Permanent part-time drivers are not casual but are full-time employees (*Northern Road Transport v. Whangarei Bus* [1984])	Permanent part-time drivers are not full-time but are casual employees (*Inspector v. Peninsular Motor* [1986])
8. Unilaterally removing penal rates can be deemed a partial lockout (*Paul v. IHC* [1992])	Unilaterally removing penal rates cannot be deemed a partial lockout (*Witehira v. Presbyterian Support Services* [1994])

Source: Items 1–6 were derived from Twining and Miers (1976:210-211).

[613] Documents to be considered as a whole

A document to be interpreted must be considered as a whole. This means, first, that all parts of the document must be considered. Thus, for example, even the preamble to an Act must be considered part of the Act. Second, all words within each section must be considered. Additional words are assumed to have been used for some purpose and it is only from the whole of a document that the general intent of the parties to it can be determined.

[614] Read in context

Words must always be read in context. Although the context in which a word appears cannot give that word a meaning of which it is not capable, it can determine which of a number of meanings a word should take. The 'context' of a word may refer to the document as a whole, or to a part of the document. Hence, if the latter, then a word or phrase can take a different meaning in different parts of the same document – because of the different contexts. This principle thus overrides the discretionary rule given in [624]: 'The same expression is deemed to be used in the same sense throughout a document.' As a consequence, Burrows (1946:25) considers that the discretionary rule [624] should be regarded as a 'consideration to be borne in mind rather than a rule'.

[615] Mischief rule

This principle rests on the assumption that agreements were made, and Acts were passed, for a purpose. This purpose was colourfully described some four centuries ago as being 'to suppress a mischief and advance the remedy'. Thus, according to Lord Coke (*Heydons Case*), it is necessary to consider:

1. what was the law before the Act was passed;
2. what was the mischief or defect for which the law had not provided;
3. what remedy Parliament has appointed;
4. the reason for the remedy.

This principle was repeated in New Zealand law in the first part of s.5(j) of the Acts Interpretation Act 1924, which stated:

> every Act, and every provision or enactment thereof, shall be deemed remedial, whether its immediate purport is to direct the doing of anything Parliament deems to be for the public good, or to prevent or punish the doing of anything it seems contrary to the public good.

While the current Interpretation Act 1999 has done away with such colourful language, the principle remains in interpretation of Acts and can equally be applied to union-management agreements. What had been agreed previously? What was the problem requiring this agreement? What was the solution? Why was that solution chosen?

[616] Liberal construction to achieve intent

This fifth principle was also expressed in the Act Interpretation Act 1924 in s.5(j), which stated that an Act should

> receive such fair, large and liberal construction and interpretation as will best ensure the attainment of the object of the Act and of such precision or enactment according to its true intent, meaning and spirit.

[617] Follow court rulings and pronouncements

Over the years, the Court has interpreted a number of common phrases. These include, for example:

a. 'shift work' (*Grant v Ross & Glendining*) – so long as at least two groups of workers will be working with the machinery at different times over a 24-hour period, *both* groups are 'shift workers' (this applies even to a group working 8 am to 5 pm);
b. 'continuous service' (*Inspector v Feltex*) – relates to unbroken service at *any* point in time, not necessarily up to the present so is *not* synonymous with 'current continuous service';
c. 'immediate family' (*Inspector v Williams*) – a person's 'immediate family' is either his/her parents, spouse and/or his/her children. It does not refer to a person's brothers and sisters, (obviously, by extension, it does not refer to cousins, etc.).

In addition, the Court has made a number of general pronouncements which should be followed, including:

> we think that the right to double payments under two clauses for the same hour worked should not be recognised unless the award contains an express provision of crystal clarity of authorising such double payments (*Inspector v NZ Co-op Dairy*).

C. Discretionary Rules

[618] Avoid absurdities

Notwithstanding the major principle outlined in [612], broad constructions of general words should be avoided if this creates an absurdity. The difficulty lies in correctly deciding between the situation where words are plain, and should be given effect to – even though they may create a seeming injustice – and the situation where the words are so absurd as to necessitate being overruled.

In effect, the absurdity has to be such as to create, or virtually create, an *impossible* situation, or one in which a literal interpretation makes total nonsense of the document.

For example, the Employment Contracts Act 1991 had a section for settling personal grievances. Section 27 stated:

> Personal grievance – (1) for the purposes of this Act, 'personal grievance' means any grievance that any employee may have against the employee's employer or former employer because of a claim – (a) that the employee has been unjustifiably dismissed; or
>
> An 'employee' is defined under s.2 as:
>
> (a) any person of any age employed by an employer to do any work for hire or reward.

A totally literal interpretation of s.27 would be that it only related to *employees* – that is, persons actually employed. Hence, an employee who is dismissed and as a consequence is *unemployed* cannot use the grievance procedure to challenge the dismissal (until such time as s/he gets a new job).

Should an employer use this argument to refuse to participate in a personal grievance, it would be rejected on the grounds that such a literal interpretation 'creates an absurdity'. The Employment Relations Act 2000 has removed the possibility of this absurdity, by stating that an employee is defined as above, 'unless the context otherwise requires'.

[619] Read according to subject matter

Words should be understood in the sense which best accords with the subject of the document and the purpose for which it was drawn up.

[620] Read according to popular meaning

Ordinary words used in non-technical documents should be given their popular, or ordinary, meaning. Thus, in a union demarcation dispute concerning who had 'rights' to the processing of venison, the interpretation of the word 'meat' arose. The Food Processors' Unions wanted 'meat' to be defined as per the Meat Act 1964, which excluded venison. The Court of Appeal (*NZ Food Processing Union v NZ Meat Processors' Union*) ruled that, other than in the Meat Act, the word 'meat' had to take its ordinary meaning (which *includes* venison).

[621] Read according to meaning when enacted

If terms or words have changed their meaning over time, it is generally taken that the meaning will be that which they bore when the document was drawn up. In years past, for example, 'crib time' meant the time spent eating a meal while still attending a machine. More recently it was used to refer to a meal break (without continuing work) taken by a shift worker.

[622] Read according to custom

While documents should be read according to custom, this rule is subject to qualification. Custom can only be invoked if some ambiguity exists, if it is used to *interpret* a term rather than to supply the term, and if the custom is of genuinely wide application and is of long standing.

[623] Technical terms to take their technical meaning

This rule is simply that 'where words with a technical meaning are used in a technical document, those words should be given the technical meaning unless there is something contrary in the context' (*Wellington Local Bodies' Officers Union v Upper Hutt City Council*). To some extent, this rule is simply an extension of the major principle that words are to be read in context. In the context of a technical document, words have a different meaning to that in the context of a general document. Thus in an engineering document the word 'cupola' would take the engineering meaning 'furnace', rather than its ordinary meaning 'dome of a building'.

[624] The same expression is used in the same sense throughout

It has been pointed out in [614] that this rule is subject to the major principle that words are to be read in context, and hence it may be described more aptly as a 'consideration to be borne in mind'. It is, however, a very sensible rule to be borne in mind when *drafting* a document.

[625] Special clauses override general clauses

In management-union documents there may be a general clause dealing with overtime, together with a special clause concerned with overtime on public holidays. When determining the rate for working overtime on a public holiday, the special clause would be the authority, not the general clause.

[626] 'Expressio unius est exclusio alterius'

This rule of interpretation, like the three following, is best known when expressed in Latin. As discussed in [607], the rule states that where some conditions or obligations are explicitly stated, then other conditions, which could otherwise have been implied, will be excluded.

In *AHI NZ Glass v North Island Electrical Union* the Court of Appeal interpreted s.116 of the Industrial Relations Act 1973. This section outlined a disputes procedure which applied to

> a dispute of rights between the parties including a dispute on:
> (a) the interpretation of this instrument; or
> (b) any matter (not being a personal grievance ...) related to matters dealt with in this instrument and not specifically and clearly disposed of by the terms of this instrument.

The Court of Appeal interpreted 'including' as per the *expressio unius* discretionary rule. As a consequence, the dispute of rights *procedure* was applicable only to those disputes of right covered by (a) and (b) above. *Other* disputes of right defined by the Act (for instance 'any dispute which is not a dispute of interest') were not covered by the procedure. Confusingly, the President of the Court of Appeal in an *obiter* (that is, not directly relevant to the decision and hence not binding) observation in *Brighouse v Bilderbeck* referred to s.40(1)(c)(ii) of the Employment Contracts Act 1991. This states that the Tribunal or Court may provide for the payment of compensation including compensation for:

i. humiliation;
ii. loss of benefit.

The President claimed the statutory word 'including' 'is not a limiting one'. In our view, and with all due respect, Cooke P. was incorrect. The word 'including', in that context, should be interpreted as limiting.

[627] 'Noscitur a sociis'

This rule states that where a word or phrase is linked together with others, then its meaning is coloured by the meanings of those to which it is linked. Thus a more general word is restricted to a sense analogous to the less general.

[628] 'Ejusdem generis'

This rule is applied in a more restrictive sense than that given in [627]. The *ejusdem generis* rule is that where a general term follows more specific terms, then the general term is taken to be of the same class or nature as the specific. Thus the word animals used in 'sheep, cows, horses and other animals' would be taken to mean animals of the same class as sheep, cows and horses. Thus goats would be included, but not tigers.

[629] 'Ut res magis valeat quam pereat'

Where two interpretations are possible, this rule states that the correct interpretation is that which does not defeat the intention of the document or render it invalid.

[630] Singular includes plural, male includes female

Legislation, and all documents, should be written in gender-neutral form. This was not so in the past and so the Interpretations Act 1999 states in s.31 that 'in an enactment passed or made before the commencement of this Act, words denoting the masculine gender includes females.' Similarly s.33 states 'words in the singular include plural and words in the plural include singular.'

[631] Punctuation may assist interpretation

Punctuation is meant to assist the understanding of the written word. The rule is that punctuation may assist interpretation but must not conflict with the plain meaning of words or cause a meaning to be placed on words that they do not have.

D. Draftsmanship

[632] Principles of draftsmanship

Clearly the need for interpretation would be greatly reduced if all documents were drafted properly. Indeed, the only interpretation necessary should be to confirm that the document is clear and unambiguous.

Before drafting documents, people should ensure they know precisely what are their intentions. Often problems arise because the parties to a document are *not* sure exactly what they intended to say.

Documents should be clear and precise to anyone competent in the subject matter. While this may sound trite, they should also be of the right length. Problems may be created by writing too much, often by putting in a number of examples. As [626] shows, this may result in misinterpretation if the examples were not very carefully chosen. Likewise, excess brevity can also result in later misinterpretation. The language used should follow the laws of grammar – and common sense. Hence, if words are repeated in the same document they should have the same meaning. Sentences should be as short as possible without destroying clarity.

After drafting a document, whoever is responsible should play devil's advocate and consider if anyone could make a valid case for interpreting it in a way other than intended. It must be remembered that many documents stand for a lengthy period. Hence it is naive to believe that because the other parties to it 'know what was intended', there could not be misinterpretation later, since the parties could well have changed. If the document is capable of two meanings, a new party to the agreement could misinterpret it by taking the unintended meaning, either deliberately to gain an advantage, or indeed in all good faith.

Chapter Seven

Bargaining

A. Introduction

[701] Coverage of the chapter

This chapter is concerned with bargaining – one of the major forms of interaction between employers and employees to determine the rules that govern the work environment. After considering aspects of bargaining and bargaining power in general, the chapter looks at the market wage concept, then looks specifically at individual bargaining and collective bargaining. The latter is considered under three headings: traditional collective bargaining and bargaining skills; productivity bargaining; and concession bargaining.

[702] Bargaining defined

In a major contribution to the literature, Flanders (1968:4) stated:

> Bargaining has been accurately defined as 'the process by which the antithetical interests of supply and demand, of buyer and seller, are finally adjusted' so as to end 'in the act of exchange.'

Flanders goes on to claim that individual bargaining may be considered true bargaining in that:

> It provides for an exchange of work for wages and, in stipulating the conditions of the exchange, adjusts for the time being, conflicts of interest between a buyer and seller of labour.

However, he considers collective bargaining is *not* true bargaining and that it is fundamentally different in that it

> does not commit anyone to buy or sell labour … it is meant to ensure that when labour is bought and sold … its price and the other terms of the transaction will accord with the provisions of the agreement.

Hence, collective bargaining is better considered to be 'collective regulation' of individual bargaining.

Notwithstanding Flanders' eminence, Fox, another leading academic, (1975:154-5) takes issue with Flanders on the basis that

> the individual agreement does not, in itself, commit either party to an act of purchase or sale, any more than does the collective agreement.

Fox may be technically correct in that there may be considered three elements in bargaining (the bargaining process, the agreement and the actual act of purchase and sale) and that with both individual and collective bargaining the final act of purchase and sale has to take place after the process and agreement. However, it is our view that Flanders is also correct in that in most cases there is a fundamental difference between individual and collective bargaining. After an individual bargain has gone through the first two elements, the final element – namely the act of purchase and sale of a *known* quantity of labour (the one individual) – is virtually assured. With collective bargaining (particularly as it occurred up until recent times) after the first two elements had been completed it was usually *not* known what quantity of labour would eventually be bought and sold. The collective bargain merely determined the minimum conditions that would have to be met, should individuals offer their labour to the employer(s). (Admittedly, in New Zealand, the Employment Contracts Act 1991 reduced the difference in that it encouraged collective bargaining to be for a specified, named, collective group of workers.)

[703] Concept of bargaining power

Bargaining power may be defined in a similar fashion to the broader concept of power in general (see [503]). Thus

> 'A' has bargaining power with respect to 'B' if the final outcome of a bargaining situation is as 'A' wishes, even if opposed by 'B'.

Chamberlain and Kuhn (1986:176), the authors of one of the modern classics on bargaining theory, adopt a similar definition, defining bargaining power as 'the ability to secure another's agreement on one's own terms.'

This definition has a number of weaknesses. It is easy to overlook the fact that parties have multiple power bases, and to fall into the trap of assuming that bargaining power is only coercive. Thus Chamberlain and Kuhn (1986:176) go on to describe management's willingness to agree to terms as depending on 'the costs of disagreeing relative to the costs of agreeing.' However, as discussed in [503] to [509], this overlooks the fact that control of *norms* and *information* can be formidable sources of power. With these covert power bases, A can determine what is on the bargaining agenda and can influence to a great extent B's expectations and wishes. A may end up getting what A wishes, without recourse to *coercive* use of power, because B was so indoctrinated and/or ignorant and/or demoralised as to be virtually amenable to anything. It would not be until B questions the norms, and/or acquires more knowledge and information that B's wishes would significantly change.

A second weakness is that in reality it is highly unlikely that any party ever has total power, or that another party ever has *no* power. Hence the concept of bargaining power is better defined in relative terms.

Taking into account both weaknesses, an alternative definition is that in a particular bargaining situation

> 'A' has more bargaining power than 'B' if the final outcome of the bargaining situation is closer to 'A''s wishes than to 'B''s wishes. The power may be manifested in an overt or covert fashion or both.

The problem still remains, that B's wishes may have been influenced or manipulated by A *prior to* the particular bargaining situation.

[704] The existence of bargaining power

From the time of the early industrial relations writings, conventional wisdom has been that bargaining power certainly exists and that in the context of individual bargaining between one employer and one worker/employee the power advantage definitely resides with the employer. As Beatrice Webb (1901:8-9) put it:

> If the capitalist refuses to accept the workman's terms, he will, no doubt, suffer some inconvenience as an employer. To fulfil his orders, he will have to 'speed up' some of his machinery, or insist on his people working longer hours. Failing these expedients he may have to delay the delivery of his goods, and may even find his profits, at the end of the year fractionally less than before. But, meanwhile, he goes on eating and drinking, his wife and family go on living, just as before. His physical comfort is not affected: he can afford to wait until the labourer comes back in a humble frame of mind. And that is just what the labourer must presently do. For he, meanwhile, has lost his day. His very subsistence depends on his promptly coming to an agreement. If he stands out, he has no money to meet his weekly rent, or to buy food for his family. If he is obstinate, consumption of his little hoard or the pawning of his furniture, may put off the catastrophe; but sooner or later slow starvation forces him to come to terms. And since success in the higgling of the market is largely determined by the relative eagerness of the parties to come to terms – especially if this eagerness cannot be hidden – it is now agreed, even on this ground alone, 'that manual labourers as a class are at a disadvantage in bargaining.'

However this view is not universally accepted, and in particular is rejected in the propaganda of the New Right.

[705] The New Right

'The New Right' is a term used to describe a political ideology developed in the 1970s and 1980s that was favourable to big business. It emphasises a strong belief in the value of the 'market', in individualism, and in government non-interventionism. It has been evidenced by 'Reaganism' in the US, 'Thatcherism' in the UK and 'Rogernomics' in New Zealand. Prime beneficiaries are big business, so it is no surprise that the New Zealand Business Roundtable (NZBR) endorses those who propagate New Right philosophies. The NZBR is described (Roper 1993:164) as:

> a moving force behind the emergence of the New Right (in New Zealand – my insert). Not only has it produced a barrage of submissions in every major area of public policy, but it has also funded visits, public seminars and publications by right-wing academics as well as setting up the Centre of Independent Studies to promote pro-business policy research.

The NZBR (1990) is dismissive of the problem of an imbalance of bargaining power, claiming it is an 'illusion.'

One of the leading gurus of the New Right in the USA is Richard Epstein, a Professor of Law at the University of Chicago. He was brought to New Zealand by the above-mentioned 'Centre for Independent Studies.' He (Epstein 1990:3) glibly discusses the possibility of inequality of bargaining power:

> Let's assume that we really believed that there was an inequality of bargaining power. Let's assume we had an employer who was entitled to 'dictate' the terms of trade in the marketplace. What would we expect to see the contract look like? The answer is the employer would never stop pressing his advantage. If it turned out the employer could dictate terms, why would he offer a wage of ten if he could drive it down to nine; and why would he settle for nine if he could drive it down to eight? The logic of a dictation, the logic of inequality of bargaining power necessarily says there is no reason to stop until the employer has finished the job. That means, in effect, you're going to observe people working for employers at a zero wage.

On the same line of reasoning, one presumes Epstein would argue there was no inequality of bargaining power between a starving Prisoner of War who sells his gold wedding ring and the prison guard who buys it for a handful of rice – because the guard did not make the POW hand over the ring for nothing.

Unless Epstein is cynically stating something he knows is false he apparently cannot grasp that it is logically possible for A to have *more* bargaining power than B, without A having to have total power, and B zero power.

The more rational and more usual line of argument against the concept that there is inequality of bargaining power is put by Brook (1990:17), a former policy analyst for the NZBR. She states that although most employers have some degree of monopsony power (the power derived from being the sole or a major purchaser – the equivalent to *monopoly* power of a sole or major producer), their ability to abuse this power

> is in most cases limited by the realization that sustained abuse, for example, in continuing to pay below market wages or provide work conditions below the 'market' level, will mean that they lose employees to other employers.

Similarly the NZBR (1990:20) uses the following as an example to demonstrate that the 'market wage' prevents employers exploiting their position:

> What forces General Motors to pay the wages it does? The answer is that if General Motors offers lower wages than other employers, it will get few employees, so its

employees get a wage that is at least as high as their services are worth to other employers.

This begs a number of questions:

- what in fact is meant by the 'market wage'?
- does it exist in reality, or is it a hypothetical concept?
- if the market wage, or a reasonable approximation, does exist – is it the 'right' wage?

B. The Market Wage

[706] The market wage

The 'market wage', also known as the 'going rate', or 'going wage', is a hypothetical concept used by economists to enable them to develop elegant models. Put simply, the market wage is the wage corresponding to the intersection of the supply curve (indicating the number of workers willing to work for a particular wage) and the demand curve (indicating the number of employees wanted by employers for a particular wage).

A superficial reading of an economics text gives the impression that this hypothetical concept is an accurate portrayal of reality. Thus Ehrenberg and Smith (1986:39) state categorically:

> We have argued that firms wishing to have workers must pay the going rate (i.e., market wage) or lose all applicants. While this may seem unrealistic, it is not.

In fact this concept, like most concepts in economic theory, is an elegant but *extreme simplification* of reality. It would be a reasonably accurate portrayal of reality *only* if certain assumptions are made. These include:

a. there is perfect knowledge (of alternative jobs, of other wages, etc.);
b. there are no impediments to the movement of labour (i.e., no economic *or* psychological costs in changing jobs);
c. all employers and employees are 'economically rational'.

In reality, *not one* of the above three assumptions is true. Not only employees, but also many employers, are ignorant of what is paid elsewhere. It is surely obvious that there are economic impediments to changing a job. In many cases there will be removal expenses, relocation expenses, as well as the loss of security benefits in the job. For many people the fear of the unknown and general inertia creates significant psychological impediments. Finally, people, whether employers or employees, are not economically rational. They are not totally *irrational*, but custom and the lack of maximising drive in many people means any theory based on 'economical rationality' is suspect. For example, in New Zealand prior to 1972 women earned lower wages for doing *identical* work to men. In general, people (including women) felt that was, if not ideal, at least acceptable. However, assuming that the average woman was able to perform to the same level as the average man, then economically rational employers would overwhelmingly employ women in preference to men. This clearly did not occur.

Thus the assumptions necessary for there to be a 'market wage' are certainly not valid. Certainly factors of supply and demand will influence the rates that are paid in the market, but there will be significant variations of the rates actually paid. Thus rather than referring to the 'market wage' it would be more accurate to refer to the 'market range'. To this end individual employers cannot totally ignore the market and the particular rates that are paid by other employers, but they have considerable discretion as to whether they pay at the higher or lower end of the market range.

[707] 'The Right Wage'

Labour economics texts imply that the so-called market wage is the wage that *should* be paid and not simply a rough indication of the market range that *is* paid. Ehrenberg and Smith (1986:51) state: 'We shall define workers as *overpaid* if their wages are higher than the market equilibrium wage for their job.' The New Right wholeheartedly support the notion that the market wage is somehow the 'right' wage. (The 'right' wage being defined as the wage that *should* be paid). However what should be paid is a value judgement and reflects a subjective view and self-interest.

Many societies accept that the 'market' – that is, the forces of supply and demand – can drive the market range to unacceptably low levels. Consequently these societies introduce both minimum wage legislation, which has a direct effect on the lower end of the market range, and unemployment benefits, which have an indirect effect. Not surprisingly the New Right want to ensure that these measures which prevent the lowering of the market range are not too effective. Thus the NZEF (1992:25) caution that 'a higher minimum wage will decrease employment opportunities', and the NZBR (1990:15) cautions not only against minimum wages but also against unemployment benefits. They point out:

> The district manager of Carter Holt Harvey in Northland was reported as saying that many married men on his staff were quitting, claiming the dole gave them a better deal … the unemployment benefit for a married person with two children, including the accommodation benefit, was more than 10 percent higher than the Guaranteed Minimum Family Income for a married person in work with two children. It is over 80 percent of the average wage in Northland.

In contrast to the New Right who believe that whatever is determined by the market is 'right', societies who support minimum wages appear to support the concept that, no matter what the levels of supply and demand, there should be a minimum level of wages. This closely follows the belief in the concept that at the very least a wage should be a 'living wage.'

Mr Justice Higgins, President of the Australian Arbitration Court made one of the most famous 'living wage' pronouncements in the so-called 'Harvester' decision. (Ex Parte H.V. McKay (1907) 2 CAR 1 at 3–4). In determining what was a 'fair and reasonable' wage, Higgins explicitly rejects the market wage, stating:

> the remuneration could safely have been left to the usual, but unequal, contest, the 'higgling of the market' for labour, with the pressure for bread on one side, and the pressure for profits on the other. The standard of 'fair and reasonable' must therefore be something else … (wages) sufficient to ensure the workman food, shelter, frugal comfort, provisions for evil days etc., as well as reward for the special skill of an artisan if he is one.

The living wage concept is not without problems. First, the actual degree of 'comfort' (or deprivation) that should be the lot of employees on the lowest rate is a matter of opinion. Further, if the living wage is set at the lowest rate allowing a employee to survive, it means an employee with dependents would be unable to survive. However, if it is set at a level allowing for dependents, critics would argue it is too high for those *without* dependents. The 'living wage' cannot be set without consideration for the market range. If it is set too far above the market range it will force some employers out of the market.

Thus the subjective view as to what level the living wage should be set will be heavily influenced by what occurs in the market. Isaac (1991:17) points out that Higgins in the Harvester decision did 'take notice of what the unskilled wage was in certain areas' before pronouncing on his view as to a living wage.

C. Individual Bargaining

[708] Individual bargaining

Until fairly recently, individual bargaining would only rate a brief mention in employment relations texts, and then as an introduction to collective bargaining. The usual practice would be first to point out the difference between individual and collective bargaining usually quoting, for example, the Webbs (1902:173):

> In unorganized trades the individual workman, applying for a job, accepts or refuses the terms offered by the employer without communication with his fellow-workmen, and without any other consideration than the exigencies of his own position. For the sale of his labor he makes, with the employer, a strictly individual bargain. But if a group of workmen concert together, and send representatives to conduct the bargaining on behalf of the whole body, the position is at once changed. Instead of the employer making a series of separate contracts with isolated individuals, he meets with a collective will, and settles, in a single agreement, the principles upon which, for the time being, all workmen of a particular group, or class, or grade will be engaged.

The texts would continue by observing that early last century workers discovered the advantages of bargaining collectively insofar as in that way some of the power imbalance could be rectified. Again, the Webbs (1902:174) would frequently be quoted:

> If the foreman had dealt privately with each man, he might have found some in such necessity that he could have driven them to take the job practically at any price rather than be without work for even half a day. Others, again relying on exceptional strength or endurance, would have seen their way to make the standard earnings at a piecework rate upon which the average worker could not even subsist. By the method of collective bargaining the foreman is prevented from taking advantage of the competition of both these classes of men to beat down the earnings of the other workmen.

However the emergence of the New Right philosophies in most Western economies, including New Zealand, has made this traditional approach suspect as the basic assumptions are challenged. Not only is there the New Right argument that there is no bargaining power imbalance between employer and employee, there is also the fact (as opposed to argument) that many more employees are now covered by individual agreements than was the case a while back (see Chapter Nineteen). Individual bargaining should no longer be regarded as an historical oddity but rather as an increasing reality.

[709] Bargaining power and individual bargaining

Paragraphs [704] to [707] above discussed the New Right argument that there is no power imbalance since wages are determined by the market and neither employer nor (potential) employee can affect the market wage. The flaw in that argument is that there is no 'market wage', but rather a 'market range.' In any particular situation the employer may *wish* to pay at the upper end of the range. In which case both parties may be happy. Alternatively, the employee may have few needs or very low expectations, or a low sense of self-worth, and be happy to accept the bottom end of the range. Bargaining power is relevant where the employer wishes to pay at the bottom end of the range and the employee hopes to receive a wage at the top end of the range.

For the same arguments expressed by the Webbs nearly a century ago, it is probably blindingly obvious to all, except highly paid apologists for the New Right, that in periods of high unemployment it is far more likely that the employer will persuade the employee to accept the bottom end of the range, than that the employee will persuade the employer to pay at the top end. If neither employer nor employee can persuade the other, it is again far more likely that the employer will be able to find *another* employee who will accept the bottom end than that the original employee will be able to find another employer who will pay at the top end. Indeed, this power difference is such that many employers do not even go through a pretence of 'bargaining' (if that is taken to mean compromise and adjusted offers and counter-offers), but rather state the conditions on a 'take it or leave it' basis.

[710] 'Take it or leave it bargaining'

In many situations of individual bargaining an employee will be offered terms simply on a 'take it or leave it' basis, with the employer making it perfectly clear that there will be no change to the original offer. There are conflicting views as to whether this approach may be deemed 'bargaining.'

One view is that a 'take it or leave it' approach is a unilateral setting of conditions by the employer, and as such is not bargaining. Proponents of this view would certainly contend that, even if it were deemed to be bargaining, it would not be 'good faith' bargaining. Thus the Labour Opposition in New Zealand before the 1993 Election proposed to introduce legislation requiring 'good faith' bargaining (see Clark (1993) and Geare (1993)). This was reiterated before the 1999 Election by both Labour (Hodgson (1999)) and Alliance (Harre (1999)).

A counter-argument is that bargaining, as defined in [702], does not require compromise or movement on the part of either or both parties. If the employer (the buyer of labour) stands firm with an offer and the employee (seller of labour) adjusts his/her level of expectations downwards, then the interests are adjusted and an act of exchange can occur.

While this 'take it or leave it' approach is commonly associated with individual bargaining, because the power imbalance is more apparent it can and has been used in collective bargaining against groups of employees. The General Electric Company in the USA used this strategy through the 1950s and 1960s. The practice was known as *Boulwarism*, after the Vice President of Industrial Relations of General Electric, one Lemuel Boulware (see [721]).

D. Collective Bargaining

[711] Derivation of the term

The term 'collective bargaining' was popularised in the classic works by Sydney and Beatrice Webb (1896, 1902). The first use of the phrase is attributed to Beatrice who used it in a less famous work published in 1891 before her marriage when she was Beatrice Potter. (Not 'Beatrix', of Peter Rabbit fame.)

The Webbs considered the major advantages to employees of collective bargaining is that the power advantage held by the employer is reduced. Their views about these advantages were clearly expressed in the excerpts above in [704] and [708].

[712] Basic definition

Collective bargaining is a process whereby parties to employment relations establish the rules by which they hope to achieve their objectives. It involves a collective group of employees – usually a union – and either a single employer or a group of employers. Representatives from these parties negotiate a final set of rules which may be referred to by a variety of titles such as the union-management agreement. In New Zealand, such agreements were defined in past statutes as awards or agreements if in the private sector, or orders and determinations if in the public sector. Since 2000, the general term is a collective employment agreement.

In most countries the union-management agreement would not, in general, commit the parties either to provide or to accept a particular amount of labour. That is, the union does not 'sell' an amount of labour but rather sets the minimum rates and conditions under which individual employees may decide whether or not to sell their own labour. In New Zealand, however, some collective employment agreements name the individuals covered.

[713] The primary issues in collective bargaining

The primary issues involved in collective bargaining are over material benefits: that is, wages, working conditions and job security, with the emphasis being on wages. The Webbs (1902:816) themselves observed that

> Powerful trade unions show no backwardness in exacting the highest money wages that they know how to obtain but ... consent ... to work for excessive and irregular hours, and to put up with unsafe, unsanitary, indecent and hideous surroundings.

While conditions today are very much better than they were in the Webbs' day – showing that negotiators *have* concerned themselves with improving conditions as well as increasing wages – in many areas the most significant improvement in conditions comes from a shorter basic working week. In many instances particularly bad conditions are introduced into negotiations in order to obtain higher wages. The line of argument is more usually 'xyz is unsafe/unpleasant, therefore give us a danger/dirt/unpleasant conditions allowance' rather than 'xyz is unsafe/unpleasant/inconvenient, therefore *change* it.' It should be noted that this line is not the prerogative of unions of manual employees. Thus, junior house surgeons who decried their long hours, saying that it affected patient care, were apparently satisfied when they were granted overtime pay.

This economic emphasis by unions is frequently criticised. Fox (1975:164) notes that the Webbs wanted unions to 'raise their sights above financial advantage and work to a fuller and richer concept of man.' All those in management or the general public who subscribe to the unitary view call for negotiations to be primarily concerned with the 'efficiency of industry' or the 'good of the nation.' However it must be stressed that it is not the function of unions to make men and women better people in the eyes of particular observers (the role of the Church?), or to make industry more efficient (the role of managers?), or to be concerned – to any greater extent than any other pressure group – with the good of the nation (the role of Government?). Unions should serve the interests of their members either as leaders or as representatives – a matter of choice for the leadership and rank and file.

In addition to the material benefits covered by collective bargaining, there is also the non-economic side to be considered. It should not be overlooked that the fact that employees have *rights* to particular conditions is an advantage just as the conditions themselves are advantages. The fact that employees play a part in the determination and administration of rules, thus having 'a voice in shaping their own destiny and the decisions on which it most depends' (Flanders 1968:26), is a significant part of collective bargaining. There is however the danger of falling into the trap of over-emphasising the importance of this aspect of collective bargaining simply because it is the situation one would like to see in existence. It would appear Flanders has done this when he continues: 'the value of a trade union to its members lies less in its economic achievements than in its capacity to protect their dignity.' As Fox (1975) has observed, it is certain that the vast majority of union members would disagree with that statement.

[714] The process of collective bargaining

Collective bargaining, or negotiation, is a central feature of employment relations and the manner in which negotiations are carried out will reflect the particular employment relations situation facing an organisation or group of managers and union representatives. However, negotiation is more than simply an eyeball to eyeball confrontation across a well-worn table. As such, it is influenced by a number of factors and, in some instances, the outcome of a negotiation may be predetermined by these factors.

A negotiation normally occurs in response to a specific issue or grievance – this may involve an individual, a group or a collection of groups, as would occur with a 'major claim.' For the most part, the issues giving rise to negotiation are initiated by unions who make a claim on management. The opposite can, of course, occur such as when management wishes to make changes to established practices.

Walton and McKersie (1965:4-5), authors of a classic text on labour negotiations, consider that negotiation

> is comprised of four systems of activity, each with its own function for the interacting parties, its own internal logics, and its own identifiable set of instrumental acts or tactics.

The four activities they identify are: distributive bargaining, integrative bargaining, attitudinal structuring and intra-organisational bargaining.

Distributive bargaining involves

> activities instrumental to the attainment of one party's goals when they are in basic conflict with those of the other party. It is the type of activity most familiar to students of negotiations; in fact, it is 'bargaining' in the strictest sense of the word.

It is frequently thought of as a WIN-LOSE situation, in that, at least on the surface, a gain to one party is a loss to another. That is, if the union bargains a wage increase up from 9 per cent to 9.5 per cent they have won a little, while management has lost a little. This is the classical type of traditional collective bargaining.

Integrative bargaining involves

> activities which are instrumental to the attainment of objectives which are not in fundamental conflict with those of the other party and which therefore can be integrated to some degree. Such objectives are said to define an area of common concern, a problem.

Integrative bargaining is sometimes described as WIN-WIN situations in that both parties can benefit. Productivity bargaining (see [725]–[733]) is integrative bargaining. It must be noted however that WIN-WIN situations still have strong elements of distributive bargaining (hence the situation could be win-WIN *or* WIN-win).

Attitudinal structuring is considered an additional major function of negotiating and involves

> influencing the relationships between parties, in particular such attitudes as friendliness-hostility, trust, respect, and the motivational orientation of competitiveness-cooperativeness.

This emphasises the long-term as well as short-term aspects of negotiation. Negotiators frequently prefer bargaining with 'professionals' – since they take a longer-term view and do not wish to make life harder for themselves in the future by causing unnecessarily antagonistic feelings towards themselves.

Intra-organisational bargaining is defined as a

> system of activities which brings the expectations of principals into alignment with those of the chief negotiator.

This area should be expanded to consider all aspects of bargaining within the party. For example, there is never *a* 'management view.' Within a firm, different managers will support different strategies and be agreeable to different concessions. The differences will be magnified if the negotiation is at industry level. Likewise there are great differences of opinion within a union with different sectional interests. These differences should be settled *before* union-management negotiations begin. This aspect has been highlighted by Dunlop (1967:173):

> One of the major activities of collective bargaining involves the determination of priorities within each side in the bargaining process. The view that a homogeneous union negotiates with a homogeneous management or association is erroneous and mischievous. A great deal of the complexity and beauty of collective bargaining involves the process of compromise and assessment of priorities within each side.

[715] The basis of the negotiation

Negotiations are over many varied issues. However, for the sake of convenience and clarity the following discussion will be concerned with *wage* negotiations. With a little imagination it should be clear how the principles would apply over the negotiation of staffing levels, or holidays, and so forth. The basis of a wage negotiation may be illustrated in a simplistic form as in Figure 7.1 below.

Each party should have a good idea of what it wants, what it expects to get, and what it is not prepared to accept. The resistance points indicate the worst situation either party will accept. They indicate the union would prefer to strike rather than accept a settlement below its resistance point and likewise management would prefer a strike or lockout rather than concede a settlement above its resistance point.

The target points represent the actual settlements both parties have in mind and, in large part, the real core of the negotiation is concerned with the identification of these points and their realignment. Thus, in making serious offers, management should have some idea of the union's target, otherwise the offer, if too far below, is likely to be rejected out of hand. Similarly, a union demand too far out of touch with management's target will be ineffective and ignored out of hand.

Initial demands and initial offers are traditionally considerably more and less respectively than the final settlement point. Outside observers sometimes call for 'sanity' and realistic demands and offers. However the tactic is not simply a game or perverse traditionalism, but has a very valid purpose of keeping each party's *true* position (with regards to target and resistance points) hidden

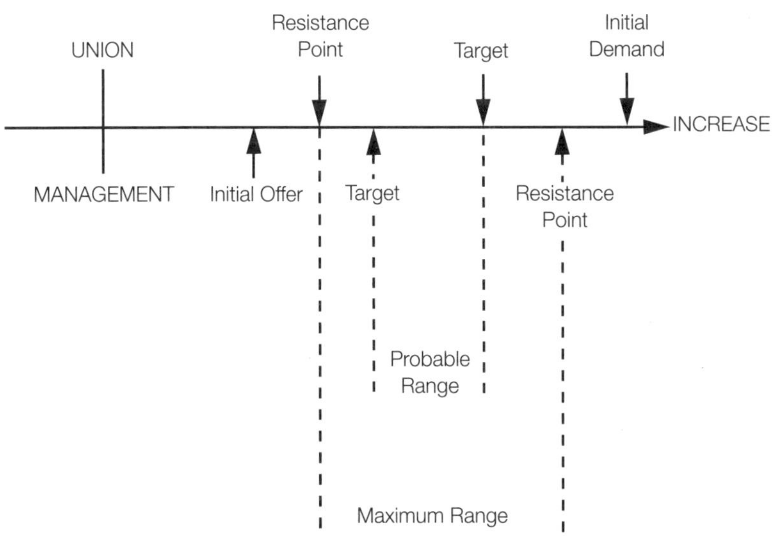

Figure 7.1. Bargaining ranges

from the other side. If the other side *guesses* one's target and resistance point incorrectly, this may be to one's advantage. Skill in negotiations involves using the other party's uncertainty and lack of knowledge to one's own advantage.

Thus, although each party can (and should) assess the other parties position, there will be a level of uncertainty. Hence Figure 7.1 reflects the actual situation, while Figure 7.2 reflects the perceived situation.

Before negotiating, each party should be certain as to its own resistance points and targets for each item under negotiation, both separately and as a group. In practice there may be trade-offs between items so that, if less than anticipated was conceded on one item, more may be conceded on another. In addition, each party should assess what it *assumes* to be the resistance points and targets for the other party. Figure 7.2 shows that neither side in reality knows accurately what are the other side's resistance point and target. The better the preparation, and the more skilful the negotiations, the greater the certainty as to the true figures.

Ideally, negotiation goes through the following processes:

a. confirming the other party's position;
b. modifying (by the quality of your negotiation) these positions until:
c. their target (possibly grudgingly) is identical with your target which becomes the point of settlement.

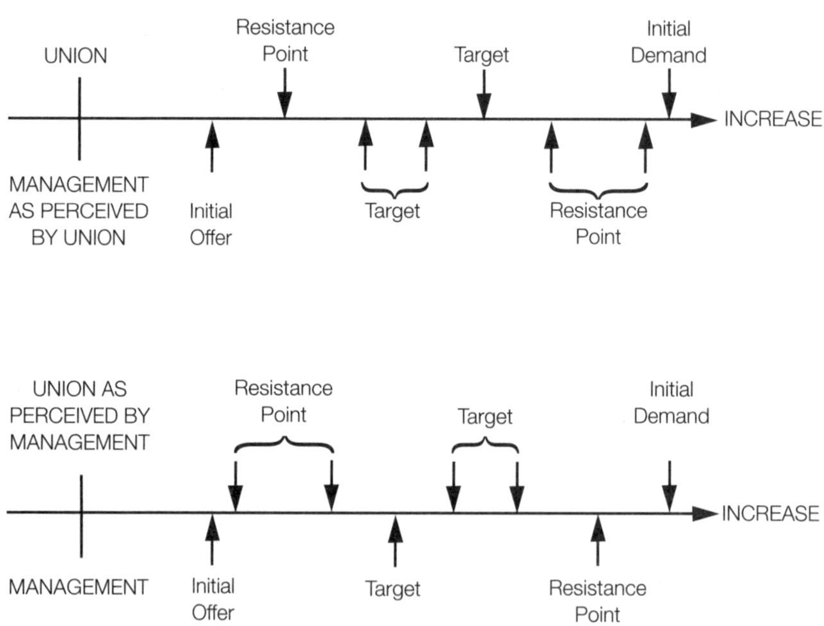

Figure 7.2. Perceived bargaining ranges

[716] Stages in the negotiation process

The stages in the negotiation process can be summarised as being:

a. preparation:
   - an assessment of bargaining power;
   - a decision as to objectives (targets and resistance points);
   - formulating strategies and tactics.

b. actual negotiation.

Following the negotiation, both parties then implement, monitor and sometimes modify the agreement. Some of the problems of interpretation (see Chapter Six) result from settlements in which the parties never completely reached agreement.

[717] Preparation

Lewicki and Litterer (1985:47) consider that 'preparation and planning are the most important parts of negotiation.'

Both sides involved in the process will be concerned to assess the relative strengths and weaknesses of their own position, and that of their opponent. Relevant factors include: their ability to sustain and survive a strike; their concern about future relationship and their dependence on good future relationships; the likelihood of government intervention and the approach taken by government in such intervention; and, at least sometimes, the logic behind the case – assuming that the logical basis of the argument is accepted by the other side.

Having gained some idea of where they stand (the past conduct of employment relations within the organisation will be critical here), both parties can decide on their respective target and resistance points. Target and resistance points should be decided upon on a *cost-benefit* basis. That is, on management's side such questions should be asked (and answered) as:

- what will it cost us in direct labour costs to concede this?
- what will it cost us if we refuse, in terms of strikes?
- will a strike benefit us long term?
- what benefits will we get if we concede?, etc.

Similarly, on the union's side:

- what will it benefit us in direct benefits if we get this?
- what will it cost us if we force management to concede?
- what will it cost us if we have to strike?
- what benefits will we get long term from the strike?, etc.

When formulating their mandate, both sides will also wish to consider which items they are prepared to give away, and in exchange for what. In this sense, the distributive bargaining model can involve 'win/win' considerations. Thus, in return for an increase in pay, or agreement not to reduce penal rates, management may want an agreement of labour flexibility. Unfortunately 'win/

lose' situations are much more common. A 'win/lose' situation may prove to be 'lose/lose', in that, while it may result in a tactical victory for one party (and in this sense they have won) they may in the final analysis be losers due to the effect on the morale of the other party who may then seek an opportunity in the future to 'get their own back.'

Observers often seem to forget, or not realise, that negotiators *should* be concerned with long as well as short-term costs and benefits. Thus when the media or politicians gleefully state for example how ridiculous it was for a union to go on strike for a small gain since it would take years at the new rate to recoup the lost wages, they do not take into account the *long-term* gains the union may have achieved as well. For instance, there may well be a greater likelihood of future demands being met since the employer realises the employees *are* prepared to strike.

Unless a side has overwhelming bargaining power, its success is very dependent on the degree of preparation. It is vitally important that the parties involved should have considered the issues likely to be raised during the negotiation. If this is not done, there is a distinct danger that someone will be caught 'with their pants down.' It is also important at this stage to agree on the composition of the negotiation team, who will be the principal advocate and who, if necessary, will act as the stooge. The danger is, however, that too much preparation is undertaken with the result that both sides become inflexible and end up in deadlock. Each party must ensure that it can 'see the wood for the trees' and that it does have some flexibility in the range of possible offers it might make. A vital part of preparation is the formulation of strategy and tactics.

[718] Strategy and tactics

Negotiation strategy may be considered the overall plan, taking into account all variables including long-term consequences. The strategy will define the basic approach.

Tactics refer to immediate short term actions and responses. In effect, tactics are used to help one achieve one's strategy. Tactics may be thought out in advance or may be almost unconscious responses. A badly prepared negotiator will use tactics (which may or may not be successful) but will not have a strategy.

[719] Actual negotiation

Conventionally, when a union makes a claim, there are a number of stages usually involved in the actual negotiations:

a. introductions and union(s) submission – it is important at this stage that everyone agrees on the terms of reference;
b. adjournment – called by management;
c. reply, counter-argument and offer;
d. union adjournment to consider;
e. above may be repeated a number of times;

f. finalisation phase and clarification of the agreement;
g. implementation phase.

In practice, the sequence of events may not follow this pattern. Much will depend on the stage of procedure involved, whether management has got a suitable mandate, and the extent to which the union is serious in its claim. Clearly, some issues may simply be presented as a 'try on.'

However, the face-to-face negotiation stage can involve a number of well-known tactics, which each side will deploy in order to strengthen their own case or weaken that of their opponents.

Tactics are a means to an end. They should never be allowed to take over and become the end themselves. If a tactic helps achieve the objective it is a 'good' tactic, if not, it is either ineffective or counter productive. Negotiators however are human and at times one may be more concerned with scoring points than the end result. If this practice becomes excessive, then the negotiator is likely to be unsuccessful.

Specific tactics include:

a. the use of adjournments – to prevent the other side from finding out too much if things are getting out of hand; to calm matters down if emotions are running high; to stop repetitive arguments; and so forth;
b. emphasising the detrimental effects of their case on their own side;
c. emphasising the benefits your case has on their side;
d. where applicable, reference to past practice, other companies behaviour, and so forth.

As stated above, *any* tactic that achieves one's objective is good. Some negotiators have achieved success with tactics such as verbal abuse, obscenities, physical intimidation and threats, which other negotiators would never stoop to use. However, while these tactics may be considered ethically and socially undesirable, at least in the short term they may be effective. In general, however, that sort of behaviour has usually proven to be unsuccessful in the longer-term.

In certain circumstances, anything may work and anything may fail. However, negotiators are in general advised:

a. not to respond to verbal attacks – at least, the response should not be on the basis of emotion, rather, there should be an appeal to reason;
b. not to let their own side give away their position. It is important that the discussion is channelled as far as possible. The side should have a principal negotiator, who should do the talking. Any one else on the team should only contribute at carefully pre-arranged points;
c. not to disagree in public. If there is disagreement, the side should seek an adjournment;
d. not to adjourn for too long. Adjournments are useful and indeed are an expected part of the negotiation process, but they can be too long, in which

case the opponents will have more time in which to regroup, or alternatively may experience acute frustration if it is felt that the other side is dragging its feet;

e. not to make serious points too early. Probably the most difficult part of the entire negotiation process is knowing when to make a commitment. This should only be done when the side has got all the facts and impressions it needs, and when the other side has had the opportunity to exercise its ritualistic function of being seen to fight long and hard for the issue at stake.

Particularly if the simplistic view is taken of employment relations that it involves 'capital' and 'labour', it is easy to overlook the fact that *individuals* are involved in negotiations. It is important to realise that personal values, ambitions, feelings and objectives can influence negotiators as well as the objectives of the parties they represent.

In practice, negotiators are human and have human frailties. Some negotiators get brow-beaten into agreeing to things that next morning they regret – indeed one tactic in negotiations is simply to tire out the opposition. Some negotiators are concerned with the image they create in negotiations and may make concessions or take stands for the purpose of furthering this image rather than the interests of those they represent. Often negotiators can paint themselves into a corner and feel they cannot move from a particular position without losing face and may end up bitterly fighting for something of little value. Finally, of course, negotiators have their own positions to think of and their own careers – with respect to both promotion and job security – and this may affect the way they negotiate and what they will agree to concede.

Hence negotiators should take into account the individuals they are negotiating against, and consider the individuals as individuals as well as being the agents for the opposing side.

[720] Effective negotiators

A profile of an effective negotiator often ends up with someone who appears to be a cross between Superman and St George, or Wonder Woman and Mother Teresa. The strengths and virtues are overwhelming. Kniveton and Towers (1978:144-6) consider effective negotiators:

a. should have unlimited patience;
b. should be persuasive;
c. should know and understand the other people in the negotiation;
d. should know themselves as others know them. In other words they should be aware of their own abilities and limitations;
e. should be able to develop good interpersonal relations with other negotiators;
f. should be able to be rigid and stick to their point of view but should be willing to move if necessary.

However this is not all, and they quote opinions that negotiators should:

a. be able to say ‘no’ effectively;
b. inspire confidence;
c. be ingenious;
d. be able to ‘Take it’;
e. be a patient listener;
f. have a sense of humour;
g. have an appreciation of the economics of the overall situation;
h. be able to organise their thoughts and speak or write with clarity of expression but without being orators.

And that effective negotiators:

a. ask a lot of questions;
b. do a lot of testing understanding, particularly when final decisions are near, so that agreements are likely to last;
c. ‘flag’ their behaviour, making it clear what they intend to do;
d. do not follow disagreements with counter-proposals;
e. do not weight their arguments too much. Too much information and facts merely provide the other side with many opportunities to attack.

All these attributes certainly help create an effective negotiator. Surprisingly, since so many attributes are listed (although some are repetitive) other, important attributes are omitted. In particular, the attribute of integrity – being able to be trusted – is paramount. Holdsworth (1987:165) states that ‘one of a negotiator’s most vital assets is a reputation for integrity.’ A second, crucial attribute is being a master of timing – knowing when to make offers/demands, when to make final commitments, when to leave a point, and when to close a negotiation.

A list of attributes for effective negotiators which is neither ridiculously long, nor apparently unachievable, should include:

a. be well prepared;
b. be prepared to listen and question;
c. be convincing yet flexible;
d. be a master of timing;
e. be trustworthy, and trusted.

[721] Boulwarism

One negotiating strategy is to employ the ‘take it or leave it’ approach (described in [710] with respect to individual bargaining) in collective bargaining against a group of employees or unions. As mentioned, General Electric in the USA employed this strategy in the 1950s, under the direction of Lemuel Boulware.

The strategy involved a multiple approach. The workforce was presented with a firm and final offer on wages, backed up with considerable argument and data in support of the company’s stance. In addition, employees’ spouses and families were also inundated with material in support of the company's offer and extensive advertising was undertaken in the press. As Chamberlain and Kuhn (1986:308) describe:

> Prior to and during negotiations the company produced, in the words of a judge who heard the case on appeal, 'a veritable avalanche of publicity, reaching awesome proportions' ... to tell its side of the issues to its employees.

Under the National Labor Relations Act 1935 (Wagner Act) employers in the USA are required to 'bargain in good faith.' Unions at General Electric filed an unfair labour practice charge with the National Labor Relations Board. After some years the Board in 1964 agreed that General Electric was *not* bargaining in good faith. In 1969 a Federal Appeals Court upheld the Board's decision, but then further confused the issue. According to Taylor and Witney (1987:398) the court held that

> a 'take it or leave it' approach was not of itself necessarily illegal. What made the G.E. conduct illegal was that at the same time, it had carried on the employee publicity campaign in the attempt to bypass the union.

General Electric abandoned Boulwarism at this time – but ironically it was not court rulings which brought this about. Rather, it was the fact that the unions had formed a Coordinated Bargaining Committee in 1966, and by 1969 were able to engineer a protracted (four month) and successful strike. The strike resulted in the acceptance of collective bargaining, as usually practised.

[722] Government and collective bargaining

Government plays a role in collective bargaining, both by legislation which directly affects the process and by providing services to the parties who are involved in collective bargaining. Legislation affecting unions obviously has an impact on collective bargaining, but in addition there can be legislation which may be designed:

a. to encourage the parties to take part in collective bargaining (e.g. the 1935 Wagner Act in the USA); or
b. to limit the scope of collective bargaining (e.g. as occurred in New Zealand under the Industrial Relations Act 1973, when negotiations were restricted by law to subjects deemed 'industrial matters' (see Chapter Seventeen);
c. to enable employers to opt for individual bargaining in place of collective bargaining – as under the Employments Contracts Act 1991 (see Chapter Nineteen).

Governments may also provide mediation services which are designed to help the parties reach a settlement. The mediators can suggest alternative lines of approach, give information as to legal matters and, probably most importantly, can help the parties to back down from extreme positions without losing face.

[723] Principal variants of collective bargaining

The term 'collective bargaining' encompasses many variants. In terms of the approaches discussed by Walton and McKersie (1965) (see [714]), bargaining may be predominantly distributive or integrative. The locus of the bargaining may be centralised (multi-employer at industry or national level) or decentralised (company or plant level). The proactive party may be the union, with the union making demands for better wages and conditions and management seeing its primary role as reacting to these demands, and reducing the level of demands. Alternatively the proactive party may be management demanding reduction in labour costs and/or seeking a change in work culture and work practices.

All variants have been practised at times over the last hundred or so years, and there has never been uniformity. However it is possible to see changes in trends, and at various times different variants have experienced a degree of attention and publicity. When the economy is strong there has been a tendency for industrialised countries to experience 'traditional' collective bargaining:

a. predominantly distributive;
b. locus tends towards centralisation though many bargains are at company/plant level;
c. the union tends to be proactive.

Kassalow's (1988:576) description of the predominant style of bargaining in the USA is fairly typical of the traditional mode:

> Beginning in the 1950s, union-management settlements in the United States came to be based on two premises: that as the economy grew, wage negotiations should (1) ensure that wages kept up with any increase in the cost of living, and (2) provide an additional increase to enable employees to share in the productivity gains of the economy.

Since the 1950s, there have been two notable variants:

a. productivity bargaining, first publicised in the 1960s;
b. concession bargaining, first publicised in the 1980s.

An eminent American scholar, Cullen (1985:318), writing about concession bargaining, suggests that the variants are not so very different to traditional collective bargaining, and considers that productivity bargaining and concession bargaining are different labels for the same thing.

Arguably there are discernable differences between the average, classic, productivity bargain and the average, modern, concession bargain – but there are also, as Cullen suggests, significant similarities. These variants are the subject of following sections.

In addition, there has been a marked trend in industrialised countries since the 1980s for collective bargaining to be decentralised. (In New Zealand this was not apparent until the 1990s, after the introduction of the Employment Contracts Act 1991.)

[724] Decentralisation of collective bargaining

Katz (1993: 3 and 12-13), when analysing collective bargaining in six countries (Sweden, Australia, the former West Germany, Italy, the UK and the USA), states:

> Reports have appeared since the early 1980s suggesting that the locus of collective bargaining is shifting downward in a number of countries, often from a national or multi-company level to the firm or plant level … the hypotheses that have been offered most frequently to explain … are that decentralisation results from shifts in bargaining power, the spread of new work organisation that puts a premium on flexibility and employee participation, and a decentralisation of corporate structure and diversification of worker preferences.

E. Productivity Bargaining

[725] Definition of productivity bargaining

Determining which collective bargaining exercises should be considered 'productivity bargains' is somewhat artificial. Employers, employees and unions do not decide all of a sudden to give up collective bargaining and start productivity bargaining. Rather, circumstances force the parties to change their approach and, later, academics consider a particular, usually very prominent agreement should be considered a productivity agreement.

In the employment relations literature (see Hunter (1964), Jones and Golding (1966), Stettner (1969), Howard and Riach (1971)) there is general agreement with Alan Fox (1966c:447) that productivity bargaining be defined as negotiations which offer a

> method by which substantial wage increase and/or other improvements in the terms of employment are financed not through higher costs and prices but by agreed changes in the work system which result in labour being used more efficiently.

Thus, productivity bargaining can be contrasted with:

a. traditional collective bargaining which is concerned with past, not specified future, productivity increases;
b. Scanlon-type plans (see [318]) which are also committed to future productivity increases, but the changes are not specified;
c. Incentive schemes (see [317]) which concentrate on stimulating extra effort, rather than specified changes in work practices.

[726] Non-genuine productivity agreements

Interest in productivity bargaining was stimulated by Flanders' (1964) classic work, *The Fawley Productivity Agreements*. While Flanders may not have coined the terms 'productivity bargaining' and 'productivity agreements', he was certainly responsible for their introduction into the literature, and into public awareness.

Politicians saw productivity bargaining as a panacea for inflation and in the era of incomes policies in the 1960s and 1970s allowed exemption from wage restraint if there was a productivity bargain.

Thus interest in productivity bargaining in New Zealand was triggered by incomes policies. The 1973 Budget stated that 'if employers negotiate wage increases above this level (five per cent) the excess must be absorbed by the firm through an increase in productivity or a reduction in firm's profits.' Later it was publicised through the media (e.g., *Otago Daily Times,* 20 April, 1974) that productivity bargaining was the way to avoid the wage freeze since, whatever the policy on wages, 'provision would also be made for the commission or other tribunal to approve genuine productivity agreements for individual firms.'

[727] Productivity bargaining and win-win

If the objective of management was simply to increase productivity and the objective of the workforce to increase job satisfaction from increased wages and shorter hours, it is possible that Flanders (1970:197) is right and all that is required from the parties is for them

> to take an enlightened view of how their functions may best be discharged, which means in particular abandoning the deeply-entrenched belief on both sides that if one wins the other must lose. They have to learn from experience that, given good will and fair dealing, they can better advance their diverging interests by appreciating that they are divergent and yet, by compromise, can be reconciled. The practical basis of reconciliation is that both sides can gain from it, not only materially but in more civilised relations.

If so, the oft-painted picture of productivity bargaining being 'win-win', and 'mutual problem solving', and generally idyllic, may have some basis in fact. A complicating factor however is that a major objective of management in productivity bargaining is to retain, regain, or increase their power in the work environment. Flanders (1970:162, 172, 204) himself acknowledged this fact. He pointed out that there has been

> a progressive loss of managerial control over pay and work and therefore over labour costs, at plant level … The paradox, whose truth managements have found so difficult to accept is that they can only regain control by sharing it … (Thus) the distinguishing, common feature of all the major, genuine productivity agreements is that they are attempts to strengthen managerial control over pay and work through joint regulation. The object may be: the restoration of control where it has been lost as in the case of overtime or incentive payments; or to bring matters, such as craft demarcation lines, which have previously been the subject of unilateral union control, under regulation by joint agreement; or to raise the existing degrees of control, for example by the introduction of new grading

> schemes or staggered work patterns. The contents of the package vary from case to case, but the proposed changes in employment practices form an integrated pattern and are invariably specified in written agreements.

Thus with respect to power and control in the workforce, there is a considerable degree of win-lose with productivity bargaining. Basically management wins (or wins back) power from work groups and/or unions. In many situations work groups are prepared to lose power in exchange for increases in job satisfaction through significant pay increases and reduction in work hours, but there is still a 'lose' element in the bargain. To the dismay of Marxist theorists, and indeed some radical unionists, many employees are prepared to trade off some power and control for more pay, better security, and/or shorter hours of work.

The win-win description is also misleading in that it fails to indicate that even when there is no 'lose' element, there is no guarantee that the wins will be approximately equal, and clearly there can be marked variations in the amount won. Put graphically, the situation may be WIN-win or win-WIN. Also, even if the end result is that both sides feel they have gained, when the actual details are being negotiated there will be normal distributive or win-lose bargaining. That is, a productivity bargain could result in a reduction in staffing, a reduction in overtime and a relaxation of demarcation rules, in exchange for job security guarantees and increased wages (with increased leisure resulting from the reduction in overtime).

The difference in approach between productivity bargaining and traditional collective bargaining is that there is a conscious effort to allow the other party to make gains – and 'win' – in exchange for compensating wins to one's self. This represents a marked change in attitude and culture. However it is totally inaccurate to assume that productivity bargaining is an easy option. Given it requires a radical change in culture it requires more effort and commitment.

[728] Advantages to the manager/employer party

Basically managers and employers use productivity bargaining to regain control or power over a number of work practices in the expectation that it will lead to increased productivity and profits. In the literature this is referred to as removing 'restrictive labour practices' – arrangements under which labour is not used as efficiently as management would desire. The expression is value-loaded and implies that such practices are not only bad, but if they are present it is labour's fault. However, Hunter (1964:277) points out:

> where such practices have become entrenched there can be little doubt that it is owing in part to managements' recognition of this aim and connivance at restrictive measures. Managements bear part of the responsibility and cannot now expect to eliminate these practices without cost to themselves.

A more accurate description of these practices is that they are 'non-managerially controlled' labour practices. Specific examples of such practices that have been reduced or eliminated by actual productivity agreements include:

(a) The working of unnecessary overtime

In the UK over 1964–5 the electricity supply industry reduced average hours worked from 49.4 down to 41.7, and Mobil Oil reduced an average of 7 hours overtime, worked per employee each week, to virtually none.

(b) Rigid application of demarcation rules

This refers to the right of particular employees to do specified work, to the exclusion of other workers regardless of ability.

(c) Excessive staffing levels

This can be caused by a variety of reasons, from having unnecessarily large groups of employees performing a work operation to having a whole class of employees who are non-productive. The Royal Commission Research Paper (1967) on productivity bargaining reported that before the Fawley agreement, craftsmen's mates were estimated as being only 40 per cent as productive as the craftsmen they assisted and actually worked only about 3.5 hours a day on average. This sort of situation has been criticised as evidence of a casual attitude towards the use of human resources, and betrays scant respect for the mates as persons: it implies that their time can be wasted with impunity. As a result of the agreements the use of craftsmen's mates was abandoned. In July 1960 there were 494 craftsmen and 275 mates. In July 1962 there were 559 craftsmen and one mate.

(d) Deliberate restriction of output

This may be done to guarantee overtime since the restriction causes a blockage in the work flow, or it may be that there is a fear that incentive rates would be cut if production increased. Elimination or reduction of non-managerially controlled labour practices should lead to overall productivity increases and profitability. Flanders (1964) estimates that maintenance workers at the Esso Plant at Fawley increased their productivity by fifty per cent, leading to greater profits.

[729] Advantages to the workforce

The major advantages to the bulk of the workforce from productivity agreements include:

(a) Larger pay increases

In the 1960s some productivity agreements resulted in spectacular wage increases. In some cases however since overtime was also reduced increases in weekly take home pay were much less than the increase in hourly rate. Thus at Fawley the average hourly rate went up by 35 per cent, but the average number of hours worked per week was reduced by 5.25 hours resulting in an increase in weekly earnings of 21 per cent.

(b) Reduction in working hours

As already cited, employees in the electricity supply industry had their working hours reduced by 7.7 hours (and their weekly earnings increased by 7.4 per cent).

(c) Increased job security

It is somewhat paradoxical that a stated advantage to employees is increased job security when it has already been stated that their managers use productivity bargaining to reduce manning levels. However the Royal Reform Research Paper (1967:27) considers that

> a guarantee against redundancy is therefore often regarded as in practice an indispensable prerequisite for any serious negotiations. Hence many productivity agreements provide workers with an explicit assurance of security against dismissal which they did not previously possess.

[730] Problems with productivity bargaining

The major problem with productivity bargaining is that the concept can appear to provide easy benefits, so parties rush into an agreement, ignoring Flander's (1970:75) warning that to rush productivity agreements through when they involve substantial changes in existing attitudes and institutions 'is to accept too many risks and to court failure.' Fox (1966c:447) observes that a popular reaction to the first successful agreement was to

> swallow the sugar and spit out the pill. The sugar was the solid achievement of the exercise … the pill was the rigorous preliminary analysis; the care and sensitive diplomacy required for the approach to unions, shop stewards and work groups; the long, wearisome negotiations that could have been threatened by a single peevish gesture.

As noted in [727], after the essential hard work and analysis has taken place, and hopefully solutions to problems hindering productivity have jointly been arrived at, there still remains the normal cut and thrust of distributive bargaining.

[731] Managerial concerns

A major concern which is still present today is that the 'buying out' of non-managerially controlled labour practices may prompt the creation of new ones. Schultz and McKersie (1967:5) point out:

> a succession of buy-outs clearly teaches an unfortunate lesson – people learn that their loose practices are worth money. This is an invitation for them to develop other bad practices in readiness for the next negotiation. Management may then wind up forever buying out newly created practices.

This problem is obviously one which managers will have to guard against, and certainly the fact that a productivity agreement has been reached does not mean that management will have an assured life of ease. But with efficient management there is no reason at all why the problem should arise. The Fawley management was quite emphatic that no new crop of restrictive practices grew up since the 1960 agreement.

A further concern, but from non-participants, is that the inflationary features (high wage rates) will spread more easily and quickly than the compensating efficient use of labour.

[732] Workforce concerns

In a similar vein, some work groups are concerned that they may give up, for example, excessive overtime working in exchange for an increased wage rate. If the increases are passed on to other work groups the original work groups may end up financially disadvantaged as it alone has given up overtime hours.

By its very nature productivity bargaining frequently results in a transfer of power and control over work practices from employees to managers. Depending on the perspective of the observer this is either good, bad or of no concern. It would appear that employees are prepared to exchange power and control for other benefits, and may well prefer increased earnings and/or increased job security and/or shorter hours to the intrinsic benefits of controlling work practices.

[733] The overall value of productivity bargaining

This technique represents a longer term outlook than traditional collective bargaining and represents an effective approach to employment relations on the part of both management and employees and unions. It is effective because it achieves their objectives – that is, it achieves what they want it to achieve and this occurs because each party realises that to be successful it cannot simply ignore the objectives of the other party. It accepts that co-operation is more desirable than conflict but realises that some degree of conflict is inevitable.

F. Concession Bargaining

[734] Concession bargaining

Cullen (1985:299) observes:

> It is usually impossible to pinpoint the moment when any bargaining trend begins, but a settlement between the United Auto Workers (UAW) and Chrysler Corporation in October 1979 was certainly one of the first of the concession bargains that have become common in American industry in recent years.

In the same paper, as noted in [723], Cullen suggests that the 1980s concession bargaining and the 1960s productivity bargaining are one and the same. However while *some* concession agreements may in fact be virtually identical to *some* productivity agreements, the average concession bargain and the average productivity bargain have fundamental differences, as well as similarities.

'Concession bargaining' often describes bargaining not too far removed from traditional collective bargaining except that managers and employers are proactive and make demands of the workforce. In general the 'concessions' come from the workforce. Frequently there are demands for wage cuts, or at least a hold on wages, and demands for reduction or elimination of penal rates.

[735] Similarities: concession v productivity

There are two major similarities. The first is the fact that driving forces behind both types of bargaining are usually *external factors*: technological change, recessions and increased competition. When things are going well, traditional collective bargaining is quite satisfactory. Whether or not concession bargaining will be sufficient to overcome the factors is a different matter. Donn (1989:199) in his study of the maritime industry believes not. He states:

> The same factors, recession and foreign competition, that had a large impact onshore combined with technological change to produce massive concessions in the maritime industry; but it is clear that collective bargaining itself cannot revive this industry, virtually no matter how large the concessions.

The second similarity is that from management's point of view both types of bargaining are intended to result in survival and hopefully increased productivity and profits.

[736] Differences: concession v productivity

One obvious difference stems from the fact that the power difference in the 1960s in favour of employers was much less marked than in the 1980s and 1990s. Hence productivity agreements resulted in perceived gains to employees. Frequently concession agreements result in perceived losses to employees. However it could be argued that the *outcomes* are a function of the state of the economy and that the bargaining *process* is similar. This, of course, is Cullen's (1985) argument, discussed in [723]. This process can also be considered different – possibly because of the power difference. Managers and employers are not approaching concession bargaining with the same philosophy of productivity bargaining – namely as an attempt to achieve objectives by allowing the other party to also achieve their objectives. Rather, the approach is to achieve one's objectives by forcing the other party to concede.

As a result long-term gains in a change of attitude and culture may be less likely under concession bargaining than under the productivity bargaining approach.

History would suggest that if one party takes advantage of superior power in too overt a fashion, this will return to haunt them in the long-term. The approach of productivity bargaining suggests possible long-term gains. The approach of concession bargaining suggests predominantly short-term gains.

Chapter Eight

Conciliation, Mediation and Arbitration

A. Introduction

[801] Introduction

The previous chapter discussed individual and collective bargaining, which are both direct methods of dispute settlement between employers and employees or their unions. This chapter discusses further methods of dispute settlement in employment relations, in which a *third party* – which may be a private individual, a government-appointed individual, a tribunal or a court – is involved.

[802] Defining the terms

In current international usage, conciliation and mediation are usually assumed to be synonymous. Thus Blain *et al* (1987:179) state that they

> use the terms 'mediation' and 'conciliation' interchangeably to mean the intercession of an outsider or third party to assist parties in resolving labour disputes.

Much earlier, Warren and Bernstein (1949:441), did differentiate between the two, claiming:

> *Conciliation* is the mildest form of intervention by a third party … [who] exerts authority only to the extent of calling conferences, keeping the discussion on a friendly basis, controlling the order of business, and carrying the proposals of one side to the other. Conciliation does not involve making positive recommendations.
>
> *Mediation* … is a more affirmative procedure. The disputants, however, remain free to reject the process or the proposals. When the conciliator fails, the mediator steps in to offer specific recommendations.

However, even Warren and Bernstein concede that the terms are often used synonymously and their suggested differentiation seems somewhat precious. We are in agreement with Paynter (1972:19) that conciliation and mediation both refer to a process where a third party

> not directly involved in a dispute is aimed at bringing the parties together again

> after a breakdown, to try to reconcile differences and reach some compromise agreement.

Arbitration, on the other hand, as Paynter (1972:19) observes,

> ascertains the facts and offers a judgement that is either final and binding upon the parties or as a recommendation to be accepted or rejected by them.

This definition applies to *conventional* arbitration. As discussed below, there is a variant (Final Offer Arbitration) with different processes and different objectives.

[803] Disputes of interest and disputes of rights

While periodically some countries explicitly define classes of disputes in legislation, there is general agreement that a dispute may be considered:

a. a dispute of *interest*
 – when it relates to the setting of terms and conditions; *or*
b. a dispute of *rights*
 – when it relates to the interpretation application or operation of an existing agreement or contract of employment which sets out terms and conditions.

'Personal grievances' (complaints by individual employees of their treatment) should be considered as disputes of rights, since they relate to how the contract of employment is applied.

Conciliation/mediation and arbitration may be used to help resolve both interest and rights disputes. Internationally, arbitration is much more frequently used with respect to rights disputes. The reasoning is that in theory if the dispute is whether or not one party is failing to abide by an established agreement, or is over the meaning of an agreement, then a third party with skills in legal interpretation can make a ruling. In practice, rights disputes are not always that clear-cut. Disputes over interpretation may result from the fact there never was complete agreement in the first place. Consequently, the 'rights' dispute is actually establishing terms and conditions – and, theoretically, is an 'interest' dispute.

[804]Objectives of conciliation/mediation and arbitration

In general, for both interest and rights disputes, the objectives of conciliation/mediation and of (conventional) arbitration are:

a. to facilitate (conciliation/mediation) or propose (arbitration) an acceptable settlement of a dispute between employer(s) and employee(s) and/or union(s);
b. to avoid recourse to strikes and lockouts – either because they are illegal or deemed undesirable;
c. to be cost-effective in terms of time and money (conciliation/mediation is intended to be cheaper and quicker than arbitration which in turn is intended to be cheaper and quicker than litigation);

d. to uphold legislative requirements wherever applicable.

With respect to interest disputes, both mediators and arbitrators may also have the objective:

e. to dispense industrial 'justice' (in terms of being fair).

However, this is not generally accepted with respect to rights disputes, where the role is deemed to be more judicial. Greenfield (1992:683) quotes the American Supreme Court, which ruled that, with respect to rights disputes,

> an arbitrator is confined to interpretation and application of the collective bargaining agreement; he does not sit to dispense his own brand of industrial justice. He may, of course, look for guidance from many sources, yet his award is legitimate only so long as it draws its essence from the collective bargaining agreement.

Hence with rights disputes, industrial justice means being 'legally correct'. In practice, a proportion of both mediators and arbitrators may have further objectives relating to their personal careers. Where they are salaried public servants, the pressure is less, but where their livelihood depends on their acceptability to both employers and employees there may be pressures to maintain a 'balance' with respect to their decisions.

B. Conciliation/Mediation

[805] Conciliation and mediation

As discussed in [802], the terms are usually used interchangeably. However, for a considerable period in New Zealand's history, conciliation and mediation referred to different practices, with this country choosing to give 'conciliation' a somewhat different meaning to that used practically everywhere else. From 1894 to 1991, by statute, conciliation in New Zealand referred to formalised collective bargaining. In 'conciliation' the conciliator (or Conciliation Commissioner) chaired the collective bargaining process, and the statute set down the number of negotiators ('assessors') that were permitted. An American observer in the 1960s considered 'conciliation' in New Zealand to be very similar to ordinary collective bargaining as in the USA.

Since conciliation has a particular meaning in New Zealand, the preferred term henceforth will be 'mediation' only.

[806] Mediation strategies and tactics

Kressel and Pruitt (1985) outline three approaches which mediators may employ:

a. reflexive: to gain understanding and build trust;
b. contextual: to create a settlement climate;
c. substantive: to promote specific solutions.

Building on their work, Phillips (1994) suggests the choice of approach will depend on the perceived personal hostility between the parties, the degree of incompatibility, and the level of experience of the disputants' advocates.

Clearly, if a mediator employs the 'substantive' approach and pushes a solution, the difference between the processes of mediation and arbitration will be very small. Indeed, the only real difference could be the degree of obligation on the disputants to accept the proposed solution. This is illustrated by an experiment in grievance mediation which was conducted in four states in the USA, as described by Goldberg and Brett (1982:257):

> If no settlement is possible, the mediator provides the parties with an immediate opinion, based on their collective bargaining agreement, as to how the grievance would be decided if it went to arbitration. That opinion is not final and binding, but is advisory in nature ... if the grievance is neither settled, withdrawn, nor granted, the parties are free to arbitrate. If they do, the mediator cannot serve as arbitrator, and nothing said or done by the parties or the mediator during mediation can be used against a party in arbitration.

C. Arbitration

[807] Conventional and Final Offer Arbitration

The discussion to date with respect to arbitration has centred on conventional arbitration in which, as stated in [804], a major objective is to propose an acceptable solution. There is, however, an alternative to conventional arbitration which has been gaining increasing publicity since the 1970s. This is Final Offer Arbitration (henceforth: FOA), which is termed 'pendulum' arbitration in the UK. Although FOA is by no means widespread, it has been utilised in the USA and the UK and was introduced into New Zealand legislation in the State Sector Act 1988. It is currently (2007) provided under the Police Act 1958 for sworn police officers in New Zealand.

[808] Conventional arbitration strategies

As discussed in [806], in practice the boundary between mediation and arbitration can become blurred. Similarly, in practice the difference between arbitration and negotiation may be much less than theory suggests. Disputants may, while presenting their respective cases to the arbitrator or arbitration tribunal or court, in effect be 'negotiating' and coming closer together. One arbitration strategy, and indeed that employed in New Zealand for much of the period 1895–1987, is for the Court to not only encourage but require the disputant parties to negotiate as near to a settlement as possible. An alternative strategy is always to go for a compromise, possibly 'splitting the difference'. This strategy clearly lends itself to manipulation. If the arbitrator or Court is known to split the difference, then rationally the disputants should tend to extreme (indeed infinitely extreme) positions.

[809] The process of FOA

FOA is a variant of conventional arbitration which requires the arbitrator to choose one or other of the two parties' final offers. The arbitrator is not allowed to compromise, and cannot be concerned with acceptability and workability, but instead must accept *either* the employees' (or their union's) *or* the employer's final offer. Hence, taken simply as a method of *arbitration* (as opposed to a method of dispute settlement), FOA is clearly inferior to conventional arbitration. The latter can operate as FOA when the situation warrants, or can make compromises when that appears more suitable. Treble (1986) points out that in the nineteenth century, opposition to the use of FOA came from the arbitrators. Weitzman and Stochaj (1980:33) analysed the views of eighteen arbitrators involved in both conventional arbitration and FOA and claim:

> two-thirds of the interviewees stated that they would prefer conventional arbitration over final-offer arbitration, because the former gives the neutral more discretion and the ability to compromise differences.

[810] The objectives of FOA

Although FOA *is* a type of arbitration, it can be best understood if one realises it was not designed to be used as arbitration, but as a creative method of dispute settlement with a very different primary objective to that of conventional arbitration. Unlike conventional arbitration, the objective of FOA is not to achieve an acceptable and workable solution. Instead the objective of its original proponents was to make the cost of failing to reach a negotiated settlement so high that both parties would be forced – by fear – to negotiate and reach a settlement. Scott, a hydro-engineer who is cited as being the first to use FOA, is of the view that 'arbitration of any kind is only an alternative to strikes and lockouts and not a substitute for negotiations. Hence there is no reason to make arbitration just or pleasant' (Perigoe, 1973:31). Thus, Scott fostered FOA not as a means of producing a just or workable solution but rather, to use the colourful language of its proponents, to be 'the hydrogen bomb poised above the bargaining table whose very terror should ensure its non-use' (Holden, 1976:28). The 'non-use' is brought about (in theory) by the fact that the losing party will have gained nothing from the arbitration process and will have to accept the other party's final offer (or demand). It is this high cost – of being forced to accept an economically crippling demand, or an offer so low that it means economic hardship for employees – that is intended to deter the parties from resorting to FOA. This in turn forces them into collective bargaining that will reach a settlement.

[811] Various forms of FOA

In general, interest disputes are not over a single issue but over a number of issues. Hence, there are a number of possible variations of FOA. Under the basic variant the arbitrator would select the most reasonable of the union's or management's final offers as a total package which could involve, for example, staffing levels, working conditions, the payment system, the level of the basic pay rate and holidays. The arbitrator has to judge on an overall basis which package is the most reasonable. This clearly could result in some issues being decided in favour of a party which, on those particular issues, was less reasonable. An alternative variant is that the arbitrator should consider each issue in turn and select the most reasonable final offer for each issue separately. There is thus compromise over the package as a whole but not for any single issue. Rogow (1973:28) is of the view that the case for FOA

> is clearer in the single issue dispute than in the multiple issue dispute. In the latter, which is the usual case, difficulties of calculating the rate of exchange and trade-off among the various disputes increase the likelihood that the Board's decision will not be an optimal one.

However, Rogow appears to have forgotten that the fundamental purpose of FOA is to increase the potential costs of failing to negotiate a settlement, not to produce an optimal decision. Thus, if one accepts the rationale behind FOA, one is logically compelled to prefer total package arbitration to issue-by-issue arbitration since there is more uncertainty and the potential costs of not settling are even greater. Indeed, the choice should possibly be for a third variant which further increases uncertainty. This has been practised in the City of Eugene, Oregon, and allows the parties to submit their final offers and a further, secret, offer to the arbitrator. Feuille and Long (1974:576) point out that 'this increased uncertainty increases the risk for both sides that one of the other party's offers may be the most reasonable and thus be selected.'

[812] The rationale for FOA

FOA is supposed to:

a. replace conventional arbitration;
b. never be used, as the cost of losing is so great the participants will choose to settle by collective bargaining.

Thus, whenever FOA is actually employed as an arbitration process it has failed in its primary purpose. It could be that the parties were very close to a settlement so that the degree of win-lose in the actual arbitration was negligible, in which case arbitration of any type would have produced a very similar settlement. Alternatively, if the parties were at extreme positions when FOA took place, then, as Wheeler (1977:299) points out, 'an unworkable result is practically guaranteed' since the extreme position of the successful party is almost certainly unworkable (determined by economic factors, membership acceptance, etc.) for the unsuccessful party.

The rationale for FOA seems to rest on three inter-dependent premises:

Premise One: that conventional arbitration is inferior to collective bargaining as a method of dispute settlement;

Premise Two: that dispute settlement processes should encourage collective bargaining;

Premise Three: that conventional arbitration has a 'narcotic effect' (Feuille, 1975:304) on the parties causing them to become 'arbitration addicts', while FOA discourages its use and encourages collective bargaining.

[813] Premise One

Those who are prepared to argue the superiority of collective bargaining over arbitration, rather than simply assume it is a given, usually base their argument on one or other of some popular myths.

The first myth is that collective bargaining represents a 'meeting of minds' (Isaac, 1958:348), resulting in an agreement with which both parties are presumably pleased, while arbitration results in an 'imposed award' which is less popular and less satisfactory. As Clegg (1975:312) has observed, a workable compromise 'cannot always be found, even in established plural societies'.

The second myth, largely dependent on the first, was also given an airing by Isaac (1958:348-9). He claimed the purpose of the parties is to 'narrow differences and thus to reach a mutually acceptable settlement' while the purpose of the parties facing arbitration is 'to take an extreme position and to stand by it. This process tends to exaggerate the differences between the parties.' The counter-arguments put to the 'meeting of minds' hypothesis are clearly equally relevant to this idealistic picture of collective bargaining being a process where differences are narrowed and acceptable settlements necessarily reached. Also, the assertion that under arbitration parties merely stand by extreme positions is not true in general and certainly has not been true for New Zealand. In its 'Arbitration era' the then legislation (Industrial Relations Act 1973) stipulated that the main arbitrating body could refuse to arbitrate over a dispute if it felt that the parties had not made adequate efforts to settle the dispute prior to arbitration. Further, the process of arbitration need not simply be one of presenting a case and awaiting a verdict, but may instead be one of continued negotiation and concession.

A third myth, clearly dependent on the above two, is that there will be more commitment to a settlement reached after collective bargaining (since the differences were narrowed and there was a meeting of the minds) than to one reached after arbitration (since the parties did not play a part in the proceedings and merely put a position and stood by it). Guillebaud (1970:53) writes that 'with compulsory arbitration there is no such commitment' to accept the decision and to see it loyally implemented.

As outlined in Chapter One, the rules in an industrial system are the intermediate steps leading to the objectives of the major parties. Hence, each of the three major parties will prefer either collective bargaining or arbitration, depending on which of the two they consider will be more likely to result in their attaining their primary objectives. As a consequence, even during the 'Arbitration era' in New Zealand (1894–1987), the process of arbitration had periods when it was supported by unions and attacked by the employers, and other periods when the exact opposite occurred. At other times, some unions would favour arbitration, while other unions favoured collective bargaining.

Thus there is no logical or theoretical reason to necessarily favour either collective bargaining or arbitration as a rule-making or rule-interpreting procedure. Preference for either method depends on the point of view from which the choice is made and the value judgements of the party making the choice.

[814] Premise Two

Premise Two is clearly not only a value judgement but is also totally dependent for its basic logic on premise one being accepted. If in fact collective bargaining is *not* necessarily superior to arbitration, there seems no logical reason why the chosen process should encourage bargaining.

[815] Premise Three

The third premise has been attributed to the then USA Secretary of Labor, W. Willard Wirtz. In 1964 he claimed that

> a statutory requirement that labor disputes be submitted to arbitration has a narcotic effect on private bargainers ... they will turn to it as an easy and habit-forming release from the ... obligation of hard responsible bargaining' (Wheeler, 1977:117).

This metaphor appealed to American writers who incorporated it into their writings by referring to 'arbitration addicts.' Since the first premise is unproven, then whether or not arbitration produces 'arbitration addicts' could be a non-issue. Indeed, if arbitration is actually a superior process to bargaining, the addiction would be a blessing not a bane. However, as illustrated by the New Zealand experience in the private sector, the availability of arbitration does not necessarily result in the parties always resorting to it. Certainly the negotiations which precede possible arbitration will clearly be influenced by the likely arbitration decision, but the strictly limited use, made of arbitration in the period 1975–87 (see Table in App-2), shows that the premise was simply not true for New Zealand. Hence there can be no suggestions that as a generalisation it is true.

[816] FOA in practice

The original proponents of FOA assumed the risk of losing everything would be such that parties would never employ FOA. However, FOA should also be judged simply as a method of dispute settlement. If everybody enjoys a gamble, and is prepared to live with the consequences, then possibly one should support FOA even if it appears theoretically unsound.

FOA has predominantly been used in the public sector in the USA, where a number of states have legislation prohibiting strikes by all public employees, and many more states have strike bans on police and firefighters (Lund and Maranto (1996)). Somewhat surprisingly, FOA has also been used extensively in setting salaries for professional baseball players. In most situations strikes are illegal (and the bans are effective) so the 'acceptability' of the FOA decisions are hard to evaluate. Certainly some writers are enthusiastic about FOA, while others are not.

The results of FOA are difficult to evaluate. Ashenfelter and Bloom (1983:539) warn that 'it takes careful analysis before box scores or win-loss records are of any value in determining the integrity or fairness of an arbitration system.' In a later paper (1984:111) they analyse results in New Jersey, a state where a 'remarkable statute provides for conventional arbitration of pay disputes if the two parties can agree to this, but requires the use of Final-Offer arbitration if they cannot.' They point out that while unions win at FOA two thirds of the time, the increases they get from FOA are lower than under conventional arbitration. They win at FOA because they are less ambitious than the employers, but they in fact do better under conventional arbitration.

Thus, it appears to be impossible to conclude from past evidence what will actually occur in the future if FOA is employed. It is possible that it will encourage more negotiated settlements than would occur if conventional arbitration were available. This, however, is not assured. If the two offers are reasonably close then the parties may in fact prefer FOA decisions, but again this is not assured. What all parties must be aware of is that there is a possibility under FOA that an extreme settlement may be made, with major adverse consequences.

[817] Conclusions

Judgements seem to be made with respect to the superiority or otherwise of various forms of dispute settlement without clearly articulating the assumed objectives of the dispute settlement process, or indeed stating from which perspective the judgement is made. If the main objective is to have employers and employees settle disputes independently, then clearly arbitration is out of favour. If, however, the objectives are different – possibly on the lines of the objectives discussed in Chapter One – then arbitration may well be superior to individual or collective bargaining or mediation, from the perspective of one particular party at a particular point in time.

Chapter Nine

Discipline and Dismissals

[901] Introduction

This chapter is concerned with disciplinary action in the work environment, concentrating in particular on dismissals. The first section is concerned with the process of disciplinary action and how it relates to the objectives of the parties and discusses the requirements for a generally acceptable disciplinary code. The second section looks at common law protection against dismissals and the third at the development of statutory protection.

A. Process of Disciplinary Action

[902]Discipline and employment relations objectives

The perceived need for discipline and dismissals, and reactions to such action when it occurs, influences, and is influenced by, the objectives of the parties and their value standards. With a few radical exceptions, all three parties agree on the need for disciplinary action on moral, ethical and legal grounds. There is likely to be fairly general agreement that discipline should be fair and just. However there may not be agreement as to precisely what is fair and just, under what circumstances discipline should be applied, and to what degree.

A major source of conflict over discipline arises from the fact that all three parties have the objective of maintaining and possibly increasing their power in the work environment. Managers wish to have the power to discipline and dismiss as they see fit. The 'right to fire' is a hallowed managerial prerogative (see [305]) which was increasingly lost through the 1960s to 1980s in the wake of stronger unions and statutory restrictions. As the union movement internationally is facing testing times, it is possible that some of this lost prerogative may be re-found. Counterbalancing that, unions also wish to retain power in this area, to have the ability to preserve job security for their members, and to be able to prevent arbitrary managerial action. The State hopes its legislation will ensure that managerial action is either obeyed or, if challenged, will be challenged only according to set procedures.

A further major objective of both managers and the State is to maintain and possibly improve productivity or efficiency; they see the unrestricted managerial right to discipline as an important means to this end. Similarly, they want to be confident that employees who have been disciplined, and their union and workmates, will either accept the discipline, or will appeal through established procedures. This objective is clearly likely to conflict with a major objective of employees and unions that employees should maintain and possibly improve their satisfaction with all aspects of their jobs. Obviously, job security and freedom from capricious or arbitrary punishment are important factors in achieving satisfaction with the job.

The conflict over power as an end in itself is a win-lose conflict, insofar as it relates to discipline. If one party increases its power to inflict disciplinary action, then the other party loses its power to restrict action, and vice versa. The conflict between objectives of efficiency on the one hand and of security and freedom from capricious discipline on the other can be settled in a manner more approximating a win-win. Obviously if the union achieves total job security, and no disciplinary action can be applied, then few if any managers would consider the situation conducive to efficiency. However, a satisfactory disciplinary code can be designed which provides a reasonable level of efficiency and an adequate level of security.

If each party determines its own objectives, really evaluates the importance of each objective, calculates the objectives of the others and works towards a mutually acceptable code, then it is much more probable that in practical situations each party will achieve its own objectives at a satisfactory level. Where a party works single-mindedly to achieve one of its objectives, for instance the 'right to fire', it will probably fail to achieve it and will suffer a significant loss of efficiency as well.

Although people are never perfectly rational, on average behaviour reflects either conscious or unconscious 'cost-benefit' calculations. For example, Union A uses the grievance procedure if their member is dismissed, while Union B strikes to get their member reinstated. Union A is not necessarily 'responsible' and Union B 'militant'. In practice, Union A has calculated or assumed that the benefits minus costs of using the procedure exceeds the benefits minus costs of a strike. Union B has calculated the reverse. Relevant facts are the probability of success in using the procedure, the time and effort involved, the willingness of the members to strike, the probability of management capitulation to a strike, and finally the likely penalties, if any, that would be imposed on the union for striking.

[903] Requirements for an acceptable disciplinary code

In the past, many organisational 'codes of conduct', or 'house rules', were purely negative documents listing offences and the penalties such offences would receive. This is problematic, since it implies that such behaviour is expected. As a reaction some organisations opted for positive codes, which simply outlined expected and desired behaviour. This approach is satisfactory up until the time someone acts in a way considered deserving of discipline. Similarly, companies which have no code of conduct or rule book may have not had a problem for many years, but when the problem arises it can be severe.

A compromise is probably the best solution. The code of conduct should:

a. outline desired behaviour and attitudes for employees;
b. outline reciprocating benefits for the organisation *then* outline the disciplinary code;
c. describe serious and less serious offences;
d. describe the disciplinary procedure, including appeals;
e. describe the penalties that may be imposed.

For the disciplinary code to be effective, ideally it should be generally accepted, and certainly it should be universally known and fairly, consistently, and rigorously implemented.

[904] Disciplinary fairness

The criterion of disciplinary fairness is of prime importance, for if the code is not fair it will not be accepted and may not be workable. A number of aspects of the code must both be fair, and be seen to be fair. One such is the penalty imposed for a particular offence. A test of this should not only be whether a reasonable employee would agree that it was fair, but also that employers would be prepared to suffer some loss to uphold the penalty. Further, the penalties must be applied without favouritism. This does not mean the penalties must be applied rigidly; mitigating circumstances *can* be taken into account. However, great care must be taken to ensure that such judgements are seen as being applied fairly. The penalty must be applied promptly and not after a great delay. This does not mean without thought and consideration, but the delay should be the minimum possible to accurately determine the facts. Finally, it is clearly unfair to punish someone unexpectedly. Hence to be fair, penalties must be known and understood.

An analogy has been made between a fair disciplinary code and a 'hot stove'. If people touch a red-hot stove they are burned – but the red glow warned them that they would be burned, and they were burned immediately, consistently and impersonally. It is suggested that discipline should be applied in the same way. That is:

a. with warning: individuals should know in advance both that they will be punished and the nature of the punishment if they behave in a particular manner;
b. immediately: so they know specifically what they are being disciplined for;
c. consistently: industrial discipline should be consistent, so there is no confusion over what is acceptable;
d. impersonally: all employees should be treated in the same manner, so it does not appear as if there has been favouritism or as if the discipline is vengeful and unfair.

While the hot stove analogy has much to commend it, it has a major flaw in that it understates the necessity of judgement. Those responsible for discipline should always consider previous offences and/or mitigating circumstances and/or consequences and use their judgement as to whether or not the best policy is to be consistent. In some situations, it will be better not to create a precedent by going against the code. In others, the *best* policy will be to create the precedent.

Thus requirements for a workable code are:

a. the rules and procedures are firmly established;
b. these rules and procedures are thoroughly known and understood by all parties: top management, supervisory staff, employees and unions. The fact that the rules and procedures are written does not mean they are known and understood. The induction process for new employees and training programmes for supervisory and management staff must ensure they are understood;
c. the rules and policies are applied consistently, taking into account mitigating circumstances and repeated offences;
d. the rules and policies are followed in detail.

[905] Typical 'House Rules'

With the large number of organisations, it is not surprising that there is a wide variation in disciplinary codes in terms of the ideal outlined above. Many organisations have no code of conduct at all. An increasing number now have House Rules, an example of which is given below, which outline offences and penalties. There will be considerable variation in the fairness and acceptability of the code and the extent to which it is implemented. As there is a statutory grievance procedure, it is unnecessary for an appeal procedure to be outlined. However, most codes, as with the example below, fail to outline the procedure to be implemented when discipline takes place. This omission is serious. It can make the action unfair from the point of view of the employee, or alternatively can result in an employee who, according to the rules, should be dismissed, subsequently being reinstated basically on a technicality.

[906] Sample House Rules

The following is an example of disciplinary rules adopted by a New Zealand firm. It is not suggested as a model, but is given merely as an example.

HOUSE RULES

A. The following will constitute serious misconduct and shall justify summary dismissal (dismissal without notice).

This list is not all embracing and any other matter of a serious nature may warrant summary dismissal as well. The list does not include all award-specified matters, but should the award make provision in certain situations then those situations shall be read in addition to the below mentioned:

1. *wilful falsification of information on job application form, engagement form or any other Company documentation;*
2. *bringing drugs or intoxicating liquors onto Company premises, or consuming drugs or intoxicating liquors on the premises;*
3. *gambling on the premises;*
4. *possession of Company property without proper written authorisation or taking Company property from the premises without written authorisation;*
5. *horseplay which results in the injury of a fellow worker;*
6. *wilful damage to Company property;*
7. *assaulting another employee on Company premises;*
8. *possession of another employee's personal property without that employee's consent;*
9. *unauthorised or irresponsible use of fire protection or safety equipment;*
10. *refusal to perform work assigned, refusal to accept reasonable overtime or walking off the job;*
11. *wilful and deliberate acts affecting quality or safety;*
12. *using Company vehicles without authorisation;*
13. *misrepresenting the Company in such a manner as to obtain personal advantages at the expense of the Company;*
14. *being absent three consecutive working days without reporting.*

B. The following actions will constitute less than serious misconduct.

In respect of the first offence a warning would ensue. In respect of the second offence, a written warning will be issued and a copy forwarded to the Local District Secretary of the respective union. On the third breach of the company's code of conduct the employee will be automatically dismissed. Any warning shall lapse twelve months after the date of issue.

1. *threatening, intimidating, coercing or interfering with other employees;*
2. *reporting late for work;*
3. *leaving his assigned place of work during working hours without permission other than for smoko, lunch break, or personal needs;*
4. *horseplay;*
5. *posting of offensive notices on the notice boards or elsewhere on the premises;*
6. *without good reason failing to report by telephone that he is unable to commence work at his usual time;*
7. *unless sick or because of some personal emergency failing to complete his stipulated hours of work;*
8. *failure to report any accident requiring medical treatment.*

This list is not all-embracing and any other matter of a less than serious nature may be treated as part of this section as well. This list does not include all award-specified matters but, should the award make provision for dismissal in certain situations, then those situations shall be read in addition to the above.

The above provisions are not restricted to repetitions of a specific form of offence but may be applied to separate offences of a clearly dissimilar nature.

****

I ___________________________________ have read the House Rules specified herein and I agree to abide by the said rules and conditions.

I acknowledge that my acceptance of these rules and conditions in addition to all employment contract provisions is a condition of my employment with the company. I also agree to perform such other work as my employer shall request from time to time.

Signed: .... Dated: ....

As mentioned earlier, these House Rules do not detail who takes the disciplinary action or how it will be taken. The list of offences contains some rules which may not win general approval. For example, penalising lateness may encourage total absenteeism. The rules above stipulate that reporting late for work on three occasions in a year results in instant dismissal. This will certainly encourage workers not to turn up at all, and instead to ring up and report a dose of flu.

The requirements on the above House Rules for the employee to sign, signifying that the rules have been read and that the employee will abide by them, makes it probable, but not certain, they have been read and understood. Management should ensure that they *are* understood.

As mentioned in [903], it is considered advantageous to have 'desired' behaviours mentioned as well as offences. The above example, typical of many, does not include those. However, some organisations include sections to this effect:

EMPLOYEE RESPONSIBILITIES

Each employee is expected to:

- *apply his/her best endeavours to the performance of the duties and responsibilities he/she is employed to carry out;*
- *contribute positively to the achievement of work objectives in his/her work area;*
- *accept responsibility for self-improvement by participating positively in relevant training and to provide training to others where appropriate;*

- *adopt work practices that promote the objective of a safe and healthy workplace;*
- *adopt a co-operative team approach compatible with the needs of the industry;*
- *comply with all lawful and reasonable instructions. (Note: to be lawful and reasonable instruction it must be within the contract of employment; not illegal and not hazardous from a health or safety viewpoint);*
- *be conscientious with regard to attendance and punctuality.*

ORGANISATIONAL RESPONSIBILITIES

The organisation's objectives are to:

- *create a work environment where co-operation, teamwork and participation are fully developed to better meet the needs of all the stakeholders in the business (customers, shareholders and employees) as well as the community as a whole;*
- *ensure that, wherever practicable, decisions on the introduction of change in the areas of new production improvements or work methods, processes, equipment, technology and training are only made on a considered basis after full consultation, avoiding unilateral or sudden actions;*
- *ensure that all actions or decisions significantly affecting conditions of work take place only after discussion and within the framework of relevant legislation, existing employment contracts and policies;*
- *develop fair and consistent procedures for negotiation and interpretation of employment agreements, disciplinary matters and the handling of disputes and grievances;*
- *make all efforts to ensure employees are free from any influences which unduly impact upon either their family, community, or personal lives whilst at work in relation to workplace issues.*

B. Common Law Protection

[907] Definition of common law

Common law is case law, or judge-made law. It can be differentiated from statutory law in that it is not in a printed Act of Parliament. However, it is also part of the overall law. Rulings made by judges are strongly influential on other judges at the same level and should determine the rulings of judges at lower levels. Hence, Court of Appeal decisions in New Zealand should determine the rulings of Employment Court judges, whose decisions in turn should determine the rulings of the Employment Relations Authority.

Where there is no applicable statutory law, common law is a *substitute* for statutory law. Where there is statutory law, almost always common law is a *supplement* for statutory law, in that it clarifies or expands on the statute.

[908] Common law as a substitute for statutory law

For most of the twentieth century, both in the UK and New Zealand, there was no statutory law limiting the power of employers to dismiss employees. However common law existed, based on an English case which was decided by the House of Lords: *Addis v Gramophone Co. Ltd.*

This case produced the decision that an employer could lawfully dismiss an employee *either*:

a. for good cause, summarily (that is without a period of notice); or
b. for any or no cause if a due period of justice had been given (or wages paid in lieu of the notice).

Common law affirms that employees may be summarily dismissed for good cause. This leaves open two questions:

a. what sort of actions give good cause for dismissal? and
b. how serious must those actions be?

Different judges at different times have expressed their views as to what sort of actions give good cause. In *Ernest Hedges v A D Paterson Construction Co* the following were suggested at 398:

a. wilful disobedience of any lawful order of the master;
b. gross moral misconduct, whether pecuniary or otherwise, which is inconsistent with the fulfilment of the conditions of service;
c. negligence in business, or conduct calculated seriously to injure the master's business;
d. incompetence or permanent disability for illness.

The second question posed above is much harder to answer. As Jamieson J. put it in *Parisian Coat Manufacturing Co. v Auckland Clerical Union* : 'the real question was not whether (the worker) was guilty of misconduct because she refused to comply with a lawful directive from her employer; the question was whether her conduct involved such a degree of misconduct that it justified the ultimate weapon of dismissal' (p. 57). Each case has to be considered on its merits.

The common law precluded any compensation or redress for dismissal *other than* wages *in lieu* of the due period of notice. The decision by the House of Lords in *Addis* (at 491) explicitly precluded compensation for hurt feelings or the injustice of being dismissed while being an exemplary employee:

> If there be a dismissal without notice the employer must pay an indemnity; but that indemnity cannot include compensation either for the injured feelings of the servant, or for the loss he may sustain from the fact that his having been dismissed of itself makes it more difficult for him to obtain fresh employment.

Thus if the due period of notice was deemed to be a week, then an employer could lawfully dismiss any employee in the category without risk of redress so long as a week's notice was given, or a week's wages paid *in lieu*. This was in effect the common law, which applied in the absence of applicable statutory law in New Zealand up until 1990. (Statutory law became effective from 1973, but was restricted to certain union members until 1991.) In the 1980s in two cases the judge expressed disquiet with the *Addis* case (*Gee v Timaru Milling*, *Horsburgh v NZ Meat Union*); and in 1990 a ruling occurred which in effect made *Addis* irrelevant. In *Whelan v Waitaki Meats*, Galen J. ruled that the Manager had not been 'wrongfully' dismissed under *Addis*. However, Galen J. found that

> the action of the defendant in terminating the employment of the plaintiff in the manner in which it did was such as to cause the plaintiff undue mental distress, anxiety, humilation, loss of dignity and injury to his feelings (pp. 98, 331).

In addition, he considered the nature of the dismissal would have caused speculation which would affect Whelan's future employment prospects. Galen J. decided that he was not bound by the *Addis* ruling and consequently awarded Whelan $50,000 compensation.

In 1991 statutory law concerning dismissal became all-encompassing (see Chapter Nineteen) and hence common law no longer applied in New Zealand as a substitute for statutory law.

[909] Variations in common law

Although *Addis*, or similar cases, determined common law in most Western countries for much of the past century, the *Whelan* case discussed above shows that common law could change.

However, in other countries common law can be very different. With respect to permanent employees in Japan, Schregle (1993:508-9) points out that Japanese common law is very different to *Addis*:

> In Japan, legal protection of workers against dismissal ... has been built up by court decisions. The result of this case law is a high degree of job security which goes far beyond the dismissal protection enjoyed by most workers in Western countries. A dismissal which is not objectively reasonable and socially appropriate is regarded as an abuse of the right to dismiss, and such a dismissal is null and void. This has led to a court practice according to which, contrary to the general principle that the plaintiff has the burden of proof, the employer is required to show the existence of just cause.

[910] Limitations of common law

With the exception of certain countries such as Japan, the common law protection, from cases such as *Addis*, clearly favours employers over employees. An exemplary employee could be dismissed at the whim of the employer with no redress other than a period of notice. While senior managers have been deemed entitled to up to a year's notice (e.g. *North Island Wholesale Grocers v Hewin*) shop floor employees could be granted as little as a day's notice, although a week was common. Although this was deemed 'lawful', it did not seem fair or just. In some countries, the State passed legislation to replace the common law. There are a variety of possible underlying motives for such action. There may have been genuine concern for 'workplace justice' and a desire to ensure dismissals were for genuine reasons. If the union movement in a country is strong, then perceived unfair dismissals may result either in strike action or in collective agreements which require dismissals to be 'for cause'.

Wheeler and Rojot (1992:368) point out that collective bargaining in the unionised sectors of Canada, Israel and the USA has ensured protection for those employees. However, given that the unionised in the USA comprises under twenty per cent of the workforce, the benefits are not necessarily widespread.

Initial legislative changes in New Zealand came after increasing strike action over dismissals, which often successfully achieved reinstatement. This, coupled with the first significant levels of unemployment post-Second World War, resulted in general support for statutory limitations in 1970.

C. Statutory Protection

[911] Statutory protection

In their study of ten countries, Wheeler and Rojot (1992) found that only in the non-unionised private sector in the USA did employees have *no* protection under common law, could be dismissed with notice and in the absence of cause. This study found that, in all five European countries studied, statutory protection extended to all employees. The employer was required to have cause for the dismissal. Similar statutory protection also applies in New Zealand.

Statutory protection almost universally requires 'cause' for a dismissal to be lawful. However, from a New Zealand perspective one of the most interesting aspects of Wheeler and Rojot's study was what it did *not* consider, namely the procedural side to a dismissal. As discussed more fully in Chapter Nineteen, the statutory protection in New Zealand requires two aspects:

1. substantive justification: the offence must be deemed sufficiently serious to merit dismissal.
2. procedural fairness: the *way* in which the employee was dismissed must also be deemed fair. This requires at the very least:
   (a) a full investigation of the facts;
   (b) specific details of the allegations against the employee;
   (c) an opportunity to refute the allegations or explain or mitigate the conduct;
   (d) an unbiased consideration of the explanation.

[912] Remedies

Although, as in New Zealand, the statute may authorise compensation under a variety of headings – loss of wages, loss of benefits, compensation for humiliation, hurt feelings, and so on – basically the remedies for unjustified or unlawful dismissal are but two:

1. financial compensation and/or
2. reinstatement.

In the ten-country study cited earlier (Wheeler and Rojot, 1992:370), it appears that in only *one* country (Italy), and in certain sections of Canada and the USA, is reinstatement a probable remedy. It is also available in the UK, Germany and France but 'it is so rarely used as to not be of any real importance'. The effect is that employers can still successfully terminate employees without cause 'if they are willing to pay a price'.

In New Zealand, reinstatement is not such a rarity, but it is not the norm. One study looked at pre-Court (mediation) cases and Court decisions from 1987–91. While the percentage of cases deemed unjustifiable was high, reinstatement was ordered only in a small minority of cases (see Table 9.1).

It is therefore more accurate to talk about statutory 'compensation' for unjustifiable dismissal rather than statutory 'protection' from unjustifiable dismissal.

Table 9.1. Reinstatement

	Cases	Unjustifiable		Reinstatement Ordered		
	No.	No.	% Of Total	No.	% of Total	% of Unjust
Pre-Court	310	245	(79.0)	35	(11.3)	(14.3)
Court	287	202	(70.4)	42	(14.6)	(20.8)
TOTAL	597	447	(74.9)	77	(12.9)	(17.2)

Source: Boon (1992)

Chapter Ten

Industrial Conflict

A. Introduction

[1001] Introduction

Feuille and Wheeler (1981:255-6) encapsulated some of the difficulties in discussing industrial conflict when they observed:

> Industrial conflict is an elusive concept with unclear boundaries, and thus the phenomena and research that fits within its rubric are subject to some debate. One of the key definitional problems is that the same word, 'conflict', can be used to describe a condition of opposing interests, methods, or goals and also used to describe occurrences that are reflections or symptoms of that condition. For example, strikes can be viewed as conflict and also as symptoms of an underlying condition of conflict.

Indeed, for many in the general public, 'industrial conflict' simply means strike action by the workforce. However, to define industrial conflict in this way is highly problematic. By implication, if there are no strikes, then there is no conflict – so presumably there is industrial harmony. Given that there *may* also be low productivity, high labour turnover, personal grievances being filed at an alarming rate, vigorous discipline and frequent dismissals being applied, 'industrial harmony' may be highly inappropriate. Hence a more suitable definition is proposed.

[1002] Definition

Industrial conflict is defined as:

> The situation that exists when one or more of the parties in employment relations fails to satisfactorily achieve all its objectives.

[1003] Inevitability of conflict

The discussion in Chapter One indicated that those who subscribe to the pluralist employment relations ideology accept that conflict is inevitable. This is seen as a rational and accurate portrayal of reality. It must be noted that pluralists do not necessarily believe in the inevitability of violent confrontations but rather in the fact that *all* parties in employment relations will never achieve *all* of their objectives.

Very few employment relations academics subscribe to the unitarist ideology as an accurate portrayal of reality, but may acknowledge that in the normative sense unitarism could be very pleasant, particularly for employers and managers. This contrasts with writers and researchers in areas such as organisational behaviour and personnel/HRM, who frequently write as if the unitarist ideology *does* reflect reality. Feuille and Wheeler (1981:257) point out that

> organisational behaviourists and especially organisational development specialists appear to accept the tenets of the Cooperation School [i.e., unitarist ideology] without any apparent assumption that organisation members are or will have opposing interests.

The significance of the definition given in [1002] is that it accepts that in a situation of conflict there may be either no overt manifestations of the conflict, or alternatively a wide variety of manifestations.

[1004] Latent conflict

It is possible for one or more of the parties in employment relations to fail to achieve its objectives without giving any overt indication. Managers may be disappointed with productivity levels, or employees may be discontented with their pay and conditions, with neither producing visible evidence of their concerns. A common assumption is that, if employees are discontented, their productivity will be low. Indeed, a meta-analysis performed by Petty *et al* (1984) concluded that individual job satisfaction and job performance are positively correlated. However, some years ago, Locke (1970:484) cautioned against taking a simplistic view and observed that 'the inadequacies of the old bromide "the happy worker is the productive worker" is now widely recognised.' It is clearly possible for employees to be happy because managerial control is inadequate and employees are able to be unproductive.

It is also possible that one party has such an overwhelming power advantage that the other is *unable* to even indicate discontent. Thus Feuille and Wheeler (1981:257) assert that

> pluralists believe that the occurrence of some overt conflict is desirable for it demonstrates that neither side has over- whelmed the other.

While very short-term conflict may be latent, it is unlikely to remain so for any reasonable period of time. So long as one overcomes the mindset that 'strikes' are the *only* possible manifestation of conflict, it is highly probable that even slave labour will manifest discontent in some way – lack of cooperation, false claims of sickness or deliberate poor quality of work.

B. Manifestations of Conflict

[1005] Manifestations

It has been suggested in the introductory paragraphs that conflict is manifested in many more ways than by strike action. The editors of one of the classics (aptly entitled *Industrial Conflict*) observed over fifty years ago (Kornhauser, Dubin and Ross, 1954:13):

> It may even be suggested that the general object of study is not the labour dispute, the strike or the lockout, but the total range of behaviour and attitudes that express opposition and divergent orientations between industrial owners and managers on the one hand and working people and their organisations on the other hand.

This viewpoint is valid, so long as it is also accepted that the State is one of the parties in employment relations and, when its objectives are not met, or when State activities are deemed by employers or employees to be the cause of their problems, manifestations of conflict will occur.

Kornhauser *et al* (1954:14) go on to list a number of activities which indicate a conflict situation:

- strikes, lockouts, removal of plant;
- work limitations, slowdowns, sabotage, unilateral changes in work standards, piece rates;
- unorganised withholding of effort, intentional waste and inefficiency;
- labour turnover and absenteeism;
- complaints, friction, infractions of rules;
- autocratic supervision and over-strict discipline and penalties;
- unnecessary and discriminatory firing, layoffs and demotions;
- unofficial speed-ups.

All the above examples of how industrial conflict may be manifested include elements, in some cases strong elements, of retribution. An attempt is made to hurt the opposition. However, conflict can be manifested by non-punitive action such as negotiation or the referral of a dispute to a disputes committee or to arbitration. This suggests that a better understanding of conflict is likely if the various expressions are classified. The system used here is to classify according to:

a. whether activities are individual or collective;
b. the purpose of the actions;
c. the extent to which conflict is the cause of the actions.

[1006] Degree of organisation of action

The most basic classification reflects the degree of organisation of the conflict. That is, there is a reasonable extent of organisation and the action may be deemed *collective*, or the action is not organised and the action is *individual*. It should be emphasised that in this context, *collective* is assumed to mean that not only is the action performed by a group, but they are organised and are acting in concert, with a common understanding.

Hence, if a group of employees individually and independently lowered their output or performance, this would be classified as a number of individual actions. However, if the group collaborated and jointly lowered their performance levels this would be deemed collective action. (Under New Zealand legislation this would be classified as a 'strike'.)

[1007] Motive behind the action

A second form of classification is based on the underlying *motive* behind the action. Specifically, the motive may be to make it easier for the party to reach its objective by *resolving* the conflict (R), or it may simply be to indicate *frustration* (F) at failing to achieve the objective. (In many cases, both underlying motives play a part.)

Discussion and negotiation is primarily to resolve the conflict. Sabotage by an employee or resignation is primarily to indicate frustration. However, a strike may be simply to help achieve a wage dispute (R) or may represent an outburst of anger and resentment (F) or frequently there will be elements of both.

[1008] Extent action reflects conflict

Some actions such as strikes can be deemed virtually one hundred per cent manifestations of conflict. Other actions are not nearly so clear-cut. Absenteeism, for example, may result from:

a. genuine and serious illness which necessitates absence;
b. mild illness which results in absence by some individuals but not in others. Absenteeism as a result of a mild cold *may* reflect a conflict situation but may simply indicate hypochondria and narcissism;
c. a dislike of certain, or all job factors. Barmby and Treble (1989:155) found that physical conditions helped explain the difference in absenteeism rates between departments within an organisation:

   > the more dirty or unpleasant the conditions are the more likely individuals are to absent themselves.

   This finding bears close comparison to one of the two strike hypotheses of Kerr and Siegel (1954):

d. a situation of total 'flexitime' attitude by the organisation and an expectation that, should the individual go absent (to watch a sporting fixture, relax on the beach, etc.), he or she would make up the work some other time. In this case the 'opportunity to go absent' may be the opposite of conflict and one of the factors contributing to high job satisfaction, indicating objectives have been met.

To further complicate matters, research has shown that government policies can greatly influence absenteeism rates. For example, Sweden has experienced two significant and almost instantaneous jumps in overall absenteeism rates. Both were caused by increases in State-funded sick-pay rates. Other potential causes of absenteeism are legion. For example, in a study of female student nurses, Parkes (1987) found that *relative weight* was a highly significant predictor of sickness and absence from work.

Hence, a third form of classification can be on the basis that the action is predominantly triggered by conflict, or can be considered the result of either conflict or external factors. Table 10.1 lists a number of individual and group actions illustrating industrial conflict.

[1009] Interrelationship between actions

Research opinion and general evidence varies as to whether or not different expressions of conflict should be viewed as alternatives. Thus Handy (1968) found that in British coalmining in the 1950s and 1960s, as strike action declined, absenteeism rose, suggesting that employees viewed both as alternative forms of withdrawal. However, in the New Zealand meat-freezing industry in the 1960s and 1970s, both strike action *and* absenteeism were very high. Drago and Wooden (1990), in their study of conflict in Australia, also found that high absenteeism is associated with larger, more costly strikes. However, there would be general agreement with Hyman (1972:55) that

> attempts to suppress specific manifestations of conflict, without removing the underlying causes of unrest, may merely divert the conflict into other forms.

Thus Turner (1969:34) points out that in the motor industry in the UK

> withdrawal from the work situation (such as accidents reported, labour turnover and refusals to work overtime) tended to increase in certain firms when strikes were held down by a managerial policy of dismissing 'ring leaders'.

Hyman (1972:55) also points out that in one factory, after severe local unemployment reduced the normally high level of turnover, the level of strike action increased dramatically.

C. Cost-benefit of Conflict

[1010] Cost-benefit

All the expressions of conflict mentioned above are designed either to *benefit* one of the parties or to inflict *costs* on another – or both. In some cases, these costs and benefits are psychological, in others they are economic. In addition to those directly involved in conflict, there are many more who may be indirectly involved. Thus, in most situations, it is impossible to accurately state the effect of any type of conflict. Two manifestations of conflict – turnover and strikes – will however be considered in this manner.

Table 10.1. Manifestations of conflict

ACTION	PURPOSE (IF CONFLICT)	EXTERNAL CAUSES?
	Individual	
a) discussion	resolve	
b) individual bargaining	resolve	
c) absenteeism	frustration	yes
d) threatening to leave	resolve	
e) turnover	frustration	yes
f) sabotage	frustration	yes
g) pilfering	resolve and frustration	yes
h) lowering production levels	resolve and frustration	
i) accidents	frustration	yes
j) filing grievances	resolve and frustration	
k) increasing discipline, by individuals	resolve and frustration	
	Collective	
a) discussion	resolve	
b) collective bargaining	resolve	
c) taking matter to arbitration	resolve	
d) strikes (stopping work)	resolve and frustration	
e) go-slows/work to rule	resolve and frustration	
f) overtime bans	resolve and frustration	
g) increased overall disciplinary standards	resolve and frustration	

[1011] Cost-benefit of turnover

Unorganised individual action can result in labour turnover. There is little governmental or managerial effort to cost this out, or give regard to the benefits accrued. Statistics simply reveal, for example, that industry X had thirty-two per cent labour turnover in a six-month period.

There is no indication as to what extent the turnover is an indicator of conflict as opposed to being influenced by external factors such as retirement or transfer. March and Simon (1958:100) have observed:

> under nearly all conditions the most accurate single predictor of labor turnover is the state of the economy … when jobs are scarce, voluntary turnover is small.

Thus to predict the cost-benefit of turnover as an indicator of *conflict*, it is first necessary to estimate what proportion of turnover is caused by conflict.

[1012] Employer perspective

The cost to an employer depends on a number of factors including:

a. recruitment and selection costs;
b. training costs;
c. loss of production resulting from:
   (i) having inexperienced employees in the production line;
   (ii) having experienced employees acting as trainers;
d. effect of turnover on overall morale and production of employees not directly involved;
e. possible effect on market position if production losses are significant;
f. the amount and penal costs of overtime that is worked to make up lost production, etc.

The New Zealand Department of Labour (1972) estimated the cost of turnover as being 150 to 399 times the worker's hourly wage. This estimate is clearly only a very rough guide and deviations could be quite considerable.

The benefit to the employer from labour turnover depends predominantly on:

a. the change of climate resulting from the turnover;
b. the quality of the replacement employees.

Williams and Livingstone (1994) point out that there is a robust negative relationship between performance and voluntary turnover, and that organisations can often benefit from turnover, by replacing the poor performers who leave with higher quality employees.

[1013] Individual perspective

The cost to individuals who leave their jobs as a result of conflict depend on:

a. time in which they will be unemployed;
b. the psychological effect of the conflict, the termination of the old jobs and the problems of getting and settling into new jobs;
c. whether they will be required to move house.

The benefits depend on:

a. the relief from the conflict in the old job;
b. the opportunities for new experiences;
c. the benefits provided by the new job.

[1014] Cost-benefit of strikes

Likewise the cost-benefits of a strike are equally complex. Strike statistics usually give the number of strikes, the number of 'working days lost' either in total or per thousand employees, and the amount of wages lost during the strike. These statistics are of some value in showing trends, but can be very misleading when used for international comparisons (since definitions of a strike differ) and be particularly misleading when used as an estimate of costs. As a measure of strike activity, the number of strikes is poor since it gives the same weight to a one-day strike by ten employees as to a month-long strike by a thousand employees. The drawback with the other two measures is that they are almost always inaccurate. Very rarely is there a finite amount of production which could be produced and sold, and very rarely would there be a finite amount of wages that would have been paid out and which are now lost forever.

[1015] Employer's perspective

The costs and benefits to an employer (whose employees manufacture a product) as a result of a strike depend on:

a. demand for the product which may be
   (i) low or nil (during recession);
   (ii) high, but could be met from stockpiles or overtime work;
   (iii) high, and cannot be met;
b. effect on market position if market demand not met;
c. difference between union demand and the final compromise;
d. savings on wage costs and other variable costs;
e. effect on future union-management relationships, etc.

[1016] Employees perspective

The costs and benefits to employees depend on:

a. amount of assistance they get during the strike (strike pay, welfare, part-time job);
b. difference between the management's offer and the final compromise;
c. effect on future union-management relationships, etc.;
d. psychological impact of the action.

The examples given above are by no means exhaustive but do underline the weakness in assuming that any measure such as 'working days lost' – which is reasonably easy to procure – is anything other than a very rough guide to the actual impact of strike action.

D. Strikes

[1017] The emphasis on strikes

The earlier sections of this chapter have indicated the wide range of actions indicating industrial conflict. This begs the question then: why the almost universal emphasis on strikes? (This chapter clearly follows the trend.) There are a number of possible explanations, as outlined below.

[1018] The relative impact of strikes

If strikes caused significant loss of production compared to other actions, it would be reasonable to concentrate on this form of conflict. However, as McHugh (1991:722) observes, 'most econometric work, however, supports the view that strikes impair productivity only modestly in the short-term.' Indeed Knight (1989:370) found that in British manufacturing:

> Some of the results actually imply instead that high strike frequency is associated with high labour productivity, and this effect is not, in general, offset by the adverse effects of strike duration. Strikes appear, in part, to have played a therapeutic role as a vent for frustration, or as a mechanism for resolving otherwise unresolvable conflicts in the majority of manufacturing industries in the sample.

It has been calculated that in New Zealand in 1973 (the last year all the figures were available) the percentage loss of working time was:

0.1 % from strikes;
1.8 % from accidents;
6.0 % from absenteeism.

Thus if *one fifth* of absenteeism results from conflict as opposed to general illness – it causes *ten times* more working time lost than does strikes.

Even if an exceptionally 'bad' year for strikes is considered – such as 1976 – the average amount of work time lost per employee through strikes was only half a day per year. This averages to forty-five seconds per day. Hence, if employees extend the morning and afternoon tea breaks by a couple of minutes, this wastes over five times the working time lost through strikes. Managers who attend one luncheon a month which extends for an extra hour and is not made up, are wasting more working time in a year than the average worker does through strikes.

For an individual *organisation*, or at particular points in time for individual *industries*, strikes may be very significant. For the economy as a whole, strikes have a fairly insignificant impact and certainly the impact on overall productivity does not justify the emphasis.

[1019] The overtness of strikes

Kornhauser *et al* (1954:8) suggest:

> Probably the basic explanation for this exaggerated view lies in the *overtness* of the strike. Glaring and palpable, it thrusts itself rudely above the surface of society.

However, nowadays very few strikes are as intrinsically noticeable as they imply. With some glaring exceptions, (the UK coal-miners, and later the newspaper strikes in the 1980s), there are few mass demonstrations and little picketing. As Hyman (1972:143-4) points out:

> for most of the time the strikers are dispersed – perhaps digging the garden, decorating the house or helping with the family shopping ... this indicates that social visibility is not merely an inherent quality of phenomena; it relates also to what people are looking for, and what is brought to their attention by the media of communication.

[1020] The media

The media certainly give strikes considerably more attention than other indications of conflict such as low productivity, absenteeisms, high turnover or frequent grievances. Some observers (Kornhauser *et al* 1954:507) see a sinister explanation, namely that since 'the media of mass communication are predominantly in the hands of management interests (advertisers) …, [we see] social interpretations and values congenial to management'. However it is more probable that the media emphasise strikes because they are more interesting and dramatic than, for example, high absenteeism. In short they are in the news because news-makers and the public agree they are newsworthy.

[1021] Strikes and the unitary ideology

A further possible reason for the emphasis on strikes is that the strike is the most obvious contradiction of the unitary ideology. Individual actions may be written off as the actions of extremists, but group action such as a strike bites hard at anyone's belief in the 'ideology of harmony of interests which assigns legitimacy to managerial power' (Hyman, 1972:161). As discussed in [108], unitarists consider any form of conflict as pathological and deny it has any validity. Strikes are the most overt manifestation of conflict.

[1022] Convenience and interest

Knowles (1954:214), after commenting on alternative forms of unrest, observes that

> strikes are the most obvious and dramatic of all these symptoms, and they provide the simplest heads under which to collect information. Partly for this reason, but partly also because strikes used to be considered a form of crime, strike statistics exist, in most countries, in considerable detail and covering a long period.

Strikes, whether used as a tactic to resolve conflict, or as an outburst of frustration, are an indicator of conflict. The conflict may not be with the 'struck' employer, but with the government – or possibly the real conflict is between another employer and another group of employees – but in almost every case there is *industrial conflict* at the root of a strike. This is clearly not true for turnover, absenteeism, accidents, and so forth.

Also, since strikes are often prohibited or illegal and indeed for many years in many countries were a crime, the official data on strikes considerably surpasses that on absenteeism, accidents, turnover or grievances. While many strikes are mundane, some are exciting: inherently much more interesting to most people than, for example, absenteeism. In short, convenience and interest probably explain much of the emphasis on strikes.

[1023] Causes of strikes

There are many varied theories as to the causes of strikes. Kaufman (1992:110-111) suggests a number of conclusions can be gleaned from the literature:

- strikes are more likely to occur the longer the duration of the preceding contract;
- the fewer the issues being negotiated (such as in a contract reopener over wages), the lower is the probability of a strike;
- negotiations that serve as a pattern setter for other firm/union pairs have higher probability of a strike;
- larger bargaining units are more likely to have a strike;
- a larger variance in the firm's financial performance is associated with a larger strike propensity;
- more highly unionised industries have more strike activity;
- firms/industries that employ a larger proportion of women are less strike prone;
- firms/industries with greater risk of injury or fatality are more strike prone;
- firms/industries that pay a higher wage rate relative to other firms/industries have a lower probability of a strike;
- considerable variation exists across two and three-digit SIC industries in the propensity to strike, holding all other measurable variables constant;
- firms that can inventory or stockpile goods are more likely to have a strike.

It is also possible to consider causes, purely from the different ideological viewpoints, as discussed in Chapter One. There is also the economists' theories and others relating to business cycles and 'long cycles'. These latter theories at least partly explain trends over medium to very long-term, but do little to explain inter-industry or intra-industry differences. Adaptions of a fifty-year-old sociological theory addresses some of these points (see [1028]).

[1024] Ideological explanations

Those holding to radical ideology see class conflict as underlying all social issues and private ownership of capital as the fundamental cause of all industrial conflict, including, of course, strikes. Normally the domain of intellectual pseudo-socialists, this ideology fails to explain why strikes are still prevalent in socialist societies and conflicts of interests and objectives occur in worker cooperatives or in union-owned industries.

Unitarists believe that strikes are pathological and industrial peace is not only a desirable goal, but in fact is already the norm. If strikes do occur, then unitarists believe this must be caused by poor or faulty communication, or by troublemakers.

If conflict is simply caused by poor communication, then this presupposes no fundamental conflict of interest and the implication is that conflict would disappear if managers would only remember to be careful enough to explain their motives and actions. If management does not tell their workforce about a proposed change in policy (which will lead to expansion) and the employees believe it will cause redundancy, then poor communications could be seen as the cause of conflict. On the other hand, if management were considering a change in policy (which they later decide not to implement) which would have resulted in wide-scale redundancy, and communicate to the employees about this possible change in policy, then good communications could be seen as the cause of conflict. Although it appears cynical, the suggestion by Kerr (1964:74) that 'misunderstandings and misuse of words have probably made a substantial contribution to industrial peace', is in fact rather perceptive.

The belief that troublemakers, or agitators, are the major cause of conflict has been a widely held myth for many years. The concept of the agitator as *prime* cause of conflict is unsubstantiated by evidence. Most often the problem of 'agitators' was created as an excuse for poor performance by managers or government, or as a focus to divert attention. However, it is certainly true that individuals, be they union officials, or unofficial work group leaders, employees, supervisors, managers, or government ministers, are able to either exacerbate or reduce overt manifestations of conflict. But, as Turner (1969:12) states:

> where industrial situations are likely to lead to conflict, they will generally find leaders to organise it anyway: and such leaders are naturally likely to be people of aggressive temperament, and so also to acquire strong views. The ability of such individuals to create conflict in the absence of circumstances that would induce it anyway seems to me to be highly marginal.

The pluralist viewpoint is that conflict is the situation where one or more of the parties fails to achieve its objectives. Employees and unions can choose from a variety of actions. Some actions best reflect their frustration at failing to achieve their objectives, others are seen as most likely to resolve the conflict situation helping them to achieve their objectives.

Thus, for example, pluralists would argue that employees choose to strike rather than discuss or negotiate, when they see they have a better 'return' from striking than from negotiation, or they realise both are futile and want to strike to express frustration at management, or at the system, or because, to an extent, striking is more fun than working.

[1025] Economic theories of strikes

The most famous economic theory of strikes is probably that proposed by Hicks (1932), relating to strikes used during wage negotiations. In brief, his theory is that employers and unions have 'concession curves' which before the strike are some distance apart but which eventually intersect, indicating the wage level agreed upon after the strike. Hicks asserts that if the parties were rational and well informed, strikes would not occur as both sides would be able to accurately predict the point of intersection of the concession curve and could save themselves the cost of the strike. (Later economists, in particular Ashenfelter and Johnson (1969), have extended the model and tested it empirically.)

Most economic models suffer in that to make them 'elegant' the modelist has to rely on assumptions (such as all actors having perfect knowledge) which are usually not true, and simplifications (such as the only purpose for a strike is immediate economic gain) which are unrealistic. In reality, no one has perfect knowledge and indeed the knowledge possessed by most people is not remotely close to 'perfect'. As argued earlier, strikes can equally well reflect frustration or a break from the monotony of the job, with strikers willingly 'paying' for the pleasure of the outburst. These are the fundamental flaws in most economic models of strikes. There are other factors, some of which can be built into models. These include the occasional need by negotiators (both management and unions) for strikes to occur, both to convince their principals (board of directors, or the workforce) that the negotiations are necessary and valuable, and to make the principals more realistic (in the negotiators' view) with respect to outcome.

The basic economic models leave unanswered such questions as to why, if strikes are a function of irrationality and lack of knowledge, these conditions seem to occur on a cyclical basis. And why should these conditions seem to occur more in some industries than others?

[1026] Strikes and the business cycle

McConnell (1990:136) points out:

> It is now well established that strike incidence varies pro-cyclically ... a one per cent increase in the unemployment rate decreases the probability of a strike by just over one per cent.

This view is generally supported by quantitative researchers, although there are exceptions. Ingram *et al* (1993:715) found that, for British manufacturing, strike incidence was *counter-cyclical* – a finding they realised was 'most surprising'.

McConnell (1990) confirmed previous research that the probability of a strike varies pro-cyclically. However, her research uncovered no evidence of cyclical variation in strike *duration*. Her study was more extensive than many quantitative works and produced some interesting results (McConnell, 1990:141). Using USA data for the period 1970–81, she found:

> strikes are most likely in industries suffering low demand in regions with low unemployment ... (Two possible explanations):
> (a) the cost of strike is low for the workers since there are many alternative employment opportunities, and the cost to the firm of lost sales is also low ...
> (b) in a booming region workers expect their industry is also enjoying booming trade and expect their wages to rise accordingly.

However, 'business cycle' explanations of strikes are inadequate. Franzosi (1989:359) asks:

> If strike waves are mainly related to national, central-state politics, though, how do we account for the fact that many strike waves seem to occur at approximately the same time in different countries?

Given that business cycles (normally around seven to ten years in length) do not coincide for different countries, an answer to Franzosi's rhetorical question possibly lies in 'long cycles', or Kondratieff cycles.

Table 10.2. Kondratieff and strike cycles

Cycle	Kondratieff Troughs	Kondratieff Peaks	Strike Activity Peaks
1	1789–92	1810–17	
2	1844–51	1866–75	1869–75
3	1892–96	1913–20	1910–20
4	1939–48	1967–74	1968–74
5	1990–98	?2017–24?	?2017–24?

[1027] Kondratieff cycles

Kondratieff cycles, according to Screpanti (1987:99), refer to

> waves in the growth rates of industrial output, consisting of a long phase of rapid growth, lasting 20-30 years, followed by an equally long phase of stagnation.

Screpanti found in a study of five countries (USA, France, Germany, Italy, and the UK) that there was a long cycle of strike activity whose peaks roughly coincide with the peaks of the Kondratieff economic cycles (see Table 10.2).

As can be seen, peaks in strike activity coincide very closely with Kondratieff cycle peaks. There are no convincing *explanations* as to why there should be such cycles. Screpanti (1987:111) does attempt an explanation postulating:

> It is possible that the sisyphean frustration remains latent and cumulates for a long time, until eventually it bursts out. This could happen at the end of the upswings; and it seems sensible to believe that precisely there explosions put an end to the prosperity phases.

However, regardless of *why* it occurs, it does appear that there is a long cycle of strike activity, underlying shorter cycles of activity and the frequent outliers.

It can be seen that the long-cycle theory predicts a trough in strike activity through the 1990s. (Fifty years on from the previous trough 1939–48.) *If* the long cycle theory is valid, this implies that HRM, NIR, the New Right (and the Employment Contracts Act 1991) are *not* responsible for the low level of strike activity in the early 1990s.

It is possible that the relationship between strike cycles and the Kondratieff cycles are coincidental. After all, with cycles of fifty years in length, there will have to be a considerable passage of time before the relationship can be confirmed with a high degree of certainty. However, if there is a relationship it still leaves unanswered the question as to why some industries are more strike-prone than others and, within industries, why some firms are more strike-prone than others.

[1028] Inter-industry strike-proneness

Fifty years ago Clark Kerr and Abraham Siegel (1954) set out to provide a general explanation of inter-industry strike-proneness. They considered a number of economic and sociological theories which, although possibly significant in explaining inter-firm differences, were inadequate in explaining inter-industry differences.

Kerr and Siegel propose two hypotheses which they consider explains why some industries are strike prone in many different countries. The first is the 'Location of the Worker in Society', with the isolated mass being at the strike-prone end of the spectrum. The 'isolated mass' can be overtly literal (for example, lumber camps, coalmining towns, isolated freezing works with workers being in camps) or less so, or less isolated (such as waterside workers who live in a particular suburb). The rationale for this is that when employees are 'trapped' in their jobs, grievances are shared and reinforced and cohesive action is relatively easy. Integrated individuals are at the opposite end of the spectrum.

The second hypothesis is the 'Nature of the Work and Worker', with hard, physical, and unpleasant work at the strike-prone end of the spectrum, with the rationale being that such employees will find aggressive actions such as strikes more acceptable. (A point which Kerr and Siegel could also have made is that the *supervisors* in those industries are also likely to be aggressive.) Industries which are at the strike-prone end for both measures will in theory be the most strike-prone.

The Kerr-Siegel explanation looked very convincing in the 1950s and 1960s, with the proposed strike-prone industries being waterside workers, coalminers and so on. As more white-collar groups become increasingly prepared to take strike action, it could appear to be losing relevance. However, given that it is far from perfect, it still provides a reasonably accurate explanation and the traditionally strike-prone industries still head the league tables. More significantly, some of the white-collar action can be explained by adapting the isolated mass hypotheses to argue that white-collar groups are becoming more of a cohesive group through bureaucratisation, loss of relative advantages over other groups and fewer opportunities for promotion. One could even argue that with RSI (Repetition Strain Injury), or as it is now known OOS (Occupational Overuse Syndrome), white-collar jobs are no longer easy and pleasant.

It must be stressed that Kerr and Siegel never claimed to explain why any particular strike took place. They are trying to explain why some *industries* are more likely to experience strike action than others. One way to use their theory is to consider there to be a lower 'flash point' in some industries than others. Hence, an unpopular or provocative action by management will be more likely to set off an explosion (strike) in strike-prone industries than in strike-free industries.

There are some industries which do not seem to conform with these theories. The most cited example is the steel industry, which internationally has a much lower strike record than one would predict from its characteristics. However, there are some peculiarities in that industry, in particular strong traditions of seniority. Eldridge (1968:175) points out:

> On the production side, a number of promotion ladders were established within particular departments. Once on a ladder, a man cannot transfer to another ladder without starting at the bottom. Well developed job hierarchies with seniority of service as the regulating principle of mobility have meant traditionally that age, prestige-giving occupations, status and pay have been closely correlated.

This would have a significant impact on the degree of 'isolated mass'. Employees are not trapped in a job for the next forty years, they are able to progress. Also, the fact that employees are in low, medium and high-status jobs, means the cohesiveness of the workforce is reduced.

It should also be stressed that discussing intra-industry differences as a means of disproving Kerr-Siegel is invalid. Edwards (1977:565) claims that in the USA long-shore industry (waterside or dock work):

> the West Coast industry has been marked by a considerable degree of industrial peace since 1948, to such an extent that a mechanisation plan was successfully introduced with union co-operation. By contrast, the East Coast industry has experienced a series of coastwide strikes since 1945 … Kerr and Siegel would need to show that East Coast workers are more isolated than those on the West Coast, or that their work is more unpleasant, to explain these facts.

The 'facts' behind Edward's contention are highly questionable. The West Coast did negotiate a mechanisation plan in 1960, but only after a series of crippling strikes from 1945 onwards which made it clear to union leaders and employers the West Coast industry was about to collapse. Notwithstanding, even if Edwards is correct in his portrayal of the facts, he is wrong in his contention. Kerr and Siegel have never contended that within a strike-prone industry firms that have more strikes are 'more massed' or have work that is 'more dangerous and unpleasant'. They describe conditions that make the *industry* – on average – more strike-prone than other industries in the same country. *Less* provocation is needed in those *industries* than in strike-free industries to generate strikes. For any particular firm, or region, there may be peculiarities which act as catalysts or triggers for strikes.

To conclude, the Kerr-Siegel hypotheses, fairly interpreted, provide a reasonable understanding of strike differences at industry level. Although their work was published over fifty years ago, it still generates empirical testing. Church *et al* (1991:76), although critical of Kerr-Siegel, acknowledge that the isolated mass hypothesis 'does help to explain inter-colliery variations in strike activity in inter-war England and Wales.' Kaufman (1983), using more sophisticated data for the USA, found support for both the isolated mass and aggressive worker hypotheses, with isolated rural industries being more strike-prone and industries with a high proportion of women (presumably less aggressive than men) being more strike-free.

[1029] Inter-firm differences

It must be noted that Kerr and Siegel are suggesting reasons for inter-industry differences in strike activity. Within any industry, there can be wide *inter-*

firm differences. Katz, Kochan and Gobeville (1983) found that in the same year grievances per 100 employees ranged from a low of 24 to a high of 450 in different plants. Some of the variables that Kerr and Siegel rejected as determinants of *industry* differences can explain *inter-firm* differences.

Within a strike-prone industry some firms will have:

a. high-quality management;
b. strong, but non-militant union leaders;
c. payment systems which do not generate conflict in themselves;
d. modern, good quality factories or mines, or equipment;
e. greater profitability and growth prospects.

Some, or all, of which may result in employees and their unions not only being more able to achieve their objectives *but* being more inclined to opt for alternative methods to resolve conflicts than strikes, and having fewer frustrations to vent.

[C] Issues

CHAPTER ELEVEN

WAGES

A. Introduction

[1101] Introduction

This chapter looks at wages in the broadest sense. The major topics considered are wage differentials, wages and the law and finally incomes policies (or wage control). The topic of wages probably best illustrates the considerable degree to which all issues in employment relations are interrelated. Already wages have been explicitly discussed with regard to evaluation [316], incentive schemes [317–8], the market wage [706], and the 'right wage' [707]. Implicitly, wages are a vital factor in any understanding of objectives – both with respect to productivity and job satisfaction, bargaining and industrial conflict. As Forth and Millward (2004:98) observe: 'For most employees, pay is the nexus of the employment relationship.'

[1102] What are 'wages'?

In any country, legislation may define what is meant by the term 'wages'. Thus in New Zealand, the *Wages Protection Act* 1983 defines wages as meaning:

> salary or wages; and includes time and piece wages and overtime, bonus, or other special payments …

To this end, *legally* the term is restricted to the above money payments.

However, in many employers' and employees' view, a broader concept may be more realistic. As discussed in [702], in its simplest form, wages are part of the wage-work bargain:

Wage
Employer → Employee
←
Work

As discussed below, the employee's part of the bargain is not simply work. However, if the employer's part of the bargain is the 'wage', then there is reasonable logic in at least notionally considering *all* the material benefits provided by the employer as *quasi*-wages.

Thus 'wages' can be conceived of as:

a. basic money wage;
b. money allowances, bonuses, overtime payments;
c. fringe benefits.

[1103] Fringe benefits

Herman *et al* (1987:199) report that in the USA 'fringe benefits' are thought to amount to around 37 per cent of pay for time worked. They report that the Congressional Research Service consider fringe benefits to be even more significant in other countries: 'In Italy, 83 per cent, in Japan 75.5 per cent, in Germany 71 per cent and in the UK 38.2 per cent.' The probable figure for New Zealand is 30 to 40 per cent.

In New Zealand, tax legislation has defined fringe benefits as including:

a. the private use or enjoyment, in relation to the employee of a motor vehicle;
b. the availability for the private use of a motor vehicle;
c. any loan;
d. any subsidised transport;
e. any contribution to any sick, accident, or death benefit fund;
f. any specified insurance premium;
g. any contribution to any superannuation scheme.

In employment relations terms, again, the concept of fringe benefits is considered to be even wider and covers:

a. time-not-worked benefits, where the employee is paid: annual and statutory holidays, meal breaks, rest periods, wash up, parental leave, jury leave, military service, call-in and call-back and travel allowances, sick leave, etc.;
b. benefits with cash value: life and health, etc., insurance premiums, company cars, interest-free or low interest loans, discounted shares, share options, paid education expenses for employee and family, paid telephone expenses, etc.

[1104] 'Real' wages and 'money' wages

During times of inflation, there is a need to distinguish 'real' wages and wage increases, from 'money' wages and wage increases. Real wages are money wages divided by a cost of living (COL) index. If inflation is 10 per cent and money wages increase by 10 per cent, then real wages remain unchanged. If money wages had only increased by 5 per cent, then real wages fell by 4.5 per cent.

Psychologically, employees accept a drop in real wages much more readily than a drop in money wages. Employers wishing to cut the real wages of their employees can do so quite easily during times of high inflation by simply increasing money wages at a lower rate than inflation. Most employers are reluctant to face the anger of their workforces by cutting money wages. Brown *et al* (2004: 509) found a mere 'six instances of nominal settlement cuts from a sample of over 30,000 settlements over a twenty-year period.'

[1105] What are wages for?

At a simplistic level it could be argued that wages are for work, as suggested above. While this may be true in some situations it is clearly not universally true. For it to be true, work must be clearly measurable and wages and work perfectly correlated. Under some 'payment by results' schemes, or where employees are on piecework, this may be true. In many cases, however, work is not clearly measurable and there are many other factors to be taken into account. The section below on differentials covers some factors which some believe either *do* determine and/or *should* determine wage levels. In brief, wages may be considered an exchange for, amongst others,

a. work which is actually done. This refers not only to the amount, but also to the complexity, the degree of responsibility and the working conditions, etc.;
b. work which could be done;
c. skills and qualifications held, which may or may not be used;
d. seniority;
e. time spent at the workplace;
f. agreeing to being available to work.

B. Wage Differentials

[1106] Adam Smith and wage differentials

One of the earliest theoretical discussions on wage differentials appeared in 1776 in Adam Smith's classic *The Wealth of Nations* (1976, ed.:116-7). Smith referred to inter-occupational differentiality – differences in wages for different occupations. His most cited view on differentials is:

> The five following are the principal circumstances which, so far as I have been able to observe, make up for a small pecuniary gain in some employments, and counter-balance a great one in others: first, the agreeableness or disagreeableness of the employments themselves; secondly, the easiness and cheapness, or the difficulty and expense of learning them; thirdly, the constancy or inconstancy of employment in them; fourthly the small or great trust which must be reposed in those who exercise them; and, fifthly, the probability or improbability of success in them.

Differentials can be discussed in both a *normative* and in an *empirical* (or descriptive, or positive) sense, as were ideologies. Normative arguments are purely subjective and outline why differentials *should* occur – according to that person's value judgement. Empirical arguments are partly subjective and partly open to research confirmation or refutation and outline why differentials *do* occur.

Adam Smith does not make it explicit in which sense he is making his observations. Thus he states, for example:

> a journeyman taylor earns less than a journeyman weaver. His work is much easier. A journeyman weaver earns less than a journeyman smith. His work is not always easier, but it is much cleanlier.

This could be considered a *normative* view. Because the work is easier, the 'taylor' (or tailor) *should* get less than the weaver. Alternatively this could be considered with respect to supply and demand. That is, because tailoring is easy, more employees want to take up that occupation, causing an excess of supply over demand, depressing the market range of wages. Similarly, fewer workers opt for weaving, with a result that wages have to be bid up by employers to attract employees into that occupation.

Smith is certainly aware of supply and demand factors, but appears to argue that wages are, and ought to be, higher in unattractive occupations, in order to prevent them from becoming 'under-populated.' The more modern and hopefully realistic view is that price is determined at least to a degree by supply and demand, rather than Smith's apparent view that prices *should* be at such a level as to control supply.

[1107] Categories of differentials

Wage differentials can be considered in a variety of categories, in each case assuming all else equal. The categories are:

a. inter-occupational;
b. inter-industry;
c. inter-firm;
d. inter-regional;
e. inter-personal.

The following sections will look first at suggested reasons why these differentials *do* occur. That is, analysing in the empirical sense. Concluding sections will consider differentials in a normative sense.

[1108] Inter-occupational differentials

This concept refers to wage differences which occur as a result of a difference in the occupation, rather than differences which are primarily caused by the industry, time or region or because of personal differences between the employees. Frequently the concept refers specifically to the skilled-unskilled differential, but this limitation is not a requirement. Some of the perceived reasons for the existence of inter-occupational differentials are given below.

[1109] Supply and demand

As discussed in [1106], differences in supply and demand for different occupations play a significant role in determining wage differentials. The supply of employees will be partly determined by job factors (those proposed by Adam Smith, amongst others) which make some jobs seem more or less attractive. Demand for employees will partly depend on demand for the product or service produced which in time will be affected by competition from substitutes and imports.

Other factors directly affecting supply of labour include all barriers to entry. These include in particular any stipulated qualifications, such as membership of the Society of Accountants, evidence of having served an apprenticeship, and government policies affecting immigration and emigration. Thus, in countries such as the USA, the skilled-unskilled wage differential has narrowed whenever immigration of unskilled labour was significantly reduced (literally making unskilled labour relatively scarce). Most of the factors discussed below (with the exception of custom) will indirectly affect supply and demand.

[1110] Custom

Although market forces of supply and demand have a significant role in determining wage ranges and differentials, evidence over the years suggests that *custom* also plays a major role. Phelps Brown (1962:132) points out:

> For nearly forty years before *The Wealth of Nations* appeared, the predominant rate for the mason and the carpenter in southern England had been two shillings a day; from about 1412 onward it had stood at sixpence a day for a hundred and twenty years. Prices do not behave like that in a stock market or a wheat pit: we cannot suppose that supply and demand came into equilibrium year after year at just the same wage; the sameness must have owed much to custom.

He also points out that custom must have played a major role in determining the skilled-unskilled (craftsman:labourer) differential:

> Between 1412 and 1914 the rate for the mason and the carpenter rose fourteenfold, but at one end of the five centuries as at the other, and during almost all the settled periods in between, it was half as much again as the labourer's. There were local differences in England, and though other countries followed the same rule in some times and places they were far from following it in all. Yet the one simple ratio of three to two appears far too widely and too long for us to suppose that it was reached each time by an equilibration of market forces: it must have been what it was primarily because men were following custom.

Although as Phelps Brown points out, the mason-labourer skill differential was around 150 per cent (or 3:2) for 500 years, customary forces received a major shock with the advent of the First World War. As Marsden (1983) shows, the skill differential in the UK dropped to 120 per cent by 1920, rose to 130 per cent soon after, then dropped to around 115 per cent during the Second World War.

If custom has determined why differentials *do* occur, then clearly custom must also strongly influence normative views. Because it is usual and commonplace, people believe it is right.

[1111] Business cycle

As Gunderson and Riddell (1988:397-8) point out:

> During a recession there is a maintenance of the demand for skilled labour but a decrease in the demand for unskilled workers, and hence a widening of the skill differential.

This occurs because skilled employees represent a larger investment in terms of recruitment costs and training expenses and so are more likely to be retained. Some of these retained skilled employees will be moved down the occupational ladder, increasing the supply of semi-skilled and unskilled, further depressing unskilled wages. During a boom period the reverse occurs, and the differential is narrowed.

[1112] Unions

The effect of union activity can be looked at in two ways:

a. the effect of unions over the years on the skilled-unskilled and other inter-occupational differentials;
b. the union–non-union wage gap.

With respect to (a), the impact of unions has almost certainly varied over time. As the earliest unions comprised craft or skilled employees, initially unions would increase differentials, as the skilled workers would be more effective in preventing wage decreases if not in creating increases. As unions for unskilled employees developed, the effect would never be to narrow differences.

In more recent times, so-called craft unions have accepted into their union more and more unskilled employees. Unskilled employees now outnumber skilled employees in many 'craft' unions. However, the union leadership comes more frequently from skilled workers. Hence at different times unions may work to:

a. widen the differential as that is in the interests of its leaders;
b. or narrow differentials, to please the bulk of the membership.

There are obvious difficulties in determining the non-union wage gap as the two are not independent of each other. If unions are able to negotiate a significant differential, employees will attempt to move from the non-union sector to the union sector, causing a relative shortage of employees in the non-union sector thereby forcing up wages. Unions were therefore responsible for directly increasing wages in the union sector and for indirectly increasing them in the non-union sector. Jarrell and Stanley (1990), using meta-regression analysis to analyse some 114 studies, estimate the differential to be in the order of 10 per cent.

Forth and Mullward (2004:111-2) in a recent study in the UK found:

> Employees covered by a simple recognised union at their workforce enjoyed no wage premium. The union premium was confined to cases where 2 or more unions were recognised by management for pay bargaining.

This would appear to indicate differing objectives between union officials and membership. The union officials are attracted to single-union deals, to increase membership and hence subscription, and hence their own power and salaries, even though the membership do not benefit.

[1113] State intervention

The State plays a major role in determining wages, wage levels and differentials (see Section C and Section D below). Many State interventionist policies *reduce* the skilled-unskilled differential. Minimum wage legislation does so by having a greater positive effect on low unskilled rates. Unemployment benefits and welfare payments also have a disproportionate effect on low, unskilled rates, as they may deter people from accepting such jobs. This reduces the relative supply of unskilled labour. Wage-control legislation frequently grants fixed across-the-board increases. Although these preserve absolute differentials, they reduce percentage differentials.

[1114] Technology and education

As technology becomes more widespread, frequently highly skilled jobs become 'de-skilled' and unskilled jobs require some skill. This has been made possible by the more general availability of education. In most industrialised countries, children from all socio-economic groups have the opportunity (although it is not always taken) for some education.

[1115] Inter-industry differentials

Inter-industry differentials relate to wage differences received by employees doing the same job (for example: driver, typist, maintenance engineer) but in different industries. Suggested reasons for such differentials relate to economic variables. These include:

a. the proportion of labour costs to total costs – if high, wages are lower;
b. whether prices are determined by competition (lower wages) or fixed by agreement;
c. the elasticity of demand for the product (if low elasticity, then wages are higher as they can be passed on as price increases).

Bell and Freeman (1991:287) consider inter-industry differentials in the USA have increased substantially in the period 1970–87 and attribute:

> about 60 percent of the rise of inter-industry wage dispersion to competitive market factors, such as changes in sectoral demographic and occupational mix, and changes in the rewards to workers with different attributes and find that industry productivity trends retain importance in industry wage change equations.

Wage controls by the State would have a dampening effect in situations where differentials are increasing, as mentioned above, or decreasing. However Watts and Mitchell (1990) consider that income policies in Australia have had little impact on the inter-industry wage structure. The impact of unions on inter-industry differentials cannot be generalised other than assuming that non-unionised industries will have a lower wage structure.

[1116] Inter-firm differentials

Inter-firm (sometimes referred to as '*intra*-industry') differentials refer to differences in wages paid to employees doing the same job in the same industry and location, but employed by different firms. These are believed to be caused by differences in the firm's production function, or proportion of labour costs to total costs. In some cases differences in quality (of the labour force, management, equipment) may result in wage differences, with higher quality firms being able to afford to pay higher wages. Also, this may attract an even better quality labour force.

In the past, unions will have definitely *reduced* inter-firm differentials by negotiating industry-wide, regional and in some cases national agreements. The modern emphasis on enterprise bargaining has put an end to this reduction, and differentials may even increase.

[1117] Inter-regional differentials

The main causes of inter-regional differentials are supply and demand, the cost and conditions of living, and competition for labour.

In regions where there is a shortage of labour, for example Alaska, which also has adverse conditions and a high cost of living, wages for labourers will be very high. Similarly, in Silicon Valley in California during the early computer boom there was extremely high demand for labour, again creating a regional differential over other parts of California.

Where there is a high cost of living, for example in London compared to the rest of England, or Auckland compared to the rest of New Zealand, there are usually regional differences in wages to compensate.

Competition for labour also plays a role. Where employers compete primarily with the agricultural sector, as is the case with rural towns, wages are lower than when employers compete primarily with other employers.

Union activity in the past tended to reduce regional differentials when industry or national agreements were negotiated. As with inter-firm differentials, current trends towards enterprise bargaining will probably result in a widening of regional differentials.

[1118] Inter-personal differentials

Inter-personal differentials refer to differences in wages paid to two employees doing the same job in the same firm and location. It is assumed that there is no clear objectively measured difference in performance, as would be the case if employees were on piece-work.

The reasons for the differentials include age. In many countries young people are paid less than adults, even though the youths may have more seniority and experience in the job (having worked from age sixteen to nineteen) than an older employee (just started at twenty-two) and may perform better. Frequently employees are paid more for seniority, or for qualifications. The rationale is presumably that these are reasonable proxies for performance.

The perceived needs of the employees are sometimes a factor. In some countries this is reflected in the net wage, rather than the gross wage, in that employees with more dependents are taxed at a lower rate.

A major cause of inter-personal differentials is often considered to be discrimination, usually on the basis of sex and race. Thus Haberfeld and Shenhav (1990:68) claim:

> Empirical evidence points to a persistent gap of approximately 40% between men's and women's average earnings in the United States, and to a gap of approximately 30% between the earnings of whites and blacks.

Some of the differences may be explained by the fact that male whites have more human capital invested in them – through education and training – and also work in higher paying jobs. However, the same authors go on to claim that:

> The 'unexplained' portion – that is, the portion of the earnings gap that is not explained by human capital and job characteristics – is found to constitute between one-third and two-thirds of this gap depending on the study.

Thus they suggest that sex and race alone account for a wage differential of between ten and twenty-five per cent. State intervention through legislation has reduced, but not eliminated, this discrimination. To an extent these differentials are a function of custom in that those who suffered from them accepted them to much the same degree as those who benefited.

C. Normative Justification for Differentials

[1119] Subjective nature

It must be stressed that all normative justifications for existing, or different wage differentials – those arguing why differentials *should* exist – are totally subjective. There is no intrinsically accurate, or nowadays even generally accepted, answer as to the correct level for any wage or difference between wages. In [1110] it was pointed out that the skilled:unskilled ratio of 3:2 lasted some five centuries. For this to occur, it would appear that most people believed that differential was the one that *should* be in existence, as well as the one that in fact *was* in existence. Since 1914, this customary belief has been severely shaken.

For example, what should be the differential between an average executive and an average factory worker? Bowie (2005:82) points out that in the USA:

> the ratio of the average executive pay to the pay of the average factory worker went from 40 to 1 in 1990 to 400 to 1 in 2002 before falling back to 200 to 1 in 2003.

Is 40 to 1 'right'? Is 200 to 1 'right'? Is 400 to 1 'right'? Was it the market that caused the change, or gross abuse of power?

Although there are many and varied views as to how the correct wage should be found – ranging from the Marxist 'to each according to his needs' (but what are one's needs?) – four in particular deserve mention:

a. market wage;
b. productivity or value of output;
c. nature of work or value of input;
d. State involvement.

[1120] Market wage

As discussed in [706] and [707], the market wage is based on invalid assumptions and does not in fact exist, but is rather a market 'range'. Further, many sections of society believe it can result in an unacceptably low wage level, in contrast to their normative beliefs that all wages should be high enough to be able to be considered a 'living' wage.

There are some distinct advantages, however, in accepting market wages (or ranges) as being the 'right' ones. Basically the argument is: 'That is what the market determines – so it must be right.' Accepting 'the market' as right suggests that there cannot be discrimination; there is therefore no need for Equal Employment Opportunity (EEO) concerns, or the need for wage legislation or wage controls. If women are paid less, then 'the market' has said that that is right. While this view has powerful champions – the New Right and many major employers – it is strongly rejected in many quarters.

[1121] Productivity or value of output

Some believe that wages should reflect the value of the product or service to the employer. Simplistic (and highly inaccurate) economic analysis suggests that this does occur in reality, by claiming wage rates are determined by the marginal productivity of labour.

A difficulty with this concept is that except for some unskilled employees it is frequently very difficult, if not impossible, to actually determine the value of the work done by an employee. Even where employees are producing units of output so that a more accurate measure is possible, the value of the product involves factors other than the employee's work. Thus paying for 'value of work' alone may seem very unfair. A simple example can illustrate:

> Two employees perform virtually identical work for two different firms producing identical products. One firm sells locally, the other has developed a much more profitable export market, with the product selling (after expenses) at 30 percent premium. Should one employee be paid 30 percent more than the other?

Strong advocates of the 'wage for value' concept may agree that the differential in the example is logical and fair. They are probably in a minority.

[1122] Nature of work or value of input

A third viewpoint is that people should be paid for the actual work they do, rather than the value of the output. It is based on the assumption that the worth of the work in a job can be objectively measured. The method used to provide such a measure is usually job evaluation.

Job evaluation can have definite benefits to an organisation. If the general perception in the organisation is that the wage differentials are fundamentally unfair, and this causes grievances, low productivity and low job satisfaction, then a job evaluation exercise may improve matters.

However, as discussed in [316], while job evaluation may be portrayed by consultants or HRM staff as *objective* this is very far from the truth. Job evaluation normally involves:

a. determining which factors should be considered in evaluating the job (a subjective view); and
b. rating each job according to those factors (also subjective).

The subjectivity does not matter if there is general consensus that it is right and fair. What does matter is when anyone believes 'their' viewpoint as to what are the relevant factors and how a job should rate against them has universal support. Job evaluation without general consensus of those involved is a fruitless and frequently expensive exercise.

Critics of current wage differentials – in particular male-female differentials – are sceptical that job evaluation will rectify the problem. In their view, current job evaluation schemes are 'wrong'. As Prue Hyman (1988:241-2) observes:

> It is argued that the skills needed in many female-dominated occupations are undervalued due to the fact that, for historical and social reasons and because experience rather than formal training courses may have been involved in their acquisition, they are seen as extensions to women's work in the home and to their traditional caring roles.

She quotes an Australian study, which asks:

> Why should the physical strength involved in many men's jobs, e.g., labourer, be valued more highly than the manual dexterity involved in many women's jobs, e.g., typist? Why should responsibility for machinery, e.g., mechanic, be considered more valuable than responsibility for people, e.g., nurses?

[1123] State involvement

Except for those who believe wages *should* be determined purely by the market, some State involvement is required. This may be to support a viable union movement, or may be more direct through legislation involving EEO issues (see Chapter Twelve), minimum wage legislation [1127] and wage control [1129] to [1133].

D. Wages and the Law

[1124] Wages and the law

The State, either through its Courts and common law, or through legislation or a combination of the two, influences wages in a number of ways including:

a. the right to wages;
b. the doctrines of indivisibility and substantial employment;
c. the right not to have to accept 'truck' or goods in lieu;
d. minimum wages;
e. anti-discrimination;
f. control of wage levels and increases (discussed in the next section).

[1125] The right to wages

Under common law, employees who perform their side of the wage-work agreement are entitled to their wages. *Martha Goldmining* at 343 states:

> The right to wages depends upon whether the consideration therefore has been performed … it must be ascertained from the contract whether the consideration for the payment of wages is the actual performance of the work, or whether the mere readiness and willingness, if of ability to do so is the consideration.

It follows therefore (*New Zealand Freezing Workers* at 598) that

> employers are not liable to pay workers for periods during which they are not working when the employer cannot be held responsible for the state of affairs. It follows that the workers cannot find a claim for payment of wages for a period during which they were not working; such a state of affairs having been caused by their own actions.

This common law might very well be superseded by legislation, but in the absence of legislation this position is generally accepted.

This common law right to payment can be affected by statutory law. Thus in New Zealand, the Wages Protection Act 1983 strengthened this right. On the other hand, legislation in New Zealand also weakened this common law right by allowing employers to suspend without pay non-striking employees, even though they were 'ready and willing to work'.

[1126] The doctrines of indivisibility and substantial employment

These two common law doctrines apply to situations where contracts of employment are not clear and unambiguous with respect to employees who perform, within any particular payment period, some work which is paid at a higher rate (H) and some which is paid at a lower rate (L). It can be assumed that the employee is 'ready and willing' to work for the full period at H but the employer cannot or chooses not to provide H work for the full period.

For many years in New Zealand, a employee could be subject to two or more different union-management documents (awards or agreements). Since 1991, most employees have been subject to only one contract, or (now) agreement. However, particular agreements may specify H and L rates for different work, without specifying how payment is to be calculated if an employee performs both types of work within one period.

If the payment period is only one hour, then the question as to whether the employee should be paid at the L or the H rate is not significant. However if, as is frequently the case, the payment period is a week, then the question is of great significance. Unfortunately the two doctrines give different answers.

The *doctrine of indivisibility* has been generally accepted as paramount for many years. As Fraser J. puts it in *Masterton* (1921):

> Where there is a provision in an award fixing a minimum wage for any class of worker, whether such wage is a daily or a weekly wage, the rule is clear that if a worker on any day or in any week, as the case may be, is employed in the work specified for any class of worker for whom a higher wage has been fixed, he must be paid that higher wage for the day or the week, not-withstanding that during the greater part of that day or week he may have been employed at lower-grade work. This is the effect of a number of decisions of this Court.

Thus, if a contract states that all employees are employed by the week and that office staff are to be paid a minimum of $470 per week and shop assistants a minimum of $440 per week, then, according to the doctrine of indivisibility, an employee who works partly as a shop assistant and partly in the office should be paid $470 per week.

On *normative* grounds, the question is whether employees who had worked in the office for four and a half days, and completed their office work and went and helped out in the shop for the busy period on Friday, should receive a *reduction* in wages when they are 'shop assistants'? On the other hand, if they helped in the office for two hours on Monday morning, then worked in the shop for the rest of the week, should they be paid $470 while other shop assistants receive $440?

The *doctrine of substantial employment* states that where a contract of employment has conflicting rates of pay, employees should be paid the rate which reflects that under which they are employed for the substantial part of the period.

These two doctrines clearly conflict, and in New Zealand there have been no binding judgements made to establish common law. However, guidelines established over half a century ago by Cornish J., in *International Paints* have been generally accepted over the years:

> The doctrine of substantiality
> (A) has been applied in cases where the lesser services – i.e., those that occupy 'by far the lesser part' of the worker's working time have been:
>
> (a) so slight in volume as to fall within the principle of *de minimis*; or
> (b) reasonably incidental to the main work; or
> (c) casual, discontinuous, or occasional, and not regular; or
> (d) done in conditions of emergency.

[1127] Minimum wage legislation

In many societies, concern that the market range of wages at the lower end is in fact 'too low' has led the State to pass minimum wage legislation. Simplistic economic theory would suggest that this would reduce employment and indeed some research suggests that is so, but not conclusively.

Raising wages has two effects:

a. it directly reduces demand for labour;
b. it increases wages, which increases demand for goods and services, which indirectly increases demand for labour.

It appears that in practice the effects of (b) can virtually counter the negative effects of (a).

Not surprisingly the New Right oppose minimum wage legislation, claiming, again not surprisingly, that their opposition is altruistic. Thus the NZBR claims (1990:17):

> Minimum wages generate unemployment by reducing the number of jobs that employers are willing or able to offer. Given the existence of the social welfare system, it is difficult to justify the existence of minimum wage legislation on equity grounds.

It may be true that some employment is lost when organisations cannot afford to pay the State minimum wages. In many instances, the minimum wage is set so low that it is highly debatable if this is so. Certainly it is probable that in New Zealand the minimum wage has little effect on employment, given that many employees are financially better off on unemployment benefits than on the minimum wage. This is accepted by the NZBR (1990), who considers the unemployment benefit discourages the unemployed from working.

[1128] Anti-discrimination legislation

In [1118] above, the role of legislation in reducing differentials on the basis of sex and race were discussed. It is irrefutable that particularly in the absence of anti-discriminatory legislation – and often even with such legislation – the female wage is lower than the male.

E. Incomes Policies (Wage Controls)

[1129] The meaning of incomes policy

The term 'incomes policy' is ambiguous, indeed it can have so many meanings that theoretically it could be regarded as meaningless. This arises from the fact that every government has an incomes policy at all times since any economic action will affect incomes to some degree and a policy of non-interference is just as much a policy as one of interference. However, by tacit convention, the term is generally used to suggest a specific policy directly affecting occasionally all, but usually only some, incomes. Such policies include setting minimum levels of wages, restricting increases in wages and occasionally other incomes, adjusting wages and other incomes, and influencing relativities. Thus the term 'wage control' is more appropriate.

[1130] The case for incomes policies

The justification for an incomes policy, specifically one aimed at restricting wage increases, rests on the belief that the policy will have a significant effect on price inflation. The case is dependent in effect on a number of assumptions. These are:

1. price inflation is a social evil;
2. wage increases are a major cause (if not *the* major cause) of price inflation;
3. a reduction in the rate of wage increases is one of the most effective ways (if not *the* most effective way) to reduce price inflation;
4. an incomes policy is an effective means of restricting wage increases and therefore is an effective means of reducing price inflation.

To a degree the same argument and assumptions are also applied, with 'unemployment' being substituted for 'price inflation.'

[1131] Price inflation

The assumption that price inflation is a social evil is widely held and reasonably easy to justify. It seriously affects those on fixed incomes, erodes savings, pensions and insurance policies. (On the other hand it helps property speculators become very rich.) If the erosion is prevented by 'inflation proofing' savings and linking pensions to the cost of living, it will fuel more inflation. The fact that price inflation tends to favour borrowers at the expense of lenders seems to run against the Protestant ethic. Price inflation can also affect trading countries if the domestic rate of inflation is greater than that of the trading parties by making exports uncompetitive.

However, governments are probably most concerned about price inflation because it is such an irritant to consumers, so much that it has become a major voting issue. Consumers usually believe price inflation makes them worse off, even if their real take-home income is unchanged, because price increases occur continuously while wage increases usually occur only once or twice a year. In fact, consumers are generally worse off during times of high price inflation even if their wage increases are equal or slightly greater, because of the phenomenon of 'fiscal drag'. This is brought about by the fact that tax scales are rarely if ever tied to, for example, the average wage, but remain fixed. Hence, if tax scales are progressive then inflationary increases in wages will put the taxpayer into a higher tax bracket.

The ultimate danger of price inflation is that it can eventually run wild, producing a collapse in confidence in the nation's currency, which in turn leads to a collapse in the whole economic system of the country. Notable examples are Germany after the First World War and Mainland China directly after the Second World War.

The second assumption is far harder to justify. Price inflation is still popularly considered to be either from 'demand-pull' or from 'cost-push'. A third type of inflation is now generally accepted, 'stagflation' which occurs when demand is falling and unemployment rising. Although 'stagflation' has only recently gained widespread acceptance, it was described over forty years ago. The Conference on Economic Progress (1959:43) noted that

> an inadequate level of economic growth in the long run, due to periods of stagnation and recession, was one of the main causes of 'the new inflation'. At the same time, 'the new inflation' contributed to stagnation and recession and thus to the low average rate of economic growth over the years. Low growth and inflation have fed upon each other.

The demand-pull theory is that excess demand over supply pulls up prices. It can only be a part explanation as it does not explain what causes the excess demand. Increases in money supply have a major influence on the level of demand but other factors are involved. These include the *expectation* of price inflation prompting panic purchasing, increases in income, and increases in credit. The cost-push hypothesis is that increases in costs (and primarily *wages* costs) faced by businesses cause them to increase their prices to compensate. If there is sufficient demand for the businesses to sell the same quantity, there will be price inflation. If there is insufficient demand for the goods or services at the higher price, there will be excess capacity, resulting in both price inflation and unemployment.

The matter is further complicated by the fact that prices of goods are often costs to other businesses. Hence demand-pull on prices leading to price inflation will result in cost-push inflation to another sector. There are also, of course, other possible causes of price inflation. One possibility is that businesses simply increase prices in order to increase the levels of their profits. If the demand is inelastic, then profits will rise after a price increase.

Hence there is serious doubt that wage increases can be claimed to be the major cause of price inflation, casting doubt on the second fundamental assumption, and hence on the third and fourth.

[1132] Unemployment

The case for an incomes policy because of its beneficial effect on unemployment is also hard to sustain. Just as with price inflation, the first fundamental assumption – that unemployment is a social evil – is generally accepted. Only a minority favour unemployment both as a ready supply of labour if demand increases and because of the motivational effect a pool of unemployed may have on the workforce. The majority accept that it causes personal hardship, suffering and often degradation and from the national point of view is also a gross waste of resources.

However, the theory that wage increases are a universal cause of unemployment is open to serious question. This view stemmed from the famous article by Phillips (1958) based on UK data from 1861–1957, in which he estimated there was a negative relationship between changes in aggregate money wages and unemployment. It was assumed the so-called 'Phillips Curve' was accurate. Paish (1969:233) has observed that 'Dicks-Mireaux and Dow conclude that a change of 1 per cent in excess demand (or roughly, of unemployment) is associated with an increase or decrease in the percentage

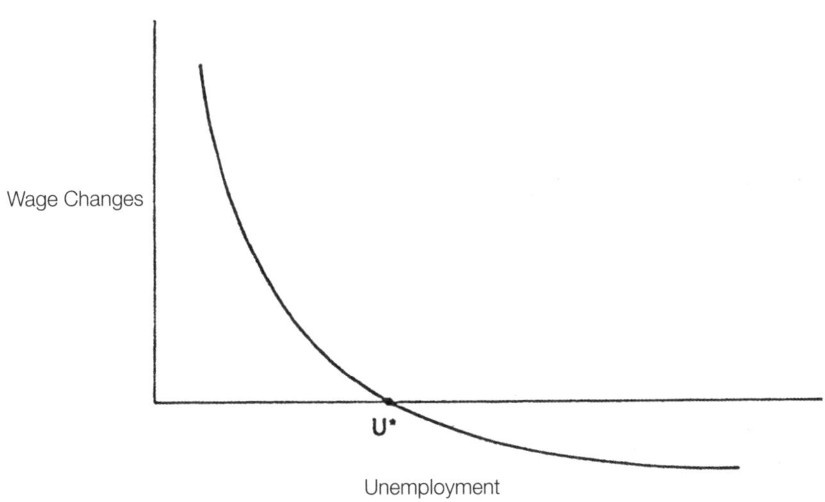

Figure 11.1. Phillips Curve

rate of wage-rate change of 3.5 per cent.' However, the relationship between inflation and unemployment became considerably blurred through the 1970s, with rising unemployment existing with rising inflation.

Cullen (1985:302) reports that in the USA:

> Union wage settlements, unemployment, and price increases struck a precarious balance during the stagflation years of the 1970s. During that decade wage increases averaged 6.8 percent a year, unemployment averaged 6.1 percent, and annual price increases averaged 7.1 percent. In the chaotic years beginning with 1980, wage increases at first advanced with inflation and then collapsed under the weight of the sharp rise in unemployment in 1982.

Gunderson and Riddell (1988:567) point out that later theorists have emphasised

> the role of inflationary expectations in the wage determination process. If wages are adjusted simply to eliminate the *current* amount of excess labour demand or supply, then the unemployment rate (or some other measure of excess demand) may be the sole determinant of wage changes. However, because wages are set or negotiated periodically, employers and employees look not only at current conditions but at the conditions *expected to prevail* during the remainder of the wage contract (or period for which the wage is set). This 'forward-looking' aspect provides the rationale for including the expected inflation variable.

The decision to employ labour is made taking into account a large number of factors. These include basic confidence in the economy, relative costs of labour and machinery, and the demand for the product or service. In turn, demand for goods and services depends on the spending power of the consumers (both at home and overseas) and the price of the goods and services. It is clear therefore that restricting wages should in theory have both positive and negative effects on unemployment.

Again, as with the argument that incomes policies will reduce price inflation, there remains the added problem that, even if the incomes policy could be demonstrated to have the intended effect on unemployment, when it breaks down, or is removed, the resulting wage-price explosion should then work in reverse, undoing any benefit that had been achieved. Conversely, of course, if the policy has no effect then the removal should have no effect.

[1133] Problems in implementing incomes policies

The major problem with incomes policies is the difficulty in enforcing them. If both employers and unions want wage increases then it is virtually impossible for the government to prevent such increases as it is unlikely they could even be detected. Where incentive schemes exist, rates can be quietly renegotiated. If straight hourly rates are paid, then additional allowances can be agreed.

When employers' demand for labour is reduced so that employers are not willing parties to the breaching of the incomes policy, the policy is still difficult to enforce. If employees and unions do not accept the restrictions and strike to affect a breach of the policy, the government is faced with ignoring the breach or has to impose penalties either on the unions and employees or the employers. Penalising strikers is difficult under any circumstances and if they were striking merely to maintain their standard of living, opposition to the penalties is likely to be so fierce as to destroy the policy. Penalising employers would probably produce less violent reaction, although many would consider it unfair.

Thus, to ensure the incomes policy is not destroyed by the major actors in the employment relations system, a reasonable degree of support for the policy must be obtained from employers, unions and employees. It must either impose very moderate restrictions or be seen as both fair and necessary.

Chapter Twelve

Equal Employment Opportunities

A. Introduction

[1201] What is meant by EEO?

Figure 12.1. 'Fair' selection? Source: EEO Trust (1992:8)

According to the New Zealand EEO Trust (1992:7), EEO means:

> eliminating barriers to ensure that all potential employees are considered for the employment of their choice, and that they have the chance to perform to their maximum … EEO is the workplace solution used internationally to deal with the problems unfair discrimination causes.

This same document uses a cartoon (see Figure 12.1) presumably to illustrate how 'fair' can also be unfair. At one level, the cartoon gives a simple message. If the test has nothing to do with the job, simply allowing everyone to compete may well be unfair. Similarly Chruden and Sherman (1980:129) reported that in the USA at that time

> Perhaps the ultimate in irrelevant requirements is to be found in one fire department that is alleged to have required each candidate to have one working testicle!

This selection requirement not only discriminates against female applicants, but if taken literally ('one', not 'at least one') it would also cause considerable consternation for the vast majority of male applicants.

The cartoon at a deeper level also illustrates a potential problem with EEO. If the job for which the animals were seeking selection was to work for Parks and Gardens retrieving lost kites from trees, the selection test is eminently suitable. It is possible that at least some of the failed applicants would blame 'discrimination' rather than their own inadequacies for the failure to get the job.

Jewson and Mason (1986:313-5) suggest that there are two conceptions of EEO – liberal and radical. The liberal conforms with the EEO Trust definition given above and argues that in principle EEO exists 'when all individuals are enabled freely and equally to compete for social rewards.' The radical view, however, 'is concerned primarily with the outcome of the contest rather than with the rules of the game.' From the radical viewpoint, EEO means, in effect, Equal Employment *Outcomes*, rather than *Opportunities*. Their research involved a UK city council, where council offices had a liberal concept and introduced fair promotion procedures, but the city councillors had a radical concept. Given the 'relatively low rates of application for promotion from black and female employees, as well as their relatively low levels of qualification', there was no dramatic increase in women and blacks at higher levels. This prompted councillors to threaten officers that their careers were on the line if they did not produce results. The result (1986:327)

> added force to existing suspicions, harboured by some officials, that councillors intended the equal opportunities policy to say one thing and do another – in effect to appear to be liberal and actually be radical. Thus their belief that the policy was an exercise in bad faith was reinforced. For councillors, this reaction confirmed their suspicions that many officers were covert racists and sexists.

[1202] EEO a recent phenomenon

While *discrimination* with respect to employment against various groups in society has undoubtedly been occurring for centuries, EEO as a deliberate concept is of recent origin. The International Labour Organisation (ILO) led the way. Vogel-Polsky (1985:255) claims:

> Equality of treatment for men and women in employment was advocated by the ILO in 1951 when the principle of 'equal remuneration for men and women workers for work of equal value' was set forth in the Equal Remuneration Convention, 1951 (No. 100), which has been ratified by 105 States. The Discrimination

(Employment and Occupation) Convention, 1958 (No. 111), extended the scope of equal treatment to all forms of discrimination in employment.

Years passed, however, before governments began – very slowly – to adopt the legislation and set up the machinery to implement these Conventions.

Laws were passed in various countries through the 1960s and 1970s and are being continually updated. Thus in the USA there was the Equal Pay Act 1963 and the Civil Rights Act 1964, in the UK the Sex Discrimination Act 1975 and the Race Relations Act 1976 and in New Zealand the Race Relations Act 1971, Equal Pay Act 1972 and Human Rights Commission Act 1977.

Some anti-discrimination laws have been introduced for unusual reasons. The USA Civil Rights Act 1964 was originally concerned only with racial discrimination. Southern State senators who opposed the Act realised that direct opposition to the Act would not be successful. They introduced an amendment, Title VII, with penalties for sexual discrimination, in the belief that although a majority would be reluctant to oppose anti-racial discrimination legislation, equally they would not accept anti-sexual discrimination legislation. The Southern senators misjudged and their amendment was included in the Act which was passed. Women in the USA owe anti-discrimination laws to the bigots not the liberals.

[1203] Coverage of EEO

With progressive legislation, more and more groups became covered by EEO legislation. For example, the New Zealand Human Rights Act 1993 s.21(1) prohibits as grounds for discrimination (but with certain specified exceptions):

a. sex, which includes pregnancy and childbirth;
b. marital status;
c. religious belief;
d. ethical belief;
e. colour;
f. race;
g. ethnic or national origins;
h. disability, which means –
   physical disability, physical or psychiatric illness, intellectual or psychological disability, reliance on a guide dog, wheelchair, or other remedial means: the presence in the body of organisms capable of causing illness;
i. age;
j. political opinion;
k. employment status;
l. family status;
m. sexual orientation.

Not surprisingly, the few groups outside EEO coverage expect inclusion. For example, conventional wisdom (see Parkes, 1987) has it that obesity creates health and work problems. Notwithstanding, McEvoy (1992:14) takes up the case for the obese and quotes an 'obesity specialist' who claims:

> The extent to which overweight people have difficulty obtaining work goes far beyond [that] which can be justified by medical data and must be due to discrimination … If sex, age, race, national origin, and religion cannot be legitimately used to bar people from employment opportunities, why should bias against the obese be allowed to stand?

[1204] Emphasis in this chapter

EEO issues cover all groups facing discrimination and some attention will be paid to a number of these. This section will concentrate on one group in particular – women – for three reasons:

a. of all the groups facing discrimination, women are by far the largest. Indeed they are not a minority in society but are a majority;
b. compared to the next large group discriminated against – racial minorities – women are making much less progress. In an international study Sloane and Jain (1990:228) consider that evidence

   > supports the view that there has been a substantial improvement in the relative position of non-white workers, particularly of non-white women. Surprisingly, in view of the latter fact, the earnings of white women have improved relatively little.

   They consider this is possibly due to the fact that in the countries they studied (USA, UK and Canada), 'non-white have a much greater propensity to bring claims than have women.'
c. Labour market changes. As Jonung and Persson (1993:260) observe:

   > The 1970s and 1980s witnessed an unprecedented increase in the labour force participation rates of women. All through the industrialised world an increasing proportion of women allocated more of their time to market work.

B. Women

[1205] Major EEO issues for women

The major EEO issues include:

a. pay;
b. access to job and promotion opportunities;
c. work places free from sexual harassment;
d. union support;
e. general responsibilities.

[1206] EEO – pay

Initially, the issue was 'equal pay for equal work' when organisations, including the Public Service, would have a male rate for the job and a (lower) female rate.

Legislation through the 1970s made such overt discrimination illegal, but still the average female wage is lower than the average male wage. In general this is seen as the issue now being 'comparable pay for comparable worth,' access to jobs and promotion opportunities.

The problems of achieving consensus with respect to comparable pay for comparable worth are considerable, if not insurmountable. The concept itself presupposes:

a. that wages *should* be (and presumably the State will ensure that they *will* be) set according to 'worth.' As discussed in [1119] to [1123] there are a variety of views as to what factors should, let alone do, determine wages. 'Worth' is by no means generally accepted;
b. assuming the problems in (a) are overcome (or ignored) the concept presupposes that comparable worth can be measured to general satisfaction. Again it has been stressed that job evaluation is a *subjective* exercise. The probability of general acceptance of job evaluation is remote.

The practical difficulties of an individual actually winning have been highlighted by Singh (1994), concerning a British case. Dr Enderby, one of a group of speech therapists (predominantly female), claimed her work was of comparable value to that of pharmacists and clinical psychologists (predominantly male) who were paid substantially more. She lost her case at the Industrial Tribunal and the Employment Appeal Tribunal. It then went to the UK Court of Appeal who referred it to the European Court of Justice (ECJ). Dr Enderby enjoyed a sort of victory at the ECJ in that it reversed the Employment Appeal Tribunal's ruling. The question of 'comparable worth' has yet to be even considered. Her employer had won the case up to the ECJ purely on the argument that, *regardless* of worth, they had not discriminated since pay was set by collective bargaining which was non-discriminatory. The ECJ disagreed and pointed out (Singh 1994:152-3):

> if an employer could rely on the absence of discrimination within each of the collective bargaining processes taken separately as sufficient justification for the difference in pay, he could easily circumvent the principle of equal pay for work of equal value by using separate bargaining processes.

However, the ECJ then gave a loophole by conceding that:

> The state of the employment market, which may lead an employer to increase the pay of a particular job in order to attract candidates, may constitute an objectively justified economic ground within the meaning of the case law cited above.

For Dr Enderby to enjoy an EEO-based increase in salary she will first have to disprove the supply and demand argument, and then prove that her job is of comparable value. (The German government submitted its view to ECJ that the job of speech therapist and that of pharmacist were too dissimilar to even be considered comparable.)

Hence change is only likely if women move out of 'women's jobs' into so-called 'men's jobs' in sufficient numbers to significantly influence supply and demand.

[1207] Access to jobs and promotion

Until the 1970s, in many industrialised countries there were overt discriminatory barriers preventing women (and racial minorities) from entering certain jobs and from being promoted beyond a certain point. In general, overt discrimination has now disappeared, but covert discrimination remains in some levels and to some degree, probably as a result of residual discriminatory attitudes. These include views such as: women are not as committed as men to their jobs; in the case of a married couple with sick children, the mother is more likely to take time off than the father; women are less likely than men to see a job as a lifetime career. Clearly in any individual case these views may be totally false.

It is possible, however, that a major factor preventing greater gender equality is that sufficient numbers of women are not applying for the jobs or the promotions. This will be due first to the real (or perceived) discrimination mentioned above, partly to insufficient home support, but also to a great extent it indicates an attitude *by* women. Women have achieved positions of tremendous power in all spheres. For example, women have reached the top in the political sphere across the world – Jenny Shipley and Helen Clark in New Zealand, Margaret Thatcher in the UK, Hilary Clinton in the USA, along with notable women politicians in Sri Lanka, India, Israel and Pakistan. In general, these women have been somewhat solitary figures and there have not been noticeable numbers of women following and emulating these role models. In the work environment, the position is similar. In the early part of the twenty-first century, New Zealand seems to have made giant steps towards having women in top positions: Prime Minister, Chief Justice, Speaker of the House, Attorney General, CEO of Telecom.

[1208] Work environments free from sexual harassment

While the guilty parties in sexual harassment cases can be both male and female, as can the victims, in the overwhelming majority of cases the perpetrator is a male and the victim a female. Sexual harassment can therefore be differentiated from normal boorish or criminal behaviour, and seen as a barrier to women participating fully in employment. If women but not men fear harassment, if they enter certain jobs, or if they assert themselves and apply for promotion, this is a form of discrimination.

Wells and Kracher (1993:423) point out there are two generally recognised forms of sexual harassment:

> *Quid pro quo* sexual harassment (where) the victim is promised an employment benefit or advantage in return for a sexual favour or is denied continued employment or some advantage for refusing to participate in sex; (and) hostile environment

> sexual harassment (where) an employee's work performance suffers because sex-related behaviours in the work place create an intolerable work environment.

To these two forms should be added a third: unwanted sexual attention. This includes persistent requests for dates, touching, sexually related comments, up to criminal acts such as sexual assaults.

The USA, probably because of numbers rather than necessarily because American males are more prone to be harassers, provides much of the data. Hauck and Pearce (1992) studied 100 arbitration awards concerning sexual harassment, with 72 per cent being between co-workers and involving lewd language or gestures.

It is however impossible to state the extent of sexual harassment, as it is widely accepted that many victims do not report the incidents. A further problem is the enormous range of behaviours which can be classified as sexual harassment, ranging from the occasional use of lewd language to blackmail and rape. At the lower end of the range, it is subjective as to whether the behaviour is offensive at all, and then, if it is offensive, whether it should be deemed merely irritating or sexual harassment. Research shows that the view of the average male and average female differs as to whether a situation (calenders portraying nudes or semi-nudes) or incidents (dirty jokes) or behaviours should be deemed acceptable or not. Furthermore, Wells and Kracher (1993:429) report:

> One survey uncovered a stunning dichotomy between men and women: 75 per cent of male respondents would be flattered by sexual advances in the workplace; 75 per cent of females would be offended.

Given male-female differences in attitudes, it is highly significant whether Courts assess behaviour from the perspective of:

a. a reasonable person (i.e., midway male-female);
b. a reasonable offender (male); or
c. a reasonable victim (female).

Wells and Kracher (1993:425) report that in the USA the Appeal Court has overruled a Federal Court who took the perspective of 'a reasonable person.' The Appeal Court stated 'what does or does not constitute sexual harassment can only be determined by viewing the alleged harassing acts from the perspective of a reasonable victim.'

Legislation will not prevent sexual harassment, but can increase the costs to employers of not preventing it, and can make more people aware that some behaviours are unacceptable – at least to sections of the workforce.

[1209] Union support

Early unions were in the most case established by men. There is absolutely no evidence that they were established by men for the betterment of all men and to the detriment of all women. They were formed, for example, by certain groups for the betterment of those certain groups. As discussed in [427], women were not craft workers and instead worked in occupations which were more difficult to unionise. Early women's unions, such as the Dunedin Tailoresses Union formed in the 1890s, often relied on male support for early leadership and administration.

Feminists attack history, blaming it for propagating what they claim is the myth that women were difficult to organise and were too timid or just not interested. Thus Forrest (1993:418-9) proclaims:

> Canadian women have been organising unions for as long as unions have been organised. When cobbled together the story of women's activism is impressive. Women *were* there: they organised unions, they went on strike, they walked the picket line, and they fought with strikebreakers.

Unions for the great part have pursued those policies considered important by the majority of their members. For most unions, pay, conditions and security are by far the most important issues.

As these conditions are improved, unions with higher percentages of women may pursue so-called women's issues. When they do, it may be for a variety of motives, or their motives may be misconstrued. Not surprisingly Forrest (1993:423) sees a conspiracy behind moves for equal pay:

> Though progressive on its face, 'equal pay for equal work' was initially adopted by unions chiefly as a way of discouraging the employment of women on jobs traditionally performed by men, most importantly, during the two world wars.

Cockburn (1989:216) in an actual study discovered 'resentment between those (women) with dependents and those without.' She also found self-interest rife in other spheres, and that women and men of ethnic minorities

> expressed deeply prejudiced views about homosexuals and were opposed to any addition of sexual orientation to the equality policy.

Given that matters such as pay equity, childcare facilities, maternity leave provisions (or even parental leave provisions) advantage only a section of almost any union and may disadvantage another section, it is unlikely these issues will receive great support. Even when unions *are* run by women, these issues are not considered paramount. Dorgan and Grieco (1993:157) studied women who had become general secretaries of unions in the UK. Only five out of seventy-eight general secretaries were women at the time of their research (and by the time of writing three had been replaced by men). They found these women placed much more emphasis on 'women's issues' but point out:

> it must be stressed that women general secretaries do not want women's issues placed *at the top* of the agenda – they would rather see terms, conditions, pay, and other matters, as usual, at the top of the agenda.

Chapter Thirteen

Participation

A. Introduction

[1301] Range of expressions

This chapter has been entitled 'Participation'. There are, however, numerous expressions which could have been selected and which would imply something similar. These include:

a. employee involvement;
b. worker involvement;
c. quality of working life;
d. worker participation in management;
e. industrial democracy;
f. worker control;
g. self-management.

The particular expression used can often indicate a personal preference for the extent of the participation. Certainly one would expect someone discussing 'employee involvement' to have a very different view as to what would be ideal to someone discussing 'worker control' or 'self-management'.

The expressions all reflect a different situation to that of a totally subservient employee receiving orders and having no power to influence the decisions on which the orders were based. However, employee involvement could simply involve employees being informed in advance of decisions or, with an increased level of involvement, being asked for their views. The term employee, rather than worker, often reflects the view that having senior managers involved in decision-making is employee involvement – this may appear slightly ludicrous when discussing 'worker' involvement or participation. At the other extreme, worker control suggests that the bottom stratum makes all the decisions.

The expression 'participation' was chosen for a number of reasons, the main one being that, although it is not currently the most popular term, it has been around for many years.

[1302] Defining participation

In everyday usage, participation refers to taking part in, or having a share in something. In employment relations, it refers to employees taking part or having a share in either, or both of:

a. profits and ownership;
b. decision-making.

There is an immense range of possibilities, all of which involve 'employee participation'. 'Employee' can refer to all employees or certain employees only, and some participation schemes relate only to senior managers. 'Participation' can be direct or by representative, and there are various *levels* of participation. For example, Gill (1993:26) found that in a survey of all twelve member States of the European Community participation varied:

a. no involvement: management plans and implements new technologies without any kind of employee representative involvement whatsoever;
b. information: management informs employees or their representatives in writing or at joint meetings;
c. consultation: joint committees are set up in which employees' representatives are not only given information by the management, but can also state their opinions and, in the case of differing views, can expect management to explain its reasoning;
d. negotiation: contractually binding conclusions which are worked out in joint negotiating committees at works level or at a higher level;
e. joint decision-making: employees' representatives have the right of veto. Decisions require the agreement of both parties.

B. Participation in Ownership and Profits

[1303] Shareholding

Shareholding gives employees an opportunity to benefit indirectly from increased profits through dividends and the increased value of shares. Technically, shareholding can be considered 'employee ownership' though obviously if the percentage of shares owned is small there is no *real* ownership or power to influence management decisions. Employees may own either tradeable shares, purchased independently of the organisation, or the organisation may make them available at discount. Employee support for shareholding is not great and this is illustrated by the fact that in most cases they have to be bribed to buy shares, either by being given 'buying privileges' for owning the shares, or by a straight monetary bribe as when shares are discounted down or there is an interest-free loan. A study of such schemes in New Zealand by Firth *et al* (1987) reveals:

> On average, employers typically offered shares at considerable discounts relative to current market prices. The mean purchase price discount at issuance was 24 percent.

In the USA these schemes are referred to as ESOPs (Employee Stock Ownership Plans). In theory as Aitken and Wood (1989:147) state, ESOPs are

> a means of improving organisational productivity and worker morale, a way of raising capital and dispersing ownership within capitalist societies, and as a form of participation in the affairs of the company that could, in theory, lead to greater power equalisation between managers and workers.

However, in practice, as Kassalow (1988:581) notes:

> ESOPs commonly develop in companies encountering economic difficulties, but they are by no means confined to such firms.

[1304] Profit-sharing

Profit-sharing occurs indirectly through shareholding – assuming dividends are paid – and can occur directly through a profit-share scheme. Some profit-share schemes were developed along the lines of Scanlon Plans (see [318]) and incorporate productivity committees or quality circles. Others simply involve a payout of profits, either as a percentage of total profits, or as a percentage above a certain amount.

Some organisations introduce profit-sharing either as a motivational tool, or those with a genuine unitarist belief may do so from a normative belief that it is 'right' for all in 'the team' to share. As a motivational device, profit-sharing has considerable drawbacks. First, the payout is only partly and very indirectly related to employee effort and performance. Second, there is a considerable time lapse between effort and payout, which will reduce any motivational impact.

In other cases organisations, as Kassalow (1988) observes, introduce profit-sharing – as with shareholding – only when in economic difficulty.

C. Participation in Decision-making

[1305] Forms of participation in decision-making

Participation can be differentiated into direct and indirect (that is, by representation), or indeed between formal and informal schemes. Thus, forms of participation include:

1. Informal

a. communication and discussion (direct participation);
b. 'defaulting' management (direct participation).

2. Formal

a. collective bargaining (by representation);
b. works councils (by representation);
c. joint management (by representation);
d. self management (by representation);
e. worker ownership (by representation);

f. (semi)-autonomous work groups (direct participation);
g. quality circles (also 'EI') (by (widespread) representation);
h. Total Quality Management (TQM) (direct participation).

[1306] Informal participation

Whenever communication and discussion occurs between different levels in the organisational hierarchy, then some degree of participation is possible. In small organisations such communication, although informal, frequently occurs and employees may influence quite a wide variety of management decisions, and often to a considerable degree. As with most participation schemes, there is no guarantee the participation will result in a different decision. With this type of participation there is also no guarantee that even the opportunity will be presented regularly.

In some cases, usually because of incompetence, management has in effect 'defaulted' and isn't making the usual management decisions. Under this situation employees make management decisions. The end result is very often to all intents and purposes, a semi-autonomous work group. However, such a group is not formalised nor was it formed by a deliberate decision.

[1307] Bargaining and participation

Through collective bargaining, and to a much lesser extent individual bargaining, employees do participate in decisions which affect them, and also influence profits, even if only to a slight extent.

Since Chapter Seven was devoted to bargaining, there will not be further discussion except simply to emphasise that to date bargaining has been the most effective form of employee participation.

[1308] Works councils

Internationally, until the 1980s, works councils were the most common type of 'popular' participative scheme. The council usually comprises managerial representatives from all levels and employee representatives from different departments. The extent to which the representatives are able to participate in decision-making can vary widely from the point where they simply hear about future decisions to ones where they can give their views, to the situation where the council has actual decision-making power, with the employee representatives being in the minority, or having a totally equal or even a majority vote.

The fact that a works council exists purely to assist communication or alternatively the fact that it has total decision-making power does not make the council a success or failure. Success, from the point of view of any of the parties in employment relations, depends on how the scheme helps the party reach its objectives.

Previously Yugoslavia was renowned for having well-developed participation schemes. As described by Kolaja (1965) in the 1960s, the average Yugoslav company workforce elected a works council which had from 15 to 120 members. This council elected a management board of from three to eleven members. The works council, together with the local people's committee, appointed the managing director and executive directors of the company. The works council met monthly, and approved production and marketing plans, allocated profits, either for distribution or investment, and was responsible for the hiring and promotion of employees. The management board met more frequently, at least weekly, and its general responsibility was the day-to-day supervision of the management of the company. The board reported to the works council, and supervised the director and his staff. The duties of the director were to implement the decision of the works council, which had a similar role to a New Zealand board of directors.

In theory (Emery and Thorsrud, 1969:34), 'exercise of initiative and decision-making are the prerogative of the workers' council and the management board of a company.' In practice, Kolaja found that, while the ordinary worker member of the council and board made nearly seventy per cent of all statements, they made a mere sixteen per cent of all decisions made by the board, and seven per cent of those made by the council. The director and, to a lesser extent, his staff, who were all *ex-officio* members of both bodies, made the decisions. By the 1970s, financial institutions with money invested in Yugoslav industry were taking an increasing share of managerial decision-making and by the 1980s there was not even the illusion of employee decision-making.

Works councils re-emerged as a new topic of interest and research in the late 1990s in Europe as a result of the adoption in September 1996 of the European Works Council (EWC) Directive. Nakano (1999:307) considers that 'by the end of 1998, roughly 540 EWCs had been established.'

Royle (1999) describes the McDonald's EWC. It would appear that little is changing in practice. The EWC was not created because rank and file employees demanded it, or not created because management thought it would be useful, but simply because the directive required it. The major objective is therefore simply to fulfil a legal obligation.

In New Zealand the *Health and Safety in Employment Act* 1992 requires occupational health and safety committees. These may be considered by respondents in surveys to be equivalent to works councils. Certainly recent research by Haynes, Boxall and Macky (2005) indicate a large percentage of firms have some sort of committee varying from twenty-eight per cent of very small firms to sixty to seventy per cent or large firms. They found that 'consistent with the British and Australian experience, joint consultation is more likely to be found in unionised [66 per cent] than non union [36.8 per cent] workforces' (p.239).

[1309] Joint management

In practice, joint management refers to participation by employees' representatives in the highest level of management, namely the board of directors. In some instances they are appointed, as for example by the government, in the case of nationalised industries in the UK. Usually employee representatives on a board of directors will be in a minority. Even if there is apparent parity, usually the shareholder directors appoint the chairman who has the casting vote.

The Yugoslav experiment also involved joint management as does the situation in Germany. The then West Germany introduced 'co-determination' in 1952 to coal and steel industries. Gradually co-determination was extended to other industries and by 1978 the coverage was extensive. See Table 13.1 below.

Co-determination incorporates three levels of participation:

a. Works council;
b. Management board – there are at least three members on this board, jointly responsible for managing the company. One of the members is the labour director, almost always a former trade union official, appointed by the supervisory board;
c. Supervisory board – this board is equivalent to a New Zealand board of directors. There are equal numbers of shareholder representatives and employee representatives. These latter are appointed by the works council and by the trade union.

The extent to which the average German employee actually participates in managerial decision-making is unclear. To a great extent work councils in Germany operate in council unions – since German unions themselves are highly centralised.

Table 13.1. Co-determination coverage 1978

Enterprises	Employee Representation	Employee Coverage
Coalmining, iron and steel	Full parity in supervisory boards; labour director on managing board; works councils	0.6 million
Large joint-stock companies with more than 2,000 employees	Quasi-parity in supervisory boards; works councils	4.1 million
Smaller joint-stock companies	One-third of supervisory board seats; works councils	0.9 million
Other private enterprises with five or more employees	Works councils	9.4 million
Public service	Staff councils	3.6 million
Private enterprises with fewer than five employees	No institutionalised employee representation	3.0 million

Source: Furstenberg (1984:617)

Jacobi *et al* (1992:243-5) claim:

> In general, works councils' participation rights are strong in relation to social policy; weaker in the case of personnel issues; and weaker still in financial and economic matters. In other words, the potential for works council intervention in managerial decision-making decreases the more closely it impinges on business policy.

Certainly co-determination is not seen as the only form of participation. They go on to state that participating management

> is intended to complement institutionalised employee representation rather than to displace it. Quality circles and teamwork are the two main models of employee participation ... Some unions and works councils at first rejected such participation initiatives, especially quality circles, but in most cases they have now accepted them.

Although joint management, or employee or union representation on Boards of Directors has been reasonably well received in Germany, elsewhere they engender little enthusiasm. A current or former union official being given a seat on the Board is unlikely to have much effect on the average employee. Hammer *et al* (1991:676-8) report on the US experience, which is fairly typical:

> Worker directorships are often described by constituents as weak or ineffective labour voice mechanisms ... One reason for this perception can be found in the opposition by conventional directors and company management to worker directors as labour interest group advocates ... When labour representatives fail to develop the skills necessary for the use of their new positions of authority, and management continues to view downward communication to the work force as the sole function of worker directors, worker board representation will likely fail to be a meaningful and long-lasting programme for employee involvement in organisational governance.

[1310] Self-management

This is the ultimate in employee participation, where employees have complete control of the management of the enterprise. Clegg (1960) points out that self-management was proposed by Communist philosophers such as Masy, anarchist philosophers such as Bakunin, and echoed after the First World War by guild socialists in England. It would be possible, especially with a small workforce, for all employees to contribute to the management of the concern, but larger organisations would operate in a similar fashion to organisations in Yugoslavia in the 1960s, as described in [1308]. That is, the workforce would elect a works council which is responsible to them. The council in turn may elect a smaller sub-council or managerial board. For a system of self-management to be operating, either the employees as a whole make all managerial decisions, or they elect representatives to make the decisions, with the employees retaining the right to replace their representatives. The likely outcome is that the management board would make the management decisions, not the average employee.

Self-management *without* workers' or employees' ownership is only likely in situations where the State enforces it, either on philosophical or nationalistic grounds.

[1311] Employee ownership

This type of employee participation ranges from the most trivial – when employees own a minute proportion of the shares of a company – to the most extreme type of employee participation when the workforce owns the organisation and thus has total managerial responsibility. This may be exercised by the workforce as a whole or by elected representatives. If the organisation is very large, then although industrial democracy could exist, the influence of an individual under such a system would be insignificant. Presumably however, the elected managers will perform to the satisfaction of the majority or they will be elected out.

One country in which there is wide-scale employee ownership is Israel. The General Federation of Labour, the Histadrut, not only controls some fifty national trade unions, but is also a major economic entrepreneur. One of the fifty national unions is a special union for employees employed by Histadrut companies. Although most Histadrut companies are small, employing around 50–300 employees, they are large enough to make the concept of 'employee ownership' somewhat artificial. Rosenstein (1970:171) observes:

> As Histadrut members, employees in these 'administrative industries' also 'own' them. But, the other hundreds of thousands of Histadrut members who are not employed in the Histadrut economy also 'own' these industries. Under such circumstances the 'ownership' of the enterprise by its employees has only nominal meaning with no practical relevance.

He goes on to point out (1970:172, 186) that, far from employee ownership being seen as the ultimate in participation, it is ineffectual, with the 'worker-owner managers' acting purely as managers and the 'worker-owner employees' acting purely as employees.

[1312] (Semi)-autonomous work groups

This form of participation differs from those previously discussed, in that employees are *directly* participating in decision-making, not through representation. Under this system of participation, small groups of employees are able to determine, with a given production plan, how, when and by whom the work is to be done. Lindestad and Norstedt (1973) describe (semi)-autonomous work groups in the automobile industry in Sweden. In one factory, seven assembly groups were organised alongside an automatic transport loop. Apart from some assembly work done before the loop, finished engines were assembled in each group.

Each production group could assemble up to six engines at the same time.

During the assembly work itself there was no mechanical control of the flow, as would be the case with the machine-paced line. Each engine was manually transported during assembly. When an engine assembly had been completed by a group, the engine was automatically transferred via the transport loop to a test station shared by all the groups. At the same time, an automatic record was made of an engine leaving the group and a new trolley was sent to the group.

Advantages of the new system were claimed to be that:

a. it was expected to be more insensitive to disruption;
b. there were many opportunities for work expansion and stimulating group work;
c. extensive and costly rebalancing need *not* be undertaken every time production volume is to be increased or reduced;
d. work content better adapted to the individual should also provide better recruitment opportunities, reduced staff turnover and less absenteeism due to illness.

Disadvantages were seen as being that:

a. the new production form takes up more space and ties up more material than a conventional assembly line;
b. investment costs are somewhat higher;
c. work efficiency (mainly speed of motion is reduced as a result of the reduced degree of specialisation).

In Sweden this form of participation was practised in a number of industries and many organisations, originally in an effort to overcome the high turnover and absenteeism plaguing Swedish industry. International attention focussed on the automobile industry and Volvo in particular. Volvo has had a number of different plants throughout Europe: some traditional, some innovative. Two plants were seen as icons: Kalmar, which opened in 1974, and Uddevalla which opened in 1989.

At Kalmar, groups built a major part of the vehicle, and at the later plant a work group of around nine built an entire car. These plants struck a chord with many social scientists, who saw them as the answer to assembly-line monotony and 'blue-collar blues'. It would appear they are passing into mythology.

However, on 4 November 1992, Volvo announced the closing down of both Kalmar and Uddevalla. Sandberg (1993) reports the last cars left Uddevalla in April 1993. Delaney and Godard (2001:418) state:

> It may be no coincidence that the Volvo experiments in Sweden, long held out as exemplars of HPWSs [High Performance Work Systems], were implemented at a time when labour markets were tight, workers had strong legal rights and protections and societal support for the programs were strong. It may also be no coincidence that, since these conditions changed, all of the experiments have been discontinued.

Volvo has clearly demonstrated that alternative methods of production are simply that – alternatives. They are not panaceas. In general, if an alternative is persisted with, there must be benefits, but there will also be costs. In a three-year study of autonomous work groups in the UK, Wall *et al* (1986:298) found that

> although implementation of this work design substantially enhanced intrinsic job satisfaction, it did not demonstrably affect job motivation, organisational commitment, mental health, work performance, and voluntary labour turnover. At an organisational level, implementation made productivity benefits possible because the autonomous workgroups reduced indirect labour costs; a side effect was increased dismissals.

[1313] Quality circles

A quality circle is basically a voluntary group of employees who meet to discuss and try to solve or reduce any production problem. The concept was seen as a Japanese innovation, and, particularly when Japanese organisations became internationally very competitive through the 1970s a lot of attention was focused on this form of participation. Hill (1991:541) points out:

> Quality circles (QCs) were hailed at the start of the 1980s as a major innovation with the power to transform British and American companies. There were three major elements in these claims. First, quality circles would increase the involvement of employees in their organisations by means of participation. Second, they would enhance business effectiveness. Finally, circles marked the commitment of companies to changing organisational culture.

Behind all this was a desire to learn the Japanese secrets. Ironically, quality circles developed in Japan after the Second World War, based on Scanlon Plans developed in the USA (see [318]). Certainly, the Japanese refined the concept. Under most Scanlon Plans, employees benefit from ideas by receiving monthly bonuses. With Japanese quality circles, employees benefit only indirectly through working for a more profitable organisation. Outside Japan, most quality circles meet during working hours. In Japan they meet outside working hours.

The Japanese are still ahead – in that quality circles in Japan are no longer a separate programme but are part of what became known as Total Quality Management, or TQM. TQM subsequently became 'Quality Management'. Quality circles are now by far the most popular form of participation or, as it is referred to in the USA, EI (employee involvement). Indeed EI and QC are now virtually synonymous acronyms.

Juravich *et al* (1993) report a variety of studies which suggest between sixty to seventy per cent of US unionised firms have quality circles and around fifty per cent of non-union firms. Although this sounds an impressive acceptance of the concept, frequently only a small percentage of the total workforce are involved in a quality circle. Further, whenever longitudinal research occurs, it is clear that there is a high failure rate with many circles disbanding (Drago, 1988).

Table 13.2. Differences between TQM and employee involvement

TQM		Employee Involvement
quality improvement	vs.	organisational effectiveness
management control	vs.	self-management
process improvement	vs.	organisation design
work simplification	vs.	enrichment/work teams
work process codification	vs.	employee discretion
quality circles	vs.	work teams
internal customers	vs.	feedback
recognition rewards	vs.	financial rewards

Source: Lawler (1994:71)

[1314] Total Quality Management

The American acronym disease has spread, with TQM being used universally.

TQM is the logical development from quality circles, in that concern for quality, productivity and continuous improvement is not left until the quality circle meeting, but, if successfully introduced, is present all the time. Lawler (1994:68-9) points out that TQM

> has become increasingly popular in the United States and Europe most likely as a result of the success of Japanese firms in a number of global markets … Great emphasis is placed on including all employees in the TQM culture. This is where employee involvement comes in. Employees are expected to take responsibility for quality in two important respects. They are expected to call attention to quality problems as they do their normal work. Perhaps more important, they are expected to accept the continuous improvement culture and look for ways that they can do their work better.

Lawler (1994) considers that while there are similarities between employee involvement and TQM, there are fundamental differences which he postulates in Table 13.2.

D. Significance of Participation

[1315] Interest in participation

Interest in participation in management decision-making as a concept fluctuates markedly over time. In the late 1960s and 1970s, the concept received a lot of attention and then it seemed as if most people lost interest in it until a recent resurgence in the 1990s.

Ramsey (1977) wrote about 'cycles of control' and returned to print on the issue sixteen years later (Ramsey (1993:77)) to reiterate his view that forms of participation are not part of an unstoppable tide, but rather that

> the pattern of history showed periods of management concession to labour pressure (though as far as possible on terms preferred by capital) followed by a retreat from these when the challenge receded; and that the resulting schemes had a high failure rate, foundering on the contradiction between the search for consensus and the reality of conflict.

In both papers, Ramsey suggests participation is a managerial response. This suggestion may be right to some extent, but it is clear from preceding discussion that the State is also a significant force in the periodic interest in participation. What is also clear is that employee support for participation is at best lukewarm, and tends to be limited to a small percentage.

[1316] Participation and objectives

The principal objectives of the parties in employment relations have been clearly set out in Chapters One and Five. 'Participation' *per se* has never been postulated as an objective. Hence if parties favour participation, it would be as a means to an end. Thus the success or failure of any type of participation, be it informal discussion, collective bargaining, works councils, quality circle or employee shareholding, can only be determined from a particular frame of reference and if one knows the objectives of the party concerned.

If any of the three parties finds that participation helps them to achieve their objectives, it is successful from their point of view. It may not be considered successful from the other parties' viewpoints. As with all employment relations issues, a party hoping to achieve its objectives should consider how other parties will react. If the parties have totally different expectations they will probably fail to achieve them and become disillusioned. Thus works councils which are seen by management as a means of communication *to* employees and seen by employees as a means of affecting management actions are likely to fail.

[1317] Reasons for the State's support for participation

In some cases the State supported a type of participation for particularly nationalistic reasons. West Germany after the war saw co-determination as a means of slowing the return of Nazis and Nazi-supporters to control of German industry. In many cases the concept is supported on normative grounds as a 'good thing' with the belief it would foster job satisfaction and productivity. In some cases, support for participation is simply a fad.

[1318] Employers support for participation

Few employers today would have the audacity to proclaim managerial prerogatives with the confidence of George F. Baer, President of the Philadelphia and Reading Railroad in 1902. Perline and Poynter (1990:180-1) recount that Mr Baer

> was urged 'as a Christian gentleman' to make concessions to the striking workers on his railroad. He responded as follows: 'The rights and interests of the labouring man will be protected and cared for not by the labour agitators, but by the Christian men to whom God in His infinite wisdom has given the control of the property interests of the country, and upon the management of which so much depends.'

However, a proportion of managers and employers do not see any reason why managers should not manage, and employees work. Those that do support participation tend to do so for one or more of the following reasons:

a. to enhance employees' identification with the firm and its goals;
b. to undermine unions. Thus Gill (1993:123) points out that quality circles and TQM have met with

    > a mixed response from trade unions. On the one hand they are welcomed because they can improve job satisfaction and lead to a greater degree of control by employees over their jobs; on the other hand they are opposed because they are seen as undermining trade union influence on the shopfloor by bypassing forms of collective representation.

c. to satisfy employees, and hopefully achieve productivity gains through lower absenteeism and turnover. Wilson and Peel (1991:467) found:

    > First, firms with profit-sharing or share ownership schemes (or both) had significantly lower absenteeism and quit rates than other firms …

    However, Fricke (1991) reports a positive relationship between participation and conflict, and Drago and Wooden (1990) a positive relationship between union-management committees and strikes. (That is, increasing participation results in increasing conflict.)
d. as a fad. Ackers *et al* (1992:280) acknowledged that for some, participation is:

    > a superficial and transient fad, attuned to the latest management fashion …

Following fads can be unproductive and some researchers believe some successful forms of participation are dependent on the *culture*. Lawler (1994:74) suggests:

> The success of some Japanese organisations that use the TQM approach suggests that it may be particularly effective in Japan because there are a number of cultural conditions that favour it. These conditions most likely include a homogeneous set of values that place an emphasis on quality, attention to detail, and discipline, as well as an acceptance of hierarchy and seniority. The United States, with its emphasis on democracy and individual rights, but with little emphasis on attention to detail and quality, presents quite a different scene and one in which the TQM approach, particularly in its pure form, does not appear to fit as well.

[1319] Employee support for participation

Over the years, the most significant employee participation in management decision-making has come through unions and collective bargaining. Chapter Four has outlined the general crisis unions face internationally.

On the one hand, there are claims that 'voice' is an important goal of employees, that employees want to participate in shaping the rules that govern the work environment (Weiler, 1990), that 'employees generally desire greater amounts of participation than firms are providing' (Drago and Wooden, 1991:195), or, as Blumberg (1968:123) asserts with almost religious fervour (in italicised print), that

> There is hardly a study in the entire literature which fails to demonstrate that satisfaction in work is enhanced or that other generally acknowledged benefits accrue from a genuine increase in workers' decision-making powers.

On the other hand, there is the view of Wall and Lischeron (1977:14) who refute Blumberg's view, stating 'how impressed we are by the lack of evidence' of the participation-satisfaction thesis.

Proponents of participation, and in particular those who claim that employees 'desire' participation, need to explain why employees never seem to make many sacrifices in order to achieve 'participation'. They will suffer considerably in conflicts over wages, over conditions, and over job security, but do not seem prepared to make sacrifices over participation.

Chapter Fourteen

Labour Market Flexibility

A. Introduction

[1401] Chapter coverage

While there may not be consensus as to what it achieves – or even what is meant by the term – there is general consensus that labour flexibility is a significant issue today, and has been so for a number of decades. New Zealand National Party's 2005 Employment Relations policy states: 'Employment law should encourage a flexible, productive high-wage economy.'

This chapter has two main sections. The first discusses labour flexibility in general:

a. what triggered demands for labour flexibility and when;
b. what is meant by labour flexibility;
c. the consequences of labour flexibility.

One aspect, or possible consequence, of the move to labour flexibility is that of retrenchment or creation of, and management of, redundant employees. Redundancy is deemed to be a topic of sufficient interest and importance that it will be considered separately in the second main section of the chapter.

[1402] Origins of concern for flexibility

According to Treu (1992:497):

> Labour flexibility first became a focus of attention in Europe around the mid-1970s as a result of the economic crisis sparked off by the massive oil price increases of 1973.

While Treu may have pinpointed the initial catalyst for concern for labour flexibility, increased attention nowadays is attributed to (Boston, 1988:129):

> The depressed character of labour market conditions during the 1980s and the protracted period of high unemployment which has afflicted most OECD countries during the 1980s has led to a widespread concern with the question of labour market flexibility.

Both Treu and Boston highlight a number of critical issues concerning flexibility:

a. concern was generated by market conditions;
b. the desire for flexibility was employer led.

Flexibility, as such, is not a major objective of employers, so much as a means to an end. As Piore (1986:162) puts it, managers and employers see the drive for labour flexibility as

> A response to a fundamental change in the business environment. The tightly integrated, hierarchical corporation was a response to a stable and predictable environment in which the corporation was able to control its market; and in which, as a consequence, long-run planning was feasible and heavy financial commitments to particular products were encouraged. The new environment is much more unstable and uncertain. Markets can no longer be effectively managed and controlled. The organisation must therefore be able to respond quickly and 'flexibly' as market conditions change.

Ferner and Hyman (1992:xx) agree:

> Conditions of escalating uncertainty have encouraged employers to seek increased flexibility in the recruitment, deployment and reward of labour, through the now familiar panoply of measures: part-time, fixed-term and other non-standard forms of employment contract; new forms of work organisation such as team-working and `just-in-time' production; and individual and performance-related pay.

Ferner and Hyman go on to claim the move to flexibility

> is driven by the requirements and strategies of employers, rather than being the expression of workplace union power … (because) the growing dominance of large corporations means that employers are less dependent on the services of interest associations acting at industry (or higher) level.

Further on in their introduction (1992:xxvii) Ferner and Hyman also point out that, in response to employer pressure

> in many countries even those whose industrial relations systems have shown great solidity and continuity, the state has played a role in deregulating labour markets.

Some of these factors are mutually supportive. Market and economic conditions have not only encouraged employers to drive for flexibility, but have also weakened unions who during more favourable times would have resisted some of the moves. The weakened condition of unions both encouraged and permitted the passing of legislation which promoted flexibility and further weakened unions.

B. Aspects of Labour Flexibility

[1403] What is labour flexibility?

Although flexibility may be accepted as an issue, there are considerable variations in meaning. Piore (1986:466) observes:

> The term takes on different meanings in different countries. In Europe, flexibility principally concerns the freedom of employers to lay off and discharge workers in response to fluctuations in economic conditions. Among North American employers, the term refers to the freedom to deploy labour within the enterprise. Traditionally economists have used flexibility to refer to the capacity of wages to rise and fall with the state of the labour market.

Atkinson (1985) suggests there are three types of labour flexibility: numerical, functional and financial, while Treu (1992) proposes four: numerical, working time, functional and pay. Clearly either definition can encompass all major aspects, depending on how broadly they are defined. For the sake of clarity, this section looks at five aspects of flexibility:

a. numerical;
b. contractual;
c. job;
d. work-time;
e. pay.

[1404] Numerical flexibility

Numerical flexibility refers to the ability of employers to increase or decrease the size of the workforce in response to changes in market demand. In general, flexibility refers to a *downward* adjustment and so in this instance numerical flexibility relates to the ability to either lay-off employees or to make them redundant (see Section C below).

Lay-offs refer to employment situations where the expectation is for a full year's work each year but, if sales are down and stockpiles rise, the employer feels free to temporarily (but in some instances for months) break the contract of employment.

[1405] Contractual flexibility

With contractual flexibility, employers can first determine what sort of employment relationship they want: a contract of service, or a contract for services (see [404]). Employers with contractual flexibility can determine whether employees under a *contract of service* are 'permanent' employees or on fixed-term contracts, and whether they are full-time or part-time.

[1406] Job flexibility

Job flexibility refers to the ability of employers to move employees from one job to another. For there to be job flexibility there must be sufficient skill levels for employees to be able to perform a variety of tasks, and there needs to be a breakdown in traditional demarcation rules. Demarcation rules may be relaxed by agreement, as in productivity bargaining (see [728]), or unilaterally by management when unions are weak or non-existent.

[1407] Work-time flexibility

In theory, work-time flexibility refers to the ability of employers to manage their organisations to operate whatever hours they choose. However (with some exceptions), most organisations have been able to operate during the hours they choose, if they were prepared to pay premium, or penal rates. In practice, the term refers to the ability to work whatever hours are chosen, with no, or at least minimal, penal rates.

Even with the payment of penal rates, some strong unions in the past were able to restrict work-time flexibility. For example, in the 1960s and 1970s in New Zealand, meatworkers and their union refused Saturday afternoon work, even though the payment would have been at double rates. They also refused to allow shiftworking. By the late 1980s, meatworkers and their union had agreed in some plants to round-the-clock operations.

[1408] Pay flexibility

Pay flexibility, in theory, refers to the ability of employers to increase or decrease pay levels to meet supply and demand. However, employers have never had real problems increasing pay levels above the norm, so, as with numerical flexibility, in practice pay flexibility refers to the ability to lower pay levels.

One form of pay *inflexibility* frequent in the past, was 'wage indexation', in which there were general wage increases, usually to match inflation.

[1409] Employers and labour flexibility

The drive for labour flexibility came from employers, so one could expect the main benefits to accrue to employers. All five different aspects of flexibility are designed to make management easier, and/or labour less costly, and/or operations more profitable.

[1410] Unions and labour flexibility

The natural inclination of unions would be to oppose moves of flexibility as they would be seen to be against the interests of their members. Numerical flexibility means members lose their jobs; contractual flexibility means full-time employees become part-time, losing income, and permanent workers become fixed-term, losing job security. Some of their members may be happy to become independent contractors, but that means a loss of membership for unions.

Job flexibility is an attack not only on the job security of work groups, but also on the independence and security of unions. Work-time and pay flexibility usually indicate a worsening of conditions, with longer hours, often for lower take-home pay.

Of all five aspects of flexibility, the one of most concern to the general public is numerical flexibility, or, as it is generally referred to, 'redundancy'.

C. Redundancy

[1411] Numerical flexibility and redundancy

If employers had total numerical flexibility and were able to increase, and more significantly decrease, the size of their workforce at will, definitions of 'redundancy' would be unnecessary. It would simply be understood that employees were dismissed as their employers no longer required their services. However, while employers may enjoy a situation of greater numerical flexibility in the 1990s than they did in the 1960s and 1970s, there are two highly significant constraints on total numerical flexibility. These are:

a. common law and statutory restrictions on the right to dismissal (see [907] to [912]); and
b. statutory or contractual requirements to pay compensation for redundancy.

These constraints result in a need for an accepted definition of *redundancy*. In the first case, this is as a defence against unjustifiable dismissal, as a genuine redundancy situation is normally accepted as a substantive justification for dismissal. (The dismissal for redundancy may still be deemed to have been performed in a procedurally unfair manner.) In the second situation, compensation will be required if the grounds for dismissal were redundancy, but not necessarily if the reason was simply that the employee was unsuitable or incompetent.

[1412] Definition of redundancy

Redundancy has been defined in numerous ways. In the late 1970s, the New Zealand Employers' Federation (NZEF) (1979:2) proposed a definition:

> Redundancy is a condition in which an employer has manpower surplus to his [sic] requirements because of the closing of the whole or any part of the employer's operation due to change in plant, methods, materials, or products or reorganisation or like cause requiring a permanent reduction in the number of permanent employees who have not reached the company's recognised age of retirement.

This definition is restrictive and illogical. The underlying motive for such a definition is obvious – the NZEF were hoping to avoid paying compensation to:

a. fixed-term employees; and
b. employees above retirement age.

A more logical approach is to have a broad definition of *redundancy*, and a restrictive agreement, if the parties see fit, to the entitlement to compensation.

The UK's Employment Consolidation Protection Act 1978, in s.81 defines a dismissal as being by reason of redundancy if the dismissal is attributable wholly or mainly to:

a. the fact that his employer has ceased, or intends to cease, to carry on the business for the purposes of which the employee was employed by him, or has ceased, or intends to cease, to carry on that business in the place where the employee was so employed; or
b. the fact that the requirements of that business for employees to carry out work of a particular kind, or for employees to carry out work of a particular kind in the place where he was so employed, have ceased or diminished or are expected to cease or diminish.

This definition is reasonably adequate, but still leaves areas open to interpretation and dispute. In particular, there is the issue of how much change is required in a job for it to be deemed to have been made redundant in terms of both content and location. A further issue is that of so-called 'technical' redundancies, where the work and conditions remain the same, but the 'job' changes in that the business has been sold.

[1413] Job content

In some situations it is clear redundancies have occurred, as when demand for the product decreases markedly, and as a consequence a percentage of the workforce are dismissed. The situation is not so clear when the job content changes and the number of employees is unchanged but the employees are to do a different job. Employers are quite entitled to expect employees to accept changes to their jobs. The issue is deciding at which point the change has become so great that it is no longer a *changed* job but in fact a *new* job.

[1414] Job location

The scenario here is very similar. Employers are free to move employees around, but only to a 'reasonable' degree. Here again, what is considered 'reasonable' depends not only on the actual case, but also on the person making the judgement. In some cases (armed forces, police), it may be a condition of the job that there will be transfers. A change in location would not be redundancy. In many cases, employees expect to remain on the same site. If the move was a few kilometres, then in general this would not be deemed redundancy – unless the employee could demonstrate severe inconvenience. This might occur if they were unable to walk to work, or unable to use public transport, or unable to meet their children after school, as they had previously.

[1415] Technical redundancy

If an employer sells their business, then their previous employees have lost their jobs. They are clearly redundant by all accepted definitions. In a 'technical' redundancy, redundant employees are fortunate enough to be given jobs by the new owner of the business. The employees work at the same job in the same location. Their job security and future prospects may be very different – either better or worse under the new owner. The original owner may have been a very profitable multi-national which chose to sell off a profitable business. The new owner could be a fly-by-night operator close to bankruptcy.

Technical redundancies are really only an issue if employers are inept enough to agree to redundancy compensation for 'all' redundant employees, including those in technical redundancies. Some inept employers who have agreed to pay all redundant employees may then either try to either renege on the agreement or pressure the State to pass legislation exempting them from their own agreement. If the inept employer happened to be a branch of the government, then it is clearly possible for the government to 'honourably' renege on its own agreements by passing such legislation. Alternatively, the legislation may be passed without any pressure from inept employers or as a consequence of inept government agreements, with the legislators simply motivated by a Puritanical belief that such redundant employees did not 'deserve' compensation.

The 1987 New Zealand Labour Government passed such legislation in the Labour Relations Amendment Act 1990 and, although initially repealed by the Employment Contracts Act 1991, it was subsequently reintroduced into the EC Act 1991.

[1416] Management of redundancy situations

The importance to the employer of a redundancy situation being well managed varies with the circumstances. If the organisation is facing bankruptcy and going out of business, it will be of marginal importance. If the organisation is continuing in business then it may vary from reasonably to very important for a number of reasons.

The first is pragmatism. A well-managed redundancy will minimise opposition and reduce the probability of industrial action and/or a reduction in productivity. A second reason is the common law requirement which, as outlined by the President of the New Zealand Court of Appeal in *Brighouse v Bilderbeck* (at 252), is:

> an application of the principle that there is implied in a contract of employment a term that the employers will not, without reasonable and probable cause, conduct themselves in a manner calculated to destroy or seriously damage the relationship of trust and confidence between employer and employee ... The obligation, which is the corollary of the employee's duty of fidelity, ... has been repeatedly recognised and enforced in a line of cases in this Court ...

The third reason develops from the second. In New Zealand legislation an employee may receive compensation and/or reinstatement for being unjustifiably dismissed. Genuine redundancy is a *substantive* justification – but, if the situation is poorly managed, this may render the dismissal *procedurally* unfair.

The fourth reason is simply to preserve good Public Relations, which should reflect well on the business.

With the exception of those employees who were about to resign anyway, it is reasonable to assume employees do not appreciate being made redundant, and indeed in some cases may find the situation extremely traumatic. Even if the employees are not themselves made redundant, having colleagues in that position will frequently create an unpleasant work environment. If the redundancy situation is well managed, this could significantly reduce the perceived degree of unpleasantness.

[1417] Issues involved in managing redundancy

Campbell and Rimmer (1994:45) state that the specific dilemmas are well-known:

> They include selection criteria (skill, seniority, disciplinary record and the like), selection methods (voluntary retrenchment, involuntary retrenchment, natural wastage and so on), length of notice and compensation. We usually presume that employers prefer to choose the selection method and criteria, to give short notice (or none at all) and to offer as little severance pay as possible. On the other hand, we tend to presume that employees prefer selection criteria which advantage them; voluntary retrenchment, long notice periods and large severance packages. Clearly these preferences are incompatible.

They themselves concede that such generalisations are not always apt, and as discussed below there are arguments for and against most of the redundancy issues, from the perspective of both employers and employees. The issues to be considered include:

a. selection methods;
b. selection criteria;
c. period of notice;
d. notification procedure;
e. compensation.

[1418] Selection methods

Given that the employer has more employees than are needed, a decision has to be made as to how numbers are to be decreased. One option is natural wastage or attrition, relying on turnover without, or with limited replacement. An alternative, or additional, option is to reduce all overtime or even normal hours of work, so that there is some work for all staff. In some situations staff accept wage and salary cuts in order to reduce potential redundancies. As discussed in [734] to [736] on concession bargaining, this approach is being utilised in the USA and other Western economies. In Japan, this approach however has been the *norm*, rather than exceptional behaviour. Schregle (1993:515) states:

> As a first step, when there is a business slump, an enterprise normally reduces or suspends the payment of dividends and cuts the salaries of top management. This measure alone, unthinkable in most American or European enterprises, indicates the high priority attributed to employment protection in Japan. The next move would be a reduction in the salaries of middle management and of the semi-annual bonuses which all employees receive.

A third option is retraining and redevelopment. However, this not only requires 'trainable' staff, but assumes the organisation as a whole is not overstaffed, but is simply changing focus.

Should the above methods either be rejected or fail to reduce the workforce to an acceptable level, then a fourth option is voluntary payoff. This can be either in the form of voluntary redundancy, or voluntary early retirement. In both cases a compensation package is normally required. Management of voluntary redundancies is required to prevent costly problems.

[1419] Selection criteria

The best known selection criterion for redundancy is on seniority, applying the 'last-on first-off' principle. This criterion is generally well supported and often demanded by unions.

Seniority has a number of advantages to employers, employees and unions. It is simple, easy to understand and reasonably easy to apply. The main difficulties in application is determining whether seniority is by *section* or by *service* in the organisation.

If there is to be compensation for redundancy, compensation usually increases with seniority. Hence 'last-on first-off' is cheaper for employers. Employees favour 'last-on first-off' for a variety of reasons. There is the force of group identity, which would suggest the newcomer should be dropped first; there is the fact that group leaders and shop-floor union representatives have often been in the group for a long time, but will not necessarily be the most able employees and hence will individually benefit from a seniority provision; and there is the force of concern for the older employees, who would be likely to find it harder to get another job.

A small-scale study in New Zealand conducted by Simmonds under the senior author's supervision produced results indicating that the 'last-on first-off' principle was not favoured. The samples are too small for statistically valid conclusions. However, as Table 14.1 below shows, a sample of forty-one freezing work employees, randomly selected from those present in the off-season, ranked last-on first-off as sixth out of six choices. Unlike Slater's (1971) study, which had an overall 'bad work record' criterion, this differentiated between absenteeism and work ability. In the study, the category 'workers with second income' did not refer to married women or to men with income-earning wives, but to freezing workers (male) who owned small farms or businesses.

Table 14.1. Criteria preferences for lay-off in New Zealand freezing works

Choice	Slaughtermen N=25	Cooling Floor N = 11	Displaced Worker N=5	Total N=41
over sixty-five	1	2	1=	1
high absentee record	3	1	1=	2
those with second income	2	3	3	3
over sixty	4	4	5	4
poor work ability	5	5	4	5
last-on first-off	6	6	6	6

There are two major concerns with 'last-on first-off.' One is that in a situation of frequent redundancies, it can condemn good young employees into a state of continual redundancies as they are never able to build up enough seniority to stay in their job. The second and most serious from the employers' point of view is that 'last-on first-off' does not take into account ability to perform and willingness to perform. This concern gives rise to a second criterion: performance.

Performance as a criterion has intuitive appeal for employers. Assessment may be on a basis of overall performance, or on skills and ability only, or on a measure such as low absenteeism. The problem with performance as a redundancy criterion is that very few employers have an accepted performance appraisal system in operation. While most employers would like to keep a small percentage of identifiably well-above-average employees and get rid of a small percentage of well-below-average employees, most would not be in a position to accurately rate the majority of their staff. These employers realise that there would be frequent, possibly justified accusations of favouritism and victimisation. Consequently, many employers are quite happy to accept 'last-on first-off.'

[1420] Period of notice

A period of notice of dismissal for redundancy may be required by legislation or employment agreements. Under common law, if wages are paid 'in lieu' of notice then no action will be taken if a shorter actual period of notice is given. There are thus two issues: the actual period of notice, and a notional period for which wages may be paid *in lieu*.

Clearly most employees would prefer six weeks' wages in lieu of notice to three weeks. Equally clearly, from a cost point of view, the reverse applies for employers. However, with respect to *actual* notice, there may well be similar views. From an employer's point of view, employees who have been made redundant tend to be both depressed and depressing, have low morale and productivity, and have an adverse effect on others. The Deloitte (1994) study, however, shows that many redundant employees do not want a long period of notice – twenty-five per cent preferred to leave that day and a further twenty-six per cent within a fortnight.

If counselling is given, this can be done with seminars off-site so that employees are not required to work while still in shock and anger. They can return for a brief period later to farewell colleagues (after having gone through the shock, anger and denial stages).

[1421] Notification procedure

Purely from the point of view of decency and good management, notification of redundancy should be done with sensitivity. From a pragmatic point of view, where, as in New Zealand, employees can take personal grievances for the *method* by which they are made redundant, sensitive notification makes very good business sense. Dismissing loyal and hardworking employees is a very unpleasant task for many employers. This is possibly a major reason why notification so frequently appears callous and unfeeling.

[1422] Compensation for redundancy

There are a number of arguments both for and against compensation for redundancy, and attitudes are not decided on the simplistic lines that employers are opposed and employees are in favour.

Whether or not redundancy compensation *should* be paid, is, like most employment relations issues, a value judgement. One argument for redundancy compensation is to alleviate the problems of unemployment. Since the late 1970s redundancies and unemployment are often seen as problems which are inevitably linked. Of course, when they do occur together, they tend to exacerbate each other. From the employers' point of view, high unemployment means redundancies will be even more unacceptable and costly, and industrial action more likely. However, redundancy during near full employment is certainly possible and redundancy in the UK was first a major matter of concern in the 1950s and 1960s when there was relatively little unemployment. Kahn (1964:19) believes:

> there are two main reasons why redundancy has been felt to be a problem only in the post-war period – and in the latter part of that period in particular. For as long as there was an overall deficiency of demand in the economy, any fresh lay-off was bound to lead to unemployment – not necessarily of those immediately affected, but of some workers somewhere in the system. Redundancy was thus overshadowed and dwarfed by the general phenomenon of unemployment. Then, with the advent of labour shortage during and since the war, the emphasis swung to the other extreme, and discussion tended to focus on those aspects of mobility which stemmed from the initiative of the worker. In other words, it was the latter's propensity to bid adieu to his boss rather than the reverse which primarily attracted attention.

Goodman (1962:2) actually went so far as to suggest:

> already it is recognised that redundancy today is harder to bear than the pre-war long stretches of unemployment. Misery is easier to share when there is meanness and squalor all around.

However, while feelings of deprivation are obviously related to others' standards of living, it seems ludicrous to suggest a redundant employee would prefer the redundancies to occur during high unemployment with little or no likelihood of obtaining another job, simply to ensure the deprivation was wide-scale.

A second argument for redundancy compensation is that it is acknowledged that employees have property rights in their jobs. Indeed, Mankidy *et al* (1994:47) point out that 'under Philippine law, a worker's job is considered as his or her property.' In Western economies, there is support for the view that employees at least have a moral right to *some* degree of ownership of their jobs. In *Lloyd v Brassey*, the oft-quoted Lord Denning M.R., stated, at 101:

> a worker of long standing is now recognised as having an accrued right in his job: and his right gains in value with the years. So much so, that if the job is shut down, he is entitled to compensation for loss of a job – just as a director gets compensation for loss of office. The director gets a golden handshake. The worker gets a redundancy payment. It is not unemployment pay. I repeat 'not'. Even if he gets another job straight away, he nevertheless is entitled to full redundancy payment. It is, in a real sense, compensation for long service.

This description emphasises the view that payment is justified, regardless of whether re-employment is immediate.

The objective of the original Redundancy Payments Act 1965 in the UK was not to mitigate the problems of unemployment. In those days unemployment was not considered a significant problem. Grunfeld (1980:1) observes the principal purpose of the Act was:

> the national economic one of facilitating industrial change and labour mobility in industry and commerce ... to mitigate the resistance of individual employees (and their unions) to the extensive changes which have accompanied and continue to accompany the adaptation of British industry to the searching demands of modern world trade.

Arguments *against* redundancy compensation include the fact that employment is in effect a wage-work bargain with no suggestion that it should last forever. If there is a contractual period of notice of termination, that should be given, but nothing further is required.

While it is accepted that redundancy, particularly during a recession, can result in redundant employees facing unemployment, the argument is that the hardship of unemployment should be addressed by unemployment benefits – not redundancy compensation. Further, if redundancy pay is to compensate for unemployment, then it should not be paid, or not in full, if redundant employees find alternative work in a short period.

The argument that redundancy payment compensates for the loss of the job is considered illogical given that, as Sachs L.J. pointed out in the case of *Hindle v Percival Boats*, redundancy compensation

> is provided by the Act for one, but only one, of life's changes of fortune as between employee and employer: that is dismissal on account of redundancy … It thus neither purports to nor does provide for other changes of fortune, such as ill health or a deterioration in the employer's views of the capabilities of the employee. Similarly it does not provide for the case where an employer wishes to see if someone else can do the job better.

The final argument against redundancy compensation, and probably the only one which gets much support (albeit reluctant) from employees as well as employers, is that it can have an adverse effect on employment prospects. This can occur in two ways. If an organisation has to make redundant a significant proportion of its employees, then redundancy compensation may affect its on-going viability. Indeed, a massive redundancy payout may result in further employees being made redundant. A second consideration is that during a slight economic recovery, when some employers would be considering expansion in staff numbers, they may be deterred from taking on new staff by the prospect of having to make redundancy payouts, should the recovery be short-lived.

Chapter Fifteen

The Future

A. Introduction

[1501] Short-term predictions

Some years ago, an eminent American industrial relations specialist, Donald Cullen, concluded an article (Cullen 1985:319) in which he made predictions about the future of American industrial relations with the following observation:

> the knowledgeable reader will treat these predictions, of course, with the disrespect they deserve. It is well established that American specialists in industrial relations have a record of predicting the future that easily matches that of economists, political scientists, and generals.

Any short-term predictions made in this book would deserve to be treated with similar disrespect, and consequently none will be made. The authors however have every confidence in their long-term predictions. (So much so that they will willingly reimburse the price of this book (subject to proof of purchase) if any of the long-term predictions fail to eventuate).

[1502] Long-term predictions

a. the *subject* of employment relations will remain;
b. the model of employment relations as defined in Chapter One will continue to reasonably accurately describe the employment situation;
c. different groups in society will be trying to achieve different or conflicting objectives as well as some objectives in common. They will continue to 'comfortise' rather than 'maximise';
d. conflict will continue to be an integral part of the employment situation.

PART TWO

EMPLOYMENT RELATIONS

THE NEW ZEALAND SYSTEM

Chapter Sixteen

Introduction

A. Coverage of Part Two

[1601] Objectives of Part Two

There are three objectives of Part Two of this book. The first is to provide a description of the current (2006) employment relations situation in New Zealand. The second objective is to provide a brief historical background to employment relations in this country. It is hoped that the history will be considered interesting and valuable in itself, but is also important in that the current situation will be better understood if there is a reasonable knowledge and understanding of what has gone before. The third objective is to develop better understanding of the concepts introduced in Part One, not only through repetition but also through applying the concepts to particular situations in New Zealand.

It is assumed that readers of Part Two have not only worked through Part One, but will refer back to relevant sections in Part One when working through these chapters.

[1602] Structure of Part Two

New Zealand employment relations history is divided into four eras. The Pre-arbitration era up to 1894 will be covered by this introductory chapter. The Arbitration era, from 1 January 1895 to 1987 will be covered in Chapter Seventeen. The end of that era could justifiably be considered either 1984 when the Industrial Relations Amendment Act 1984 abolished compulsory arbitration of interest disputes, or 1987, when the Labour Relations Act was passed. The latter was selected as being more significant, hence more appropriate. Chapter Seventeen covers both the private sector and the public sector in different sections, as the overriding legislation was very different for both sectors.

Chapter Eighteen covers the Collective Bargaining era, from 1987 to 1991. After the State Sector Act 1988 was passed, the differences in legislation covering the two sections, Private and Public, were minimal.

Chapter Nineteen covers a new era, termed Laissez-Faire, introduced in the Employment Contracts Act 1991. It was very quickly suggested that the Act was 'an employers' charter' (Anderson, 1991) and, given the remarkable similarity between the Act and proposals put forward by the New Zealand Employers' Federation (NZEF) and the New Zealand Business Roundtable (NZBR), the suggestion is reasonably apt. However, the Act is not so much anti-employee or anti-union as simply abrogating responsibility for ensuring equity in the workplace. As the discussion in Part One suggests, the power difference between employers and employees, and between employers and unions is such that so-called neutral legislation will result in a considerable advantage to employers. Although New Zealand society accepted for virtually one hundred years that employees needed assistance for there to be fair contests, in the Laissez-Faire era since 1991 that century-old assumption is apparently now viewed as wrong.

The Employment Relations Act 2000 made little impact. The Amendment in 2004 was more significant, but not sufficient to suggest the Laissez-Faire era has ended.

B. The Pre-arbitration Era

[1603] The beginnings

Employment relations began in New Zealand as soon as employer-employee relationships began with European settlement. The first significant employment relations event is popularly considered to be the action of one Samuel Parnell, a Wellington carpenter, who in 1840 refused to work for more than eight hours in a day. Parnell is the one remembered, but Sutch (1966:24) claims 'E. Ticehurst and W. Taylor, also Wellington carpenters, have been credited with similar organising about the same time.'

Although New Zealand was, and is, a 'farming country', the vast proportion of the working population from the very earliest days of European settlement have been wage earners. Sutch (1966:27) considers that in 1867–8, for every one farmer in New Zealand there would be four farm labourers, six miners, five general labourers, five craftsmen, two domestic servants and two office or factory workers.

[1604] Key factors

There were a number of key factors which set the stage for the arbitration era. These included the discovery of gold, the development of unions, exploitation of women, the Sweating Commission, and the Maritime strike.

[1605] Gold

Discovery of gold, first at Coromandel in 1852 and more significantly in Otago in 1861, led to a massive increase in population as thousands poured into the gold fields. (Between the 1858 and 1874 censuses, New Zealand's population *tripled*.) As work on the gold fields ran out, many of the miners remained as unskilled manual labour.

[1606] Development of unions

Records and knowledge of the very earliest unions in this country are limited. A Wellington 'Benevolent Society of Carpenters and Joiners' was established in 1842 and actual unions appeared in the next decade. In the 1860s, unions were formed which have survived to the modern times – Printers, Engineers and Tailors. As theory suggests, the first unions were craft unions composed of skilled tradesmen, who were better educated and better paid than factory workers. By the 1870s, there were sufficient groups of permanent wage workers for unionism to become more widespread. Again as theory suggests, many unions were formed to fight a particular issue and collapsed if the strike was lost or even, but less often, if the issue was won. Most of the issues involved actions by employers to reduce wages or worsen conditions, rather than an effort by workers to improve wages or conditions. The cost-cutting by employers was in response to a depression which set in during the 1870s. Roth (1973:9) points out that

> the bootmakers struck work so frequently that they became known as 'the fighting bootmakers' , but of about fifty strikes before 1895, not one was for a rise of wages. 'We consistently struck against reductions,' said their Dunedin President.

World-wide unionism was on the rise in the late 1880s, and New Zealand was no exception. Although admittedly only approximations, figures by Roth (1973:10) illustrate this:

> in 1888 New Zealand unions had perhaps 3,000 members; by the end of 1889 this number had risen to 20,000 and by October 1890 a total of 63,000 unionists was claimed, although this was undoubtedly an exaggeration. The number of unions increased from fewer than 50 in 1888 to 75 in 1889 and more than 200 in 1890.

In October 1889 the Maritime Council was established in Dunedin by some of the more powerful unions – those of seamen, watersiders and miners. Unions of railway, clerical and manual workers and storemen joined soon afterwards. This was the first national organisation of unions.

[1607] Exploitation of women

While unions were developing, and giving some assistance to their members, there were still many groups of workers who were not unionised. These were frequently those most in need of assistance. Women (and children) working in factories were frequently the most exploited and also most unprotected.

By 1888 public condemnation of the exploitation of women was on the rise. In Dunedin, the Reverend Rutherford Waddell preached sermons against the 'sin of cheapness' and the evils of 'sweating', when workers were required to work at piece-rates so low that even after a sixty-hour work week and taking work home to do at night, women frequently received wages below subsistence level. The *Otago Daily Times* printed editorials condemning the practice and, to be fair, the occasional leading businessman condemned the exploitation and supported the concept of unions. Woods (1963:33) records:

> in 1890 Mr Hallenstein read a paper on trade unionism at a conference of Chambers of Commerce held in Dunedin in which he put forward the view that the new trade unionism was of vast importance to the industrial development of the country and should be regarded favourably by employers.

Some progress was made and a Tailoresses Union was formed in 1889, with 700 members. Its officers were men, the Rev. Waddell was President and Captain Millar (General Secretary, of the Seamens Union), was Secretary. However conditions in general were still so poor that a Royal Commission, popularly known as the Sweating Commission, was set up early in 1890.

[1608] Royal Commission 1890

A majority of the Royal Commission decided that a sweating *system* as occurred in London did not exist in New Zealand, but that there were many instances where individual factories 'sweated' their labour. The Royal Commission, (as reported in the *Appendix to the Journals of the House of Representations* (1890)) gave strong support to unionism:

> the evidence as a whole goes to show that in whatever branch of industry a union has been formed the condition of the operatives has improved, wages do not sink below a living minimum, and the hours of work are not excessive.

[1609] Maritime strike 1890

In August 1890 a seamen's strike in Australia spread to New Zealand, apparently at the employer's instigation. The Maritime Council called a seamen's strike which spread to the other affiliates of the Council (excepting the railwaymen). The Maritime Strike of 1890 lasted 56 days, and ranks alongside the strike of 1913 (58 days) and the 151-day strike of 1951 as one of the major strikes in New Zealand's employment relations history. In 1890, as in 1913 and 1951, the workers suffered a heavy defeat. There were instances where preference of employment was given to strike-breakers, where former union leaders were blacklisted and former unionists forced to sign so-called 'Yellow Dog Contracts', promising never to join a union. Roth (1973) cites such instances both in coalmining and in the railways. As Roth points out, the maritime strike resulted in the union movement being crushed. From the heyday of 1890 when there were reportedly 200 unions and a membership of 63,000 (a probable exaggeration), support had fallen by 1894 to a mere 70 unions and an estimated membership of 8000.

[1610] Political action

By the end of 1890, there was general concern at the plight of non-unionised workers, recognition that unions gave satisfactory protection, but the union movement had been totally crushed. One solution was political action.

The election in December 1890 was the first on a 'one-man – one-vote' basis.

(Women got the vote in 1893.) The Liberal Party was elected to Government and tended to be sympathetic to wage earners and, although the Labour Party had not yet been formed, there were some 'labour' politicians.

While it may seem that wage earners turned to politics only after industrial defeat, Roth (1973:18) disagrees. He states:

> it has been said that industrial defeat caused the workers to turn to political action, but this is not strictly accurate. Already the first Trades and Labour Congress in 1885 had discussed the need for working men representatives in Parliament, and the Maritime Council too had never spurned politics. There is no doubt that unionists would have taken an active part in the elections regardless of the Maritime Strike, but the almost simultaneous defeat of the strike and the Liberal victory at the polls created the illusion that only political action was able to right Labour's wrongs.

However, it was through political action that New Zealand employment relations achieved significant change. In 1891, William Pember Reeves introduced a bill to provide for compulsory conciliation and arbitration, which was strongly supported by unions and wage-earners, but opposed by employers. Although it was supported in Parliament, the bill was rejected in 1892 and 1893 by the Legislative Council. (The Legislative Council was the 'Upper House' equivalent to the British House of Lords. Since the government of the day could 'stack' the Council, it could not indefinitely delay Bills. The Council was only abolished in 1950.) In 1894, the Legislative Council passed the Bill which became the Industrial Conciliation and Arbitration Act 1894 and took effect on 1 January 1895, introducing the Arbitration era.

Chapter Seventeen

Arbitration Era

A. Introduction

[1701] Time frame

This era in New Zealand's employment relations history lasted from 1 January 1895 to 31 July 1987 – over ninety years of great change elsewhere. The era went from before automobiles to after space travel.

[1702] General approach

Although the major private-sector legislation at the end of this period could be clearly identified as being based on the original Industrial Conciliation and Arbitration Act 1894 (ICA Act 1894), there were a considerable number of changes along the way. There were six ICA Acts (1894, 1900, 1905, 1908, 1925 and 1954) and an ICA Compilation Act in 1905. In addition, there were forty-five ICA Amendment Acts (ICA Am Act). Near the end of the era came the Industrial Relations Act 1973, and seventeen IR Am Acts. Although the IR Act received considerable fanfare (the *New Zealand Official Year Book* (1973:894) asserted that it was 'the first major restructuring of New Zealand's industrial legislation and institutions since 1894. It provides a new charter for the conduct of industrial relations'), the reality was that the IR Act was not that different, and should have been labelled the seventh ICA Act.

Many of the changes and amendments over the years were trivial, but some were significant. Given both the length of the period, ninety-two years, and the enormous number of pieces of legislation, this chapter cannot hope to do anything other than highlight some significant features of the period.

[1703] Chapter coverage

The rest of this introduction will give a brief overview of historical incidents during the era. The next section discusses the principal private-sector employment relations legislation. Following sections consider the public sector, and a number of employment relations topics.

[1704] Strike-free period

From 1894 to 1906, there were no strikes in New Zealand. To some, this showed the benefits of the legislation, to others the costs. New Zealand is periodically visited by overseas experts who bestow on the country the benefit of their insights. Roth (1973:25) quotes two visitors in this period, who both decided the unions had been the victims, rather than the beneficiaries of the ICA Act. Ramsey MacDonald claimed 'a trade union in New Zealand exists mainly to get an award out of the Arbitration Court', and a certain V.S. Clark stated that unions here were 'litigious rather than militant organisations, the creatures and instruments of state regulations.'

While the legislation had a significant impact on unions, other relevant factors should not be ignored. These include: the 1890 defeat (see [1609]), the small scale of industry, the scattered population, and the difficulties in travel and communications.

Undoubtedly, the Court of Arbitration was conservative in the latter half of the strike-free period and evidence shows that wages increased by only a small amount. However, without the ICA Act conditions for employees would probably have been worse.

[1705] Dissatisfaction with arbitration

In November, 1906, the first strike for twelve years occurred. Union strength had revived and over the next few years their dependence on the Act diminished and more unions were prepared and able to strike. In 1908, the Blackball miners' strike occurred when union leaders were dismissed after disputes over conditions, a major complaint being that only fifteen minutes were permitted for lunch. The ringleader, Hickey, (1925:12) later recounted that when the matter went to the Court of Arbitration – for the union to be prosecuted (and fined) for striking – reference was made by his solicitor to the lunch allowance of fifteen minutes as being far too short:

> His Honour remarked with a frown that he thought fifteen minutes ample time. He then glanced at the clock, noticed the time was 12.30 and stated the Court stood adjourned for lunch till 2pm.

The strikers received strong support throughout the country and after three months the company reinstated the dismissed men and allowed thirty minutes for lunch.

[1706] Red Feds

The success of the Blackball strike rejuvenated the union movement. The miners' unions did not register under the ICA Acts. Leaders in the strike became leaders in a Federation of Miners. In 1909, the name was changed to 'New Zealand Federation of Labor' (spelt deliberately in the American fashion). By 1911, other unions had joined the Federation, including the brewery workers (under

Savage) and labourers (under Fraser) – both future Labour Prime Ministers. From 1912, the Federation became known to the public as the 'Red Fed'.

[1707] Waihi Strike

Waihi gold-miners went on strike in 1912 in protest over the registration of a breakaway union. Once registered, the breakaway union (considered by the strikers to be employer-dominated) would have sole bargaining rights. During the strike the Liberal Government was defeated by the Reform Party (conservatives) under Massey. The new government sent large contingents of police to Waihi and the strikers were prosecuted. The 'arbitrationists' or 'strike-breakers' were brought in under police protection. When they outnumbered the strikers, the arbitrationists attacked them with the apparent support of the police, beating, looting and in fact killing one of the strikers. They then drove out many strikers and their families from the town.

The Red Fed had been supporting the Waihi strikers with considerable financial aid, but did not call for supporting strikes. By the time such action was considered, their funds were low and there was little probability of success.

[1708] The 1913 Strike

In January 1913, the Red Fed called a Unity Conference, which was attended by some eighty organisations representing 27,000 members. This conference established a United Federation of Labour (UFL) and a Social Democratic Party.

The seamen and watersiders' agreements were due to expire in February 1914 – the height of the export season. In October 1913, provocative action by mine owners and waterfront employers precipitated a strike. From a strategic point of view, the strike was at the most convenient time for employers, and the UFL was not properly prepared. Massey's Reform Government enrolled farmers as special constables, who rode into Wellington armed with axe handles. Sutch (1966) claims that instructions to the 'specials' indicate their commanders saw them as instruments of aggression rather than control. 'Specials' rode into and battened strikers, their wives and children. 'Arbitration unions' were registered and the actions of the police and specials led to a General Strike being called, which involved about 16,000 strikers. Eventually the unions and the UFL were beaten, but the employers refused to allow the strike to end until the unions were crushed. At one stage employers refused to accept the terms that they had originally put forward. When the strike was over, many strikers were blacklisted from joining the new arbitration unions.

[1709] The inter-war years

The years between the two world wars were notable for wage cuts imposed both by the Court of Arbitration and by employers. For the 1932–3 season, freezing companies proposed massive cuts in wages. When the slaughtermen struck, they were replaced by non-unionists and the 'chain' system of slaughtering was introduced to replace 'solo-butchering'. This reduced the skill level required by a considerable margin, and meant replacement of striking freezing workers was much easier.

During this period, the employers' industrial power had increased to the point where they saw no advantage in arbitration. From 1932 to 1936, except for female employees, arbitration was only available if both employers and unions agreed. The depression and high unemployment resulted in wide-scale rejection of arbitration by employers who could impose their conditions on the unions.

In 1935 the first Labour Government was elected. They introduced compulsory unionism in 1936. Although this was intended to benefit unions, it was opposed by the Alliance of Labour, the central organisation which had replaced the UFL. The Alliance of Labour thought compulsory membership would take the militancy out of unions. Internal conflicts within the Alliance led to its collapse and in April 1937 the New Zealand Federation of Labour (FOL) was formed. The FOL lasted fifty years until in 1987 it merged with the Combined State Unions (CSU) to form the New Zealand Council of Trade Unions, the CTU.

[1710] The 1951 dispute

The 1951 dispute of 151 days accounted for the greatest loss of working days through strikes in New Zealand's history. This dispute started on the waterfront over a refusal by employers to pass on increases granted by the Court of Arbitration. The watersiders imposed an overtime ban. Such action was defined as a 'strike' under the wartime *Emergency Regulations* which were still in force. Overtime bans were not defined as strikes under the ICA Act, and hence many refer to the incident as 'the 1951 Lockout'. The strike spread to freezing workers, miners, drivers, hydro workers and others.

As with the seamen in 1890, and the miners in 1913, the watersiders' tactics and strategy were found wanting. Before the 1951 strike, the watersiders had led a walkout of the FOL in some major unions, alienating themselves from the FOL. Hence, in the 1951 strike, the unions had to face the employers and the government, with half the labour movement opposed to them. Government action was fierce and repressive, with an inactive Opposition. Nash, the Leader of the Opposition Labour Party, sat on the fence during the five-month strike, and is remembered for being 'neither for nor against the strike'.

As in 1913, the employers ensured that the final defeat was overwhelming. In this case, when the watersiders accepted the employers' conditions, the employers added to them. The major unions involved – the watersiders and freezing workers – were crushed and new unions registered. Many watersiders were blacklisted and some emerged later as leaders of a variety of unrelated unions, such as that of clothing workers.

B. Principal Legislation

[1711] Philosophy of the legislation

Woods (1963:38) considers that

> during the four years 1890 to 1894 four main motives were operative amongst the supporters of compulsory arbitration – a general desire to avoid strikes; a desire on the part of trade unions to secure a recognised status; a desire amongst most sections of the community to eliminate child labour, to regulate the employment of women, and to secure a general improvement in social conditions; and a desire to avoid industrial stoppage and to secure third party intervention in industrial disputes.

The ICA Act 1894 was described as

> an Act to encourage the formation of industrial unions and associations and to facilitate the settlement of industrial disputes by conciliation and arbitration.

Originally it was not unitarist, in that it set out to create unions, but pluralist only to the extent that it favoured collective bargaining in a formalised sense (that is, conciliation using the New Zealand definition, see [805]), rejecting the idea of strikes. Elsewhere it has been claimed (Geare, 1989:213) that during much of the period until 1987 the legislation in fact was paternalistic and the underlying ideology increasingly unitarist.

[1712] Two sectors

In s.91 of the ICA Act 1894, it was specified that, with certain exceptions, the Act would not apply to the Crown or Government departments. Thus although there had always been a public and a private sector, the ICA Act emphasised this difference, and the separation remained until 1988. The public sector in New Zealand during this period employed around twenty per cent of all wage and salary earners. Three of the largest unions in the country were public sector unions. The largest employer in the country was the government, and even when broken down into the Post Office, State Services, and so forth, governmental employer bodies rank at the top. In the latter years, wage increases in the public sector were often blamed for being a major cause of inflation. All this would tend to suggest that public sector employment relations would have received a reasonable degree of attention. However, in general, this was not the case and indeed the same may be said for other industrialised countries. The situation is self perpetuating. Probably because, in the early period of employment relations study (late nineteenth to early twentieth century), the public sector was less militant than the private sector, it was seen as 'less interesting.' Consequently there was less study done of the public sector, less was written about it, and hence programmes and courses on employment relations tended to ignore it, concentrating for many years on blue-collar (male) factory workers. Certainly the fact that in New Zealand the major piece of employment relations legislation excluded the public sector helped ensure it was ignored by academics. Thus, the prominent texts of the 1970s which related to aspects of employment relations such as industrial and employment law have either ignored the public sector (Mathieson, 1970) or specifically excluded it (Szakats, 1975), even when the titles of the texts implied total generality. While this chapter will tend to concentrate on the private sector, it will not ignore the public sector which is discussed in Part Three.

[1713] Institutions

During the 'Arbitration era', the main arbitral body had a variety of name changes. In summary:

1895–1973	Court of Arbitration
1973–1978	Industrial Court and Industrial Commission, with the *same* representatives from the New Zealand Employers' Federation (NZEF) and Federation of Labour (FOL) in each. (The law was changed in 1976 and stipulated that there be *different* representatives from the NZEF and FOL – but the required order in Council to put that into effect was not made.)
1978–1987	Arbitration Court

The Court of Arbitration was both an arbitral and legal body and had jurisdiction for the settlement and determination of any industrial dispute referred to it under the provisions of the ICA Act. Thus, it was the final arbitral body in situations where agreement had not already been reached. In addition, the Court had the right to give its opinion on any question connected with the construction of any award or industrial agreement, or on any particular determination or direction of the Court, or on the construction of any Act relating to matters within the jurisdiction of the Court. This meant the Court was able to interpret awards and industrial agreements. It was not obliged to do so, and was able to decline to give its opinion.

The Court of Arbitration consisted of a Judge, a representative of the unions of employers, and a representative of the unions of workers; in practice in more recent years, the NZEF and the FOL have represented workers.

From 1971 a joint committee established from the executives of the NZEF and the FOL had been working on a revision of the industrial legislation. Although no agreement was reached over many major issues, they did produce one idea, considered radical, that there should be a split in the functions of the Court of Arbitration so that the legal functions of interpretation and enforcement were not to be carried out by a body which has an arbitral role.

After eighty years with a Court of Arbitration, the idea of having an Industrial Commission to arbitrate and determine awards, and an Industrial Court to interpret and enforce them, could seem innovative. However, since

Australia had made a similar move some twenty years earlier, it was probably simply imitative.

In order to clearly differentiate between the arbitral function of the Industrial Commission and the interpretative function of the Industrial Court, a distinction was made between the two major classes of disputes: (a) interest: establishing conditions in awards and agreements; (b) rights: interpreting and enforcing awards and agreements.

The degree of separation between the two bodies was lessened by the fact that key members of the Industrial Commission were also members of the Industrial Court. The Industrial Commission consisted of five members:

a. three who do not represent any sectional interests;
b. one from the NZEF;
c. one from the FOL.

The Industrial Court retained the same structure as the Court of Arbitration.

From 1973–6 it was required by the IR Act 1973 that the NZEF and FOL nominees on the Industrial Court be the same as those on the Industrial Commission. Thus two of the principals on both the Commission and the Court were the same individuals.

In 1977, the two bodies were recombined back into the Arbitration Court. Its makeup was identical to the old Court of Arbitration.

[1714] Registration of unions

The principle behind the legislation for the whole of this period was voluntary registration of 'industrial unions of workers' under the Act, and the acceptance of conciliation and arbitration as alternatives to strikes or lockouts if peaceful negotiation failed to settle a dispute. Although registration was theoretically 'voluntary', the term is somewhat misleading. The then Registrar of Industrial Unions (Woods, 1963:15) wrote that registration 'is entirely voluntary, but the advantages of registration, while not coercive are strongly persuasive.' In fact, from the mid 1930s the pressure on unions to register, and remain registered, was highly coercive. This resulted from a combination of the advantages, and the danger in *not* being registered (stemming from compulsory unionism [1715], and the blanket clauses [1719]). The coercion is explained in [1725]. As a result of this coercion, only a very insignificant percentage of societies chose *not* to register and to remain outside the 'system.'

The original idea behind union registration was to grant them sole bargaining rights and protection from takeover by another union. No union could amend its rules to include under its membership coverage persons already covered by another registered union, except with permission from the Registrar or Court. Hence absorption of one union by another was impossible. Permission was granted very rarely, and the applicant union had to have already been acting for the employee in question, over a period of time – even though they should in theory have been in a different union. The Court attempted to ensure that membership clauses were clear and different and hence confusion did not arise. However, as work changed the question as to which union a particular worker should belong was not always easily answered and demarcation problems occasionally arose.

[1715] Compulsory unionism

From 1896–1936 there was no compulsion to join a union. There was an advantage in that some awards had preference clauses included which gave preference of employment to union members, provided they were as qualified as non-members to do the work. This was not a great advantage: employers decided who was equally, or better, qualified, and hence could always find some reason to favour the non-member. In 1936 union membership was compulsory by law. It is interesting to note that, shortly before compulsory unionism was introduced into this country, the concept was considered and rejected by the National Council of the Alliance of Labour (the forerunner of the Federation of Labour) because it was considered that the overall effect was disadvantageous to the union movement (it reduced militancy). At the same time, according to Rudman (1974:68-9), the NZEF was also against the concept because they felt 'the privilege was more substantial than the surrender' – that is, they considered the overall effect to be overly advantageous to the union movement. However in 1951 (and again in 1961), when the National Party threatened to abolish compulsory unionism they found that both the FOL and the NZEF favoured its retention. This time the FOL thought the union movement benefited more by having compulsion as it increased numerical strength and funds; and the NZEF now thought employers also benefited more, as it reduced conflict within the workforce and union militancy.

In 1961 the National Government – after having backed down a decade earlier from a promise to abolish compulsory unionism – did abolish legally imposed compulsory unionism. It replaced this with a provision that an 'unqualified preference clause' could be inserted in an award or agreement.

The unqualified preference clause would be inserted if either one of two conditions was met. The first was that the insertion of such a clause was agreed to by the assessors (negotiating team) at conciliation (see Chapter Seven). This occurred in virtually every situation. It should be noted that agreement was by all assessors. Hence, employers as well as unions were responsible for the insertion of such clauses. The second condition was that not less than fifty per cent of the employees involved wanted to become or remain union members. For practical reasons the law allowed fifty per cent of the votes cast to be taken as fulfilling the requirement. Thus, if the majority of employees did not want unqualified preference, then at the AGM they could instruct the union assessors not to agree to unqualified preference.

If an unqualified preference clause was in an award or agreement, it meant that any employee employed by an employer bound by that award or agreement had to join the union within fourteen days of being asked, and had to remain in the union. Failure to do so meant both the employee *and* the employer were in breach and could be fined.

If unions were able arbitrarily to restrict entry, they could, in effect, prevent certain individuals, or individuals of a certain race, political belief or religious orientation, from gaining employment by means of the unqualified preference clause. Individuals who were not permitted to join the union could still be asked to join (and then have their application turned down). They, and more significantly, their employer, would then be in breach of the award or agreement. To avoid a series of $500 penalties, the employer would dismiss the employees. To prevent such an abuse of the system, the legislation gave all employees the right to join the union unless either they were of 'general bad character' (not specified) or, though this occurred only rarely, the Court had set a maximum membership on the union and this maximum had been reached. In the past, union exclusion of individuals occurred with government-backed unions blacklisting former 'militants.'

Certain employees felt unable to be members of unions because of their beliefs. Under the law, employees were exempted from joining the union if they had sincere conscientious beliefs, on either religious or other grounds, against joining a union. Table 17.1 gives the grounds and usual occupations of employees, considered for exemption in the year ending 31 March 1982.

Table 17.1. Conscientious objectors

Grounds for Objection:		
(a) Religious belief		176
The workers being:		
Exclusive Brethren	116	
Seventh Day Adventists	16	
Other religions	44	
(b) Other grounds		37
TOTAL		213
Usual occupations:		
Clerical		93
Engineering		21
Retail		17
Farming		16
Reps – Travellers		14
All others		52
TOTAL		213

Source: Department of Labour Report, 1982.

Religious objection to unionism results, apparently, from a literal interpretation of the Bible, in particular 2 Corinthians, chapter 6 verse 14: 'be ye not unequally yoked together with unbelievers.' However, it would seem that conscientious objectors do not seem to follow the rest of the Bible so conscientiously and literally. Thus Matthew, chapter 5 verses 29–30 is ignored with very few (if any!) obeying the injunctions:

> If thy right eye offend thee, pluck it out, and cast it from thee ... And if thy right hand offend thee, cut it off, and cast it from thee ...

Most prefer to take this section figuratively. It could also be queried how the religious objectors felt able to be 'unequally yoked' with the rest of New Zealand society, and live in the country at all.

Objectors were obliged to pay a sum of money equal to the union fees to the consolidated account, so they did not save money by not joining the union. In reality, most people who objected to joining the union did so because either they did not feel they got value for money, or they realised they would get many of the benefits any way as non-members. Wanting to save, by not paying union fees, was not a ground for exemption.

From 1976 a series of ministerially enforced ballots were held, with very disappointing results for the Government. Of the first six ballots, support ranged from ninety-six per cent in favour to a low of seventy-five per cent in favour of retaining compulsory unionism through the unqualified preference clause. The unqualified preference clause in the New Zealand Clerical Workers Award (affecting seven unions) was made invalid on the ground the unions had failed to provide membership lists. When a ballot was held, a majority was in favour of unqualified preference – although clerical workers were presumed to be amongst the most anti-union of work groups.

A 1983 amendment introduced voluntary unionism by law as from February 1984. As an election was due that year, with an almost certain Labour victory, there was very little union reaction to the move. The incoming Labour Government had promised a return to unqualified preference but in the event were slow to act. It appears that they wanted to use the promise of a return to unqualified preference as an inducement for support and good behaviour for as long as possible. Thus voluntary unionism by law was not abolished until July 1985. At that time unqualified preference was reintroduced, but the clause was titled 'union membership' rather than unqualified preference.

[1716] Industrial matters

From the original ICA Act 1894 through to the IR Act 1973 in operation in 1987, the legislation was designed to settle 'disputes'. The various Acts only operated once a 'dispute' existed.

However, a dispute is not simply a 'difference of opinion', but has instead a particular meaning defined under the Act. Under New Zealand law a dispute had to be between union(s) and employer(s) *and* had to be over an 'industrial matter'.

Over the years the definition changed somewhat, but not to a major degree. Industrial matters under the IR Act were:

> all matters affecting or relating to work done or to be done by workers, or the privileges, rights, and duties of employers or workers in any industry, not involving questions that are or may be the subject of proceedings for an indictable offence; and includes –
>
> (a) all matters affecting the privileges, rights, and duties of unions or associations or the officers of any union or association; and
> (b) all matters affecting or relating to the preferential employment or the non-employment, of any person or class of persons, whether a member or members of a union of workers or not, but not so as to prevent any employer from engaging any person who at the time of engagement is not a member of a union; and
> (c) all matters that by this or any other Act are declared or deemed to be industrial matters – but does not include any matter relating to the compulsory membership of a union of workers by a person, as a condition of his employment, before such employment commences.

Judgements regarding industrial matters do not exhibit a high level of consistency. For example, the Court of Appeal in *Magner v Gohns* was split on a 3:2 basis over the interpretation.

There are three general approaches to the interpretation of the definition – broad, narrow and pragmatic. Judges in the past have taken all three. Judges are of course also dependent on earlier judgments, which either assist them or shackle them, depending on the degree of agreement.

Narrow interpretations of 'industrial matters' were taken by judges who upheld the idea of 'managerial prerogatives'. (See [305]). Hence they saw it as their duty to ensure that their interpretations prevented the intrusion of unions or the Court into managerial prerogatives.

Judges favouring narrow interpretations also tended to write words into the definition, either explicitly or implicitly, in order to justify their interpretation. Thus they converted 'work done or to be done' into 'work *actually* done', (*Clancy v Butcher Shop Employees Union*) and 'privilege' was converted into 'privilege written into an award or contract of service' (*NZ Bank Officers*), thus ignoring unwritten, but traditional, perks and privileges.

A more legitimate restriction – in that it did not require a re-writing of the legislation, although it is open to debate – was to claim that the definition applied only to employees when they were *actually* employed, thus defining as non-industrial such matters as pensions or redundancy pay. The alternative approach favoured by those taking either a broad or pragmatic view is that it is a privilege to an *employee* to be guaranteed benefits when he or she became an *ex-worker*.

Those favouring a broad interpretation tended to consider that most, if not all, issues likely to be raised by a union were covered by the definition.

For example, a decision to introduce new technology would clearly affect the work to be done by employees. The provision, or not, of holiday homes would affect employee privileges. The granting of pensions to retired employees, or their widows and widowers, can be taken to be a privilege or right of employees notwithstanding that they were no longer employed, since as Kitto J. observed in *R v Hamilton Knight* at 332:

> A claim for pensions after the termination of employment is a claim that the rewards of the employment shall include not only immediate remuneration but also, in certain events, a pension either for the employee alone, or for him in the first instance and for his widow after him.

The pragmatic approach to the interpretation of the definition produces a very similar result to the broad approach. It took the view expressed in *Australian Tramways* by Isaacs and Rich (at 695) that legislation concerning conciliation and arbitration in Australia (and New Zealand) was created to settle industrial disputes which at that time

> was not then a technical term; it expressed in popular language a situation with respect to industry that had often happened, and was happening with increasing frequency and ever-broadening application.

And so:

> To hold that a 'dispute' causing serious industrial disturbance and public loss could not be dealt with by the Arbitration Court unless the claim refused directly affected both the employees and the employers would, in my opinion, seriously curtail a very beneficial power intentionally given to the Commonwealth Parliament, and I personally cannot concur in such a view.

Although the broad, narrow and pragmatic interpretations give very different results, this does not necessarily indicate that the judgements are affected by bias. Obviously the different value systems held by different Judges must influence their interpretation, though they could still be attempting to interpret the legislation fairly according to accepted rules. Unfortunately it does not always appear that way. Judges who favour the narrow approach (rather than those who are clearly just following earlier judgements) give a strong impression they will support the concept of managerial prerogatives come what may. Similarly, Judges who favour the pragmatic approach, notwithstanding their admirable sense of employment relations reality, at times tend to give the impression that they are prepared to overlook the law when it seems to them that it deserves to be overlooked.

Near the end of the Arbitration era, there were two significant cases in New Zealand. Both judgements took a *narrow* interpretation, and tended to rely on Australian cases for support. The *NZ Bank Officers* case arose from a conflict created when the ANZ Bank decided to raise the interest rate on the loans it made to some, but not all, staff members. The judge's decision was that the issue was not an industrial matter, and he claimed (at 384):

> The award contains nothing to create any rights or duties in relation to the availability of staff loans. We have had no evidence to suggest that there is any general contract of service which incorporates any such provisions or which creates any obligation on the part of the bank to make loans on favourable terms to individual employees. We regard the matter of staff loans as not one which relates to the relationship of master and servant, but to be at best peripheral or collateral to that relationship. We repeat that once the employee seeks a loan from the bank the relationship then arising is that of lender and borrower, or mortgagor and mortgagee.

The union's case would have been more effective if counsel had stressed the difference between a privilege and a right. A privilege is not guaranteed to all – that would make it a right – and thus it should not be expected to appear in the award. Since the issue was deemed by the Judge not to be an industrial matter, there was no dispute, only a conflict, and the system could do nothing to help resolve the matter.

The decision in the *NZ Bank Officers* case resulted in stopwork meetings and strikes and finally, over a year after the dispute started, Roth (1979:2) reports:

> The ANZ Bank agreed to reduce interest rates on staff loans but negotiation broke down when the Bank denied the right of the Bank Officers Union to represent its members on matters outside the award. ANZ staff in several centres voted to take industrial action but on 10 October the trading banks acknowledged the Union's right of representation.

The second case was the *Law Practitioners* (1980), which involved the issue as to whether or not the establishment of new technology or new machinery, which may result in fewer jobs or job opportunities, is an 'industrial matter' within the meaning of the law. The Court in this case ruled that the introduction of Visual Display Units (VDUs) into law offices was again *not* an industrial matter – even though clerical workers would lose their jobs as one employee with a VDU could do the work of a number using typewriters. The clerical workers accepted their defeat without further action.

A conflict does not disappear simply because it is defined as being over a 'non-industrial matter', and it is naive and unrealistic to assume it would. The consequence is that unions, if strong enough, will use normal negotiation tactics such as strikes to win their case. The clerical workers in the *Law Practitioners* case accepted the decision against them, but in the same period the meat workers demonstrated that they would not be fobbed off with the notion that the installation of new technology was a managerial matter which should not concern them.

It can be argued that attempting to define 'industrial matters' at any stage is a mistake. Any definition allows the introduction of bias into interpretation. Purely on pragmatic grounds, whatever system of employment relations is in place should be equipped to help settle conflicts, whether on managerial prerogatives, social issues, political issues, wages, conditions or whatever. If a system involving conciliation and arbitration is considered to be better than one using strikes and lockouts, then the system should be able to cope with all conflicts.

[1717] Disputes

The difference between interest-type and rights-type disputes was discussed in [803]. Until 1973, the legislation did not formally differentiate between the two types and the Court of Arbitration was the final arbitral body for both types. The IR Act 1973 formally defined disputes. The statutory definition of a dispute of interest and a dispute of rights was close to, but did not coincide with, the popular meanings. Thus, a dispute of interest was defined as a dispute:

> created with intent to procure a collective agreement or award settling terms and conditions of employment of workers in any industry, whether or not the agreement or award is to be in substitution for an existing agreement or award …

A dispute of rights was defined as:

> (a) A dispute concerning the interpretation, application, or operation of a collective agreement or award; or
> (b) A dispute concerning a matter of the interpretation, application, or operation of an enactment or contract of employment, being a matter related to a collective agreement or award; or
> (c) Any dispute that is not a dispute of interest, including any dispute that arises during the currency of a collective agreement or award; or
> (d) A personal grievance.

These definitions create problems. The definition of a dispute of interest is restrictive. Not only must the dispute be over setting terms and conditions, but it must also be to procure a collective agreement or award (both defined under the law).

Awards set minimum conditions, in general for a district(s) or the country as a whole. For example the NZ Printers Award set minimum conditions for *all* printing firms in the country. This was very significant. All employees in that industry had a minimum level of wages and conditions. All employers knew that competitors could not (legally) pay less than award rates and thus undercut other employers.

Frequently a particular firm, or the employees, would want to negotiate 'above-award' conditions. Such a dispute is not a dispute of interest. Thus the Court of Appeal in the AHI case observed at 248:

> the dispute in the present case, although a dispute as to terms and conditions of employment, was not a 'dispute of interest.' That is because it was not a dispute 'created with intent to procure a collective agreement or award.'

It would thus appear that a dispute to gain above-award provisions would be a dispute of rights under (c), in the definition above. As discussed in [626] when interpreting the procedure to settle disputes of right, the Court of Appeal in the AHI case concluded the procedure would not cover an above-award dispute.

[1718] Settlement of disputes of interest

Disputes of interest, through the whole of this era, could be settled by:

a. 'voluntary negotiation' – or collective bargaining.
b. conciliation – where the term has the meaning peculiar to Australia and New Zealand (see [805]) involving *formalised* collective bargaining with a chairman. The chairman (there were no women employed in this role) was variously referred to as Chairman of the Conciliation Board, Conciliation Commissioner and Conciliator.
c. arbitration – by the Court of Arbitration, or later the Industrial Commission, or later yet the Arbitration Court.

The end products of a dispute of interest *should* have been entitled:

a. negotiated agreement;
b. conciliated agreement;
c. arbitrated award.

Unfortunately the end products were not titled according to logic or method of settlement. At different times during this period an 'award' could have been produced by:

a. voluntary negotiation, resulting in an industrial agreement which was then rubber-stamped into being an award;
b. conciliation;
c. arbitration.

Table App-1 in the Appendix lists the various classifications. The important thing to note was that an *award* was not necessarily the product of arbitration. In the later years of the era (see Table App-2), arbitration was very rare.

A collective agreement could be a *principal* document, used instead of an award. (Principal) collective agreements usually involved major employers who were prepared, or wished, to have different conditions to the average (usually smaller) employer. In addition the collective agreement could be a *secondary* document, used to supplement an award. In later years this type of document was frequently referred to as a *second-tier* agreement. In some cases the secondary agreement involved wages; in other cases it would involve a matter which the union wanted, but was unable, to introduce into the award. The union would negotiate the matter with individual employers until eventually a large enough number had agreed for it to be accepted by the employers' negotiators into the award.

[1719] *Blanket clause*

One of the major features of this era was the long-standing provision known as the 'blanket' clause. The 'blanket' clause, according to Woods (1963:66), was not 'inserted in the Act' until 1937. However, the 1925 Act stated:

> The award, by force of this Act, shall extend to and bind as subsequent party thereto every trade-union, industrial union, industrial association, or employer who, not being an original party thereto, is at any time whilst the award is in force connected with or engaged in the industry to which the award applies within the industrial district to which the award relates.

As far back as 1900 the Court of Arbitration had the power to extend the award to cover other parties engaged in the industry, but it was not automatic. The blanket clause meant that unions did not need to negotiate with every small employer in the industry or district. The union(s) could negotiate with the major employers and a selection of small employers. The blanket clause in the award then extended all the provisions to every other employer. This also had advantages to employers who knew that competitors should, by law, be paying stated minimum wages and providing stated minimum conditions. As discussed below in [1725], it also helped make deregistration a powerful weapon for the State.

The blanket clause did not automatically apply to industrial agreements, which bound only the parties to them. However, an industrial agreement could cover the majority in the industry and, if so, could be 'rubber stamped' by the court and transformed into an award. The blanket clause would then become operative.

[1720] Settlement of disputes of rights

A dispute of rights referred to a dispute over the interpretation, application or operation of the award or agreement (variously termed). That is, there was a disagreement over what the document actually *meant*, or one or other party (usually the employer) was not *applying* or *operating* the award correctly and was failing to abide by one of the minimum conditions and so for example would be paying below award wages, or was failing to pay the correct penal rate for overtime, or was not giving adequate holidays.

Since 1951, legislation provided for a disputes committee to try to settle the matter. Failing this, the matter would go to the Court. The dispute, as with disputes of interest, would be between union(s) and employer(s).

[1721] Settlement of personal grievances

Pressure for legislation to provide a procedure to settle personal grievances, particularly with regard to grievances over dismissals, came during the late 1960s. Employers came to support the idea only after stronger unions found they could successfully contest dismissals by going on strike. Employees and unions became more supportive when, in 1968, unemployment reached significant levels for the first time since the Second World War.

In 1970, the ICA Amendment Act introduced a procedure to settle grievances because of a claim an employee had been 'wrongfully' dismissed. The Minister of Labour, the Hon. J.R. Marshall, then made the exercise a pointless waste of time by announcing that any dismissal with notice was not a wrongful dismissal. Consequently it was not until the IR Act 1973 that a useful procedure was introduced covering 'unjustifiable' dismissals, in s.117.

The procedure in the model clause involved a series of steps to be taken if the grievance was not settled by an earlier stage. In brief, the procedure, if not settled at a particular step, was:

a. worker to supervisor;
b. worker to union secretary;
c. grievance in writing;
d. grievance to grievance committee (committee comprised equal numbers, up to three, for each side and optional chairman);
e. grievance to Arbitration Court.

In effect, if the parties agreed to have a chairman, they were agreeing to abide by his decision provided that consensus could not be reached. The decision was 'of the committee' – but since in a disagreement the voting patterns of the employer and employee sides matched, the chairman's decision was vital. There was no appeal over the decision.

The legislation specified that, by reason of the personal grievance, employees could not strike, and employers could not subsequently dismiss any other employee.

If the employee was found to have been unjustifiably dismissed, the settlement could, but need not, include one or more of:

a. the whole or part of lost wages;
b. reinstatement;
c. compensation.

Analysis of what is currently meant by 'unjustifiable' is given in Chapter Nineteen.

[1722] Anti-discrimination

The IR Act 1973 did not deal with general forms of discrimination. That was left to two other pieces of legislation, the Race Relations Act 1971 and the Human Rights Commission Act 1977.

From as early as 1903, penalties could be imposed applicable to the private sector, which provided for penalties to be imposed on employers who dismissed employees because they took part in union-related activities. However, it was only since the enactment of the IR Act 1973 that there had been actual protection for the employees from the effects of the employers' actions. Prior to 1973, the employer could be penalised, but the employee would receive no compensation or reinstatement. The IR Act 1973 did provide in s.150 (referred to by the

Chief Judge of the Arbitration Court in *Auckland Shop Employees* (at 170) as 'the anti-victimisation section') for reinstatement of, and/or compensation to, employees dismissed as a result of union or industrial-related activities. The general protection against unjustifiable dismissal, discussed above, greatly reduced the significance of the anti-victimisation protection.

Research by Geare (1987) revealed that only 48/263 (20.6 per cent) of smaller unions, with membership up to 4999, and only 12/29 (41.4 per cent) of larger unions had union rules which gave protection under s.150 to their shop-floor representatives. In total, only 60/262 (22.0 per cent) unions gave protection.

Once s.117 (unjustified dismissal) was available, s.150 (anti-victimisation) became superfluous. Action could be taken only under one or other section not both. Under s.150, an employer always had the defence that while the dismissal may have been unjustifiable, it was for a reason *other than* the union related activities. Thus an arbitrary and unfair dismissal of a union representative was not 'discrimination' if, for example, it was because of *racial* as opposed to *union* discrimination.

[1723] Strikes and the law

It is often inferred that the 'opposite' to a strike is a lockout. That is, a strike is caused by employees, or unions, who stop work and a lockout is caused by the employer or managers who prevent employees from working. This view is a distortion of reality, even though it is reinforced by the legislation which has penalties for employees, unions and union officials for strike action, and penalties for employers for lockouts. However this is just window-dressing. Lockouts during this era were virtually non-existent, because there was rarely any need for employers to use lockouts, even if they wanted a stoppage of work. If they really wanted a stoppage, then in practically all cases they could trigger strikes either by their actions or by their refusals to act. Hence, the fact that there is legislation against lockouts as well as strikes does not mean that both parties are treated equally. If there must be penalties in the legislation then to be fair they should be applied to individual managers and employers, as well as to union officials and employees, in the event of a strike. No rational person has ever alleged that strikes are caused 100 per cent by employees, unions or union officials, with management being totally blameless. However, the penalties for strikes implied that was so, as 100 per cent of the penalties apply to employees, unions and union officials.

The legal situation with regard to strikes during the era was complicated and often misunderstood. This is largely the result of the fact that over the years since 1895 the legislation became progressively more repressive and in addition became more explicit regarding strike action. As a result, a particular strike could be deemed illegal or subject to penalty from a number of different sections or Acts.

Strangely, a strike was not defined until the ICA Am Act 1908. This amendment defined a strike as:

The act of workers

a. discontinuing that employment, whether wholly or partially;
b. breaking their contracts of service;
c. refusing or failing after any such discontinuance to resume or return to their employment – with intent to:
   (i) compel or induce an employer to agree to terms of employment;
   (ii) cause loss or inconvenience to any such employer in the conduct of his business;
   (iii) incite, aid, abet, instigate or procure any other strike;
   (iv) assist workers in the employment of any other employer to compel or induce that employer to agree to terms of employment or comply with any demands made upon him by any workers.

The 'intent' part of the definition remained unchanged through the ICA Acts.

In 1939, under *Emergency Regulations* (1939/204), two further acts of workers were deemed strikes:

- refusing or failing to accept their usual work; and
- reducing the normal output.

The Regulations remained in force until December 1951, so the 1951 Waterfront Dispute (see [1710]), which was triggered by an overtime ban, was a strike under its jurisdiction – since the action meant they not only reduced their normal output but refused to accept their usual (overtime) work. The ICA Am Act 1951 incorporated the additional acts.

[1724] Strike penalties

In the first few years of the era, strikes were permitted except when a dispute was at conciliation or arbitration. The prohibition for strikes before conciliation remained with a specific penalty provided from 1908 to 1981.

Very shortly before strikes were explicitly banned a combination of sections made them illegal under many circumstances and subject to penalty. From the ICA Act 1900, s.86, it was provided that

> notwithstanding the expiration of the currency of the award, the award shall continue in force until a new award has been duly made …

We might imagine this coupled with the provision established in the ICA Am Act 1903 in s.109:

> if during the currency of any award, any employer, worker, industrial union, association … has taken proceedings with intent to defeat any of the provisions of the award … (they) … shall be deemed to have committed a breach of the award and liable accordingly.

In this coupling, it can be seen that an award is in existence until the instant the new one supersedes it. Thus at *all* times a current award exists. Hence, any strike action over hours of work or wages or conditions must cause a breach of an award, subject to penalty. Originally these provisions referred only to awards, but later similar provisions were introduced for industrial agreements.

After 1905, the ICA legislation explicitly made strike action or the aiding of a strike an offence. The penalties for striking under this section were greater than for breaching the award, and so attention from then on focussed on explicit penalties. Over the years, the levels of penalties increased.

After 1908, there were additional penalties for strikes in certain specified industries, if fourteen days' notice had not been given. These were industries considered 'essential', not necessarily 'strike-prone', and included the production and supply of coal, coal gas, natural gas and electricity, the supply of water and milk and the slaughtering and distribution of meat for domestic consumption.

In 1972, the National Government presented their *Industrial Relations Bill* which continued the historical pattern by increasing the prohibition of, and penalties for, strikes. One of the issues in the 1972 General Election was whether these increased penalties should be introduced. Not surprisingly, those measures (subsequently introduced in 1976–77) had engendered a lot of hostility. The National Party was defeated in the election and the Labour Government removed the measures proposed by National, and also some of the existing provisions against strikes. This action prompted the belief that strikes had been legalised. However, what the Labour Government removed from the legislation were equivalent to the later and more severe penalties imposed under the ICA Acts. Equivalent provisions to the first restrictions on strike action over disputes of interest still remained, in fact in a somewhat more comprehensive form.

Under the IR Act 1973 strikes were illegal and subject to penalty when a dispute was before conciliation; and strikes were banned when a dispute was before a disputes committee, or there was a personal grievance, and in those instances could be penalised as breaches. A strike while the dispute was before the Court could result in proceedings for contempt of Court, as the Arbitration Court had all the powers inherent in a Court of record. In addition there was always the penalty of deregistration. Notwithstanding, at the first meeting of the Industrial Relations Council (see [1748]), the Minister of Labour (*Press Association Report*, 1974) announced, with scant regard for the facts, that 'the Industrial Relations Act, under which this Council is set up, has ruled out penalties for industrial action.'

[1725] Deregistration

In [1714] above, it was observed that the pressure on an unregistered society to register was coercive. This was a function of the blanket clause and compulsory unionism or unqualified preference. These provisions, which individually were seen as benefiting employees and unions, combined together to form a tremendous weapon for the State *against* unions.

Assume, for example, a group of employees decided to remain in an unregistered society, rejecting both the benefits and restrictions of registration. If they were highly skilled and had total solidarity, the society could survive. If, however, the society faced State disapproval and there was a small group of dissidents, then the dissidents could themselves register as a union. The dissident union (comprising, say, 15 out of 1000 in the Auckland district) could negotiate an award and have the unqualified preference clause included. According to the blanket clause, *all* employers in Auckland of employees of that type were covered. The members of the society would now have to join the 'union' if they wanted work. Quite probably, the union rules would suggest some of the officers, and members of the society would be banned from membership of the union, and hence prevented from gaining employment.

Deregistration clearly put a union in the same precarious position as an unregistered society, with the additional handicap that State disapproval was apparent. When waterside unions were deregistered in 1951, it was easier to create new unions as the work was unskilled. Sutch (1966:380) states that the government

> took men recently released from prison, made them officials of scab unions, and persuaded rural Maoris, recently arrived displaced persons, methylated spirit addicts (and other persons 'known to the police') to be the nuclei of these unions.

Roth (1973:81) points out that in Auckland

> not only the leaders but virtually the entire membership of the old union, some 2,000 men, were deliberately excluded by the new union, and despite repeated protests this ban remained in force for some considerable time.

The Minister of Labour had the power under s.130 of the IR Act 1973 to deregister any union:

> if in respect of any discontinuance of employment the Minister is satisfied that it has caused or is likely to cause serious loss or inconvenience and that it has been brought about wholly or partly by any union of employers or of workers or by any member or members thereof, the Minister may, by notice in the Gazette, cancel the registration of the union, or cancel any award or collective agreement so far as it relates to the union, or cancel the membership of any specified class of members of the union.

This ultimate penalty for strike action was first used in 1939 when according to Mathieson (1970:121) 'it was hurriedly introduced, at least partly in order to deal with a particular stoppage then in progress by Auckland freezing workers.' It must be noted that a union could be deregistered for just *one* strike, for which it was only partly responsible, so long as the Minister was satisfied that it was likely to cause serious inconvenience.

The IR Act 1973 contained additional provisions with regards to deregistration which were more severe than those under the ICA Acts. From 1973, a deregistered union could have its assets taken over.

[1726] Suspension

Suspension for employees during strike action was not introduced until late in this era. Since 1973, an employer could suspend (on *no* pay) non-striking employees if, as a result of a strike, the employer was unable to provide normal work to the non-striking employees.

For an employer to use this section, there must have been employees on strike and there must not have been work available. Hence, if the employer dismissed all the striking employees, there would no longer be a strike taking place and so the employer would be unable to suspend other employees. Further, the employer could not anticipate a strike and suspend others who were not going to be involved. The suspension would be invalid and the non-striking employees entitled to pay. Similarly, the employer had to prove work was not available, and could not suspend purely in order to put pressure on the striking employees.

This provision was primarily to prevent the situation where one group of employees in a continuous operation went on strike, effectively closing down the whole operation. If the remaining employees were on full pay, they could have subsidised the striking employees, putting considerable pressure on the employer.

In addition, in theory, if non-striking employees were suspended without pay, this was supposed to make the strikers feel guilty and hasten their return to work. In practice, the suspended employees were likely to strongly resent the actions of the employer, and were likely to finally return to work with strong grievances.

From 1981, an employer was able to suspend the employment of any employees who were a party to the strike. Suspended employees lost all rights to remuneration but their service was deemed continuous.

The major significance of this provision was that employers could choose not to allow 'rolling' strikes, whereby part of the workforce or sections of the industry strike while other sections continue working, and to suspend all the employees. The employer would have to prove the suspended employees were 'party' to the strike, which would be straightforward in the event of the union announcing a rolling strike.

[1727] Mediation

From 1972, a mediation service was provided. The service started slowly, with only one mediator initially appointed to cover the whole country, and his appointment followed a considerable delay. While the law provided a grandiose description of the role of mediator, the mediator's function was primarily as a 'fire-fighter' – offering services to parties to help settle conflicts, chair disputes committees and personal grievance committees. Later, mediators were also used to chair committees of inquiry. The number of mediators increased slowly during this period – reaching six.

Mediators were explicitly excluded from disputes of interest during conciliation or arbitration. Some commentators have claimed (Howells and Cathro, 1986:22) that mediators were 'barred from interest disputes'. This is incorrect and highlights the confusion created by the legislation. An 'interest dispute' is one setting wages and conditions. It could be an above-award claim or concerning an incentive scheme in one department of a firm. Mediators could be involved in such disputes. A 'dispute of interest' is a particular type of interest dispute – namely one created with intent to procure an *award* or (registered) *collective agreement* – as opposed to an informal departmental or company level agreement.

Mediators frequently act as arbitrators, either explicitly – when chairing personal grievance committees or disputes committees – or in a *de facto* role as mediators. This *de facto* role occurs when they strongly 'suggest' an outcome separately to each party.

C. Public Sector

[1728] Union development in the public sector

It was during the last quarter of the nineteenth century that unionisation began in the public sector. The New Zealand Educational Institute (NZEI) was formed in 1883, its aims originally being professional ('to advance the cause of education') rather than unionist. Later it became more union-conscious, with the aim to 'uphold and maintain the just claims of its members.' The Amalgamated Society of Railway Servants was formed in 1886 and the Post and Telegraph Officers' Society in 1890. There had in fact been a strike by telegraph staff in 1880 following the abolition of overtime payments in 1879. Keating (1974:28) reports that the strike failed because

> one operator divulged all he knew to a superior officer, so the administration ... made arrangements in advance for staff replacements ... The leaders were dismissed and even prevented from getting employment in Australia, but were re-employed later after public protest.

The Public Service Association was formed in 1890 but collapsed within a few years, having failed to achieve its main objectives: classification and recruitment policy. The present Public Service Association (PSA) dates back to 1913.

[1729] Political patronage

One of the major criticisms of the Civil Service of the time was the extent of political patronage in the area of appointments: that is, the appointment by government of persons to positions, irrespective of their actual merit, qualifications or experience. Of course, many such appointments would have been genuine, with the interest of the Civil Service at heart. However, the opportunity for granting favours for services clearly existed. In 1886, the Civil Service Reform Act stopped outside appointments by ensuring that entry to the Civil Service was by competitive examination. However, Government first ignored the legislation, then in 1887 amended the Act, to allow for appointment without examination. As Robertson (1965:1) observes, it was not until the passing of the Public Service Act 1912 that there was real effort to establish a career service 'free from the abuses of political patronage and "back door" appointments.'

[1730] Public Service Act 1912

The Public Service Act 1912 (which followed yet another Royal Commission, although the Bill was put before the Commission had reported) provided for a Public Service Commissioner and two Assistant Commissioners, independent of Government, but responsible to Parliament. It divided the Public Service into four divisions: Administrative, Professional, Clerical and General. All employees were to be graded (with a right of appeal), with the whole service regraded every five years.

In 1927 the Public Service Amendment Act made a significant change to conditions of employment by specifying that appointments were to be made on the basis of *merit* – and that seniority should only be considered when two applicants were equally efficient and suitable.

Since judgements on merit are frequently subjective and often made by people with little or no training in performance appraisal, such concerns are often valid, see [315]. Unless employers can gain acceptance that their appraisal systems are fair and accurate and skilfully and honestly applied, then merit rating will always be open to criticism on the grounds that it may be deliberately manipulated to favour one individual or that, although the rating may have been done scrupulously honestly, it reached the wrong conclusions through lack of objective data.

Just prior to, and during, the Second World War, large-scale recruitment was necessary, mainly of temporary staff. From 1935 to 1946, temporary staff as a proportion of the total staff increased from 22.3 per cent to 55.9 per cent. An amendment to the Public Service Act in 1946 allowed for temporary employees to become eligible for permanent appointments. The number of temporary staff dropped from 15,969 in 1946 to 2343 in 1949.

[1731] Legislation through 1960s to 1980s

In the 1960s and 1970s there were three further Royal Commissions: one in 1962 on the general running of the State Service, which led to the passing of the State Services Act 1962 (SS Act 1962), and two on Salary and Wage Fixing Procedures in the State Service. The first was in 1968, leading to the State Services Remuneration and Conditions of Employment Act 1969 (SSRCE Act 1969), and the second was in 1972. The SSRCE Act was later replaced by the State Services Conditions of Employment Act 1977 (SSCE Act 1977). These latter Acts, together with the SS Act 1962 and its Amendments, formed the basic legislation governing the State Services. Some sections of the State Service (Police, Post Office, etc) were not covered by the SS Act 1962, and the salaries of certain top executive officers in the State Service were determined under the Higher Salaries Commission Act 1977, rather than the SSCE Act 1977. The Higher Salaries Commission determined the salaries of the highest paid executive officers in Air New Zealand Ltd, the Bank of New Zealand, the New Zealand Wool Board, and so forth – and surprisingly the salaries of *all* teachers in universities. (The reason for this was not that university staff were 'highly' paid but because university staff were 'neither fish nor fowl', being not quite private sector but also not public sector.)

[1732] State Services Act 1962

The SS Act 1962 was concerned with employment conditions other than wages. It was to a great extent equivalent to a private sector company rule book.

The SS Act 1962 differentiated between the appointment of *outsiders* to posts in the Public Service and the appointment of *officers* (full-time Public Service employees who have worked out their probationary period) to different posts within the Public Service.

An outsider would only be appointed to a post in the Public Service if the person had 'clearly more merit for the position to be filled than any officer who is qualified and available for the position', this being determined by:

a. work experience and competence shown in performance of duties previously carried out by him; and
b. personal qualities, characteristics, and attributes relevant to the position to be filled; and
c. relevant educational or other qualifications.

Since it was difficult to do merit-rating accurately and fairly, and that was generally accepted, the system encouraged the attainment of qualifications on the grounds that they were objective attributes (even if not necessarily particularly useful).

Every officer in the Public Service had the right of appeal to the Public Service Appeal Board in opposition to

> the promotion of any officer or the appointment of any person who is not an officer, to any position on the permanent staff of the Public Service if (in either case) the appointment of the appellant to the position would have involved his promotion.

However, there could be no appeal against the promotion or appointment of any officer to the specified top positions in the Public Service. Outsiders appointed to one of these top positions had to demonstrate that they had 'clearly more merit' than officers who had applied for the post.

Following recommendations made by the 1962 Royal Commission, the SS Act 1962 greatly increased the number of posts exempt from appeal from six to, at that time, eighty-six. Not surprisingly Robertson (1965:11) reports:

> The employee organisations protested strongly about this legislation on the grounds that it took away from public servants appeal rights which had been present for many years.

By making posts exempt from appeal, the possibility of political patronage was increased. It must be recalled that the purpose of the Public Service Act 1912 was to free the Public Service from political patronage. Robertson (1965:11) claims the argument for making these top posts exempt from appeal was that 'a judicial tribunal (such as the Public Service Appeal Board) cannot have the same competence to decide between people as a group of experts with the most intimate knowledge can have.'

The Public Service Association (PSA) was, not surprisingly, very angry at the loss of the right to appeal, but failed to reverse the decision.

The Public Service was divided into occupational classes and further subdivided into grades according to the assessment of the relative levels of responsibility and skill which were or could be required by persons of that class. Every officer was placed into a grade in an occupational class, with salary payable according to grading. The State Services Commission (SSC) – the 'employer' – was responsible for conducting a continuous review of the classification and grading of the Public Service.

The SS Act 1962 also spelt out a list of offences with which employees could be charged. These included failing to comply with the Act, disobeying orders, being negligent, indolent, inefficient or incompetent, perpetual absenteeism or lateness, misuse of liquor or drugs, improper use of property or stores, improper disclosure of information or conduct which brought the Public Service into disrepute.

Thus the State as an employer (or its delegated employing authority the SSC) had powers (in theory) over its employees not held by private sector employers – most notably the power to 'fine' (for offences such as 'indolence') and the right to deduct the penalty from future wages or salaries. Like so much in legislation, however, there is a marked difference between statutory rights and rights which are actually exercised, and which could be exercised without incurring strike reaction.

Officers in the Public Service could be transferred by the SSC from one locality to another. This provision was one reason why the public sector favoured uniform wage and salary rates throughout the country rather than the regional differences that occurred in the private sector.

According to the SS Act 1962, the employment of any officer was subject to three months' notice on either side and any officer's employment may have been terminated on the grounds of redundancy if three months' notice was given. In practice, however, it was generally accepted that one of the 'fringe benefits' of employment in the public sector was job security. Redundancy was not a threat for officers in the Public Service.

[1733] Negotiation and arbitration

During the 'Arbitration era', employees in the public sector had their conditions of employment embodied in orders and determinations.

The employing authority would issue a 'determination' to those service organisations (unions) whose members would be affected by the determination. The service organisation would either:

a. accept the determination;
b. attempt to negotiate improvements;
c. apply for arbitration.

The main arbitral body in the latter periods was the Public Sector Tribunal. In operation the Tribunal had the same structure as the Arbitration Court: A chairman (who was a judge of the Arbitration Court), an employers' and an employees' representative.

[1734] Wage-fixing

There were two types of pay review within the State Services: wage-fixing and wage adjustment. Under wage adjustment, there was a general movement in the pay scales in the State Services to compensate for general movements in pay scales outside the State Services.

With wage-fixing, the objective was to set for each occupational class a pay scale which would enable the State Services to recruit and retain an efficient staff, take account of special responsibilities or conditions applying to employment in the occupational class, and be fair to the tax-paying public and to employees in the State Services.

In order to satisfy the above aim, the rewards of employment in the State Services were to be kept broadly in line with those of employment outside the State Services.

The Act made it clear that in wage-fixing particular emphasis went on ensuring that a job in the public sector received roughly the same rewards as an identical job in the private sector. Unfortunately for the ease of wage fixing, only a small percentage of jobs were identical in both sectors, and there were many jobs where no comparisons could be made between sectors. In these situations horizontal comparisons within the public sector could be made. (That is, with similar level jobs in other occupations.)

The rationale for wage-fixing is the normative view that the 'right' wage is that received by an average, roughly comparable private-sector employee. It is based on the assumption either that the private sector wage is 'right', or, if it is 'wrong', that it does not matter so long as there is consistency.

In practice, wage-fixing was a slow, expensive and time-consuming activity. Consequently wage-fixing for any particular occupation would occur only every five years or so. Particularly in times of high wage and price inflation, such delays would mean a considerable loss of income. (If wages are increasing at fifteen per cent per annum, wages double every five years.) Thus interim *wage adjustments* were needed.

[1735] Wage adjustment

Wage adjustments were used to compensate those in the State Services whose wages were not 'fixed' in any particular year.

For the period 1969–77, wage adjustments occurred every six months. By the time a survey had been completed and interpreted, and the wage adjustment approved, a number of months would have passed. Thus, unless backdating occurred, employees in the State Services would be disadvantaged.

In practice, interim wage adjustments were backdated, normally to the mid-point between surveys. The reason comes from how surveys work in practice. For example, assume that in April 1978 both the public and private sectors were completely in line, and then the October 1978 survey showed the private sector was ahead by ten per cent. The survey results would not be available for some time, and hence State Servants' pay could not be adjusted until, probably, January. Thus three months' backpay is required unless the State Servants were to be disadvantaged. This was the minimum. However, the private sector increases would not have all occurred on 30 September. Some would have occurred in May, some July, some September, and so on. Thus the increases had to be assumed (in the absence of detailed information) as having taken place on average midway between the surveys.

From 1977, wage adjustments occurred only once a year. At that time, the Government was trying to enforce a twelve-month rule for private sector employees. Although State Servants were simply 'catching-up', the appearance was that they were able to get two increases a year instead of one.

[1736] Inflationary aspect of wage fixing and wage adjustments

The system of having two sectors, private and public, with public sector wages being adjusted relative to 'average' private sector movements created a number of inflationary pressures.

The scenario of a uniform national State rate throughout the country, while the private sector had regional differences, meant that in low-wage areas of the private sector the State rates were higher. This tended to inflate the private rates. In high-wage areas, the State rates would not be competitive so there was a tendency to increase the State rates in occupations where there was a shortage, in order to recruit labour. This increase in State rates would apply in all areas, exacerbating the situation in low-wage areas.

The inflationary effect of the uniform rate throughout the country was similar to the inflationary effect of the State using average increases to make wage adjustments. Some occupations would be better off in the public sector (encouraging wage and salary demands in the private sector) and some would be worse off – leading to problems of recruitment, which in turn led to increases in the public sector.

The system of backdating was price-inflationary, insofar as it injected large amounts of money into the economy, thus increasing demand for goods and services while having no effect on supply. Basic theory suggests this would result in price increases.

The system of having two sectors, private and public – with the basic philosophy that the public sector should follow but also be roughly comparable to the private sector – was thus inherently inflationary. The obvious solution was to combine the two sectors under common employment relations legislation.

In 1983 it was predicted (Geare, 1983a:249):

> Although a merging of the sectors is not immediately likely, the possibility is increasing particularly with the amount of legislation covering both sectors and since 1976 the fact that the public sector, for the first time, is put on a similar basis to the private sector as regards strikes and lockouts.

As it happened, the merging took place in 1988.

D. General Employment Relations

[1737] The industrialised setting

The industrial setting in New Zealand during this period had a strong influence on employment relations. The era was so long that there would clearly be enormous differences from the early years, when New Zealand was basically a pioneer country, to the later years, when New Zealand was reasonably industrialised.

Writing in the middle of this era, Hare (1946:77-9) pointed out that in the 1936 census the four main centres included:

> just over a third (38.5 percent) of the population, but these cities are situated hundreds of miles apart and have no near rivals in size. Of the smaller towns, ten in number, none exceeded 26,000 in 1936, and these are not urbanised industrial centres, for their primary purpose is to serve the needs of the surrounding agricultural communities. Even counting these smaller centres together with the population of the four main cities, the urban population in 1936 formed only just over one half of the total population of New Zealand. The other half live under rural conditions and agriculture is their predominant occupation.

Hare goes on to point out that a second major factor influencing the industrial setting and development was the physical nature of the country: mountainous and rugged with rivers subject to flood. Thus transport by land is slow and costly and 'the rivers are too swift and mostly too small to provide easily navigable inland waterways.'

To this end, for a considerable portion of this era, the industry that did exist was small scale and localised. Unions developed in a similar fashion – although the legislation helped preserve small localised unions.

[1738] Unionisation

Table 17.2. Level of unionisation

	1981 (Census)
Total population	3,175,737
Not actively engaged	1,844,525
Actively engaged	1,331,210
Of the actively engaged, there are:	
Self-employed, employing labour	79,880
Self-employed, not employing labour	95,670
Unpaid, unspecified	11,020
Unemployed	60,860
Wage and salary earners	1,083,770
Of the wage and salary earners, some are in:	
Registered private sector unions	520,000
Unregistered private sector societies	7,000 (approx)
Public sector unions	163,000 (approx)
Total in unions/societies	690,000
Percentage in unions	63.7%

The degree of unionisation increased significantly after compulsory unionism was introduced in 1936. Roth (1973:112) estimated the level of unionisation at fifty-nine per cent in 1945, dropping to fifty-five per cent in 1970.

Later, Howells (1980:134) stated:

> The growth in public sector employment since 1970 has probably reduced this figure for union penetration because union membership in this area is not compulsory. Nevertheless, union membership is still likely to be over 50 per cent of the total labour force in New Zealand.

Using data from the 1981 census, the level of unionisation (public and private sector), and counting unregistered 'societies' (which are 'unions' except they did not register under the ICA Acts), the figure was probably closer to sixty-five per cent. This is shown in Table 17.2 above.

The degree of union penetration exceeded that of Australia by 10–15 per cent, Britain by 15–20 per cent and the United States by 25–35 per cent at least. However, it still means that approximately 370,000 wage and salary earners were apparently not in a union. This number of non-unionists is surprisingly large, considering that virtually all private sector unions had compulsory memberships through the unqualified preference clause. Compulsion was less universal in the public sector, but 80–85 per cent of those eligible to join the major union, the PSA, were members nonetheless (*PSA Journal*, 1981, 68(11)).

[1739] Central union organisations

In October 1987, the New Zealand Council of Trade Unions (CTU) had its inaugural conference, combining the Federation of Labour (FOL) and the Combined State Unions (CSU). During the bulk of the Arbitration era, the significant central body was the FOL.

The FOL provided the workers who were representative on the court, negotiated for General Wage Orders (see [1746]), lobbied the government, provided a service to unions, and would negotiate for them on request. The FOL was always strongly influenced by individuals: Fintan Patrick Walsh, Sir Tom Skinner, Jim Knox and Ken Douglas among them.

The majority of unions in the private sector were affiliated to the FOL. Over the years, power struggles between individuals or unions resulted in some unions disaffiliating or refusing to affiliate. Thus the Bank Officers were not affiliated, but did affiliate with the CTU; the Electrical Workers, under Tony Neary, had a number of well-publicised rows and disaffiliations; and there was a classic example in 1950 when the watersiders and supporters formed a rival central organisation, the Trade Union Congress, which collapsed after the 1951 strike.

The FOL was headed by a National Executive of nine members, elected for one year, with the exception of the President and the Secretary who were full-time officers elected for five years. The executive was elected at the annual conference of affiliated unions by the delegates at the conference. The number of delegates a union had was dependent on its membership. At the district level the FOL was represented by twenty District or Trades Councils (and a smaller Committee). One delegate from each Trades Council, together with the National Executive, formed the National Council which met twice a year. The power within the FOL lay with the National Executive and in particular with the President and with the Secretary.

Unions affiliated to the FOL benefited significantly from the increased power base. This was most important if they were involved in a confrontation with the Government.

The Combined State Unions (CSU) was the central organisation in the public sector. Within the public sector, where two or more services were involved with employer bodies, the employee organisation concerned was the CSU. Until late 1978 this body was known as the Combined State Services Organisation (CSSO). The change in name to 'unions' (also followed by the Post Office Union, previously Association) indicated a growing white collar militancy. The CSU was considerably less significant than the FOL, predominantly because of the dominance of the Public Service Association (PSA) in the public sector.

[1740] Number and size of unions

In the private sector there were a large number of unions, many of them very small. Table App-3, gives the number and size of private sector unions for a number of years. It is clear, however, that most workers were *in* large unions – even though most unions were themselves small. Data on public sector unions is less readily available. Table App-4 gives the public sector unions (or 'service organisations' as they were known) in 1985.

There were frequent complaints by employers over the 'number of unions', but in reality their complaints were over the fact that most large organisations would have to deal with one or more industrial unions and a number of occupational unions (clerical, drivers, cleaners, etc.) and craft unions (engineers, electricians, etc.).

[1741] Characteristics of New Zealand unions

New Zealand unions and union officials have been subjected to a considerable degree of criticism over the years. Much tends to be inconsistent and irrational. Almost with the same breath, critics would accuse unions of being *too weak*, and unable to control their members, of being *too strong*, and of now running the country. Alternatively critics said unions were *apathetic* – doing nothing – and at the same time would suggest they were sabotaging the economy and our way of life. When their arguments were exposed in this way, such critics usually recanted and claimed they were only referring to a small percentage of unions.

As discussed earlier, New Zealand unions were very dependent on legislation for their creation and survival. The legislation was also responsible for their approach. Hare (1946:193-4) was critical that 'very few unions engage in any activities other than those closely involved in industrial affairs.'

Partly because they were unable to provide welfare services, unions had less need for finance than overseas unions, who would be providing these welfare services. Consequently the restrictions which existed during those times in relation to union levies and subscriptions were not of great significance during the period to 1964. However, the effect was significant insofar as unions and union members had become conditioned to low subscriptions – and to financially insecure unions.

From the Second World War till the end of the era, the question of communist domination of unions would surface intermittently. In most cases the 'communist threat' was either political vote-chasing, an excuse for managerial incompetence, or a ploy in union in-fighting. Honest, rational, observers did not take the threat seriously. Roth (1978:51) reports:

> In reply to a Social Credit accusation that the National Party was conducting a campaign of 'political scaremongering by seeing a red under every trade union bed', the Minister of Labour denied that there was significant Communist influence in industrial disputes. 'The Communists are certainly not a dominant concern,' he told the press, 'although I do get concerned about one or two instances. When you are sitting at the desk dealing with up to ten disputes a day, you don't see much Communist influence.' The Prime Minister, however, disagreed with his Minister of Labour and insisted that 'a few reds stir up a lot.'

It is apparent that some union leaders took a communist stance (and frequently at other stages an anti-communist stance) – purely as power plays within the union movement. A former President of the FOL, Fintan Patrick Walsh, is a good example. In his younger days as a seaman, he was a communist and a militant who was a suspect in the presumed murder of a non-unionist who disappeared, presumably overboard, on a trip to Australia. When he took over the Seamen's Union he had resigned from the Communist Party but he was still very close to it. He became very powerful in the FOL, where the main challenge came from members of the Communist Party. In 1947 Walsh was beaten to the Vice-Presidency of the FOL by Bill Richards, by 137 votes to 136. Roth (1973:67-9) wrote that in response Walsh rallied his supporters

> and crushed the opposition in a series of hammer blows which all but destroyed the trade union movement as an effective force for social change … Socialism was becoming a dirty word, and to demand higher wages made one suspect of being part of a sinister Communist plot. Walsh and Fraser, who collaborated more closely than ever in this period, used the Communist smear very effectively to quash left-wing opposition in the Labour Party and in the unions.

The 'leftist' unions – drivers, carpenters, watersiders – formed a rival organisation to the FOL, the Trade Union Congress. Although Walsh did not become President of the FOL until 1952, he saw the TUC as an attack on his power base. Thus from the 1940s till the early 1950s, Walsh was a virulent anti-communist. But from the late 1950s, Walsh saw 'right-wing' unions as the major threat to his power, and his former allies against the communists were now seen as dangerous right-wingers. The arch-enemy was the Vatican, not the Kremlin. Walsh suspended the Labourers' Union, which prompted the disaffiliation of the North Island Electrical Workers, and Wellington Rubber Workers. Finally, just before his death in 1962, Walsh had turned full circle and was again expressing socialist ideology.

[1742] Managers, employers and the NZEF

By the later stages of the Arbitration era, there were a large number of managers and employer-managers in New Zealand. Indeed, Table 17.2 above shows 79,880 as self-employed, employing labour. The large number was a function of the small size of many business operations, matching the large number of small unions present in those times.

Table 17.3 shows that in 1982 over fifty per cent of all establishments employed less than ten employees. However, just as was discussed with regard to unions and union membership, the data looks very different when analysed with regard to percentage of those employed. Table 17.3 covers 9498 establishments employing approximately 295,000. Hence if all 2120 employing '1–4' are assumed to employ four employees, and all 2745 employing '5–9' are

Table 17-3. Manufacturing establishments, by size of workforce

Establishments		
Staff employed	No	%
1–4	2120	22.3
5–9	2745	28.9
10–19	1937	20.4
20–49	1595	16.8
50–99	577	6.1
100–599	470	4.9
600–999	31	0.3
1000+	23	0.2
Total	9498	100.0

Source: New Zealand Official Year Book 1982.

assumed to employ nine employees, then the maximum possible that the small establishments (51.2 per cent of all establishments) could employ is only 33,185 or 11 per cent of employees. Table App-5 gives the size of establishments over a number of years.

The major employer organisation during this time was the New Zealand Employers' Federation (NZEF). This body had four regional divisions – the Auckland, Wellington, Canterbury and Otago-Southland Employers' Associations.

At national level, the NZEF was run by a National Executive comprising thirty persons with an Executive Director. The National Executive of thirty was composed of twelve from the regional divisions, fourteen from employer sectors and the Presidents of the Associated Chambers of Commerce, Federated Farmers and Manufacturers' Association together with the immediate Past President of the Employers' Federation. The National Executive elected a President from the thirty.

The NZEF operated as a counterpart to the FOL (and later to the CTU). It nominated the employers' representative on to the Arbitration Court, provided an advocacy service for award negotiations, and made submissions on proposed new legislation. At regional level, the Employers' Associations provided information, training courses, advisory services, advocacy services for local award negotiations and personal grievance hearings, and, to a degree, provided general consulting services to employers.

[1743] Strikes

As outlined in Chapter Ten, although industrial conflict can be manifested in numerous ways, attention is usually centred on strikes. In addition to the major reasons cited in that chapter, it is no wonder that most attention focuses on strikes when the legislation is concerned only with strikes (admittedly with a broad definition of 'strike') and lockouts, and official statistics concentrated on strikes. As noted, from 1895–1906 there were no strikes in New Zealand. For the next few years every strike that occurred was documented each year in the *Official Year Book.*

Subsequently, reasonably comprehensive data has been made available every year on strikes – their duration, days lost, wages lost and stated causes. Data on other forms of conflict, however, are not readily available. The official year books provide strike data only. Less freely available publications provided turnover statistics, but stopped after 1979. Statistics for days lost through accidents were available up until 1973, then ceased. (Absenteeism data have *never* been available on a comprehensive scale.)

A number of generalisations can be made about strikes in New Zealand during this era:

a. although in almost all cases strikes were either explicitly illegal or at least open to penalty, strike intensity was high on a periodic basis. (See Table App-6);
b. with some notable exceptions, strikes were usually short. Over 70 per cent of post-Second World War strikes were of under two days' duration;
c. for much of the period, strike-prone industries were those suggested by the Kerr-Siegel hypothesis (see [1028] and Table App-7);
d. it is possible by using *selected* data to demonstrate almost any proposition. Hence any attempts to indicate *trends* or the effectiveness of government action by using short-term data reflect either incompetence or deliberate dishonesty. Discussions on Kondratieff cycles [1027] and Table App-6 suggest strike intensity is very cyclical *long term*.

[1744] Incomes policies: General wage orders

Wage-fixing and wage adjustment in the public sector were described in [1735]–[1737].

In addition, for over sixty years New Zealand had an unusual characteristic in its employment relations system – namely that the main arbitral body in the private sector had the right to increase (or indeed decrease) all wage rates under its jurisdiction through 'General Wage Orders' (GWO).

While the amount of the general increase would obviously affect individual award negotiations, an individual employer could see wage rates increase because of the general wage order, and then because of the award negotiations, could subsequently face so-called 'second tier' (but actually 'third tier') bargaining for an increase in level of above-award payments.

Table 17.4. General wage orders

Date	% Change (Unless Specified)	Empowering Legislation
1922	–3 (approximate)	ICA Am Act 1921–22
1931	–10	Finance Act 1931
1940	5	Rates of Wages Emergency Regulations 1940
1942	5 (up to £5/wk)	Rates of Wages Emergency Regulations 1940
1951	15	1950 Regulations under Economic Stabilisation Act 1948
1952	10 (to £12/wk)	1953 Regulations
1954	Substituted 13 for 10	"
1956	Substituted 18 for 13 (to £13/wk)	"
1959	Substituted 24 for 18	"
1962	2.5	"
1964	6	"
1966	2.5	"
1968	Nil, then 5	"
1970	3	General Wage Order Act 1969
1971–77	Period of Wage Restrictions	
1978	7 (to $100/wk)	General Wage Order Act 1877
1979	4.5	Remuneration (General Increase) Regulations under Remuneration Act 1979
1980	4	"
1981	5	Stabilisation (cost-of-living) Regulations 1980, under Economic Stabilisation Act 1948
1982–84	Period of Wage Freeze	

Originally general wage adjustments applied only to the private sector, but from the 1970s they have applied to the public sector as well. The last general increase was made in 1984, and the regulations were repealed in 1986. As shown in Table 17.4 above, the first GWO was made in 1922 and was for a *reduction* of three per cent, and was followed by a *reduction* of ten per cent in 1931. With the exception of a nil order in 1968 (see below), all other GWOs were for an *increase* in wages.

[1745] The 1968 GWO

One GWO has become notorious – the 1968 GWO. The order was made under the Economic Stabilisation Act 1948. The Court was supposed to give a GWO that would assist in providing 'economic stability'. The Court was required to consider cost-of-living, economic conditions, production output and income levels.

The NZEF argued for a nil order, the FOL for a five per cent increase. The Court, specifically the Judge and the employers' nominee, voted for a nil increase over the employees' nominee, who voted for five per cent.

This decision brought widespread protest, with thousands of employees taking part in stopwork meetings and demonstrations. A major employer granted a five per cent increase to all its employees and the Employers' Federation finally instructed the employers' representative to support a similar increase. After a second application the employers' and employees' representatives (a majority) supported a five per cent General Wage Order over the vote of the Judge. This joint action was later termed an 'unholy alliance' by R.D. Muldoon, then Minister of Finance, and later Prime Minister (1975–84).

One result of the 1968 Nil Order was to cause resentment by unions against the system and create realisation of their power to operate outside the system. The extent of 'wage drift' (the difference between actual rates paid and those prescribed in awards and agreements) indicated that unions had been operating outside the system for many years.

It has been estimated that in 1947 the average weekly wage payment for ordinary time exceeded minimum rates by about eight per cent. By mid 1965 this margin had increased to some thirty per cent. Thus the Nil Order, the uproar and the five per cent order did not start any trend; it merely emphasised what the union movement already knew, that direct action in a time of high demand for labour brought quicker results and better returns than arbitration.

[1746] The Remuneration Act 1979

In July 1979 the union movement, through the Federation of Labour, applied for a minimum living-wage order under the GWO Act 1977. To prevent this occurring, the Government repealed that Act and passed the Remuneration Act 1979. This was a most peculiar piece of legislation. Although introduced to prevent the minimum living-wage order, it went much further and gave the Executive power to overturn a settled union-management agreement. It was announced not through Parliament but over television.

Although it was probably unintentional, the Act actually encouraged *arbitration*, at the expense of collective bargaining and conciliation, in that no regulation could cancel or reduce rates decided on by the Arbitration Court (or Tribunals in the Public Sector). Thus, ludicrous though it may be, unions and employers who agreed to a thirteen per cent increase could be overruled. However, if they went to the Arbitration Court with an unsettled dispute with, for example, the union demanding 13.01 per cent and the employers offering 12.99 per cent, the Court's decision could not be overturned. (The Government, of course, could later have amended the legislation to close that loop-hole.)

The first use of the Act led to a one-day general strike and the Act was repealed in 1980. This meant the end of permanent legislation allowing for general wage adjustments. However, the Economic Stabilisation (cost-of-living increase) Regulations 1980 under the Economic Stabilisation Act 1948 allowed the Arbitration Court to make increases in 1981 (five per cent) and 1984 ($8/week), under a similar situation to that in the 1950s and 1960s. As stated, the Regulations were repealed in 1986, ending the facility to make general wage adjustments.

[1747] Incomes polices: General restrictions

There are two general periods of restrictions, detailed in Table 17.5:

a. 1971–1977 – restrictions and guaranteed minima;
b. 1982–1984 – wage freeze.

The introduction of incomes policies in New Zealand followed an almost text book approach:

a. problems with price inflation and balance of payments;
b. wage increase targeted as cause;
c. pleas for restraint;
d. pleas ignored;
e. controls introduced;
f. actual and perceived instances of avoidance reduce support for controls;
g. marked increase in 'incomes – policy avoidance' schemes;
h. personal greed of politicians 'reluctantly' granting themselves increases produces widespread increased contempt, and controls collapse. (For example, in 1974 the Labour Government (and National opposition) accepted around forty-four per cent increases. The 1975 National Government was equally avaricious, but managed to get the increase with somewhat less publicity.)

The Wage Freeze introduced in 1982 was finally ended by the 1984 Labour Government, three months after taking office.

Table 17.5. Wage restrictions and stipulated increases

Date	Empowering Legislation	Permitted Increases through Negotiation	Increases Granted by Authority (Cost of Living)
1971			
25 March	SRA 1971	7% plus catch-ups	Nil 4.8% min. guarantee for those negotiating less
21 July	SRA 1971	Nil	9.2%, absorbing the 4.8%, as min. guarantee
1972			
26 October	SRR 1972	Nil	4.2% (Private Sector) 2.8% (Public Sector)
In November 1972 the Labour Party became the Government and abolished the Remuneration Authority and for around nine months allowed union-management negotiations to take place.			
1973			
11 August	ESR 1973	Nil	8.5% to max of $5.80/wk (Private) 6.2% to $4.60/wk (Public)
1974			
11 February	ESR 1973	Nil	2.7%
1 July	WAR 1974	2.25%	9& (in addition to the up to 2.25%)
1975			
15 January	WAR 1974	Nil	4.0% max of $3.00/wk
9 July	WAR 1974	Nil	11 cents/hr
1976			
27 January	WAR 1974	Nil	9 cents/hr
25 June	WAR 1974	Nil with exceptions	7.0% to max of $7.00/wk
1977			
14 March	WAR 1974	Nil	General order of 6.0% on ordinary pay only – (not on cost of living orders)
From August 1977 to June 1982 there were no general wage restrictions. However the last 'round' of increases ended in November 1981.			
1982			
23 June	WFR 1982	Nil	$8/week 1 June 1984
The Wage Freeze ended 30 November 1984			

Key: SRA 1971: Stabilisation of Remuneration Act 1971
SRR 1972: Stabilisation of Remuneration Regulations 1972
ESR 1973: Economic Stabilisation Regulations 1973
WAR 1974: Wage Adjustment Regulations 1974
WFR 1982: Wage Freeze Regulations 1982

[1748] Participation

There is only sketchy information about the actual extent of participative schemes during this era. As an *issue* however, participation, other than collective bargaining, was a non-event.

Of the commonly regarded employee-participation schemes, works committees seem to have the longest history. Workshop Committees established in Railway Workshops in 1936 'consisted of six shop foremen, six representatives of the workmen ... and the manager of the workshop as Chairman.' Works Councils, known as Works Efficiency Councils, were compulsorily established during the Second World War in the freezing industry. Hare (1943:49-50) claimed these were a failure since 'many of the managers of the meat freezing works were opposed to them' and most workers apparently did not realise they should be striving for self-actualisation, being only interested in making 'good money' while they could. The idea of taking a consultative part in the day-to-day running of the business had no place in their minds.

In 1973, the New Zealand Department of Labour reported on a survey of firms employing twenty or more employees. The Department received replies from 2027 firms and found:

a. 147 had works committees;
b. 61 had autonomous work groups;
c. one had joint management.

A further ninety firms had participation in profit schemes, direct or through shareholding. A number of the firms had more than one type of scheme operating. In all, a total of 186 firms out of 2027 (9.2 per cent) had some type of employee participation in decision-making scheme. If profit-sharing is included, a total of 253 out of 2027 (12.5 per cent) had a type of scheme.

Works Committees are clearly the most popular type of scheme. These vary from a staff meeting, where employees are given information, to groups with some decision-making power.

At two different times there have also been legislatively-imposed participation at State policy level. A little known Act, the Industrial Relations Act 1949, created an Industrial Advisory Council (IAC), and the later, much better known, Industrial Relations Act 1973 created an Industrial Relations Council (IRC).

Both comprised, in effect, the members of the executive of the FOL and NZEF, together with a Chairman. In 1949 it was the Minister's appointee, in 1973 the Minister of Labour. Both attempts at participation at policy level were dismal failures and neither Council at any stage did anything of significance. The IAC did not meet at all during the crisis years of 1950 and 1951, nor in 1971 and 1972 when by their own initiative the FOL and NZEF were making joint submissions on new legislation. (Ultimately the IR Act 1973.)

Table 17.6. Total redundancy provisions by levels principal documents only

Level	1976		1978		1980	
	No	(%)	No	(%)	No	(%)
0	269	(69.5)	369	(55.6)	306	(47.6)
1	56	(14.5)	120	(18.1)	82	(12.8)
2	6	(1.4)	43	(6.5)	79	(12.3)
3	24	(6.2)	69	(10.4)	106	(16.5)
4	3	(0.8)	9	(1.4)	8	(1.2)
5	29	(7.5)	54	(8.1)	63	(9.6)
TOTAL	387	(100.0)	664	(100.0)	643	(100.0)

Source: Geare (1983b).

[1749] Redundancy

Redundancy became an issue in New Zealand employment relations when unemployment became a major problem in 1976/1977 – for the first time since the Great Depression.

At no stage during this period has there been any legislation guaranteeing redundancy payment. Labour Governments implied they would introduce such legislation. The 1972–75 Labour Government introduced the Severance and Re-employment Bill 1975 – but 'did not have time' to pass the legislation. While in Opposition 1975–84 they promised to introduce legislation to establish a fund which would guarantee a minimum payout. This was one of a number of issues in their 1984 Manifesto ignored by the 1984 Labour Government.

The National Government introduced legislation – but it was to set *maximum* levels of payment, rather than guaranteeing minimum. From 1976, the legal maximum payout was approximately one week's pay per year's service for a maximum of twenty years. In practice, actual payments exceeded the legal maximum and '3+2' was common: three weeks pay for the first year's service and two thereafter, for a maximum of nineteen. In 1982 the legal maximum was increased to '4+2' which reflected common practice. This remained in force until December 1986.

Research (Geare, 1983b:6) indicated that there was a wide range of redundancy provisions in collective agreements and awards. These were assigned into six levels:

Level 0: no positive benefit to workers
Level 1: union to be advised, but no time specified
Level 2: union to be advised, if possible, with period of notice
Level 3: union to be advised with required notice period
Level 4: agreed that redundancy pay will be negotiated

Level 5: redundancy payment level specified *or* agreement that no actual redundancy to occur until payment accepted.

As shown in Table 17.6, redundancy provisions increased quite markedly over the period 1976 to 1980.

E. Other Legislation

[1750] Health and safety

The original Factory Act in New Zealand actually predated this era, coming in 1891, just following the Coal Mines Act 1891 and preceding a Shops and Shop Assistants Act 1892. Factory inspectors were appointed in 1892 and Woods (1963:27) reported that 'in the first three months inspectors required improvements and alternatives in 913 factories.'

The Factories Act 1891 was superseded by a number during this period, including 1901, 1921 and 1946 before the Factories and Commercial Premises Act 1981. (FCP Act 1981). Although there were factory inspectors, and undoubtedly these Acts did prevent some of the worst excesses, their influence was probably marginal. Hare (1946:147-150) points out that the Factories Act 1921, in force until 1946, was

> mainly concerned with the regulation of hours of work, overtime and minimum wages; the regulation of the physical conditions under which work is carried on occupies a place of subordinate importance.

and goes on:

> in some respects the Factories Act of 1921 is less advanced than the first Factories Act of 1891.

Campbell (1993:3) has observed that 'many significant developments in (health and safety) legislation have been responses to a disaster.' This was not only in the early days. As late as 1959, a Construction Act was passed following an enquiry into a collapse of scaffolding on the DIC building in 1957.

The 1946 Act remained in force for thirty-five years and its successor the Factory and Commercial Premises Act 1981 saw out not only the rest of the Arbitration era, but the next era as well.

[1751] Holidays and leave

Legislation requiring a minimum level of annual holidays, regardless of award or agreement, was introduced in 1944. This Act was superseded by the Annual Holidays Act 1981. This provided for eleven statutory holidays per year which, unless otherwise provided in the contract of employment, were to be specified days (Christmas, New Year, etc). In addition, workers/employees were entitled to three weeks' annual holiday on pay.

Near the end of this era, maternity-leave provisions were introduced and these were superseded by the Parental Leave and Employment Protection Act

1987. This guaranteed maternity leave (fourteen weeks) and paternity leave (two weeks). In addition, extended leave may be taken. Except in special circumstances (temporary replacements not reasonably practicable), the position was to be held open.

[1752] Minimum wages

The concept of a minimum wage for those not covered by an award or agreement was introduced by regulation in 1942 and by the first Minimum Wage Act 1945.

Brosnan and Wilkinson (1989:18-20) point out that the value of the minimum wage fell from eighty-three per cent of average earnings in 1947 to 'only 30 per cent in 1984.' The 1984 Labour Government did increase the amount in 1987 to $210 per week, it was only fifty-three per cent of average earnings. At that time however, some '20 per cent of awards had a minimum rate lower than the Statutory Minimum.'

[1753] Wage protection

In the UK, legislation against the 'truck system' stems from 1465 where, according to Mathieson (1970:390), it was first applied to woollen cloth making. General legislation was enacted in 1831: the UK Truck Act 1831. The 'truck system' is where employers pay in goods (or 'kind') rather than money, or alternatively with vouchers which employees have to use in company shops.

New Zealand introduced the Wages Protection Act only in 1964. This was also 'anti-truck' and required payment to be in money. It also prevented employers making deductions from wages for breach of contract or because of overpayment. The 1964 Act was superseded by the Wages Protection Act 1983.

[1754] Equal Pay Act 1972

This Act made a contribution towards pay equality for women by making it illegal to have men's and women's rates in the same collective document. Prue Hyman (1993:47) claims the Act had 'highly limited' effectiveness.

[1755] Race Relations Act 1971 and Human Rights Commission Act 1977

These Acts legislated against discrimination on the basis of race, colour, ethnic or national origins, sex, marital status and religious or ethical belief. Although obviously relevant to industrial matters, they also extended to other areas of social life. It is to be hoped that these Acts had more effect than simply to introduce abominations such as 'bar person' into the English language. While legislation can prevent blatant discrimination, unfortunately it is extremely difficult to prevent covert discrimination.

Chapter Eighteen

Collective Bargaining Era

A. Introduction

[1801] Time frame

In marked contrast to the Arbitration era, this, the Collective Bargaining era, lasted only briefly. It is also difficult to accurately define. It could be said to have begun on 1 August 1987, when the Labour Relations Act 1987 (LR Act) came into force and to have ended on 15 May 1991, with the Employment Contracts Act 1991 (EC Act). However, two of the major features of this era were the abolition of compulsory arbitration for interest disputes – which was in fact introduced in 1984 by the IR Am Act – and the bringing-together of the private and public sectors which came about partially in 1986–7 (for State Owned Enterprises) and totally in 1988. However, given the paramount importance of the LR Act for this era, the time frame will be assumed to be 1987–91.

[1802] General approach

As with Chapter Seventeen, this chapter is not intended as an exhaustive review of the period, but rather is intended to highlight both the significant changes from the Arbitration era, and those features that were retained. Where the legislation is worded in a similar fashion to that in the Employment Contracts Act 1991, or the Employment Relations Act 2000, the main discussion will be with respect to the later Acts.

[1803] Chapter coverage

Section B will outline the LR Act, with emphasis given both to major changes from the Arbitration era and to major features which were retained. Later sections discuss other relevant legislation and briefly examine significant employment relations issues.

[1804] The era in historical perspective

The Labour Party won an early election in July 1984. Ostensibly led by David Lange, it appeared to many that the driving forces were Roger Douglas and Richard Prebble, with David Lange chosen as leader as he was seen as more 'charismatic' and a more entertaining public speaker. The Labour Government proceeded to create confusion by being significantly more to the Right than the previous (supposedly right-wing) National Government, and very rapidly introduced economic changes consistent with New Right thinking.

The changes in employment relations, however, were strongly criticised by the New Zealand Business Roundtable (NZBR) as being totally inadequate, particularly with respect to promoting flexibility into employment relations. Thus the NZBR in its submission to the Labour Select Committee on the LR Am Bill in June 1990 claimed:

> When the Labour Relations Act was introduced in 1987, there was widespread concern among New Zealand businesses that the reforms embodied in that Act were insufficient to ensure that companies and workers could adapt to the increasingly competitive economic environment. In particular, the New Zealand Business Roundtable and others expressed concern that the rigidities that the Act perpetuated in the labour relations system would have a high cost in terms of productivity, growth, job security and workers' incomes.

Thus, to an extent, the LR Act was under threat from its very beginning. As discussed later (see [1818]), the LR Act certainly allowed for flexibility and innovative agreements. Ironically, soon after the Employment Contracts Act 1991 (EC Act) was passed, examples of innovative agreements which had been made under the LR Act were being cited as examples of the success of the EC Act.

B. Principal Legislation

[1805] Labour Relations Act 1987

Shortly after the introduction of the Labour Relations Act 1987 (LR Act) Geare (1989:213), one of the authors of this book, claimed that:

> Unlike the cosmetic changes brought about by the IR Act 1973, however, the LR Act 1987 *does* introduce significant, indeed radical, changes in industrial relations.

Even with hindsight, and given the far more radical changes that were to occur in 1991, this author still believes the comment is accurate. Certainly some major features of the legislation that had been in place were retained, but not only was the underlying ideology and purpose of the Act different, there were indeed other changes, some major as well as those less significant.

One less significant, but almost obligatory change was the name of the major arbitral institution. Once again the Arbitration Court was split into two institutions – the Labour Court, which now comprised a judge alone, and the Arbitration Commission. To nullify the effects of streamlining the Court, the Commission was boosted to five persons. In theory, there were to be three non-aligned members with a union and an employers' representative. Of the three supposedly 'non-aligned', only one had a 'neutral' career (he was a former Conciliator).

[1806] Major changes

The major changes identified include:

a. ideology and purpose of the legislation;
b. availability of interest arbitration;
c. requirement for one document only;
d. union size;
e. deregistration;
f. concept of managerial prerogatives;
g. legality of strikes and lockouts;
h. conciliation/mediation;
i. personal grievances.

A further major change in the era – but not directly attributable to the LR Act is the bringing under the LR Act of the State Sector. (See [1822]).

[1807] Ideology and purpose

As discussed in Chapter Seventeen, while the ICA Act 1894 was supportive of unions, being partially entitled 'an Act to encourage the formation of Unions' during much of the 92-year period, until 1987 the legislation in fact was paternalistic, with the underlying ideology becoming increasingly unitarist. The trend towards anti-unionism and increased punitive measures against strike action did not of course proceed steadily but with irregular jerks and jumps, and indeed at times appeared briefly to reverse itself. When the Labour Party became Government in 1984 however, strikes were all either explicitly unlawful or liable to penalties, arbitration was available as a guaranteed 'back stop', and certain issues (the introduction of new technology for example) were interpreted by the Courts as being managerial prerogatives and hence not negotiable under law. Also, in the Arbitration era senior government ministers often became personally involved in labour-management disputes. The Labour Government made it clear through policy statements, position papers and speeches its belief that, ideally, employment relations problems should be settled by management and unions, with minimal third-party involvement. The Minister of Labour was nicknamed 'Sideline Stan' by the Opposition to deride his lack of intervention in industrial disputes. The Minister, however, took the nickname as a compliment and a recognition that he was doing the right thing. He was quoted in one local paper (*Otago Daily Times*, 1988) as saying he 'believed that such intervention is ultimately damaging to good industrial relations and that only the union and employer parties can reach satisfactory settlements.'

The LR Act 1987 was more pluralistic, insofar as it made strikes lawful in certain circumstances, it did not accept that some issues were managerial prerogatives and hence non-negotiable, and it encouraged unionism and collective bargaining. It was also less paternalistic, doing away with the automatic right to arbitration.

The purpose of the Act was clearly to encourage collective bargaining.

Algorithm. Settlement of disputes of interest

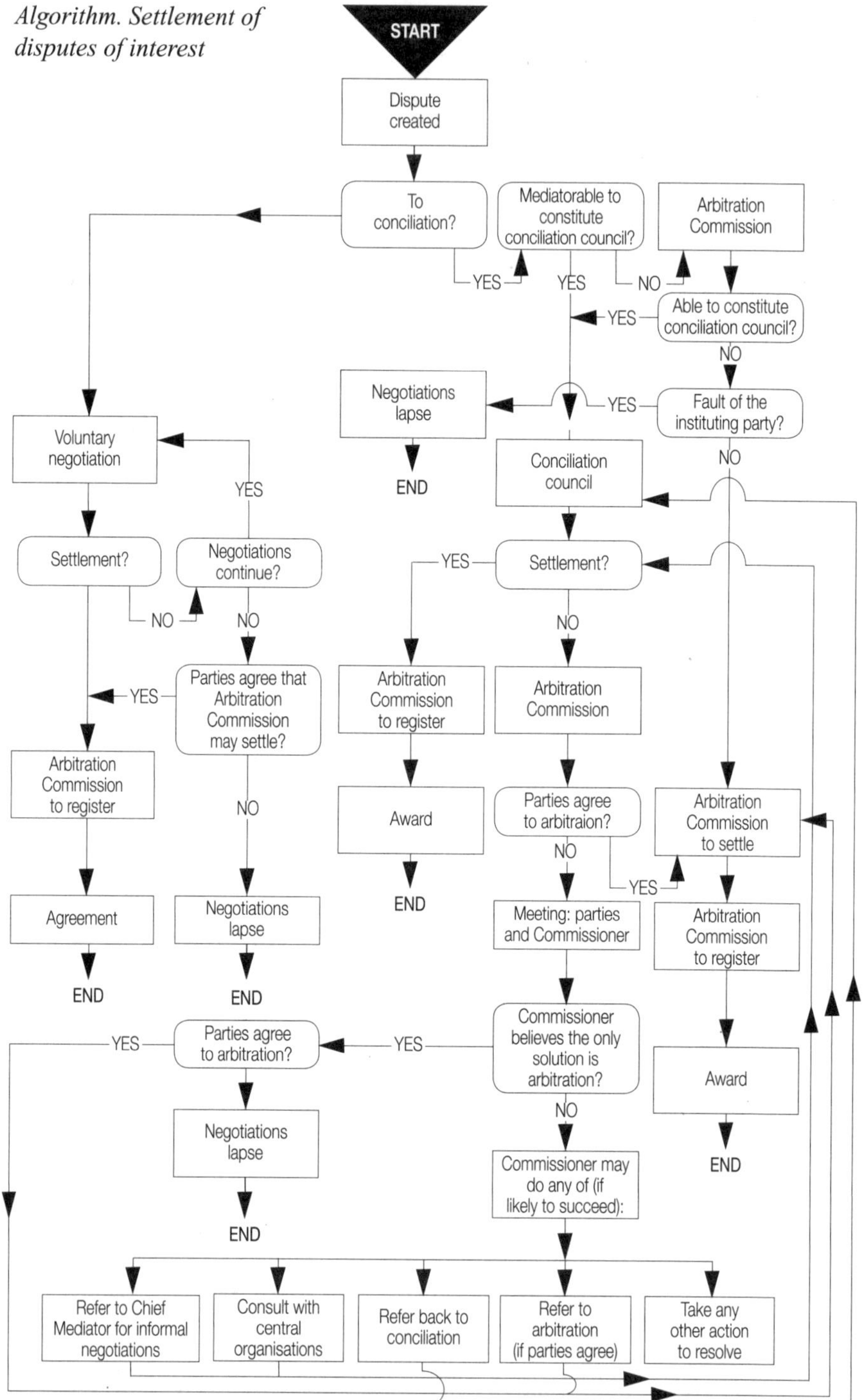

[1808] *Arbitration for interest disputes*

As introduced in 1984 by the IR Am Act, the LR Act abolished compulsory arbitration for interest disputes. Arbitration would be available, but only if both parties agreed. If, however, the workforce and union were weak, the employer could refuse to go to arbitration and thus maintain the *status quo*.

As indicated by the algorithm opposite, the system at this point could tolerate having no settlement. Somewhat confusingly, now the parties could choose to have voluntary negotiations and then, if negotiations failed, go to the Arbitration Commission, while other parties could go through conciliation but one or both could then refuse to go to arbitration.

If negotiations lapsed, then, as in the Arbitration era, the legislation provided that the expired award or agreement would continue in force for one year automatically and for a second year on application of either party. The award or agreement would then be cancelled unless either party put in a request for a third year. Three years after the award or agreement had 'expired', it would be cancelled. All employees would then be bound by the minimum conditions in other legislation (Minimum Wage Act, etc.).

Just before the 1990 General Election, the Labour Government nullified this major feature of their employment relations policy and reintroduced compulsory arbitration from 31 August under the LR Am Act 1990. Compulsory arbitration would apply only if the award had expired for two years and negotiations failed to reach settlement. Arbitration would be Final Offer Arbitration (see [809]). This desperate move to win back support failed and National won the election and their LR Am Act (No. 2) 1990 repealed this reintroduction.

[1809] *Single document*

The Labour Government considered it very important that employees be covered by one document only. In the previous era, employees could be covered by an award and a (registered) agreement, both of which were enforceable. The LR Act was designed to discourage so-called second-tier bargaining, and the *intent* of the legislation was that unions would choose to negotiate an agreement with employers who were 'special cases' and use the award for the average employer.

Contrary to some views, the LR Act did not ban, prevent, or eliminate second-tier bargaining. Thus, Deeks *et al* (1994:70) state that 'the 1987 Labour Relations Act eliminated two-tier or secondary bargaining.' In fact this was not so, and second-tier bargaining could continue. However the Act *discouraged* such bargaining by:

a. making strikes over second-tier bargaining illegal;
b. not allowing the resulting document to be registered and hence any second-tier agreement was not enforceable through the system;
c. allowing the employer to opt out of the award.

However, if the employer was reasonably prepared to agree to the second-tier proposals in addition to the award, second-tier *bargaining* could continue quite happily. Second-tier *agreements* could come into effect, but could not be registered and enforced through the system.

[1810] Union size

A major change from the past era was the minimum number of members required for registration. Under the ICA Act 1954 a single district union only required *fifteen* members for registration, and a New Zealand union only required twenty. The LR Act 1987 suddenly required a minimum of 1000 members for any union to be registered. (Two years were allowed for unions to reach the figure, either by amalgamation or simple increases in membership, to avoid being deregistered.)

The purported reason for this arbitrary move was that unions *ought* to be large to provide good service. Interestingly, Harbridge and Webber (1987:86) consider that their research identified that, during the period of voluntary unionism in 1984–5,

> while a few small unions with less than 200 members were unable to cope and became defunct, the vast majority of these small unions lost a very small percentage of their members compared with large unions. In some way, an individual worker's decision to accept or reject union membership must be a reflection of the perceived effectiveness of that union to the worker. In this case, it is reasonable to assume that members of small unions were happy with the services given them by their unions. Accordingly, in view of that data presented, there may be no sound basis for legislating small unions out of existence.

The real reason for the change is unknown. *Ostensibly* it was because of a belief that larger unions provide better service. However, *if* larger unions did in fact provide better service then union members could push for amalgamations. There was no need to *force* this on them. It is also quite likely that the Labour Government was overly influenced by, and possibly copied, the so-called Hancock Report from Australia, which recommended that the minimum size for Australian unions registered federally be 1000. The third possibility is that the Government wanted to prevent employer-dominated site unions from being forced on employees. (This latter is the most logical rationale for the legislation.)

[1811] Deregistration

Deregistration was no longer a punishment for strike activity. Unions would be deregistered only if they failed to submit required paperwork, or if they failed in the two-year period to reach and maintain the 1000 membership.

[1812] Managerial prerogatives

As discussed in [1716], in the previous era some issues were considered to be 'managerial prerogatives' and not 'industrial matters' and hence not acceptable subjects for dispute.

If this view was generally accepted, then it could clearly be very convenient from the point of view of management. Managers could introduce change unilaterally with no opposition. Whatever one's normative view of managerial prerogatives, from a pragmatic viewpoint it is sensible to have a system which can settle conflicts over such issues. The definition of 'industrial matters' under the ICA Act and the IR Act could be, and frequently was, interpreted narrowly. The LR Act was more pragmatic and did not arbitrarily try to exclude any subject from the employment relations arena.

[1813] Legality of strikes and lockouts

The LR Act was designed to encourage collective bargaining over arbitration and as a logical consequence strikes and lockouts were now legalised under conditions.

Strikes and lockouts remained unlawful if they concerned:

a. dispute of rights;
b. personal grievance;
c. demarcation;
d. union membership, or change of union coverage;
e. cancellation of a union's registration.

However, they were lawful if they were over a 'dispute of interest' – that is, a dispute leading to an award or agreement with the following provisos:

a. if a current award or agreement existed, it was to expire within sixty days;
b. if the industry was defined as 'essential' then fourteen days' notice had been given. If the industry was meat processing, three days' notice had been given.

Strikes and lockouts were also lawful if they were over:

a. a redundancy agreement;
b. a 'new matter.'

[1814] Conciliation/mediation

The LR Act combined the two functions of conciliation and mediation under one service: the Industrial Mediation Service. Initially, the change was purely cosmetic. The individuals who had been 'conciliators' under the IR Act were now called mediators, but their main function continued to be to chair conciliation councils. It is not known whether the Labour Government intended to phase out conciliation, but this move certainly prepared the ground for the National Government in 1991. The individuals who had been called mediators under the IR Act continued to be so named and largely performed the same function. There was now obviously no restriction on mediation being involved in disputes of interest.

[1815] Personal grievances

The personal grievance procedure had much in common with the procedure under the IR Act 1973, but there were a number of changes.

More thought had gone into the procedure, with a requirement for written statements both from the union on behalf of the grievant and from the employer. This tended to restrict the grievance and employer response from 'growing'.

Grievances could now be specifically over *sexual harassment*. The sexual harassment could be perpetrated by the employer or representative, or by a co-worker, client or customer. (In the latter case, the employer would only be at fault if there had been a failure to take whatever steps were practicable to prevent a recurrence.)

If the committee came to agreement, or there was a majority agreement (other than with the chair), no appeal was allowed. However, if the decision of the committee was the chair's (a mediator) then there could be an appeal to the Court.

Before the Act was passed, it had been suggested that the remedies for unjustifiable dismissal would be considerably strengthened, *requiring* reinstatement as well as lost wages. In the event, the LR Act was somewhat stronger than the IR Act – but nothing like as strong as predicted. The Act provided for reinstatement (if, in fact, desired) but only 'where practicable.' The employer had at least two strategies. One was to hire a replacement, thus putting the union in the position of being responsible for the *replacement* losing his/her job. A second was simply to argue that the events were such that the employer-employee relationships could not be maintained. The Act also required the payment of lost wages – but not if the employee was also partly at fault.

In many cases, court rulings under the LR Act still apply under the Employment Contracts Act 1991 and are reviewed in [1944] to [1946].

[1816] Disputes of right

Under the IR Act 1973, a dispute of right was defined more widely and included 'personal grievances.' The definition under the LR Act was simply that a dispute of right was one over 'the interpretation, application, or operation of an award or agreement.'

The new Act, under s.187, stated that every award or agreement must contain a procedure to settle disputes of rights without stoppage of work. A possible 'model' is provided in the Sixth Schedule to the Act.

The model was that either the union or employer could invoke the procedure. The dispute was referred to a disputes committee of equal numbers from each party, together with an independent to chair the committee. This person was either mutually agreed upon, or a mediator or mediator's nominee. A majority decision of the committee (excluding the person in the chair) was the decision. If the committee was equally divided, the person chairing could make a decision or refer the dispute to the Labour Court. If the decision was by the chair's casting vote, any party could appeal the decision to the Labour Court. To limit appeals, the Court took the same approach as taken by the Arbitration Court in *Thornton Electrical*:

> we as usual approach such appeals on the basis that we should not lightly overturn a disputes committee decision unless it be shown to be manifestly wrong.

Subject to the above right of appeal, the decision of the committee was binding on the parties to the dispute.

Section 189 states that if a party failed to observe the procedure, then the other party could refer it to the Labour Court for settlement. Unfortunately, the disputes procedure outlined in the Act did not guarantee prompt action. Either party could procrastinate in nominating its representatives to the committees, or delay agreement on the chairman. Obviously such action was not in the long term employment relations interest of either party. However, it could be considered in the economic interests, at short term, of one party. The Act also specified that no strikes, lockouts or dismissals may occur because of the dispute.

[1817] Significant features retained

Notwithstanding the changes already documented, there were a number of significant features from the Arbitration era which were retained into this period. These included:

a. system of regional and national awards;
b. blanket provisions;
c. compulsory unionism.

As mentioned in [1804], the major critics of the LR Act – the NZBR and the NZEF – attacked the Act for not providing sufficient flexibility, basically because the award system was retained and the blanket provisions extended award coverage to all employers in the region or country.

[1818] Flexibility

There are two aspects to flexibility in the system with respect to contracts of employment:

a. the type of agreement;
b. the similarity or difference in settlement levels.

The LR Act allowed for enterprise bargaining. Originally, only the union had the legal right to initiate enterprise bargaining, leading to an agreement rather than an award. To our knowledge, there was no instance where an employer who wanted enterprise bargaining, other than to give *more* than award conditions, was unable to persuade the union(s) involved to negotiate for an agreement. The reality was that the vast proportion of employers were quite satisfied operating under an award. The LR Act 1990 gave employers of more than fifty employees the legal right to initiate enterprise bargaining if they wished.

Table 18.1. Collective document structures

Major Collective Document	Early 1991	Mid 1992
(Near) national award	80%	10%
Regional/local award	8%	2%
Contract exclusive to firm	9%	80%
Contract exclusive to parent company	3%	8%

Source: McAndrew (1992).

Research by McAndrew (1992) on the changes in bargaining structure from under the LR Act to under the Employment Contracts Act 1991 illustrate the extent to which awards predominated right through this era. The results shown in Table 18.1 are based on replies from 557 organisations out of a random sample of 1800.

If 'flexibility' means that in the majority of cases the major collective document was firm-specific, then clearly there was *not* a great deal of flexibility. Nearly ninety per cent of firms were under an award. However, the *system* did not prevent more firms negotiating firm-specific documents; it was their own lack of motivation.

A second measure of flexibility is the similarity or difference in settlement levels between awards and agreements in any wage round. Harbridge (1990:241) points out that claims of inflexibility were frequently based on folklore, or statistics that were 'badly astray'. For example, the system was attacked on the grounds that ninety per cent of all settlements were for a wage increase, plus or minus one per cent either way of the settlement in the Metal Trades Award. In reality, sixty-nine per cent of awards fell in that range.

Harbridge (1990:244) attributes the concern over this mythical 'ninety per cent of all settlements' to Max Bradford (a former director of advocacy for the NZEF and subsequently a National MP, and chair of the select committee for the EC Act 1991), and refers to the 'Bradford' statistic.

Of course, even if ninety or even one hundred per cent of wage settlements were within one per cent either way of a major settlement – rather than only sixty-nine per cent – that is not necessarily a matter of any concern. As discussed in Chapter Eleven, it is highly problematic to define the right wage, or the right increase. Rightly or wrongly, most wage *increases* have a function of cost-of living-increases and productivity increases. If overall productivity increases are low, then wage increases are basically a function of cost-of-living – which is a constant. It could be argued that, as occurred, sixty-nine per cent of award changes falling between six and eight per cent indicated high flexibility. A final observation was that the *opportunity* for greater flexibility by way of second-tier agreements remained. As discussed in [1809], somewhat ironically this was discouraged rather than encouraged by the legislation.

C. General Employment Relations

[1819] Unions

Union numbers were clearly affected by the 1000 membership rule, although this did not affect most union *members* – who were already in unions of 1000 plus size (See Table App-3). Unions were losing members because of redundancies and lay-offs. However, compulsory unionism was reintroduced in 1985 and remained in force for this period. The only difference (and it was insignificant) between the situation from 1985–91 and that which was in effect from 1961 was that the 'unqualified preference clause' was renamed the 'union membership clause'.

[1820] Strikes

Table App-6 shows the change in strike intensity during this period. Theory suggests that strikes during this period were heading down to a Kondratieff trough (see [1027]).

Economic conditions, including widespread threat of plant closures and redundancies, discouraged unions and workgroups from taking much industrial action.

[1821] Redundancy

As was the case in the previous era, there was no legislation introduced to guarantee compensation for dismissal through redundancy. There was one piece of legislation relevant to redundancy introduced by LR Am Act 1990. This became s.184A. It related to so-called 'technical redundancy', where one employer would sell the whole or part of a business as a going concern. The Act now specified that if employees were offered employment and the conditions remained unchanged, including service-related conditions and those relating to redundancy and superannuation, then:

> nothing in any award, or agreement or registered redundancy agreement shall require the employer to pay compensation for redundancy.

In other words, the law would retrospectively 'rescue' incompetent employers who had negotiated and agreed to redundancy provisions in awards and agreements, and even negotiated specific redundancy agreements which had not precluded so-called 'technical' redundancies. It is not known whether the concerns felt by the Government for employers who had negotiated poor agreements was heightened by the fact that possibly the Government had done likewise. However, this raises very strong ethical concerns if it is indeed true that the Government, through its agents, negotiated agreements and then passed legislation to allow the Government to 'honourably' renege on its own agreements.

In the 1970s to mid 1980s the attitude of the courts in general was that, in the absence of a redundancy agreement, and so long as the common law notice was given, then if the redundancy was genuine (and not a subterfuge to get rid of a troublesome or unproductive employee) the dismissal would be deemed justified and no compensation would be payable. (See *Canterbury Hotel v Fabiola Fashions Limited* and the Court of Appeal in *City Taxis Society Ltd v Otago Clerical Workers*.) Even in a case (*New Zealand Retail Employees* – Decision) where the 'employer's failure to recognise the proper steps in the grievance procedure was contemptuous and deserves censure', the then Chief Judge ruled (at 54) that 'The Court has no power to award any form of payment … unless it finds she was unjustifiably dismissed, and this we cannot do.' By the late 1980s, courts began to require employers to demonstrate the genuineness of alleged redundancy situations rather than simply accepting their word. Dismissals purporting to be for redundancy were found to be unjustified in *Macleod* because the court stated 'we saw no factors or figures whatever to support or confirm any downturn in business or its extent.'

[1822] Court decisions under the LR Act

Research (Geare, 1983b) shows that in 1980 less than ten per cent of collective documents had full redundancy agreements and of 851 collective documents:

509	(59.8%)	made no reference to redundancy
271	(31.9%)	specified only that notice be given
8	(0.9%)	required negotiation
63	(7.4%)	full redundancy agreements

Some of the 271 documents requiring that notice be given specified that the notice was to 'allow discussions to take place'. The Court in *Cornhill Insurance Co. Ltd v NZ Insurance Guild IUW* assessed the ruling of a committee chairman who had considered a clause stating that, in the event of redundancy, the company was obliged 'to notify the union in writing of the impending redundancy to allow discussions to take place.' The chairman:

a. directed that the parties commence further discussion immediately;
b. directed that the company's representatives have given authority to conclude a fair and amicable settlement;
c. ruled that the dispute might be referred back to the committee should the parties be unable to resolve their differences.

The Court, however, overruled the chairman and ruled that, having notified the union and having allowed discussions to take place,

> the employer has done all that it was obliged by the award to do. The employer cannot be compelled to do anything further, however unsatisfactory the results may be to the union and to some of its members. The award imposed no obligation to pay redundancy pay and neither the Disputes Committee nor this Court has any power to give judgement for such a payment.

Other agreements had clauses which explicitly permitted involvement by committees and the Court. In *Wellington Local Bodies' Officers' IUW v*

Wellington Hospital Board, the clause stated the employer 'shall negotiate with the union a mutually agreed redundancy contract. In the event of any dispute hereunder the matter shall be dealt with under Clause 18 (Disputes).' The matter was not settled in negotiation and went to the Disputes Committee, then the Arbitration Court, and finally on to the Court of Appeal. This is totally reasonable and not contentious.

However, the percentage of documents which had clauses requiring negotiation was very low and this clearly left little scope for judicial involvement. Possibly coincidentally, in *Wellington Local Bodies v Westland Catchment Board* judicial activism began. The clause in that case required nothing more than that notice be given to the union prior to the employer informing the redundant employee. The President of the Court of Appeal (Cooke, P., as he was then) stated that:

> It is true that paragraph (b) makes no express provision beyond the requirement for notice, but it is of some significance that notice is required to be given to the union before notice is to be given to the affected officer. Plainly the intention must have been to allow negotiations to take place between the union and the employer.

With due respect to the President, we do not find his 'logic' or argument compelling. The employer agreed to give notice to the union before notifying the employee. That *could* be to allow negotiations to take place, but equally it could simply be to allow the union the opportunity to appear to be up with the play and involved with decision-making. It could be to allow the union time to prepare a response to the employee. However, to claim that an agreement to notify *necessarily* becomes an agreement to negotiate redundancy payments – and in the event of non-agreement, also becomes an agreement to allow the Court or Court of Appeal the right to set the level of pay – seems to be evidence of blatant judicial activism. An interesting fact about that case was that the counsel for the appellant was Mr T.E. Goddard, who shortly afterwards became Judge Goddard, and later Chief Judge of the Court.

The President's approach must have seemed like an overt invitation to allow judicial activism. The next case involved a cleaner who was dismissed for redundancy as the company was in financial difficulties. Cost saving could be made by replacing the employee with a contract cleaner. There was no redundancy agreement, but the employer offered, *ex gratia*, some redundancy compensation. The case of the cleaner was considered under the personal grievance procedure. Chief Judge Goddard found that the dismissal was substantively unjustified (on the grounds that a redundancy would only be justified if the commercial viability of the employer depended on it) and also procedurally unfair (on the grounds that the circumstances warranted significantly greater redundancy compensation). Chief Judge Goddard appeared to have a strategy to make his decisions extreme, almost expecting them to be overturned, but counting on the fact that there would be openings left by the Court of Appeal's decisions, allowing him creative interpretations in the future. So, in *G. N. Hale & Son Ltd v Wellington Caretakers IUW*, he ruled that since the dismissal 'was not, at the time, commercially necessary to ensure the ongoing viability of the respondent … it was, therefore, unjustifiable.' This assertion was not surprisingly rejected by the Court of Appeal in *G. N. Hale & Son Ltd v Wellington Caretakers IUW*, who pointed out that 'a worker does not have the right to continued employment if the business can be run more efficiently without him.' All five judges of the Court of Appeal gave decisions. There was total agreement on the point that so long as the employer genuinely believed there was a redundancy situation then redundancies were justified and it was not for the Court to substitute its business judgement for that of the employer. However, very significantly, two of the five also gave the view that justification could also turn on whether the circumstances called for reasonable compensation and whether it was given. That (minority) view was seized upon by the Chief Judge, when the case went back to the Labour Court (*Wellington Caretakers IUW v G. N. Hale & Son Ltd*). The Chief Judge acknowledged that:

> There is no right to compensation for a dismissal on grounds of redundancy unless that right is conferred by a redundancy agreement or by an award or collective agreement [or by statute].

However, Judicial activism had now created the situation that for the dismissal for redundancy to be considered 'procedurally fair', and hence the dismissal to be considered justifiable, compensation 'may' be required.

D. Other Legislation

[1823] State Sector Act 1988

The State Sector Act 1988 brought the Public Service and Education Service under the LR Act 1987. Earlier the State Owned Enterprises Act and the SOE Am Act 1987 (together with the State Services Conditions of Employment Amendment Act 1987) had achieved the same purpose for state enterprises. These included:

Air New Zealand Limited
Airways Corporation of New Zealand Limited
Coal Corporation of New Zealand Limited
Electricity Corporation of New Zealand Limited
Government Property Services Limited
Land Corporation Limited
New Zealand Forestry Corporation Limited
New Zealand Railways Corporation
New Zealand Post Limited
Post Bank Limited
Telecom Corporation of New Zealand Limited

Tourist Corporation of New Zealand Limited
Tourist Hotel Corporation of New Zealand
The Shipping Corporation of New Zealand Limited

Thus, by 1988 New Zealand had both the private and State Sectors under one employment relations system, and under one major piece of legislation, the LR Act 1987.

In some areas, however, differences remained. The SS Act 1988 did in fact allow unions to opt for compulsory arbitration. Unions who put in a request to the Public Service Commission (the employer) in the first three months that the Act was in force (April–June 1988) were given a guarantee that compulsory arbitration would be available, should a dispute not be settled by negotiation. To discourage unions from 'backsliding', this offer was made as unattractive as possible. The union had to give up the right to strike, and agree to a no-strike clause, and in addition the arbitration offered would be Final Offer Arbitration (see [809]).

[1824] Employment Equity Act 1990

The Employment Equity Act 1990 was a short-lived piece of legislation, and was introduced as part of the backsliding (see [1808]) which occurred in the Labour Party just before their defeat in the 1990 Election. This Act was repealed late in 1990 by the incoming National Government.

The pay equity provisions of the Employment Equity Act 1990 (EE Act 1990) enabled any union, or group of twenty or more women, to request the Employment Equity office to conduct a pay equity assessment in respect of a particular female occupation. The difficulties in determining 'pay equity' even simply on a theoretical level have been discussed in Chapter Twelve.

On normative grounds, one may agree with the motives behind pay equity. However, in the context of the Labour Government's employment relations philosophy and the LR Act 1987, the EE Act 1990 was totally incongruous. Indeed, it raises suspicion that the Act was simply a desperate attempt by an unpopular and self-destructing government to win a few votes.

The EE Act could have worked in the Arbitration era, when there was some centralised control over wage rates. Given the move to collective bargaining, equal pay legislation becomes extremely difficult to enforce – assuming the initial problem of determining comparable worth had been overcome.

Chapter Nineteen

Laissez-Faire Era

A. Introduction

[1901] The Laissez-Faire era

The Laissez-Faire era for New Zealand employment relations began on 15 May 1991, when the Employment Contracts Act 1991 (EC Act) came into force. The label 'laissez-faire' is intended to reflect the high degree of State non-involvement in employment relations issues, especially when compared to the two previous eras. Part One made reference not only to the major impact State support has on union strength and viability (see [209]) but also the concept of power, relative power and bargaining power (Chapters Five and Seven). These issues should make it apparent why it is possible for apparently contradictory statements to all be 'true' from different perspectives.

Thus, from a *legal* perspective, it was not unreasonable (*United Food Workers' Union v Talley*) for Hardie Boys J. to argue that 'the Act is not anti-union; it may fairly be described as union-neutral.' However, from a *union* perspective, given that the Act removed considerable support, some of which had been present for half a century, and other support which had been around for a whole century, the Act may fairly be described as anti-union and anti-employee.

The then President of the CTU stated (Douglas, 1994:230):

> Public opinion polls have been universal in finding that a majority of New Zealanders are opposed to the Act. They oppose it because it is unfair: it gives too much power to employers and it allows the vulnerable to be ripped off.

Likewise, the then Secretary of the CTU, Foulkes (1993:186), considered the Act had clear intended impacts, one of which was 'a deunionised workforce'.

The NZBR and NZEF (1992:i) tacitly admit that the Act marginalised unions, but of course from their perspective this was 'highly beneficial', allowing 'employers and employees much greater freedom to decide on the terms of their contracts.'

[1902] General approach

Given that for the 1990s the EC Act was the predominant employment relations legislation, it will be discussed in more detail than the ICA Acts or LR Act. The following section will discuss the purported purpose of the Act, and suggest the probable underlying purpose before highlighting the major changes. A later section will describe the Act in detail. Two further sections will cover current employment relations issues and other relevant legislation.

[1903] Background

As mentioned in Chapter Eighteen, the LR Act 1987 was under attack, almost from its introduction, for not going anything like far enough in its reforms. Internationally (and particularly in the USA with Reaganomics, and the UK with Thatcherism) the 1980s saw an increasing acceptance of New Right philosophies. With high unemployment, frequent redundancies and State policies which were frequently anti-union, unions were weaker and the relative power of employers and senior managers compared to that of employees and unions steadily increased. This resulted in the rich becoming relatively richer, as illustrated in Table 19.1 below.

Table 19.1 reflects the economic times and New Right thinking. As shown in Table 19.2, unemployment, which had been very low internationally until the late 1970s, rose markedly through the 1980s. This weakened unions by both reducing their membership and to an extent their will to resist, as some employees feared that direct action could cost them their jobs.

Table 19.1. Average annual percentage increase in wage or salary

	Chief Executives	Managers	Workers
Canada (1975–87)	14	10	8
USA (1981–88)	10	6	4

Source: Kochan and Verma (1989).

Table 19.2. Unemployment internationally

	1970	1975	1980	1985	1990	1995	2000	2005
New Zealand	0.2	0.4	2.3	4.1	7.8	6.3	6.3	3.6
Australia	1.4	4.4	6.1	8.2	6.9	8.6	6.8	5.1
USA	4.9	8.5	7.1	7.1	5.4	5.6	4.0	7.0
UK	2.6	4.1	7.4	11.2	6.8	8.8	5.9	4.7
Japan	1.2	1.9	2.0	2.6	2.1	3.1	4.7	4.5
OECD Average	–	–	–	7.8	6.1	7.5	6.5	6.7

Source: Various Bulletins of Labour Statistics, OECD Surveys

[1904] Employment and Unemployment

Statistics concerning employment and unemployment must be treated with care. The concepts are by no means unambiguous. Table 19.3 gives figures for those employed. However, 'employment' covers both part-time (1–29 hours per week) and full-time (thirty hours plus) employment. From 1991–9, total employment has increased by 265,000 or eighteen per cent. The Table also shows that in the same period part-time employment has increased by thirty-five per cent, while full-time employment has increased by only thirteen per cent. The figures do not tell us if those in part-time employment are there by choice, having moved from unemployment to a part-time job which is what they want, or whether their previous full-time employment has been down-graded to part-time.

Unemployment figures are even more misleading. Official figures differ. *The New Zealand Official Year Book* (1997:343) points out that there are three main sources of unemployment data in New Zealand, which differ from each other in their scope, collection methods and the way they define unemployment. They are:

- Statistics New Zealand's Household Labour Force Survey (HCFS);
- Statistics New Zealand's five-yearly Census of Population and Dwellings; and
- The Department of Labour's job seeker register.

Table 19.3 shows that in 1999 there were 1,136,000 people over the age of fifteen who were 'not employed'. Many of these people do not want employment

Table 19.3. Employment

Year	Working Age Population*	Employed (full time)	Employed (part time)	Total	'Not Employed'
	000s	000s	000s	000s	000s
1990	2502	1187	300	1487	1015
1991	2565	1161	311	1472	1093
1992	2593	1164	318	1482	1111
1993	2607	1169	318	1487	1120
1995	2704	1309	356	1665	1039
1996	2812	1326	374	1700	1112
1997	2844	1301	389	1690	1154
1998	2867	1331	404	1735	1132
1999	2864	1343	410	1753	1111
2000	2881	1375	410	1785	1096
2001	2900	1410	408	1819	1081
2002	2930	1441	429	1871	1059
2003	2966	1480	435	1914	1052
2004	3148	1526	440	1966	1182

* Labour force aged 15 plus

Source: Various New Zealand Labour Force Statistics

because they are retired, studying full time, are full-time parents or for some other reason not interested in being in employment. Although these people are 'not employed' they are not deemed to be 'unemployed'. Table 19.4 below gives a variety of official measures of 'unemployment'. In 1999 while there were 139,300 officially unemployed, there were 196,200 who were registered as 'unemployed', and 222,200 'jobless'.

With this level of confusion it is not surprising that politicians can refer to the same data and come out with very different conclusions. The June 1999 issue of the *New Zealand Journal of Industrial Relations* included a Special 'Election Forum'. The spokespersons from the four main parties all referred to the effect the Employment Contracts Act had had on employment.

Table 19.4. Alternative measures of unemployment

Average for year ended March	Registered Unemployed (1) (2)	Officially Unemployed (3)	Surplus Worker (4)	Jobseeker (5)	Jobless (6)
	000s	000s	000s	000s	000s
1987		64.0	103.9	80.9	115.4
1988	90.0	69.5	108.9	88.3	121.1
1989	128.5	98.0	143.8	120.3	157.5
1990	149.2	112.4	164.2	134.8	175.9
1991	165.7	135.7	196.2	164.1	212.5
1992	201.0	172.9	245.3	202.2	259.9
1993	217.1	166.8	237.1	195.2	251.3
1994	206.8	157.1	226.2	184.6	241.5
1995	178.3	130.2	191.8	157.2	207.4
1996	153.8	110.8	168.1	134.9	182.6
1997	154.0	114.5	173.3	142.4	190.8
1998	170.5	126.9	188.8	156.2	206.8
1999	196.2	140.9	206.3	172.4	225.6
2000	230.0	125.3	188.0	157.0	207.3
2001	218.6	110.2	167.1	139.8	184.0
2002	185.7	103.8	163.6	132.9	182.5
2003	162.3	102.4	158.6	131.4	176.5
2004	133.8	92.0	144.7	121.6	164.2

(1) Those people who were registered as unemployed with the New Zealand Unemployment Service, excluding vacation workers.

(2) As from April 1998 are those people who were registered as unemployed with Work and Income New Zealand

(3) Those people who were without a paid job, available for work and actively seeking work.

(4) Those people who were without a paid job and available for work

(5) Those people who were without a paid job and seeking work by active or passive means.

(6) Those people who were without a paid job and either available for but not actively seeking work, or actively seeking but not available for work

Source: Personal communication from Statistics New Zealand (correcting Table from Labour Market Statistics, 1998), Various New Zealand Labour Force Statistics

The National Party representative considered (Bradford, 1999: 56):

> The benefits of flexibility have been clearly apparent … Since 1991 employment has risen by 256,000 …

However, Labour saw things differently. Hodgson (1999:178-9) pointed out:

> In the five and a half years before the Employment Contracts Act was introduced unemployment averaged 5.8 per cent. In the eight years since it has averaged 8.0 per cent … another, unwelcome trend in the past year 19,000 full-time jobs have gone, to be replaced by 30,000 part-time jobs.

Alliance, (Harre, 1999:195) concentrated on unemployment:

> The Government has taken a hands-off policy to the creation of jobs. This has led to a jobless figure of 221,000.

Although the EC Act was generally perceived as favouring employers, marginalising unions and reducing protection for employees, there was very little opposition because the economy had already achieved similar results. The general attitude of many employees to the situation in New Zealand is encapsulated in the evidence given in *Adams v Alliance* (at 1103), referring to an employment contract rather than the Act itself:

> Our backs are to the wall, it's a new world out there … The mill's fortunes have been very shaky for a long time now. There are plenty of us here who have seen the receivers in and out and redundancies. Of course you wonder how much longer your job is going to be secure. People at the mill have been feeling vulnerable and insecure. It's got to the point now where people will do anything to keep a job. Two or three years ago no-one would have signed this contract.

B. The Employment Contracts Act: Background

[1905] The expressed purpose of the Act

In its title, the Employment Contracts Act 1991 explicitly states its purpose is 'to promote an efficient labour market' and this is an honest statement. There will be different views as to what makes a labour market 'efficient', but most would understand the government's view that efficiency is clearly related to flexibility. There was no attempt to suggest that the Act was designed to promote concepts such as 'fairness' or 'harmony' in the labour market.

The Act then goes on to claim its purpose is in particular:

a. to provide for freedom of association;
b. to allow employees to determine who should represent their interests in relation to employment issues;
c. to enable each employee to choose either:
   (i) to negotiate an individual employment contract with his or her employer; or

(ii) to be bound by a collective employment contract to which his or her employer is a party;

d. to enable each employer to choose:
   (i) to negotiate an individual employment contract with any employee;
   (ii) to negotiate or to elect to be bound by a collective employment contract that binds two or more employees;
e. to establish that the question of whether employment contracts are individual or collective or both is itself a matter for negotiation by the parties themselves;
f. to repeal the Labour Relations Act 1987.

Apart from (e) and (f), the listed purposes could be described as an example of *suggestio falsi, suppressio veri*. That is, they imply what is not true (the Act gives freedom and choice), and conceal what is true (that many employees will be in a position where they can be virtually dictated to by their employer). Indeed, (c) and (d) possibly go beyond just *suggestio falsi*. While it could be argued that (e) clarifies the position, an interpretation of (c) by itself would be that an employee can decide to have either an individual employment contract (IEC) or a collective employment contract (CEC). It is not clear from (c) that the reality is that the employee can choose *to try to get his or her employer to agree* to negotiate either an IEC or a CEC. If the employee *can* choose, then this makes (d) an impossibility, as the employer will have to accept the employee's choice.

[1906] Underlying objectives for the Act

The New Zealand Business Roundtable (NZBR) and the New Zealand Employers' Federation (NZEF) began lobbying for the sort of changes which finally appeared in the EC Act from before the LR Act 1987 was enacted.

The primary objective the National Government wished to achieve through the EC Act may have been the efficient labour market, as they claimed. The primary objective(s) which the NZBR and NZEF wish to achieve through the Act is unknown, but would appear to be to regain managerial prerogatives. To do this, the NZBR and NZEF needed to remove or reduce constraints on their behaviour. The major constraints were:

a. unions;
b. the national award system and the blanket clauses;
c. interest arbitration.

[1907] Attack on unions

Position papers by lobbyists implied that at least some unions and union officials were troublemakers (NZEF, 1990:5, 7):

> There is justification for the view that some unions are third party interventionists with their own agendas.

Moreover, in general they were:

> A major block in many employer/employee relationships, as they are unable to respond in a specific way to individual needs.

In an interesting use (or abuse?) of language, the NZBR (1991:6) allege that when unions have power they could *abuse* it, while when employers have power they are (presumably) too noble to do anything other than *use* it:

> This amounts to a concern that existing unions will either *abuse* their market power, or resort to force, to perpetuate arrangements that may not meet the interests of workers. There is a related concern that, regardless of union pressure, employers may *use* their market power to constrain the options available to workers [our emphasis].

In a turnaround from their position in the 1950s, 1960s and 1970s, when it had supported the concept, the NZEF (1986:28) began objecting to compulsory unionism from the mid 1980s, stating:

> Neither workers nor employers should be compelled to join unions.

The NZBR had never, as an organisation, endorsed compulsory unionism as had the NZEF. However the *organisations* (or predecessors), of which the members of the NZBR were the Chief Executives or General Managers, had all been members of the NZEF and had supported compulsory unionism. The NZBR (1989:6) also attacked compulsory unionism – ostensibly out of altruism:

> The major problems with compulsory unionism are that it does not cater for workers whose needs differ from the norm and who would fare better under individual employment contracts rather than collective bargaining, and it reduces the pressures on unions to serve their membership efficiently and democratically and to accept change.

And also out of concern for equity and efficiency (1991:1):

> The Business Roundtable has advocated freedom of contract and freedom of association as the only effective means of promoting both equity and efficiency in employment relations.

The EC Act removed all legislative support for unions, and in fact tried to suggest unions do not exist, by never referring to unions as 'unions'. Instead it refers to 'employee organisations' – which may include unions, social clubs, works councils, productivity groups, production units, or any group of employees. The EC Act abolished monopoly bargaining rights for unions and made compulsory union membership unlawful: not explicitly, but indirectly by ensuring no employee organisation has monopoly rights and no employee organisation has compulsory membership. Even if *all* employees *and* the employer want to establish that union membership is compulsory, the EC Act does not allow them to have the freedom to negotiate such a condition. Not surprisingly, unions have been significantly affected. As shown in Table 19.5 below, the decline in union membership which occurred from the late 1980s was initially a function of the economy, with redundancies and closures, but accelerated after the passing of the EC Act.

As the economy moves out of the slump it has been in from the late 1980s to early 1990s, the influence of unions will again increase. From the early 1990s, however, unions and the CTU have been effectively marginalised. Even Angela Foulkes, the then Secretary of the CTU, and hence a person one would imagine would wish to emphasise the continued significance of unions and the CTU, accepts (1993:186) that the EC Act had

> clear intended impacts – which were essentially a deunionised workforce, an extension of managerial authority in the workplace and the emergence of enterprise bargaining.

[1908] Attack on the national award system

One of the often-cited features of New Zealand employment relations prior to the EC Act was the system of national awards. In fact, this description is a gross simplification. Collective documents included awards and agreements. 'Awards' could be on a single industrial district basis (Otago-Southland), on a multi-district basis (New Zealand except for Westland), or on a national basis, but for many years could also refer to any arrangement involving a number of employers who chose to use a formal conciliation council for their negotiations. 'Agreements' were arrangements between single employers and a union or unions. Notwithstanding, it is true that a small number of national awards, such as the New Zealand Metal Trades Employees' Award, covered a large number of employers and a far greater number of employees.

The significance of awards was greatly enhanced by the so-called 'blanket clauses' (see [1719]), which meant that any award could be deemed to include all relevant employers in the industrial district or districts. This occurred whether or not they bothered to take part in the negotiations for the award. Thus, when the New Zealand Printers' Award was negotiated, all the major printing employers and a few of the smaller printing employers would be involved in the negotiations. After the award was settled, several hundred small printing concerns would receive a copy of the new award, which would bind them and their employees. This provision clearly has significant pragmatic advantages since, in the vast majority of cases, the settlement was deemed reasonable and under the award system there was one set of negotiations rather than dozens or hundreds. The argument against the blanket provisions was that individual employers did not negotiate the rates which would apply specifically to themselves.

The argument for national (and regional) awards was that they provided a floor of minimum conditions which would apply to all. The argument is related to concepts of 'fairness.' As discussed in Chapter Eleven, there is no generally accepted concept of what 'fair pay' is, or what 'fair conditions' are. In practice,

Table 19.5. Trade unions, membership and union density, 1985–2003 (selected years)

	No. of Unions	Total Membership	Union Density (%)
December 1985	259	683,006	43.5
September 1989	112	648,825	44.7
May 1991	80	603,118	41.5
December 1991	66	514,325	35.4
December 1992	58	428,160	28.8
December 1993	67	409,112	26.8
December 1994	82	375,906	23.4
December 1995	82	362,200	21.7
December 1996	83	338,967	19.9
December 1997	80	327,800	18.8
December 1998	83	306,687	17.7
December 1999	82	302,405	21.1
December 2000	134	318,519	21.6
December 2001	165	329,919	21.6
December 2002	174	334,783	21.4
December 2003	181	341,631	21.4

Source: Crawford et al (1999:365), May et al (2003)

many people assess that what they pay or are paid is fair if it equates to the 'going rate', or the 'market rate'. There was therefore a large degree of support for a system which guaranteed, for example, that all carpenters would be getting a basic $11 per hour. However, relativities are not the only means of assessing what is fair pay. One could also argue that a fair rate of pay should be then determined by, for instance, the employer's ability to pay or the value of the contribution made by the employee.

Arguably there is no one clear-cut 'correct' method of determining what should be paid. The award system relied on one method and had (and has) many supporters. They are not necessarily right, but neither are the critics. The NZBR and NZEF – who attacked the award system, arguing that individual circumstances and ability to pay precluded against it – never came out with the suggestion that a very profitable organisation should be required to increase its wages since it could pay more.

One of the main arguments used against the award system was that it was inflexible. As discussed in [1818], this was a half-truth. There was always flexibility upwards, and no award prevented *above*-award conditions being paid. Many employers did in fact pay above-award rates, usually on their own initiative, but occasionally only after employee or union pressure. The award simply prevented worse-than-award conditions being lawfully paid. Prosecutions for breaches of award indicated that illegal practices by employers were not uncommon.

The blanket provisions in particular were attacked, particularly by the NZBR who claimed (1989:16):

> Moves should be made to eliminate the blanket coverage provision so that only parties wishing to be covered by awards are involved...

The NZBR went on (1990:4):

> Employers have to date been largely unable to initiate changes in bargaining arrangements, so as to achieve employment packages tailored to the needs of individual workers and workplaces. Blanket coverage (the rule that an award binds employers of the workers covered by the relevant union whether or not that employer participates in award negotiations) is an important factor here.

These attacks were clearly influential. The blanket coverage provisions were repealed and while national awards were not made illegal, strikes to encourage employers to agree to multi-employer awards have been made illegal, and the repeal of the blanket provisions make awards much less effective from the union and employee perspective.

[1909] Attack on interest arbitration

As discussed in the previous two chapters, compulsory interest arbitration was available for those who had accepted the ICA Acts (and later the IR Act) from 1895 to 1984. From then, interest arbitration was available if both parties agreed (except for a few months in 1990).

In practice, especially in more recent years, as shown in Table App-2, arbitration was used very rarely. The vast majority of settlements were reached by negotiations. The negotiations may have been conducted informally (leading to agreements) or formally at conciliation (leading to an award). However, it is almost certain that the *availability* of arbitration influenced settlements. As put by the NZBR (1990:11):

> In New Zealand, unions in fact made little use of compulsory arbitration from around 1968 ... However, the availability of compulsory arbitration can be argued to have remained a constraint on settlements through this period, as unions and employers have strong incentives to follow precedents set by the Arbitration Court, and in particular to adhere to relativities set historically between awards.

Arbitration clearly favours the weaker party. When New Zealand unions were in a relatively strong position they saw little need for arbitration. Not surprisingly, in the 1990s situation with weakened unions, high unemployment, and a general fear of redundancy, employers scorned arbitration as unnecessary interference. Those views were not expressed through the 1960s and 1970s.

The EC Act completed the moves initiated in 1984 and abolished the Arbitration Commission. There was no formal institution available specifically for interest arbitration. However, the Employment Tribunal (which replaced, and was much the same as, the mediation service under the LR Act) was able to provide arbitration services.

[1910] Rationale for the attacks

None of the changes called for by the NZBR or NZEF were explicitly stated to be primarily for the benefit of employers, senior managers or shareholders. However, the claim was made by the Labour Market Manager of the NZEF (Clark, 1990:1) that employers were so disadvantaged they were desperately in need of succour:

> Since about 1970 a number of changes have occurred which have gradually but inexorably eroded the position of employers so that in terms of the employment relationship they are now severely disadvantaged in general and in some situations are open to exploitation by a small number of unscrupulous unions and workers.

The NZBR and NZEF argued that the changes they called for were first for the benefit of New Zealand as a whole – by increasing efficiency and productivity, thereby leading to increased employment and national wealth and happiness. Furthermore (surprisingly), the changes were for the benefit of *employees*. Notwithstanding the claims of researchers (Brosnan and Wilkinson, 1989), who believe that the least advantaged employees were almost totally reliant on national awards and compulsory unions, the NZBR (1990:7) claimed that their proposed (and accepted) changes were for the benefit of employees and, in particular, the least advantaged:

> This conception of 'protection' ignores the fact that it is *workers* who have probably suffered most from an inability to strike enterprise deals – workers who have been denied the right to negotiate productivity packages with their employers, and, most of all, workers 'out of the mainstream' whose interests have never been catered for in national awards – most usually, working mothers, Maori, Pacific Islanders, school-leavers, the disabled, and those living in relatively depressed regions.

In an attempt to demonstrate that employees did not need unions to give them protection from exploitation, the NZEF Labour Market Manager (Clark, 1990:5) somewhat contradicted the NZBR view by claiming that

> Much of our workforce is relatively well-trained and all our people have access to a high quality education system by world standards … few workers these days are helpless by any stretch of the imagination.

This claim by the NZEF that much of the workforce is 'relatively well-trained' and the education system is 'high quality' contrasts vividly with the usual employers' propaganda and complaints of poor education and literacy amongst the workforce. A report in the *Otago Daily Times* (1993) stated:

> Many job applicants lack primary school basics, Wellington manufacturers say. The Wellington Manufacturers' Association wants applicants who can read, write,

> add up and think for themselves. Its President, Mr David Moloney, said in a report on education and training in New Zealand there was likely to be a shortage of people with these skills in the future.

It is not easy to accept that individuals who cannot 'read, write, add up or think for themselves' would be able to negotiate equitable employment contracts for themselves.

Clearly both Mr Clark and Mr Moloney were taking extreme positions to support a particular argument at a particular point in time – but equally clearly, such divergent claims affect their credibility as spokesmen for employers.

Notwithstanding, the end result of this lobbying, as already stated, was that the National Government virtually produced *the* major piece of employment relations legislation to the specification of one of the parties. Having been granted their wish list, the NZBR and NZEF were constrained to claim the EC Act was a success.

In a joint publication (NZBR and NZEF, 1992:i) the two groups alleged:

> The Employment Contracts Act has ushered in a new and highly beneficial era of employment relations by removing a great deal of statutory interference in employment relations and allowing employers and employees much greater freedom to decide on the terms of their contracts. In general, the results have been a pronounced shift to enterprise-based collective and individual contracts, greater trust, cooperation and information sharing between firms and their staff, and better incentives for performance including the removal of restrictive and uneconomic conditions. The Act is making an outstanding contribution to productivity growth and its contribution to employment growth is likely to become increasingly apparent in the period ahead.

Given that business cycles *are* cycles, economic conditions in New Zealand will improve as the country comes out of the slump. The actual impact made by the EC Act, as opposed to the economic conditions and other changes, will remain a matter of debate.

C. The Employment Contracts Act: Content

[1911] Introduction to the EC Act

The EC Act was introduced on May 1991 and remained in force until 2 October 2000 when it was repealed by the Employment Relations Act 2000 (ER Act).

[1912] Coverage of the EC Act

The EC Act applied to all employment contracts irrespective of whether the employee was employed in the private sector, in the public sector, by a State Owned Enterprise or by a local authority.

An employment contract was defined under s.2 as a *contract of service*; but included a contract for services between an employer and homeworker (see [402]).

Thus the issue as to whether a person was an 'employee' or an 'independent contractor' (see [404]) involved not only taxation and accident compensation issues but whether the EC Act applied. An employee would have the right to take a personal grievance against dismissal while an independent contractor would not.

[1913] Freedom of Association

Part One of the Act was entitled 'Freedom of Association', and established:

a. employees have the freedom to choose whether or not to associate with other employees for the purpose of advancing the employees' collective employment interests;
b. no person may, in relation to employment issues, apply any undue influence, directly or indirectly, on any other person by reason of that other person's association, or lack of association, with employees.

The reality was that in most situations employees could choose to associate with other employees, but whether they could 'advance their collective employment interests' was a question of power. The law did not *prevent* employees from trying to act collectively, and did not prevent them from negotiating a collective employment contract (CEC). It did *not* however give them the right to *choose* to do so. They could choose to *try to do so*. If their employer wanted individual employment contracts (IECs) and was more powerful, the employer had 'the choice'.

Conversely, if an employer wished to operate with one CEC only, and with no IECs then, as s.18 of the Act explicitly stated, 'the number and mix of employment contracts' was a matter of negotiation: the employer could lockout all employees not party to the CEC.

Those employees would then be forced to associate with their fellows, at least to the extent of being party to a CEC, or remain locked out. If the CEC was being negotiated by a union as bargaining agent, the locked-out employees could be required to pay a 'negotiating fee' to the union, if they wished to be party to the CEC.

Interestingly, the NZEF justified the fact that s.63(e) made a strike unlawful if it 'is concerned with the issue of whether a collective employment contract will bind more than one employer' on the basis of 'freedom of association'. The ILO (1994:86) investigated complaints against the EC Act 1991, and finally came down with only three recommendations. The third was:

> The Committee reiterates that workers and their organizations should be able to call for industrial action in support of multi-employer collective employment contracts, which is currently made expressly illegal under section 63(e) of the Act.

The NZEF (1994:6) responded:

> Freedom to associate and not to associate are recognised and protected for both employees <u>and</u> employers.

> Therefore strike action to achieve a multi-employer agreement cannot be undertaken as it is a means to force employers to associate with those they do not wish to.

Apparently the NZEF saw no inconsistency between their rejection of employees being able to strike to force employers into multi-employer contracts, and their acceptance of employers being able to lock out employees to force the employees into a multi-worker CEC – even though that would 'force employees to associate with those they did not wish to.'

[1914] Voluntary membership

Section 6 of the Act stated that 'membership in employee organisations will be voluntary.' In practical terms, this section of course refers to *union* membership. It made illegal what had been one of the major features of New Zealand employment relations since 1936 – compulsory unionism, either by law (1936–61) or by agreement or ballot (1961–91 except for 1984–85).

As discussed in Chapter Four, the desirability or otherwise of voluntary unionism is purely a value judgement, and there are arguments both for and against. In recent years there has been much propaganda in favour of legally-imposed voluntary unionism put out by both the National Party and NZEF. It should be noted that the National Party has been in Government for much of the last forty years. Their *rhetoric* has been consistent: they called for voluntary unionism:

a. in 1951 – but backed down after strong protests from the NZEF and the unions;
b. in 1961 – but only replaced compulsory unionism by law with compulsory unionism by agreement. The NZEF again objected to voluntary unionism;
c. in the mid 1970s – but only initiated compulsory ballots which came out in favour of compulsory unionism.

But only in 1983 (clearly as an electioneering tactic – a move later reversed by the 1984 Labour Government) and only in 1991 did the National Government actually *introduce* voluntary unionism by law.

[1915] Bargaining under the EC Act

Coupled with the right to collectivise, the Act also provided under sections 9 and 10, the right for parties to either negotiate in their own right or be represented by a person, group or organisation. Under s.12(2):

> Where any employee or employer has authorized a person, group, or organization to represent the employee or employer in negotiations for an employment contract, the employee or employer with who the negotiations are being undertaken shall … recognize the authority of that person, group, or organization to represent the employee or employer in those negotiations.

Bargaining behaviour, and outcomes, were limited by s.57(1):

Where any party to an employment contract alleges –
(a) that the employment contract, or any part of it, was procured by harsh and oppressive behaviour or by undue influence or by duress; or
(b) that the employment contract, or any part of it, was harsh and oppressive when it was entered into, – that party may apply to the Court for an order under this section.

Under the EC Act there was no statutory requirement to 'bargain in good faith', as is now the case. The EC Act presented a simple picture – parties were free to negotiate whatever they chose – while on the other hand there was a very confused and confusing set of conflicting and ambiguous clauses. This led the Chief Judge to observe (*NZ PSA:* 1320):

> It may be that the difficulty with the bargaining process … cannot readily be overcome by the legislation as it is. It may be that it is the policy of the legislation that collective bargaining should not be easy, only possible.

[1916] Major problem areas

Specific questions left open to interpretation were:

a. what sort of bargaining behaviours were required by the statute? and
b. what sort of bargaining behaviours were prohibited by the statute?

In particular, with regards (b) –
(i) what behaviours indicated a failure 'to recognise' the bargaining representative of the other party?
(ii) what behaviours were deemed to indicate that 'undue influence' or 'duress' is being applied, and what were 'harsh and oppressive' behaviours or contracts?

[1917] Bargaining behaviours required by statute

The EC Act, as outlined above, required the recognition of the representative of the other party. Apart from that, there were no positive requirements at all. In *Adams v Alliance* the Chief Judge determined at 1023, 'the employer must negotiate, if at all, with that representative … [but] the employer need not negotiate at all.' This view was reinforced in the *obiter* observations of the then President of the Court of Appeal in *Eketone* at 787: 'Certainly an employer is free not to negotiate with anyone …'. Thus in the early years under the Act, there was certainly no claim that the *statute* required any one to negotiate at all, let alone 'in good faith.' But, by 1997 the Chief Judge (as one of three in a sitting of the Full Court) had a very different 'interpretation'. In *NZEI v State Services Commissioner* it was stated at 391:

> There can be no doubting the existence of a duty to bargain in good faith as between parties to an existing continuous contract of employment.

In *Harrison v Tuckers* the Chief Judge, sitting alone, went further in creating negotiating obligations. While acknowledging (at 458) that these may not be justified 'on a strict construction' of the EC Act, he constructed his own definition of 'negotiation', claiming that negotiation

> involves the concept of deliberating together as contracting equals … for negotiation to take place in good faith, I take negotiation to mean each side regards the other as an equal contributor to the form, content and other qualities and aspects of the proposed contract.

[1918] 'Recognising' the representative

The statutory requirement under s.12 is to 'recognise' the bargaining representative of the other party. Again the seminal case was *Adams v Alliance*. An uncontroversial determination was made at 1010:

> the obligation contained in s.12 to recognise the authority of the representative to represent the employees in the particular negotiations means that the employer must accept that the representative is able to conduct and conclude the negotiations on behalf of the employees whom that representative has established an authority to represent, subject only to any necessary ratification.

The Chief Judge went further and ruled at 1023:

1. the employer must negotiate, if at all, with that representative;
2. the employer may not insist upon negotiating with the employees direct or with some other representative;
3. the employer need not negotiate at all;
4. the employer may request or offer direct negotiation with employees;
5. the employer must not in doing so exert undue influence on the representative not to act or to cease acting;
6. the employer must not exert undue influence in relation to any employment issue on any person by reason of that person's association (or lack of it) with employees.

As already discussed, he has since gone on to apparently contradict point 3, with later rulings there is an obligation to negotiate (and in good faith). The crucial point with respect to recognition lies in point 4: while the employer may not insist on negotiating with employees, it is permissible to *offer* negotiation, should they wish. The Chief Judge elaborated on his views (at 1024):

> There remains the question whether it is proper for any employer, once negotiations are underway, to go behind the representative's back and endeavor to negotiate with the employees direct. The answer in my view must be that just as employees are at liberty to express a wish to be represented in negotiations, so they are entitled to stand firm in that resolve and refuse to negotiate with the employer direct when the employer approaches them to do so. But if they are persuaded by means falling short of undue influence of the kinds referred to in s 5(b) and in s 8 to agree to direct negotiations after having originally appointed a representative to act on their behalf, there is nothing to prevent them from doing so.

As an interpretation of s.12, both in terms of the words used and the intent of the legislature, the above seems uncontentious.

However, interpretation of s.12 changed markedly over the next few years, triggered by *Eketone v Alliance*, which was an appeal against the decision of *Adams v Alliance*. By the time the Court of Appeal heard the appeal, the case was no longer 'live', and the observations made were rightly acknowledged by the President (at 786) and by Justice Hardie Boys (at 788) as being 'necessarily *obiter*'. The President (at 787) was not prepared to 'express a final opinion' but sounded 'a note of warning only' that:

> I am disposed to think that once a union has established its authority to represent certain employees ... then the employer fails to recognize the authority of the union if the employer attempts to negotiate directly with those employees. To go behind the union's back does not seem consistent with recognizing its authority ... Certainly an employer is free not to negotiate with anyone; but if he wishes to negotiate I doubt whether he can bypass an authorized representative.

There were three major cases which appeared before the Employment Court, all of which were later appealed to the Court of Appeal. The first, in 1994, was *NZ Med. Lab v Capital Coast Health*. This was heard before the Full Court, with the Chief Judge and Judge Travis.

Notwithstanding the fact that *Eketone* was obviously *obiter*, the case was 'dead' and both the President and another Justice expressly stated their observations were *obiter*, the Employment Court managed to decide at 125-6:

> We do not agree that the observations in *Eketone* can properly be seen as obiter ... In any event we agree with those views.

At 127-8 the Employment Court ruled that

> a direct approach to employees may constitute a breach by undermining the authority of the authorised representative.

Further (at 128), the Court implied that communicating with employees during negotiations is failing to recognise their representative:

> It seems to us that there may be situations in which a lawful communication has the effect of causing employees to lose confidence in their representatives and of driving a wedge between them and their representative, whether a union or not.

The following year the Chief Judge also ruled on *Ivamy v NZ Fire Service*. Here he went further and (at 49) ruled that:

> once negotiations for an employment contract have begun and the employees' representative has established its authority to represent the relevant employees, no further communication on the subject of the negotiations should be addressed by the employer to those employees except such as may be authorised or required by the Employment Contracts Act 1991 to be personally addressed (notices of lockout or of suspension of striking workers are immediately obvious examples).

Later that year, the Court of Appeal ruled on *Capital Coast Health* and dismissed the appeal, thereby apparently upholding the Chief Judge's viewpoint, although it was stated (at 320) that in some regards the Employment Court 'erred in law'.

The Court of Appeal thus confirmed the Employment Court's position that any attempt to negotiate with employees is a failure to recognise their representative, and that *some* communications may also be in breach of s.12. Factual information which is *not* 'intended to persuade' is apparently permissible. Justice Hardie Boys did not discuss why anyone would want to bother to give information that was not calculated to persuade!

The third case (*NZ Airline Pilot's Assn*) was heard by the Employment Court, just after the above ruling from the Court of Appeal was made public. The Chief Judge made what was later referred to by the Court of Appeal (*Airways Corp. of NZ*: 135) as an unwarranted 'extensive shift' in the interpretation of the law, and the Court of Appeal went on to state the Chief Judge 'erred in law'.

The Court of Appeal has overturned the general ban on employers communicating with their workforce, and allowed (at 136) some communications on the grounds that

> They do not in our view amount to negotiation or attempted negotiation but rather fall into the category of factual information relating to the negotiations. Nor do they strike us as so disparaging of ALPA as to call in question its authority to represent the controllers.

The above quotation refers to communications not being 'so disparaging' as to call into question the authority of the representative. Hence, only communication deemed to be disparaging of the representative should be ruled to be in breach of s.12(a). However, the Court of Appeal reinforced the ban on *attempting* to negotiate with employees, once they have a representative. 'Offering to negotiate' would certainly be seen by the Employment Court as equivalent to 'attempting to negotiate' and thus would be deemed illegal.

[1919] Undue influence and duress; harsh and oppressive behaviour and contracts

What degree of influence amounts to 'undue' influence and duress, and what level of behaviour is harsh and oppressive is clearly a value judgment on the facts of each case.

Again *Adams v Alliance* is the seminal case, and also once again the original approach taken seemed reasonable. The Chief Judge declared (at 998) with regard undue influence that:

> it is necessary to be conscious of the need for the existence of a causative relationship between the behaviour or undue influence or duress and the making of the contract … it is not to the point that harsh and oppressive behaviour was exhibited towards workers if those workers were entirely unmoved by it and entered into the contract for reasons unconnected with it.

The Chief Judge was somewhat ambivalent as to whether a lawful strike or lockout could be deemed duress. He stated (at 1027) that 'there exist highly persuasive authorities' for the proposition that a lawful strike or lockout could *not* be deemed duress, but also claimed 'the contrary opinion has been advanced.' Hence (at 1028):

> The Court will therefore necessarily approach with caution any suggestion that a strike or lockout which is lawful for most other purposes can amount to or constitute economic duress …

With regards to 'harsh and oppressive behaviour', the Chief Judge (at 1027) considered:

> The behavior complained of must strike the Court as reprehensible, as morally blameworthy and as meting out intolerable treatment. It will normally have elements of deliberation and of unwarranted severity. Deceptive or misleading statements of the kind alleged and aggressive marketing by strong personalities do not strike me as amounting to the behavior described in the subsection. Abnormal behavior without abuse of power or position is not enough.

Within a very short space of time the Chief Judge had what appears to be a much lower threshold for behaviour to be harsh and oppressive. In *United Food Workers v Talley* (1992) at 454, he claimed:

> What converts the defendant's conduct from oppressive to harsh and oppressive is the employees' misplaced dependence upon TFL and their trust in the first defendant enhanced by his offer of what is called his 'LV Martin guarantee.'

When the case went to the Court of Appeal, the Chief Judge's decision was upheld, albeit without much support.

In *Harrison v Tuckers*, the Chief Judge progressed even further. In that case employees signed a contract 'not only with reluctance but under protest' (at 464). The Chief Judge made a number of determinations with regards the meaning of 'harsh and oppressive' which were a long way removed from his earlier cited determination in *Adams v Alliance*. He now considered that a contract which did not have a premium for overtime worked was *by definition* harsh and oppressive, at 467:

> To require employees to agree in advance to do additional work for no additional return is harsh and oppressive, as the employee's ability to refuse the work is more theoretical than real in the case of low paid workers in potentially vulnerable employments.

It should be noted that this statement is somewhat confused. The clause does *not* require the employees to do 'additional work for no additional return' – it required them to do additional work for a proportionately identical additional return. The Chief Judge has decided that a *penal* rate of return is required, and that apparently anything less is harsh and oppressive.

From the start to the finish of the decade, common law in effect rewrote the EC Act. No matter if one is a supporter or critic of the EC Act, the level of judicial activism should be of concern.

[1920] Employment contracts

The remainder of Part Two outlined employment contracts. As s.18 had outlined, the number and mix of contracts was a subject for negotiation. Note, this did *not* mean parties must discuss and reach a compromise. One party, if it has sufficient power, may simply inform the other party that it intended to have, for example, only one CEC covering all employees.

Section 19 stated that if there was no applicable CEC an employee may negotiate an IEC. If there was an applicable CEC the employee may also negotiate an IEC so long as the terms and conditions were:

> not inconsistent with any terms and conditions of the applicable collective employment contract.

Thus an employee may have signed a CEC, as one of a number of employees who are all parties to it, and also negotiated and signed a separate IEC. The CEC could stipulate that the wage be 'in a range from $8 to $11 per hour' or 'to be specified in separate IECs' while the IEC states that for the particular employee the wage will be $9.50 per hour.

There was initial confusion as to what was meant by an 'applicable' CEC, leading to a public debate between the Minister of Labour, Bill Birch, and the President of the Council of Trade Unions (CTU), Ken Douglas. In a letter to the *Dominion Sunday Times* on 17 June 1991 Bill Birch emphasised that 'applicable' referred to the individual employee and not to the workforce in general. This is actually made explicit in s.2 of the Act, which defined 'applicable CEC' as meaning a CEC:

> that is binding on the relevant employee, employees, employer, or employers (as the case may require) at the relevant point in time.

The concern of the CTU was that after a union had negotiated a CEC binding on a group of employees, the employer may hire *other* employees on IECs, paying them lower wages and thereby possibly undercutting union members for jobs. However this possibility was perfectly acceptable under the Act.

A second area of confusion was what was meant by 'not inconsistent'. In the past in New Zealand most awards specified *minima*. Hence individual arrangements which were better than award were legally perfectly acceptable and did not breach the award. Some commentators assumed that so long as the IEC was *no less favourable* than the CEC, it would be deemed 'not inconsistent'. However this view appears incorrect. In a judgement of the Court of Appeal, in *NZ Meat Processors' Union v Alliance* (1990) Richardson J. at 98,293 ruled, admittedly with respect to inconsistencies between individual contracts and awards, that

> where there is a true inconsistency, where the contractual provision and the award cannot stand together, the award must prevail whether the result is perceived as favourable or unfavourable to the particular worker.

Hence, if it was intended to have IECs together with an applicable CEC, parties should ensure that the CEC specifies it was establishing *minima*, or it should specify a *range*, or it should state that it is not specifying a particular condition which instead will be specified in IECs.

[1921] Personal grievances

Part III of the Act on Personal Grievances closely followed previous legislation in the definition of personal grievances. The most significant change was that under s.26(a):

> (a) All employment contracts must contain an effective procedure for the settlement of personal grievances

That is, either a personal grievance procedure was in reality included in every employment contract (whether a CEC or an IEC) or, if a procedure was not included, then the model procedure in Schedule A was *deemed* to be in the employment contract. Thus *all* employees, whether at managerial level or not, whether union members or not, whether they have written employment contracts or not, were covered by the procedure and had the right to take a case to the Tribunal and Court.

This change in statutory law obviously had a marked detrimental effect on union membership. Under the LR Act only union members had access to the personal grievance procedure. This clearly provided a major 'selling point' to unions. Admittedly unions could still provide advocacy services to members, but union membership no longer conferred unique rights to the procedure. It is purely a matter of conjecture whether the anti-union aspect of this change was considered a primary objective or merely seen as fortuitous.

[1922] Strikes and lockouts

The law with respect to strikes and lockouts was not changed significantly from the situation under the LR Act. However the economic climate, particularly high unemployment, together with very low job security for many employees meant that *behaviour* with respect to strikes and lockouts was very different in the 1990s to what it was even in the late 1980s and certainly very different from the 1960s and 1970s. While there was some strike action in 1991–2, employees tended to be passive with a great deal of concern just to keep a job. As already cited from *Adams v Alliance* (at 1103):

> People at the mill have been feeling vulnerable and insecure. It's got to the point now where people will do anything to keep a job. Two or three years ago no-one would have signed this contract.

After the passing of the EC Act, lockouts became more frequent and certainly much more publicised. It is submitted that this was not a direct result of the Act – although publicity and propaganda about the Act being an 'Employers' Charter' may have prompted some employers to consider lawful options more closely. Macfie (1992:321) considers the major reason for the rarity of lockouts was the 'highly regulated and centralised system of award bargaining', which meant that employers would have had 'to act in a highly organised and disciplined manner.' One probable reason why lockouts were so scarce through the 1960s, 1970s and 1980s was that during periods of inflation there was rarely if ever a *need* to lock out. Employers could simply adhere to the *status quo* – which in real terms meant a significant reduction in real wages and conditions, thus prompting employees to strike. Also the depressed economy since the late 1980s, where wages had hardly been increasing at all, may have prompted more use of the lockout as a negotiating weapon in the 1990s.

Part V establishes that under certain conditions strikes and lockouts are lawful and continues to include a wide range of behaviours as both a strike and a lockout.

[1923] Institutions

Part VI established two newly entitled institutions – the Employment Tribunal and the Employment Court. The Tribunal had very similar functions to that of the Mediation Service under the LR Act and the Court had very similar functions to the Labour Court under the LR Act.

Presumably in order to suggest it was bringing in something new and different, the EC Act referred to 'adjudication' rather than 'arbitration'. The words are synonymous.

[1924] The Employment Tribunal

Section 79(1) stated that the Tribunal should have jurisdiction amongst others:

> (a) to provide mediation assistance in all matters properly brought before it;
> (b) to adjudicate on personal grievances, under personal grievance procedures contained or implied in employment contracts, which are properly brought before it;
> (c) to adjudicate on disputes, under disputes procedures contained or implied in employment contracts, which are properly brought before it;
> (d) to adjudicate on all actions commenced under section 48 of this Act for the recovery of wages or other money;
> (e) to adjudicate on all actions for the recovery of penalties under this Act for a breach of an employment contract or for a breach of any provision of Part II or Part III or Part IV of this Act.

Section 79(2) went on:

> (2) In all matters before it for adjudication, the Tribunal shall have jurisdiction to determine them in such manner and to make such decisions or orders,

> not inconsistent with this or any other Act or with any applicable collective employment contract, as in equity and good conscience it thinks fit.

The Tribunal consisted of 'mediator' members, who provided mediation, and 'adjudicator' members, who provided adjudication. Some members of the Tribunal were mediator/adjudicator members and could provide both services.

The Tribunal in effect had the powers of a Court when involved in adjudication. As mediation is informal, and by consent, those powers during mediation would be inappropriate.

[1925] Drafting inadequacies

The drafting inadequacies of this section of the EC Act were discussed in [605]. There were a number of glaring instances of muddled thinking, bad drafting, and illogicalities.

[1926] The Employment Court

The constitution of the Employment Court followed the trend established by the LR Act in streamlining. For many years the Court comprised a Judge and two 'panel members' – one representing employers, one the central union body. The LR Act allowed for a Judge alone to act, except for demarcation issues and for personal grievances. The EC Act did away with 'panel members' altogether. The Court comprised a Judge alone, or in exceptional cases, as the Full Court, it comprised three Judges.

[1927] The EC Act in perspective

The EC Act was 'sold' to the public under a barrage of propaganda, including a pamphlet to each home from the Minister of Labour which included a considerable amount of *suggestio falsi, suppressio veri*. Individuals were told that they would have 'to agree' to changes in terms and conditions. Many (naively?) believed this meant that if they didn't want changes, the changes would not occur. Subsequently, some found they could be locked out until they 'agreed', or had their take home pay cut (a partial lockout) until they agreed. Employees under IECs had no protection from lawful lockout action by an employer who later wished to have a CEC. After the event, *Witehira* suggested such partial lockouts were unlawful. However full lockouts were (and are) lawful.

In [1904], there was discussion of the Act's stated purpose and in [1905] the underlying objectives were hypothesised. Clearly some, maybe all, readers will disagree on whether the suggested alternatives *were* the real objectives. Even if there is agreement, there will be differing views as to how justified were the *real* objectives. Part C discusses employment relations issues during this period. It must be emphasised that while the outcomes were *influenced* by the EC Act, the Act was not the sole cause. The economic situation – redundancies, high unemployment – and economic competition were all highly significant.

[1928] Background to the Employment Relations Act 2000

The Employment Relations Act 2000 (ER Act) was introduced amid claims from employers, employer groups and the right wing opposition that the Act would return New Zealand to the 'bad old days' of the 1960s and 1970s. The Minister of Labour, Margaret Wilson, claimed the Act 'reinforced to employees basic rights which had been denied them for over a decade.'

In fact, the most significant change introduced by the statute was in the object of the Act. As discussed in [1904], the purpose of the EC Act was to 'promote an efficient labour market'. The object of the ER Act is

> to build productive employment relationships through the promotion of good faith in all aspects of the employment environment and of the employment relationship

Certainly the EC Act in statute form did not suggest anything about 'good faith.' However, by the end of the early 1990s 'good faith' had become part of the common law for the EC Act. In 1998, the Court of Appeal in *Sky Network* emphasised that 'there must be good faith and fair treatment.' In [1917] it has already been observed that the Employment Court in different cases pointed out that 'good faith' was required in negotiations. Thus, the *major* impact of the ER Act in 2000 was to put in the statute what was in existence in common law.

[1929] The Employment Relations Amendment Act 2004

The Amendment Act (Am Act) was enacted in October 2004 and came into force on 1 December 2004, again amidst strident opposition from the same groups who objected to the ER Act. This time, however, there was a not-infrequent refrain that there was nothing wrong with the ER Act and 'if it ain't broke don't fix it.' This justifies the prediction made in 1993 that the changes proposed for the ER Act would be 'cosmetic rather than creative' (Geare, 1993:203). As Thickett, Walsh and Harbridge (2004:56) observe, 'overall, the Employment Relations Act has not brought about wholesale improvements to terms and conditions of employment.'

While the Am Act does introduce somewhat more substantial changes to the status quo than did the parent Act, and is more supportive of collective bargaining and unionism than the ER Act, it is still a long way short of a return to the situation pre-EC Act. This does not prevent opponents seeing an ominous inclination to edge towards such a return.

It is worth noting, even after the 2004 Amendents, the significant changes introduced by the EC Act which have been left largely (or totally) unaffected:

- compulsory unionism illegal;
- monopoly bargaining and membership rights of unions removed;
- individual bargaining permitted;
- national award systems de-emphasised (although strike action to regain multi employer agreements is now legal);

- blanket provisions removed;
- personal grievance procedure available to all employees – non-union and managers.

[1930] Good Faith

Good faith, under s.4 (1A) is wider in scope than the implied mutual obligations of trust and confidence, and 'requires the parties … to be active and constructive in establishing and maintaining a productive employment relationship …'. The failure has to be:

(a) … deliberate, serious and sustained; or
(b) intended to undermine either bargaining, and agreement or an employment relationship.

This amendment is an apparent rebuff to the Court of Appeal in *Coutts Cars v Baguley*. There the Court of Appeal stated at 672:

> We do not see that the new statutory obligation on employers and employees to deal with each other in good faith introduces any significantly different obligation that the Courts have placed upon parties to employment contracts over recent years

The Court of Appeal was comparing the statutory requirements in 2000 to deal with parties in good faith, with the common law situation in which it is implied that in all employment agreements, parties have a mutual obligation to deal with each other in such a way as to maintain trust and confidence.

The section is very short on specifics as to what exactly the difference happens to be. Should there be a failure to comply with the duty of good faith, a new s.4A allows for penalties to be imposed. Fines can be up to $10,000 for organisations.

[1931] Freedom of association

The situation introduced by the EC Act remains, with employees being allowed to associate, that is form unions, but compulsory unionism remains illegal.

There is a prohibition on preference because a person is, or is not, a member of a union but a new s.9(3) states that:

> To avoid doubt, this Act does not prevent a collective agreement containing a term or condition that is intended to recognise the benefits –
> (a) of a collective agreement;
> (b) arising out of the relationship on which a collective agreement is based.

Undue influence must not be exerted on a person to induce them to become or remain a member, or cease to be a member of a union.

[1932] Union and union members

Unlike the EC Act, which never mentioned unions, the ER Act gives them at least the psychological benefit of recognition, even if the benefits of the arbitration era are not provided.

Unions are given the sole right to negotiate a collective agreement, which would appear to be a significant benefit to the union movement. However, any registered society comprising only fifteen individuals can become a union for this purpose. Consequently, as Table 19.5 shows, the number of unions has increased markedly since 2000 – from 82 in December 1999 to 181 (121 per cent) in December 2003 – but union membership over the same period grew from 302,405 to only 341,631 (13 per cent).

Union members are entitled to two paid union meetings a year of a maximum duration of two hours each. The employer must be given fourteen days' notice.

Under part 7 of the Act, union members are also allowed paid education leave to improve employment relations. For an average sized firm (51–280 employees), the leave entitlement is one day in total for every eight employees, (one hour each, equivalent).

Under ss.55 and 65A, employees who are members of a union are to have automatic deduction of their union fees, unless the collective or individual agreements explicitly exclude it.

This is a distinct administrative and financial benefit to unions, but indirectly can be seen as a major benefit to some employers as well. With automatic deduction of fees, union representatives are much less likely to visit the workplace.

[1933] Bargaining fees for unions

In a move towards an 'agency shop' situation (see [421]), the Am Act introduced ss.69 D-W which allows a bargaining fee clause to be inserted in collective agreements. However the insertion is far from automatic and, even when included, it is not mandatory.

The employer and union must first agree to the clause. After agreement there has to be a secret ballot of all employees doing the work under the coverage clause of the collective agreement. Should a majority of the voters vote in favour of the bargaining fee, it will be included in the collective agreement. The fee must not be greater than the union membership fee.

Payment of the bargaining fee is not compulsory and employees who notify their employer that they do not agree to pay the fee are exempt. Clearly the legislature and the union movement are relying on the apathy of a large percentage of the population. Historically there is always a big difference between the numbers who will voluntarily 'opt-in' compared to the numbers who remain in if they are so placed, but given the right to 'opt-out'.

[1934] Union representatives

Under ss.20–25, provision is made for union representatives to have access to workplaces for purposes related to members' employment or the union's business.

Access must not be 'unreasonably denied', but the representative must exercise the right to enter at reasonable times, in a reasonable way and complying with reasonable procedures and safety requirements. (Access may, however, be denied to workplaces with fewer than twenty employees, none of whom are union members, and where the employer is of a religious society or order which precludes union membership and the employer holds a certificate of exemption.)

[1935] Collective bargaining

The original 2000 ER Act required collective bargaining to be conducted in 'good faith.' Partly this is naïve wishful thinking. Under s.4 (1)(b):

> The parties must not … do anything –
> (i) to mislead or deceive each other; or
> (ii) that is likely to mislead or deceive each other.

Taken literally, this is an absurdity. Any offer or demand in collective bargaining outside the parties' real target is clearly intended to mislead and deceive the other party. One assumes that legislation intended this to mean:

> Other than normally accepted practices which mislead and deceive the other party, parties should keep such practices to a minimum.

The 2000 Act accepted that even though the parties were acting in good faith, they may be totally unsuccessful in bargaining. The Employment Relations Amendment Act 2004 indicates a loss of patience.

Section 32(1) as amended now requires the union and employer to continue bargaining over other unsettled matters, even though they are deadlocked on one issue. This is unfortunately too simplistic. It may appear sensible to say to the parties 'get on and settle the other issues', but it totally ignores the fact that in most if not all negotiations the issues are interrelated. How one matter is settled has a major influence on how others will be settled.

Section 33 was repealed and replaced. A union and employer are now required to conclude a collective agreement unless there is a genuine reason based on reasonable grounds not to. The section goes on to state a genuine reason does not include:

> (a) opposition in principle to collective bargaining; or
> (b) disagreement about including a bargaining fee clause.

[1936] Undermining collective bargaining

The Am Act introduces ss.59 A, B and C, which state that undermining collective bargaining by automatically passing on terms and conditions to the individual agreements or on different collective agreements is a breach of good faith, and hence subject to penalty as discussed above.

In an unusual break from normal practice, the Am Act in this area was actually more extreme than in Bill form. In the Bill, it was only a breach of the duty of good faith if the passing-on of terms and conditions was done by the employer:

(a) with the intent to undermine *and*
(b) with the effect of undermining.

In the Am Act, the requirement for a breach was significantly increased in that the 'and' was changed to an 'or'. Thus an employer could (although the probability is incredibly low) be adjudged to have breached the duty of good faith because of particular actions, even if there was no guilty intent. It should be recalled that for the bulk of the last century strike action was punishable by fine, imprisonment or deregistration – but punishments were imposed in only a tiny percentage of possible cases.

[1937] Individual employee's terms and conditions

The significant aspect of this section is that, rhetoric aside, the ER Act still permits individual bargaining and individual agreement.

[1938] Fixed term employment

Fixed term employment is still permitted under the Act, but is constrained. The employer must have genuine reasons based on reasonable grounds for employing an employee on a fixed term basis. Specifically, the following are *not* genuine reasons:

- excluding or breaching the rights of the employee under the Act;
- establishing the suitability of the employee for permanent employment;
- excluding or breaching the rights of the employee under the Holidays Act 2003.

Hence, 'rolling over' fixed term contracts so that the employer can get rid of the employee at will is illegal.

The practice of most (or all?) New Zealand universities to employ academic staff for a three-to-five-year term to determine their suitability for employment before either 'granting tenure' or 'confirming appointment' is illegal.

However, under s.66(1) it is legal to appoint an employee for a fixed term to:

- replace an employee on paternity leave;
- conclude a specific project such as:
  - completing a PhD;
  - installing a new computer system.

[1939] Rights under restructuring

One area in which the changes introduced by the Am Act are less cosmetic than usual is in the rights accorded so-called 'at risk' employees should there be restructuring.

'At risk' employees are defined in Schedule 1 A as those who provide:

- cleaning or food catering services (any sector);
- caretaking (education sector);
- laundry services (education, health, aged care sectors);
- orderly services (health, age-related care sectors).

The Am Act recognises that these are the employees that most frequently get made redundant, as the work they do is given to independent contractors or outside contracting organisations. However, rather than confront the problem of redundancy head-on, the legislature has chosen to introduce these convoluted provisions.

If the employer of these 'at risk' employees proposes to restructure so that their work is to be performed by a new employer, the employees may under s.69 A, E and G:

a. bargain with the original employer for alternative arrangements (if these are unsatisfactory);
b. elect to transfer to the new employer on the same terms and conditions; or
c. elect to be made redundant by the original employer. If so, under s.69 G the employee may have entitlement to redundancy pay from the original employer if entitlement was excluded for technical redundancy.

If the employee elects to transfer and is subsequently made redundant by the new employer then the employee may either negotiate satisfactory redundancy payment, or under s.69 J have those entitlements decided by the Authority. Technically this is not another situation of the Authority adjudicating over interest issues. Since the entitlements are deemed the employee's rights, this is the Authority settling a rights dispute.

These provisions clearly make the contracting out of work much more difficult for an employer. It is not unreasonable to assume that an employer is much more likely to want to contract out work where the employees are not highly productive than when they are highly productive. The potential contractor is unlikely to be enthusiastic at having to take on less than optimal employees. It is probable that under the new legislation employers will attempt to shed as many of their less productive staff as possible before contracting out the work. The Am Act may, in fact, have very adverse effects on this 'at risk' employee.

[1940] Strikes and Lockouts

The Act recognises that 'good faith' does not preclude certain strikes and lockouts being lawful. The definition of strikes and lockouts and their legality has not changed significantly since the LR Act 1987.

A strike, under s.81(1), means an act that –

(a) is the act of a number of employees who are or have been in the employment of the same employer or different employers –

(i) in discontinuing that employment, whether wholly or partially, or in reducing the normal preference of it; or

(ii) in refusing or failing after any such discontinuance to resume or return to their employment; or

(iii) in breaking their employment agreements; or

(iv) in refusing or failing to accept engagement for work in which they are usually employed; or

(v) in reducing their normal output or their normal rate of work; and

(b) is due to a combination, agreement, common understanding, or concerted action, whether express or implied, made or entered into by the employees.

A lockout under s.82(1) means an act that –

(a) is the act of an employer –

(i) in closing the employer's place of business, or suspending or discontinuing the employer's business or any branch of that business; or

(ii) in discontinuing the employment of any employees; or

(iii) in breaking some or all of the employer's employment agreements; or

(iv) in refusing or failing to engage employees for any work for which the employer usually employs employees; and

(b) is done with a view to compelling employees, or to aid another employer in compelling employees, to –

(i) accept terms of employment; or

(ii) comply with the demands made by the employer.

[1941] Lawful strikes and lockouts

Any strike or lockout is lawful if there are reasonable grounds for believing it is justified on the grounds of safety or health.

Otherwise, a strike or lockout is lawful if it relates to collective bargaining and at least forty days have passed since bargaining was initiated.

[1942] Unlawful strikes and lockouts

A strike or lockout is specifically *unlawful* if it occurs while a collective agreement is in force (when a declaration has been made by the court to allow such action over an aspect of the agreement) or if it

- relates to a personal grievance;
- relates to a dispute;
- relates to a bargaining fee clause;
- (whether otherwise lawful or not) is in an essential service and the required notice has not been given.

[1943] Suspension

The Act permits the lawful suspension of both striking employees and non-striking employees. Non-striking employees may be suspended only when their normal work is not available because of the strike action of other employees.

[1944] Personal Grievances

The section on personal grievances is not substantively different from the original section in the IR Act 1973, other than the change introduced by the EC Act 1991 allowing all employees access to the personal grievances procedure.

A 'personal grievance' under s.103 means any grievance that an employee may have against the employee's employer or former employer because of a claim –

(a) that the employee has been unjustifiably dismissed; or
(b) that the employee's employment, or 1 or more conditions of the employee's employment (including any condition that survives termination of the employment), is or are or was (during employment that has since been terminated) affected to the employee's disadvantage by some unjustifiable action by the employer; or
(c) that the employee has been discriminated against in the employee's employment; or
(d) that the employee has been sexually harassed in the employee's employment; or
(e) that the employee has been racially harassed in the employee's employment; or
(f) that the employee has been subject to duress in the employee's employment in relation to membership or non-membership of a union or employees organisation.

[1945] Procedural fairness and substantive justification

Early Court decisions stressed that there was a significant difference between the new phrase 'unjustifiable' and the common law 'wrongful'. A course of action would be deemed unjustifiable when that which was done could not be shown to be in accord with justice or fairness (see *Auckland City Council v Hennessey*).

It has also been stressed that it was not only *what* was done that had to be demonstrably fair, but also *how* it was done. Thus a dismissal could be lawful under common law, but procedurally unfair (*BP Oil*), or could be substantively justified under statute law, but procedurally unfair (*NZ Food Processing Union v Unilever*).

The two concepts of substantive justification and procedural fairness are closely intertwined, and there is inevitably a degree of overlap (*Cherrington v Auckland Farmers*). Common law originally suggested that for a dismissal to be deemed justifiable it had to be both for a substantively justified reason, and conducted in a procedurally fair manner.

As a minimum, any agreed procedure with regards dismissals must be faithfully followed, and 'natural justice' must be observed. Natural justice was defined in *Hillier* as requiring the employer to:

> inquire into the allegations in a fair and reasonable manner. This necessarily involves the employee being adequately informed of the allegations, so that he is able to prepare any answer he wishes to make. It involves the employee being given adequate opportunity to present his answer. It means that the employer must not reach a decision adverse to him on the basis of allegations of which he has not been informed, and to which he has had no opportunity to respond. And it means that the employer must approach the inquiry with an open mind … Adherence to the outward formalities of fairness means nothing if the decision is already made, or if the employer's mind is for other reasons turned against the employee so that the outcome of the inquiry is unlikely to be affected whatever he may say in his own defence.

As a consequence, any reasons *not* communicated to the employees cannot later be claimed to be operative grounds for dismissal (*Batey*). The Court has ruled (*Northern Butchers' Union v Peach*) that if a decision to dismiss was unjustly made, it remains unjust however appropriate the result of the decision may come to appear in hindsight.

In the case of lesser offences, there should also be a warning and a request to improve performance and conduct in general (*Canterbury Clerical Workers' Union v Tuckers*).

It should be noted that perfection was not required. The Chief Judge made clear in *NZ Food Processing Union v Unilever* that 'What is looked at is substantial fairness and substantial reasonableness according to the standards of a fair-minded but not over-indulgent person.' It is generally advisable to avoid later accusations of pressuring and unfairness, so employers should ensure employees have representation at disciplinary meetings.

For a dismissal to be deemed substantively justified by the Court, it must be agreed that the offence or behaviour would in general warrant dismissal. Typically there would need to be:

a. unsatisfactory work performance;
b. long-term sickness;
c. an incident of serious misconduct;
d. a number of incidents of less serious misconduct which together could be deemed sufficiently substantive.

While unsatisfactory work performance can be deemed substantive justification, *Trotter v Telecom* at 681 outlines an exhaustive list of questions to be answered to ensure such dismissal is fair.

> (1) Did the employer in fact become dissatisfied with the employee's performance of his or her duties?
> (2) If so, did the employer inform the employee of that dissatisfaction and require the employee to achieve a higher standard of performance?
> (3) Was the information given to the employee readily comprehensible in the sense of being an objective criticism of the work so far and an objective statement of standards requiring to be met?

(4) Was a reasonable time allowed for the attainment of those standards?

(5) Following the expiry of such a reasonable time and following reasonable information of what was required of the employee, did the employer turn its mind fairly to the question whether the employee had achieved or substantially achieved what was expected, including:
   (a) using an objective assessment of measurable targets;
   (b) fairly placing the tentative conclusions before the employee with an opportunity to explain or refute those conclusions;
   (c) listening to the employee's explanation with an open mind;
   (d) considering the employee's explanation and all favourable aspects of the employee's service record and the employer's responsibility for the situation that had developed (for example, by not detecting weaknesses sooner or by promoting the employee beyond the level of his or her competence); and
   (e) exhausting all possible remedial steps including training, counselling, and the exploration of redeployment?

A major difficulty is determining the degree of seriousness of the behaviour. The ultimate test is the opinion of the Court, after making the inquiry and hearing the representations. One instance of serious misconduct may be sufficient. One instance of simple misconduct is unlikely to be sufficient, whereas several instances of simple misconduct following warnings may be sufficient (*Wellington Road Transport Union v Fletcher*). Thus the Court has to make up its mind whether or not that type of misconduct is usually reasonable and sufficient grounds for dismissal (*McMurtrie v West Coast Area Health*).

The Court accepts that punishment can be severe without being unjustifiable (*Bates v Dunlop*), and notes that it is not for the Court to substitute its judgement as to what penalty should or should not actually have been imposed (*Read v Air NZ*).

In addition to 'offences', there are situations in which a dismissal may be deemed substantively justified. These have included, but not without counter-judgements, repeated ill-health (*Campbell v Vacation Hotels Ltd*) and redundancy. Redundancy is considered below in [1960].

While many decisions considered procedural fairness and substantive justification as separate issues, this lost favour with the Employment Court. In *Drummond v Coca Cola Bottlers*, at 232-3 the Chief Judge stated:

> It is now well settled that it is incorrect to look at a dismissal separately from the point of view of substantive justification and procedural fairness, especially in that order for it is likely to lead to a mindset that on certain assumptions the dismissal must be justified, leading to a reluctance to defeat the making of those assumptions by criticism of what is sometimes described as 'mere procedure'. The true inquiry is one that looks at the dismissal overall but it would be no exaggeration to say that the inquiry into procedure should come first. Thus it is

> that an employer who has not conducted a fair inquiry into a serious allegation such as an allegation of dishonesty cannot be allowed to insist that it had an honest belief in the truth of the allegations.

[1946] Test of justification

For the first time there is now a statutory test to justify dismissal, rather than relying on common law. The new s.130A appears to be an unnecessary 'change' and a somewhat gratuitous rebuff of the Court of Appeal. The Select Committee on the Bill argued the amendment was necessary since:

> The Court of Appeal's judgement in W & H Newspapers v Oram (2000) ERNZ 448 has been perceived as meaning that dismissal is justified, provided that the employer thought the action was reasonable or that the action constituted what a fair and reasonable employer could have done.

To be fair to the Select Committee, it is possible that some individuals who did not bother to read the Oram decision may have actually believed that the Court of Appeal could have ruled that justification is assured so long as the employer thought its action was reasonable. The Oram decision, of course, does not contain anything like that.

Prior to Oram, the common law standard was as expressed by the Court of Appeal in *Northern Distribution Union v BP Oil NZ Ltd* (1992) 3 ERNZ 483 at 487:

> Definition is not possible, for it is always a matter of degree. Usually what is needed is conduct that deeply impairs or is destructive of that basic confidence or trust that is an essential part of the employment relationship. In the context of a personal grievance claim under the Labour Relations Act, questions of procedural and substantive fairness are also relevant. In the end, the question is essentially whether the decision to dismiss was one which a reasonable and fair employer would have taken in the particular circumstances.

In *Oram* (at 457) the Court of Appeal made a minimal change which they justified, using 'could' rather than 'would':

> ... personal grievance, once the employee has established a prima facie case of unjustifiable dismissal, the onus is on the employer to justify the dismissal. The Court has to be satisfied that the decision to dismiss was one which a reasonable and fair employer could have taken. Bearing in mind that there may be more than one correct response to a fair and reasonable employer, we prefer to express this in terms of 'could' rather than 'would', used in the formulation expressed in the second *BP Oil case* ([1992] 3 ERNZ 483 (CA) at p. 487).

In practical terms, this amendment will probably have absolutely no effect on managerial behaviour or on how the Authority or Employment Court determines if a dismissal was justifiable or not. It will have an effect on how *decisions* of the Authority or Court are written up.

[1947] Remedies for personal grievances

Where the Authority or Court determines that an employee has a personal grievance it may provide under s.123 for any one or more of:

> (a) reinstatement of the employee in the employee's former position or the placement of the employee in a position no less advantageous to the employee;
> (b) the reimbursement to the employee of a sum equal to the whole or any part of the wages or other money lost by the employee as a result of the grievance:
> (c) the payment to the employee of compensation by the employee's employer, including compensation for –
> (i) humiliation, loss of dignity, and injury to the feelings of the employee; and
> (ii) loss of any benefit, whether or not of a monetary kind, which the employee might reasonably have been expected to obtain if the personal grievance had not arisen …

These have been the remedies since 1973. The ER Act specifies that reinstatement is to be the primary remedy, and if the employee seeks reinstatement and is found to have a personal grievance the Authority 'must' provide for reinstatement 'wherever practicable.' The qualifying phrase is significant. In many cases the employee does not really want reinstatement, and asks for it in order to try to get a better financial settlement. This would occur where the dismissal had procedural faults and the employee would realise that a procedurally fair dismissal would be likely in the near future. In other situations, even if the dismissal was totally unjustified, the employee could be reluctant to return because the employer-employee relationship would be so poor. Other instances where reinstatement may be deemed impracticable would be where the dismissal had taken place a year or more in the past, or where the employer claims strongly that a normal employer-employee relationship is impossible.

Table 9.1 shows reinstatement ordered by the Tribunal under the EC Act. (Cases under the EC Act were heard long after the Act had been repealed.) They show that reinstatement has been a remedy in only a small percentage of winning cases. McAndrew, Morton and Geare (2004:107) report that under the ER Act the Mediation Service reported profile of settlements 'was not markedly different than those mediated in the Tribunal era either. Less than 2.5 per cent involved reinstatement of the employee.'

[1948] Disputes

A 'dispute', previously known as a 'dispute of right', refers to a dispute over 'the interpretation, application or operation of an employment agreement.' Disputes may be settled between the parties, or by utilising the mediation service or Employment Relations Authority.

[1949] Institutions

There are three institutions:

- the Mediation Service;
- the Employment Relations Authority which replaced the Employment Tribunal under the EC Act; and
- the Employment Court, which remains as it was under the EC Act.

[1950] The Mediation Service

The Mediation Service was greatly expanded in comparison to the number of mediation members of the Employment Tribunal, but with a corresponding lowering of status.

The Mediation Service is very broad and is designed to support employment relationships in a wide variety of ways, including:

- telephone, internet and e-mail services;
- pamphlets;
- specialist mediation.

[1951] Employment Relations Authority

Under s.157, the Authority:

1. is an investigative body that has the role of resolving employment relationships problems by establishing the facts and making a determination according to the substantial merits of the case, without regard to technicalities;
2. must, in carrying out its role,
   (a) comply with the principles of natural justice; and
   (b) aim to promote good faith behaviour; and
   (c) support successful employment relationships; and
   (d) generally further the object of this Act.

The Authority took over the adjudicating role of the Tribunal, but was intended to be more investigative and to reduce the lawyer-dominated adversarial process in the Tribunal. Although reducing the use and resulting cost of lawyers was deemed a major priority, the legislature apparently could not see that a remarkably effective way of doing this would be to go back to the ICA legislation and forbid persons holding a practising legal certificate from appearing before the Authority or Court, unless all parties agreed.

Initially, the Authority believed it was entitled to deny parties the right to cross-examine. However the Court, in *David v Employment Relations Authority*, ruled that this denied natural justice. The ER Act was amended to state that natural justice did not require the Authority to allow cross-examination, but 'the Authority may, in its absolute discretion, permit such cross-examination.'

Under s.161 the Authority has exclusive jurisdiction to make determinations about employment relationship problems generally. Numerous examples are given, and include:

- disputes about the interpretation, application, or operation of an employment agreement;
- matters related to a breach of an employment agreement;
- personal grievances;
- matters about whether the good faith obligations imposed by this Act have been complied with in a particular case;
- matters about the recovery of wages or other money under section 131;
- actions for the recovery of penalties;
- compliance orders.

[1952] Employment Court

The Employment Court is the same Court as established by the EC Act 1991. This means it is a Court of Record, and under s.187 has exclusive jurisdiction, amongst other matters:

- to hear and determine elections under section 179 for a hearing of a matter previously determined by the Authority;
- to hear and determine actions for the recovery of penalties under this Act for a breach of any provision of this Act;
- to hear and determine questions of law referred to it by the Authority;
- to hear and determine any questions whether any person is to be declared to be an employee within the meaning of this Act;
- to order compliance;
- to hear and determine proceedings founded on tort and resulting from or related to a strike or lockout;
- to hear and determine any application for an injunction.

D. Other Legislation

[1953] Health and Safety in Employment Act 1992

The Health and Safety in Employment Act 1992 (HSE Act) came into force on 1 April 1993. The HSE Act centralises applicable legislation – around thirty statutes and some health and safety provisions. Kiely and Langton (1994:195) point out that the past record does not read well:

> In 1990 five people were killed every fortnight at work; 17 accidents per week were investigated by the Department of Labour; five employees each week were left with permanent disabilities and 200 employees each week were laid up with work related injuries; undoubtedly a serious concern from a social and economic perspective in that it cost the nation 300 million dollars in Accident Compensation payments. And the cost of lost production and retraining is estimated at around 1.5 billion dollars per annum – a staggering two per cent of GDP. Not surprisingly, the Act is designed to shift the financial commitment and responsibility from the government to the employer by imposing proactive duties reinforced by hefty liabilities and penalties.

They go on to point out that in the first year of operation there were 12 prosecutions for serious offences (one dealt with) and 205 other prosecutions of which 65 had been dealt with.

[1954] Wages protection

The Wages Protection Act 1983 continues in force. Aspects have become relevant with regard to deductions for union dues. Under this Act s.5(1) specifies that:

> An employer may, for any lawful purpose, –
> (a) With the written consent of a worker; or
> (b) On the written request of a worker –
> make deductions from wages payable to that worker.

Originally employers who made *overpayments* to employees had to get written permission from those affected to recover the overpayments from future wages, or take the employees to Court. Section 6 now allows employers to recover overpayments if

> By virtue of the methods or equipment normally used by that employer in arranging the payment of, or paying, wages to the worker concerned, it was not reasonably practicable for that employer to avoid making that overpayment; and there is prompt notification to the employees.

[1955] Human Rights Act 1993

The Human Rights Act 1993 has gone on from, and repeals, the Race Relations Act 1971 and the Human Rights Commission Act 1977. In some cases (in particular sexual harassment cases), employees will be able to take action either under the Human Rights Act or the ER Act. They must choose one or other, they cannot take action under both. Clearly if awards are deemed greater, or the treatment deemed more professional and/or sympathetic if action is taken under one of the Acts, then employees will tend to gravitate to that Act.

The Human Rights Act extends the prohibited grounds for discrimination to cover almost every conceivable area barring obesity, height (or lack) and body odour. From 1 February 1999 it has been prohibited to discriminate on the basis of age (being defined as sixteen years or more). Hence retirement will have to be voluntary, or the employee will have to be dismissed on performance grounds.

[1956] Holidays Act 2003

The new Holidays Act 2003 came into force on 1 April 2004. April Fools' Day seemed appropriate. The Act was poorly thought through and poorly drafted, and had to be amended within the year.

The philosophy behind the original Act was that employees who worked on a public holiday should receive time and a half (that is, fifty per cent in addition to the pay they should normally receive for a 'normal day') plus a day in lieu.

The crafters failed to take into account the fact that a number of collective agreements entitled employees to penal rates for working on the public holiday. The Act required they be paid time-and-a-half of the rate they would have been paid for *that* day – not for a 'normal' day. This meant in one case four-and-a-half times the payment for working a public holiday.

A second problem that became apparent was that the original Act required that someone who was rostered to work on the public holiday, but did not work because of sickness, would be entitled to time and a half for *not* working.

The Amendment Act addresses these issues. Where there has been contractual agreements, the employees is paid the greater of the agreed rate plus penal rates, or relevant daily rate *less* penal rate plus half again. When an employee is sick when rostered to work on a public holiday, the employee is paid as if the holiday had been observed.

E. Employment Relations Through the Laissez-Faire Era

[1957] Unions

If the EC Act had not been passed, New Zealand unions in general would nonetheless have been in a weaker position in 2000 than they had been in 1990, and considerably weaker than in 1970. The economic conditions of the time would have ensured that. Through 2000 to the present, economic conditions are starting to favour unions as the economic upturn leads to expectations of improved wages and conditions and more employee recognition that strong unions can be effective. The ER Act 2000, and Amendment in 2004 may contribute to this – but equally without them the union movement would have been stronger in 2005 than 2000.

However, the EC Act, through the introduction of voluntary unionism by law, its attack on the national award system and the abolition of monopoly bargaining rights for unions, has contributed to a considerable reduction in union membership and union power. Alan Jones (then Industrial Relations Manager for New Zealand's largest company and a Board Member of the New Zealand Employers' Federation) claimed in a paper (1992:12) that a major effect of the legislation is 'the shift of power from unions and union officials to employees.' He accepted that unions have been weakened, but failed to admit the result is a significant increase in power accorded to employers. Instead he presented, apparently in all seriousness, a claim that the power has gone to employees.

There was not a uniform weakening of unions. Those unions which in the past were weak and most dependent on legislative support were most affected. These include unions of retail shop assistants, clerical workers and cleaners. (Indeed the New Zealand Clerical Workers' Union collapsed.) Stronger unions, such as the meat workers or engineers, had already been adversely affected over the previous ten years by the economic factors mentioned earlier, and the legislative changes resulting from the EC Act had less impact. Those sections of society who were disproportionately hurt were the young, women and Polynesians. As Brosnan and Wilkinson (1989:86) observed in a case study of the low paid, the then strength of the cleaners' unions owed 'much to the national award system and compulsory unionism.' As stated above, the destruction of the national award system appears to have been part of the agenda, particularly for the NZEF and NZBR. The EC Act went a long way to achieve that goal.

[1958] Strikes

As mentioned in [1820], theory suggests that the early 1990s should have witnessed a trough in strike activity, and certainly that is what occurred.

As emphasised in Chapter Ten, *conflict* will always occur in work environments, but conflict does not have to be manifested by strikes. However, the probability is very high that as the international economy improves over the next few years, and the New Zealand economy also picks up, that strike activity will also increase. There has been nothing to imply that there have been widespread fundamental changes in human behaviour and motivation to suggest other than that. When the power inequality lessens, 'pay back time' will be high on the agenda for a number of unions and workgroups. Hince and Harbridge (1994:246) point out that in recent years the 'rich are getting richer' and the 'poor are getting poorer.' They also suggest (1994:251) that

> Evidence is emerging that the Employment Contracts Act regime is creating a low-trust threshold in industry. In 1993 a private polling consultant, Heylen Research, commissioned by the Department of Labour to report on aspects of attitudes to the statute, surveyed 2,000 workers in 1995 enterprises. It reported that 43 per cent of employers thought workers trusted them, but only 15 per cent actually did; that 66 per cent of employers thought staff felt more secure in their jobs but only 14 per cent thought they were; and that 51 per cent of employers thought staff had gained job satisfaction but only 23 per cent of staff thought so. Such data does not augur well for the long-term success of workplace reform and changed bargaining structures that have occurred during this period.

[1959] Scope of bargaining

It was suggested in [1905] and [1907] that a major underlying objective of the proponents of the EC Act was the destruction of the national and regional award system. The evidence suggests that that objective was achieved very rapidly. As Table 19.6 (based on the 1993 survey) shows, multi-employer documents became a thing of the past, under the EC Act. Under the ER Act, there has been a slight revival, but 'MECA's' (multi-employer collective agreements) will probably never be as popular as awards.

Table 19.6. Employment contract structures 1991–93 (private sector)

	1991	1992	1993
Award/Multi-employer CEC	59	9	6
Single Enterprise CEC	13	35	35
IEC	10	35	37
Combination CEC and IEC	–	5	8
No formal contract	18	16	14
Total	100	100	100

Source: Whatman et al (1994)

[1960] Redundancy under the EC Act

As in the two previous eras, there is as yet no legislation guaranteeing compensation for dismissal through redundancy.

Specific 'redundancy' legislation has tended to be negative and anti-compensation, rather than the reverse. Thus the provision in the LR Am Act 1990 discussed in [1821], which allowed employers to retrospectively renege on a redundancy agreement if it was a so-called 'technical' redundancy, was retained in the EC Act 1991 in s.176(5). Furthermore, the EC Act in s.46(3) stated:

> where a provision of any contract deals with the issue of redundancy but does not specify either the level of redundancy compensation payable or a formula for fixing that compensation, either the Tribunal nor the Court shall have the jurisdiction to fix that compensation or specify a formula for fixing that compensation.

Section 46(3) did not have the restraining effect expected by the legislature. In the next major case (*Bilderbeck v Brighouse,* 1993), the Chief Judge ruled that the employment contracts did not even mention redundancy so s.46(3) did not apply and the Court could set compensation. He also claimed that s.46 applied only to 'dispute proceedings' (interpretation, application or operation of an employment contract) and not to personal grievances. Under that logic, virtually any dispute to which s.46(3) applied could be reworded as a personal grievance rendering the section ineffective.

The Chief Judge ruled that although there was a redundancy situation – and although the employees had no redundancy agreement and had been given the required notice (and that three of the four were re-employed by the new owner of the company) – since there had been no consultation, and because the compensation offered was deemed by the Chief Judge to be inadequate, the dismissals were all unjustified. When the case went to the Court of Appeal (*Brighouse v Bilderbeck,* 1994) there was a unanimous ruling that

> There is no general requirement for an employer to pay compensation in every redundancy situation.

Notwithstanding, a 3:2 majority of the Court of Appeal upheld the Employment Court's decision, and the judicial activism at Court level was given Court of Appeal approval. However, one of the two dissenters in the Court of Appeal decision on *Brighouse*, Richardson, J., became president of the Court of Appeal when Cooke, P., retired. Richardson was opposed to judicial activism and when a similar case to *Brighouse* came to the Court of Appeal (*Aoraki Corp. Ltd v McGavin*), Richardson, P., called all seven permanent judges to, in effect, review *Brighouse*.

In *Aoraki*, as with *Brighouse*, the redundancy situation was genuine, but the compensation was deemed inadequate and there were procedural deficiencies. In a valiant (but vain) attempt to curb the judicial activism, the Court of Appeal made a number of significant rulings:

> (a) It cannot be mandatory for the employer to consult with all potentially affected employees in making any redundancy situation … (However) in some circumstances an absence of consultation where consultation could reasonably be expected may cast doubt on the genuineness of the alleged redundancy … So, too, may a failure to consider any redeployment possibilities.

(The *caveats* in the above would all be seen as loopholes by the judicially active.)

> (b) … except where the employment contract requires payment of compensation when an employee becomes redundant, in which case the Court will enforce that contractual obligation, the statute does not empower the tribunal or Employment Court to require any such payment.

In addition, the Court of Appeal pointed out that compensation for a grievance is only for that specific grievance. In some dismissal cases procedural deficiencies may cast doubt on the substantive justification for the dismissal. Compensation in those cases will be for hurt and humiliation *and* the loss of the job. But:

> In a genuine redundancy the remedies for procedurally flawed dismissal are compensation for the resulting hurt and loss of benefit. They are necessarily limited to the effects of the procedural deficiencies. So there can be no compensation in a genuine redundancy situation for the loss of the job except as provided in the employment contract itself.

While commentators (Harbridge & Kiely, 1998) at the time saw the *Aoraki* decision as one which 'marked a sharp break with the Court's activist approach to redundancy in the *Brighouse* decision', it simply required more creativity on the part of activists. Every comment in a decision is seen as a possible loophole and opportunity for further activism.

In *Aoraki* the Court of Appeal accepted that consultation 'may' be needed in some circumstances. Chief Judge Goddard appeared to believe consultation 'will always' be needed. In *Phipps* he ruled that the question is whether a redundancy is genuine and unavoidable. He claimed:

> It could not be either and certainly could never be both in the absence of the necessary consultation with the employee.

The Chief Judge also has firm views as to what constitutes consultation, which he outlined in *Cammish*:

> Consultation is to be a reality, not a charade. The party to be consulted must be told what is proposed and must be given sufficiently precise information to allow a reasonable opportunity to respond. A reasonable time in which to do so must be permitted. The person doing the consulting must keep an open mind and listen to suggestions, consider them properly, and then (and only then) decide what is to be done. However, consultation is less than negotiation and the assent of the persons consulted is not necessary to the action taken following proper consultation.

The period of notice will also come more into focus. In *Rolls v Wellington Gas Company Ltd*, a Mr Rolls had been made redundant. While his title was Commercial Sales Manager, he was the only employee in that sales department and was basically an independent salesman. When made redundant he was paid according to the formula and given four weeks' notice. There was nothing in his contract which stipulated a particular period of notice. Nowhere in the Tribunal decision, is there any indication that either Mr Rolls or his advocate had any complaint about the notice period given. However, the Chief Judge determined that, in his view, the appropriate period should have been three months or thirteen weeks. He also determined that 'It was of course distressing and humiliating for the appellant to be dismissed without being given his contractual period of notice …'. Consequently, the Chief Judge granted a further $5000 compensation.

[1961] Redundancy under the ER Act and ER Amendment

As mentioned above, the ER Act was largely cosmetic, although it brought under statute law the well-established common law principle that there should be 'good faith' in all employment relations dealings.

Notwithstanding, the Employment Court in *Baguley v Coutts Cars Ltd* attempted to use the change in law to distinguish *Aoraki*. If successful, they would be unrestrained in terms of activism. When the case (*Coutts Cars Ltd v Baguley*) was appealed, the Court of Appeal (672) ruled that 'it has long been the law that the special nature of the employment relationship incorporates mutual obligations of trust and confidence' and that they did not see the obligations on employers 'as differing significantly from those referred to in the judgements of this Court in *Aoraki Corp Ltd v McGavin.*'

The ER Act, however, failed to replicate s.46 of the EC Act which had effectively prevented the Court from determining the outcome of 'failed' negotiations over redundancy issues. In the *Canterbury Spinners* (2001) cases there was a clause requiring the employer to 'negotiate a level of redundancy compensation'. The employer and the union failed to agree and the matter went to the Employment Relations Authority which ruled that it did not have authority to set the amount, as s.161(2) states:

> The Authority does not have jurisdiction to make a determination about any matter relating to –
> (a) bargaining; or
> (b) fixing of new terms and conditions of employment …

The Court reverted back to the judicially active line of cases discussed above in [1822] and determined that the Authority did indeed have jurisdiction. The Court ruled that it was not fixing new terms and conditions (i.e. settling an interest dispute), but was settling a rights dispute since the clause had established a right to redundancy compensation and the Authority was simply to determine the level. This view was supported by the Court of Appeal.

[1962] 'Planning with Confidence'

As argued above, *Aoraki* will not allow employers and employees 'to be able to plan with confidence'. If employers and employees want a reasonable degree of certainty with regards to redundancy situations they should ensure that employees have written contracts detailing:

a. compensation (if any) for redundancy;
b. procedures to be undertaken if redundancy occurs including notice, whether or not consultation will occur, what services if any will be provided.

Moreover they should adhere to this agreement.

Those without agreements should have as little confidence now as to what the Employment Court may rule, as they had at any time in the 1990s.

APPENDICES

Table App-1. Classification of major documents

1) ARBITRATION ERA 1895–1987		
	Private Sector	**Method**
ICA Acts	1) Industrial Agreements 2) Awards	1a) Voluntary Negotiation (CB) 2a) Conciliation *or* 2b) Compulsory Arbitration *or* 2c) 'Rubber Stamping' of Industrial Agreement
IR Act	1) Collective Agreements 2) Awards	1a) Voluntary Negotiation (CB) 2a) Conciliation *or* 2b) Compulsory Arbitration
	Public Sector	
	1) Determinations	1a) Imposed by employer *or* 1b) Voluntary Negotiation
	2) Orders	2a) Arbitration
2) COLLECTIVE BARGAINING ERA 1987–91		
	Both Sectors	
	1) Agreements	1a) Voluntary Negotiation (CB) 1b) (possibly) Voluntary Arbitration
	2) Awards	2a) Conciliation *or* 2b) Voluntary Arbitration
3) LAISSEZ-FAIRE ERA 1991–		
	Both Sectors	
	1) Individual Employment Contracts	1a) Voluntary Negotiation (IB) *or* 1b) Managerially Imposed
	2) Collective Employment Contracts	2a) Voluntary Negotiation (CB) 2b) Managerially Imposed

Table App-2. Settlement of disputes of interest under IR Act 1973

Year ending 31 March	Awards: (Some Arbitration)	Awards: (Registered Conciliated Agreements)	Collective Agreements: (Registered Voluntary Settlements)
1975	35	192	181
1976	20	265	383
1977	9	245	246
1978	8	280	434
1979	8	303	416
1980	23	251	482
1981	9	385	530
1982	9	343	70
1983	6	109	414
1984	0	0	32
1985	0	67	59
1986	11	358	538
1987	5	316	560
TOTAL	143	3,114	4,345

Source: Various Reports of the Department of Labour, Wellington, 1975–87

Table App-3. Number of unions and workers represented, 1895–2003

NUMBER OF UNIONS

	1895	1925	1955	1970	1985	1991	1998	2001	2003
< 100	53	211	154	127					
%	69.7	53.1	37.6	36					
100-999	23	166	191	148					
%	30.3	41.8	46.6	41.9					
< 1000	76	377	345	275	146	4	50	131	147
%	100	94.9	84.2	77.9	65.5	5	60	79	81
1000-4999		19	53	56	47	48	21	22	21
%		4.8	12.9	15.9	21.1	60	25	13	12
5000-9999		1	9	18	18	8	3	4	5
%		0.3	2.2	5.1	8.1	10	4	2	3
10000 +			3	4	12	10	9	8	8
%			0.7	1.1	5.4	25	11	5	4
TOTAL	76	397	410	353	223	80	83	165	181
%	100	100	100	100	100	100	100	100	100

WORKERS REPRESENTED (in 000s)

	1895	1925	1955	1970	1985	1991	1998	2001	2003
< 100	2.1	7.0	9.5	5.6					
%	26.4	9.5	2.3	1.5					
100-999	6.0	51	67	53					
%	73.6	51.4	22	14					
< 1000	8.2	61	74	58	41	2.9	14	18	21
%	100	60	24.3	15.5	8.5	1	5	6	6
1000-4999		30	115	117	93	99	42	46	45
%		30	37.9	30.9	19.2	16	14	14	13
5000-9999		9.2	60	125	130	64	20	29	35
%		9.2	19.8	33.1	26.5	11	7	9	10
10000 +			54	77	224	436	229	235	239
%			18	20.5	45.8	72	75	71	70
TOTAL	8.25	100.54	304.28	378.47	490.21	490.21	603.12	329.92	341.63
%	100	100	100	100	100	100	100	100	100

Source: Various Yearbooks, Harbridge (1993), various Department of Labour reports

Table App-4. Public sector unions – 1985

Union	Membership
Assn of Teachers in Technical Institutes	2,114
Assn of University Library Staff	310
Dockyard Unions	227
National Union of Railwaymen	9,300
NZ Dietetic Assn Inc	200
NZ Educational Institute	18,761
NZ Free Kindergarten Teachers Assn	954
NZ Hospital Engineers Assn Inc	157
NZ Institution of Medical Lab Technology	1,040
NZ Locomotive Engineers Assn	1,833
NZ Nurses Assn Inc	14,057
NZ Post-Primary Teachers Assn	13,156
NZ Public Services Assn	69,718
NZ Railway Officers Institute	4,154
NZ Railway Tradesmen Assn	2,428
NZ Society of Radiographers	265
NZ Teachers Colleges Assn	311
NZ Workers Union (Public Sector Membership)	8,500
Post Office Union	38,100
Teacher Trainee Assn of New Zealand	2,800
Technical Institutes Allied Staff Assn	658
Total	189,043

Table App-5. Manufacturing establishments, by size of workforce

Establishments employing:						
Year	10 or under	11–20	21–50	51–100	Over 100	Total
1924–25						
No:	2972	720	570	155	121	4538
%:	65.5	15.9	12.6	3.4	2.7	100
1939–40						
No:	4218	957	772	212	183	6342
%:	66.5	15.1	12.2	3.3	2.9	100
1954–55						
No:	5350	1473	1020	310	213	8366
%:	64.0	17.6	12.2	3.7	2.5	100
1969–70						
No:	6466	1846	1382	506	373	10573
%:	61.2	17.5	13.1	4.8	3.5	100
Year	0–5	6–9	10–49	50–99	100+	Total
Feb. 1987						
No:	11733	2664	4056	612	498	19563
%:	60.0	13.6	20.7	3.1	2.5	100
Feb. 1991						
No:	12902	2327	3461	468	369	19527
%:	66.1	12.0	17.7	2.4	1.9	100
Feb. 1995						
No:	13359	2372	3083	382	365	19561
%:	68.3	12.1	15.8	2.0	2.0	100
Feb. 1998						
No:	14552	2169	3003	344	341	20409
%:	71.3	10.7	14.7	1.7	1.7	100

Table App-6. Working days lost in stoppages, per 1000 wage salary earners – five year averages 1921–2004

Year		Year	
1921–25	281	1966–70	175
1926–30	64	1971–75	95
1931–35	108	1976–80	96
1936–40	67	1981–85	31
1941–45	81	1986–90	427
1945–50	254	1991–95	54
1951–55	436	1996–00	30
1956–60	40	(2001–04)	36
1961–65	70		

Source: Various New Zealand Department of Statistics, Prices, Wages & Labour, Various Year Books and Key Statistics

Table App-7. Work stoppages (selected years)

Year	Total Stoppages	Person-Days of work lost (000s)
1921	77	120
1930	38	31
1940	57	28
1950	129	271
1951	109	1,157
1960	60	36
1970	77	85
1981	291	388
1985	383	756
1986	215	1,329
1988	172	382
1990	137	331
1991	71	99
1992	54	114
1993	58	24
1994	69	38
1995	69	53
1996	72	70
1997	42	25
1998	35	12
1999	32	17
2000	21	11
2001	42	54
2002	46	34
2003	28	19
2004	34	6

Source: Various Key Statistics 1920–2004

Table App-8. Industries responsible for five + per cent of 'working days lost' in each year for 1925, 1955, 1970, 1985, 1990, 1991, 1995, 1997, 2000, 2003

Industry	1925	1955	1970	1985	1990	1995	1997	2000	2003
Meat Export Works	6.2		39.5	28.6	65.3				
Other Slaughtering, Preserving of Meat									
Paper, paper products, printing and publishing				7.2					
Transport equipment				5	5.2				
Building		63.6							
Construction other than building				11.6					
Water Transport		17.5	6.8*		13.5				
Land Transport				6.1					
Licensed Hotels			21.9						
Waterfront			6.5						
General Engineering			5.3			44	55		
Coal Mining		19.9							
Rubber		7.7							
Finance, Insurance, etc				5.8					
Community, Social and Personal Services					7.9				
Education*						42			
Government Administration and Defence*							10	2	
Transport, Storage and Communication Services*						8	16		
Manufacturing**								78	91
Health and Community Services**								16	2
Other*							9	4	7
Total Person Days Lost (000s)	0.6	52	277.3	756.4	330.9	53.3	25.6	11.5	19.5

** Classification Data Available for 2000, 2003*
*** New Classifications 2000, 2003*
Source: Various Labour Market Statistics (2004), Various Year Books (1988–1997), Monthly Abstract of Statistics (126-85)

References

Ackers, P., *et al*., (1992), 'The Use of Cycles, Explaining Employee Involvement in the 1990s', *Industrial Relations Journal*, 23(4):268-283.

Ackers P. and A. **Wilkinson,** (2003), *Understanding Work and Employment*, Oxford University Press, Oxford.

Adams, R. (1992), 'The Role of the State in Industrial Relations', in Lewin, *et al.* (eds), (1992).

Aitken, M. and R. **Wood**, (1989), 'Employee Stock Ownership Plans: Issues and Evidence', *Journal of Industrial Relations*, 31(2):147-168.

Allen, V.L., (1976), 'Marxism and the Personnel Manager', *Personnel Management*, 8(12):18-22.

Anderson, G., (1991), 'The Employment Contracts Act 1991: An Employers' Charter?' *New Zealand Journal of Industrial Relations*, 16(2):127-142.

Ashenfelter, O. and D. **Bloom**, (1983), 'The Pitfalls in Judging Arbitrator Impartiality by Win-loss Tallies Under Final Offer Arbitration', *Labour Law Journal*, August:534-539.

Ashenfelter, O. and D. **Bloom**, (1984), 'Models of Arbitrator Behaviour: Theory and Evidence', *American Economic Review*, 74:111-124.

Ashenfelter, O. and G. **Johnson**, (1969), 'Bargaining Theory, Trade Unions and Industrial Strike Activity', *American Economic Review*, 59:35-49.

Atkinson, J., (1985), 'Flexibility: Planning for an uncertain future', *Manpower Policy and Practice*, 1:25-30.

Bacharach, S.B. and E.J. **Lawler**, (1981), *Bargaining: Power, Tactics and Outcomes*, Jossey Bass, California.

Bachrach, P. and M.S. **Baratz**, (1962), 'Two Faces of Power', *American Political Science Review*, 66(4):947-952.

Bachrach, P. and M.S. **Baratz**, (1963), 'Decisions and Non Decisions', *American Political Science Review*, 67(3):632-642.

Bain, G.S., (1970), *The Growth of White Collar Unionism*, Oxford University Press, Oxford.

Bain, G.S. and H.A. **Clegg**, (1974), 'A Strategy for Industrial Relations Research in Great Britain', *British Journal of Industrial Relations*, 12(1):91-113.

Barbash, and M. **Meltz**, (eds) (1997), *Theorizing in Industrial Relations*, ACIRRT, Sydney.

Barmby, T. and J. **Treble**, (1989), 'A Note on Absenteeism', *British Journal of Industrial Relations*, 27(1):155-158.

Beaumont, P.B., (1991), 'Trade Unions and HRM', *Industrial Relations Journal*, 22(4):300-308.

Beaumont, P.B. and R.I.D. **Harris**, (1990), 'Union Organising Attempts in Britain in the 1980s', *Industrial Relations Journal*, 21(4):274-286.

Bell, D., (1970), *The End of Ideology*, Free Press, New York.

Bell, L.A. and R.B. **Freeman**, (1991), 'The Causes of Increasing Interindustry Wage Dispersion in the United States', *Industrial and Labour Relations Review*, 44(2):275-287.

Bellemare, G., (2000), 'End Users: Action in the Industrial Relations System?' *British Journal of Industrial Relations*, 38(3):383-405

Bennett, J.T., (1991), 'Private Sector Unions: The Myth of Decline', *Journal of Labour Research*, 12(1):1-12.

Bennett, J.T. and B.E. **Kaufman,** (eds), (2002a), *The Future of Private Sector Unionism in the United States*, M.E. Sharpe, Armonk, New York.

Bennett, J.T. and B.E. **Kaufman**, (2002b), 'Introduction' in Bennett and Kaufman, (eds), (2002a).

Blain, N., J. **Goodman** and J. **Loewenkers**, (1987), 'Mediation, Conciliation and Arbitration', *International Labour Review*, 126(2):179-198.

Blumberg, P., (1968), *Industrial Democracy*, Constable, London.

Boon, B., (1992), 'Remedies for Unjustifiable Dismissals under the Labour Relations Act 1987', *New Zealand Journal of Industrial Relations*, 17(1):101-107

Boston, J., (1988), 'The State, Wage-fixing and Labour Market Reform: Some International Perspectives', *New Zealand Journal of Industrial Relations*, 13(2):121-142.

Boston, J., J. **Martin**, J. **Pallot**, and P. **Walsh**, (1996), *Public Management: The New Zealand Model*, Oxford University Press, Oxford.

Bowie, N., (2005), 'Kantian ethical thought', in J. Budd and J. Scoville (eds), *The Ethics of Human Resources and Industrial Relations*, LERA, Champaign, Illinois, 61-88

Boxall, P.F., (1993), 'The Significance of Human Resource Management: a Reconsideration of the Evidence', *The International Journal of Human Resource Management*, 4(3):645-664.

Brass, D.J., (1984), 'Being in the Right Place: A Structural Analysis of Individual Influence in an Organisation', *Administrative Science Quarterly*, 29:518-539.

Bridgford, J., (1990), 'French Trade Unions: Crisis in the 1980s', *Industrial Relations Journal*, 21(2):126-135.

Brook, P., (1990), *Freedom at Work*, Oxford University Press, Auckland.

Brosnan, P. and F. **Wilkinson**, (1989), *Low Pay and the Minimum Wage*, NZIIR, Wellington.

Brown, J.A.C., (1954), The *Social Psychology of Industry*, Penguin, Harmondsworth.

Brown, D., P. **Ingram** and J. **Walsworth**, (2004), 'The Price is Right? Pay Settlements and Nominal Wage Rigidity in Britain', *British Journal of Industrial Relations* 42(3):507-525

Budd, J.W. (1992), 'The Determinants and Extent of UAW Pattern Bargaining, *Industrial and Labour Relations Review*, 45(3):523-539.

Budd, J.W., R **Gomez** and N.M. **Meltz**, (2004), 'Why a Balance is best: The Pluralist

Industrial Relations Paradigm of Balancing Competing Interests,' in Kaufman (ed.), (2004a).

Budd, J. and J. **Scoville,** (eds), (2005), *The Ethics of Human Resources and Industrial Relations*, LERA, Champaign, Illinois.

Burrows, R. (1946), *Interpretation of Documents*, Butterworths, London.

Campbell, D., and M. **Rimmer**, (1994), 'Managing Retrenchment: Award Standards or Enterprise Agreements', *Australian Bulletin of Labour*, 20(1):45-65.

Campbell, I., (1993), 'Regulating Workplace Health Hazards in New Zealand: A Historical Note', *Occasional Papers*, Department of Management Systems, Massey University.

Carey, A., (1967), 'The Hawthorne Studies: A Radical Criticism', *American Sociological Review*, 32(2):403-416.

Chamberlain, N., (1948), *The Union Challenge to Management Control*, Harper and Row, New York.

Chamberlain, N. and J.W. **Kuhn**, (1986), *Collective Bargaining*, 3rd Edn, McGraw Hill, New York.

Charness G, and D. **Levine**, (2000), 'When are Layoffs acceptable? Evidence from a Quasi-Experiment,' *Industrial and Labour Relations Review*, 53(3):381-400

Chruden, H.J. and A.W. **Sherman**, (1980), *Personal Management: The Utilisation of Human Resources,* South-Western Publishing Co, Cincinnati.

Church, R., Q. **Outram** and D.N. **Smith**, (1991), 'The "Isolated Mass" Revisited: Strikes in British Coal Mining', *Sociological Review*, 39:55-87.

Clark, H.C., (1938), *National Income and Outlay*, Macmillan, London.

Clark, Rt. Hon. H., (1993), 'Employment Relations – The New Direction Under Labour', *New Zealand Journal of Industrial Relations*, 18(2):153-162.

Clark, M., (1990), 'Managing Change in Industrial Relations', Paper presented to IIR Conference, Auckland.

Clark, P.F., J.T. **Delaney** and A.C. **Frost,** (eds), (2002), *Collective Bargaining in the Private Sector*, IRRA, Champaign, Illinois.

Clegg, H.A., (1960), *A New Approach to Industrial Democracy*, Basil Blackwell, Oxford.

Clegg, H.A., (1970), *The System of Industrial Relations in Britain*, Basil Blackwell, Oxford.

Clegg, H.A., (1975), 'Pluralism in Industrial Relations', *British Journal of Industrial Relations*, 13(3):309-316.

Clegg, H.A., (1979), *The Changing System of Industrial Relations in Great Britain*, Basil Blackwell, Oxford.

Clegg, S., (1975), *Power, Rule and Domination*, Routledge and Kegan Paul, London.

Clegg, S., (1979), *The Theory of Power and Organisations*, Routledge and Kegan Paul, London.

Cockburn, C., (1989), 'Equal Opportunities: The Short and the Long Agenda', *Industrial Relations Journal*, 20(3):213-225.

Collins, D., (1998), *Gainsharing and Power*, Cornell University Press, Ithaca.

Commons, J.R., (1911), *A Documentary History of American Industrial Society*, A.H. Clark, Cleveland.

Commons, J.R., (1934), *Institutional Economics: Its Place in the Political Economy*, Macmillan, New York.

Conant, J.L. and D.L. **Kaserman**, (1989), 'Union Merger Incentives and Pecuniary Externalities', *Journal of Labour Research*, 10(3):243-253.

Conference on Economic Progress, (1959), *Inflation – Cause and Cure*, Washington.

Craft, J.A., (1990), 'The Communists as a Source of Union Power', *Journal of Labour Research*, 11(2):145-160.

Cullen, D.E., (1985), 'Recent Trends in Collective Bargaining in the United States', *International Labour Review*, 124(3):299-322.

Cully, M., S. **Woodland**, A. **O'Reilly** and G. **Dix**, (2000), *Britain at Work: As depicted by the 1998 Workplace Employee Relations Survey*, Routledge, London.

Dahl, R.E., (1957), 'The Concept of Power', *Behavioural Science*, 2:201-218.

Deeks, J., (1976), 'Ideology and Industrial Relations in New Zealand', *New Zealand Journal of Industrial Relations*, 1(2):26-31.

Deeks, J., J. **Parker** and R. **Ryan**, (1994), *Labour and Employment Relations in New Zealand*, Longman Paul, Auckland.

Delaney, J.T. and J. **Godard**, (2001), 'An industrial relations perspective on the high performance paradigm', *Human Resource Management Review* 11:395-429

Deloitte Touche Tohmatsu, (1994), *Survey of People's Experience of Redundancy*, Deloitte Touche Tohmatsu, Wellington.

Department of Labour, (1972), *Labour Turnover*, Department of Labour, Wellington.

Department of Labour, (1982), *Report 1982*, Department of Labour, Wellington.

Dickens, W.T. and J.S. **Leonard**, (1985), 'Accounting for the Decline in Union Membership, 1950–1980', *Industrial and Labour Relations Review*, 38(3):323-334.

Disney, R., (1990), 'Explanations of the Decline in Trade Union Density in Britain: An Appraisal', *British Journal of Industrial Relations*, 28(2):155-177.

Donn, C.B., (1989), 'Concession Bargaining in the Ocean-going Maritime Industry', *Industrial and Labour Relations Review*, 42(2):189-200.

Dorgan, T., and M. **Grieco**, (1993), 'Battling against the odds: the emergence of senior women trade unionists', *Industrial Relations* 24(2):151-164.

Douglas, K., (1994), 'The Industrial Conciliation and Arbitration Act: 100 years on', *New Zealand Journal of Industrial Relations*, 19(3):228-230.

Drago, R., (1988), 'Quality Circle Survival: An Explanatory Analysis', *Industrial Relations*, 27(3):336-351.

Drago, R. and M. **Wooden**, (1990), 'The Determinants of Strikes in Australia', *Journal of Industrial Relations*, 32(1):32-52.

Drago, R. and M. **Wooden**, (1991), 'The Determinants of Participatory Management', *British Journal of Industrial Relations*, 29(2):177-204.

Drucker, P.F. (1968), *The Practice of Management*, Pan Books, London.

Dubin, R., (1957), 'Power and Union – Management Relations', *Administrative Science Quarterly*, 2:60-81.

Duncan, H.G., (1972), 'Interpretation of Awards and Agreements', Unpublished Paper.

Dunlop, J.T., (1950), 'Framework for the Analysis of Industrial Relations: Two Views', *Industrial and Labour Relations Review*, 3(3):383-393.

Dunlop, J.T., (1958), *Industrial Relations Systems*, Holt, New York.

Dunlop, J.T., (1967), *'The Social Utility of Collective Bargaining'* in L. Ulman, (ed.), (1967).

Dunlop, J.T., (1993), *Industrial Relations Systems*, (Revised Edition), Harvard Business School Press, Boston.

Dunn, S., (1990), 'Root Metaphor in the Old and New Industrial Relations', *British Journal of Industrial Relations*, 28(1):1-31.

Edwards, P.K., (1977), 'A Critique of the Kerr-Siegel Hypothesis of Strikes and the Isolated Mass: A Study of the Falsification of Sociological Knowledge', *Sociological Review*, 25(3):551-574.

EEO Trust, (1992), *Making the Most of a Diverse Workforce*, EEO Trust, Wellington.

Ehrenberg, R.G. and G.T. **Milkovich**, (1987), 'Compensation and Firm Performance in Kleiner *et al*. (eds), (1987).

Ehrenberg, R.G. and R.S. **Smith**, (1986), *Modern Labour Economics*, Harper Collins, New York.

Eldridge, J.E.T., (1968), *Industrial Disputes*, Routledge & Kegan Paul, London.

Emery, F.E. and E. **Thorsrud**, (1969) *Form and Content in Industrial Democracy*, Taristock, London.

Epstein, R.A., (1990), 'Liberating Labour: The Case for Freedom of Contract in Labour Relations', Paper presented to *Centre for Independent Studies*, Auckland.

Farber, H.S., (1990), 'The Decline of Unionisation in the United States: What Can be Learned from Recent Experience?' *Journal of Labour Economics*, 8:75-105.

Farnham, D. and J. **Pilmott**, (1986), *Understanding Industrial Relations*, Holt, Rinehart and Winston, London.

Ferner, A. and R. **Hyman**, (eds), (1992), *Industrial Relations in the New Europe*, Blackwell, Oxford.

Feuille, P., (1975), 'Final Offer Arbitration and the Chilling Effect', *Industrial Relations*, 14(3):302-310.

Feuille, P. and G. **Long**, (1974), 'The Public Administrator and Final Offer Arbitration', *Public Administration Review*, 34:575-583.

Feuille, P. and H.N. **Wheeler**, (1981), 'Will the Real Industrial Conflict Please Stand Up?' in Stieber *et al*, (eds), (1981).

Fiorito, J. and W.E. **Hendricks**, (1987), 'Union Characteristics and Bargaining Outcomes', *Industrial and Labour Relations Review*, 40(4):569-584.

Firth, M., S. **Keef** and R. **Mear**, (1987), 'Some Preliminary Evidence on Employee Share Ownership Schemes in New Zealand Listed Companies', *New Zealand Journal of Industrial Relations*, 12(1):23-30.

Flanders, A., (1964), *The Fawley Productivity Agreements*, Faber, London.

Flanders, A., (1968), 'Collective Bargaining: A Theoretical Analysis', *British Journal of Industrial Relations*, 6(1):1-26.

Flanders, A., (1970), *Management and Unions*, Faber, London.

Flanders, A., (1973), 'Measured Daywork and Collective Bargaining', *British Journal of Industrial Relations*, 11(3):368-392.

Forrest, A., (1993), 'Women and Industrial Relations Theory: No Room in the Discourse', *Relations Industrielles/Industrial Relations*, 48(3):409-440.

Forth, J. and N. **Mullward**, (2004), 'High-Involvement Management and Pay in Britian', *Industrial Relations* 43(1):98-119

Foulkes, A., (1993), 'The Culture of Tripartism: Can European models be adapted for New Zealand Use', *New Zealand Journal of Industrial Relations*, 18(2):185-193.

Fox, A., (1963), 'What Does Morale in Industry Mean?', *Socialist Commentary*, March.

Fox, A., (1966a) 'Managerial Ideology and Labour Relations', *British Journal of Industrial Relations*, 4(3):366-378.

Fox, A., (1966b), *Industrial Sociology and Industrial Relations*, HMSO, London.

Fox, A., (1966c), 'Productivity Bargaining', *New Society*, 22 September:446-448.

Fox, A., (1971), *A Sociology of Work in Industry*, Collier Macmillan, London.

Fox, A., (1975), 'Collective Bargaining, Flanders and the Webbs', *British Journal of Industrial Relations*, 13(2):151-174.

Fox, A., (1979), 'A Note on Industrial Relations Pluralism', *Sociology*, 13(1):105-109.

Franzosi, R., (1989), 'One Hundred Years of Strike Statistics: Methodological and Theoretical Issues in Quantitative Strike Research', *Industrial and Labour Relations Review*, 42(3):348-362.

Freeman, R. and J. **Pelletier**, (1990), 'The Impact of Industrial Relations Legislation on British Union Density', *British Journal of Industrial Relations*, 28(2):141-164.

French, J.R. and B.H. **Raven**, (1959), 'The Basis of Social Power', in Swingle, (ed.), (1959).

Fricke, J.G. (1991), 'Labour Management `Trust Relations' as Reflected in Collective Agreement Clauses', *Relations Industrielles/Industrial Relations*, 46(2):447-463.

Fried, Y. and L. **Slowik,** (2004), 'Enriching Goal-Setting Theory with time: An integrated approach', *Academy of Management Review* 29(3):404-422

Fryer, R.H., (1973), 'The Myths of the Redundancy Payments Act', *Industrial Law Journal*, 2:1–16.

Furstenberg, F., (1984), 'Recent Trends in Collective Bargaining in the Federal Republic of Germany', *International Labour Review*, 123(5):615-63

Galbraith, J.K., (1967), *The New Industrial State*, Hamilton, New York.

Gall, G., (1993), 'What Happened to Single Union Deals? A Research Note', *Industrial Relations Journal*, 24(1):71–75.

Gaski, J.F., (1986), 'Interrelationships among a Channel Entity's Power Sources', *Journal of Marketing Research*, 29:62-77.

Geare, A.J., (1976), 'Productivity from Scanlon-Type Plans', *Academy of Management Review*, 1(3):99-108.

Geare, A.J., (1977), 'The Field of Study of Industrial Relations', *Journal of Industrial Relations*, 19(3):274-285.

Geare, A.J., (1983a), *The System of Industrial Relations in New Zealand*, Wellington, Butterworths. (First Edn).

Geare, A.J., (1983b), *Redundancy in New Zealand*, NZIPA Research Monographs, Wellington.

Geare, A.J., (1986), 'An Examination of Certain Aspects of Industrial Relation Ideologies: A Theoretical Analysis and an Empirical study of Managers', Unpublished PhD, University of Otago, Dunedin.

Geare, A.J., (1987), 'Statutory Protection against Victimisation for Union-related Activities – The Case of New Zealand', *Employee Relations*, 9(1):27-31.

Geare, A.J., (1989), 'New Directions in New Zealand Labour Legislation', *International Labour Review*, 128(2):213-228.

Geare, A.J., (1993), 'The Proposed Employment Relations Act', *New Zealand Journal of Industrial Relations*, 18(2):194-204.

Geare, A.J., (1994), Ideology in Industrial Relations, *New Zealand Journal of Industrial Relations*, 19(2):117-130.

Geare, A.J. and **Edgar**, F.J., (2005), Job Satisfaction data collected in 2005 (unpublished) as part of a wider study on New Zealand managerial and worker ideologies.

Geare, A.J., J.J. **Herd** and J.M. **Howells**, (1979), *Women in Trade Unions: A Case Study of Participation in New Zealand*, VUW, Wellington.

Gilbert, R., (1993), 'Workplace Industrial Relations 25 Years after Donovan: An Employer View, *British Journal of Industrial Relations*, 31(2):235-253.

Giles, A., (1989), 'Industrial Relations Theory, The State and Politics' in Barbash and Barbash (eds), (1989).

Gill, C., (1993), 'The Involvement of Trade Unions in Quality: Evidence from E.C. Enterprises', *New Technology, Work and Employment*, 8(2):122-133.

Godard, J., (1991), 'The Progressive HRM Paradigm: A Theoretical and Empirical Re-examination, *Relations Industrielles/Industrial Relations*, 46(2):378-399.

Godard, J., (1997), Whither Strategic Choice: Do Managerial IR Ideologies Matter?, *Industrial Relations*, 36(2):206-228.

Godard, J. and J.T. **Delaney**, (2000), 'Reflections on the 'High Performance' Paradigm's implications for Industrial Relations as a Field', *Industrial and Labor Relations Review*, 53(3):482-502

Goldberg, S.B. and J.M. **Brett**, (1982), 'Grievance Mediation: An Alternative to Arbitration', *Proceedings 35th Annual Meeting, Industrial Relations Research Assn*: 256-259.

Goll, I., (1990), 'Environment, Corporate Ideology and Employee Involvement Programs', *Industrial Relations*, 29(3):501-512.

Goodman, G., (1962), *Redundancy in the Affluent Society*, Fabian Society, London.

Goodman, R.A., (1968), 'On the Operationality of the Maslow Need Hierarchy', *British Journal of Industrial Relations*, 6(1):51-59.

Gottfredson, G.D., (1996), 'The Hawthorne Misunderstanding (and how to get the Hawthorne Effect in Action Research)', *Journal of Research in Crime and Delinquency*, 33(1):28-48.

Gouldner, A., (1971), *The Coming Crisis of Western Sociology*, Heinemann, London.

Gray, R.B., (1971), 'The Scanlon Plan – A Case Study', *British Journal of Industrial Relations*, 9(3):291-313.

Greenfield, P.A., (1992), 'How do Arbitrators Treat External Law?' *Industrial and Labour Relations Review*, 45(4):683-696.

Grunfeld, C., (1980), *The Law of Redundancy*, Sweet and Maxwell, London.

Griffith, J.A.G., (1981), *The Politics of the Judiciary*, (2nd edn), Fontana, Isle of Man.

Guest, D., (1987), 'Human Resource Management and Industrial Relations', *Journal of Management Studies*, 24(5):503-521.

Guest, D., (1990a), 'Human Resource Management and The American Dream', *Journal of Management Studies*, 27:377-397.

Guest, D., (1990b), 'Have British Workers Been Working Harder in Thatcher's Britain? A Re-consideration of the Concept of Effort', *British Journal of Industrial Relations*, 28(3):293-312.

Guest, D., (1991), 'Personnel Management: The End of Orthodoxy', *British Journal of Industrial Relations*, 29(2):149-175.

Guillebaud, C.W., (1970), *The Role of the Arbitrator in Industrial Wage Disputes*, James Nisbet, Welwyn.

Gunderson, M. and W.C. **Riddell**, (1988), *Labour Market Economics*, McGraw-Hill Ryerson, Toronto.

Haberfeld, Y. and Y. **Shenhav**, (1990), 'Are Women and Blacks Closing the Gap? Salary Discrimination in American Science during the 1970s and 1980s', *Industrial and Labour Relations Review*, 44(1):68-82.

Hall, D.T. and K.E. **Nougaim**, (1968), 'An Examination of Maslow's Need Hierarchy in an Organisational Setting', *Organisational Behaviour and Human Performance*, 3:12-35.

Hammer, T.H., S.C. **Currall** and Robert N. **Stern**, (1991), 'Worker Representation on Boards of Directors', *Industrial Labour Relations Review*, 44(4):661-680.

Hancock, **Report** (1985): Committee of Review into Australia Industrial Relations Law and Systems, *Report*, AGPS, Canberra.

Handy, C.B., (1976), *Understanding Organisations*, Penguin, Harmondsworth.

Handy, L.J., (1968), 'Absenteeism and Attendance in the British Coal-Mining Industry', *British Journal of Industrial Relations*, 6(1):27-50.

Harbridge, R., (1990), 'Flexibility in collective wage bargaining in New Zealand: facts and folklore', *New Zealand Journal of Industrial Relations*, 15(3):241-250.

Harbridge, R. and P. **Kiely**, (1998), 'The Rise and Fall of Judicial Activism', *Employment Law Bulletin*, 8:60

Harbridge, R. and S. **Webber**, (1987), 'Trends in Official Union Membership: 1983–1985', *New Zealand Journal of Industrial Relations*, 12(2):81-87.

Hare, A.E.C., (1943), *Workers Councils in New Zealand*, Victoria University College, Wellington.

Hare, A.E.C., (1946), *Report on Industrial Relations in New Zealand*, Victoria University College, Wellington.

Harre, L., (1999), 'Why Collective Bargaining? The Alliance View', *New Zealand Journal of Industrial Relations*, 24(2):181-196.

Hauck, V.E. and T.G. **Pearce**, (1992), 'Sexual Harassment and Arbitration', *Labour Law Journal*, 43(1):31-39.

Haynes, P., P. **Boxall** and K. **Macky,** (2005), 'Non-Union Voice and the Effectiveness of joint Consultation in New Zealand', *Economic and Industrial Democracy*, 26(2):227-254

Herman, E.E., A. **Kuhn** and R.L. **Seeber**, (1987), *Collective Bargaining and Labour Relations*, Prentice-Hall, Englewood Cliffs.

Herzberg, F., (1964), 'The Motivation-Hygiene Concept and Problems of Manpower', *Personnel Administration*, 27:3-7.

Herzberg, F., (1966), *Work and the Nature of Man*, World Publishing Co., Chicago.

Herzberg, F., B. **Mausner** and B. **Snyderman**, (1959), *The Motivation to Work*, Wiley, New York.
Hickey, P.H., (1925), *'Red' Fed. Memoirs*, Wellington Media Collective, Wellington.
Hicks, J.R., (1932), *The Theory of Wages*, Macmillan, London.
Hill, C. and P. **Brosnan**, (1983), 'Who Cares About Industrial Relations?', *Management*, August: 74.
Hill, S., (1991), 'Why Quality Circles Failed, but Total Quality Management Might Succeed', *British Journal of Industrial Relations*, 29(4):541-568.
Hince, K., and R. **Harbridge**, (1994), 'The Employment Contracts Act: An Interim Assessment', *New Zealand Journal of Industrial Relations*, 19(3):235-255.
Hodgetts, R.M., (1975), *Management: Theory, Process and Practice*, W.B. Saunders, Philadelphia.
Hodgson, P., (1999), 'Labour's Labour Relations', *New Zealand Journal of Industrial Relations*, 24(2):173-180.
Holden, L.T., (1976), 'Final Offer Arbitration in Massachusetts: One Year Later', *Arbitration Journal*, 31(1):26-35.
Holdsworth, W.J., (1987), *Advocacy and Negotiation in Industrial Relations*, Law book Company, Sydney.
Hood, C., (1991), A Public Management for All Seasons, *Public Administration*, 74:9-32.
Horner, J., (1974), *Studies in Industrial Democracy*, Victor Gollancz, London.
Horwitz, F., (1991), HRM: An Ideological Perspective, *International Journal of Manpower – The Best of Strategic Human Resource Management: Part 2*, 12(6):2-9.
Howard, W.A. and P.A. **Riach**, (1971), 'Productivity Bargaining in the Public Sector', *Public Administration*, 30(2):117-134.
Howells, J.M,. (1980), 'New Zealand', in R. Blanpain (ed.), 1980.
Howells, J.M. and S.H. **Cathro**, (1986), *Mediation in New Zealand*, Dunmore Press, Palmerston North.
Hunter, L.C., (1964), 'Productivity Agreements', *Scottish Journal of Political Economy*, 11:260-286.
Hyman, P., (1988), 'Equal Pay for Work of Equal Value – Job Evaluation Issues', *New Zealand Journal of Industrial Relations*, 13(3):237-255.
Hyman, P., (1993), 'Equal Pay for Women after the Employment Contracts Act: Legislation and Practice – the Emperor with no Clothes', *New Zealand Journal of Industrial Relations*, 18(1):44-57.
Hyman, R., (1972), *Strikes*, Fontana, London.
Hyman, R., (1975), *Industrial Relations: A Marxist Introduction*, Macmillan, London.
Hyman, R., (1978), 'Pluralism, Procedural Consensus and Collective Bargaining', *British Journal of Industrial Relations*, 16(1):16-40.
Hyman, R., (1982), 'A Review Symposium', *Industrial Relations*, 21(1):100-114.
I.L.O., (1994), 'Complaint against the Government of New Zealand', Report.
Ingram, P.N., D. **Metcalfe** and J. **Wadsworth**, (1993), 'Strike Incidence in British Manufacturing in the 1980s', *Industrial and Labour Relations Review*, 46(4):704-717.
Ironside, M. and R. **Seifert**, (2002), 'Changes in the Employment Conditions and

Labour Processes of Selected Public Sector Employees Resulting From the Implementation of Neo-Liberal Reforms in the UK: A Model and an Assessment of the Evidence, Published Paper', *Celebrating Excellence: The Proceedings of the 16th AIRAANZ Conference*, 1:263-272.

Isaac, J.E., (1958), 'The Prospects for Collective Bargaining in Australia', *Economic Record*, 34:347-361.

Isaac, J.E., (1991), 'The Arbitration Commission: Prime Mover or Facilitator?', in Savery and Dufty, (eds), (1991).

Jackson, M., (1977), *Industrial Relations*, Croon Helm, London.

Jacobi, O., *et al*, (1992), 'Germany: Co-determining the Future?' in Ferner and Hyman, (eds), 1992.

Jacoby, S.M., (1993), 'Review Symposium', *Industrial and Labour Relations Review*, 46(2):399-403.

Jarrell, S.B. and T.D. **Stanley**, (1990), 'A Meta-Analysis of the Union–Nonunion Wage Gap', *Industrial and Labour Relations Review*, 44(1):54-67.

Jewson, N. and D. **Mason**, (1986), 'The Theory and Practice of Equal Opportunities Policies: Liberal and Radical Approaches', *Sociological Review*, 34(1):307-334.

Jones, A., (1992), 'What were we afraid of? The Employment Contracts Act – the Past, the Present, the Future', Unpublished Paper, Wellington.

Jones, K. and J. **Golding**, (1966), *Productivity Bargaining*, Fabian Research Series 257.

Jonung, C. and I. **Persson**, (1993), 'Women and Market Work', *Work, Employment and Society*, 7(2):259-274.

Juravich T., H. **Harris** and A. **Brooks**, (1993), 'Mutual Gains? Labour and Management Evaluate their Employee Involvement Programs', *Journal of Labour Research*, 14(2):165-185.

Kahn, H.R., (1964), *Repercussions of Redundancy*, George Allen & Unwin, London.

Kassalow, E.M., (1988), 'Concession Bargaining: Towards New Roles for American Unions and Managers', *International Labour Review*, 127(5):573-592.

Katz, H.C., (1993), 'The Decentralization of Collective Bargaining: A Literature Review and Comparative Analysis', *Industrial and Labour Relations Review*, 47(1):3-22.

Katz, H.C., T.A. **Kochan** and K.R. **Gobeille**, (1983), 'Industrial Relations Performance, Economic Performance and QWL Programs,' *Industrial Labour Relations Review,* 37(1):3-17

Kaufman, B.E., (1983), 'The Determinants of Strikes over Time and Across Industries', *Journal of Labour Research*, 4(2):159-175.

Kaufman, B.E., (1992), 'Research on Strike Models' in Lewin *et al* (eds), (1992).

Kaufman, B.E., (1993), *The Origins and Evolution of the Field of Industrial Relations*, I.L.R. Press, Cornell

Kaufman, B.E., (2002), 'The Future of US Private Sector Unionism', in Bennett and Kaufman (eds), (2002a).

Kaufman, B.E., (ed.), (2004a), *Theoretical Perspectives on Work and the Employment Relationship*, LRRA, Champaign, Illinois.

Kaufman, B.E., (2004b), *The Global Evolution of Industrial Relations*, ILO, Geneva.

Kaufman, B.E., (2004c), 'Employment Relations and the Employment Relations System: A guide to Theorizing', in Kaufman (ed.), (2004b).

Keating, E.J., (1974), Trade Unionism in State Organisations', in Howells *et al* (eds).

Kelly, J. and C. **Kelly**, (1991), 'Them and Us: Social Psychology and the New Industrial Relations', *British Journal of Industrial Relations*, 29(1):25-48.

Kerr, C., (1964), *Labour and Management in Industrial Society*, Doubleday, New York.

Kerr, C. and A. **Siegel**, (1954), 'The Inter-industry Prosperity to Strike – An International Comparison', in Kornhauser *et al*, (eds), (1954).

Kiely, P. and S. **Langton**, (1994), 'The Health and Safety in Employment Act 1992 – An Overview', *New Zealand Journal of Industrial Relations*, 19(2):195-211.

Kirkbride, P.S. (1985), 'The Concept of Power: A Lacuna in Industrial Relations Theory', *Journal of Industrial Relations*, 27(3):265-282.

Kirkbride, P.S. (1987), 'Bargaining Power and Industrial Relations', *Personnel Review*, 16(2):3-11.

Kirkland, L., (1986), 'It Has All Been Said Before …' in Lipset, (ed.), (1986).

Kleiner, M.M. et al, (eds), (1987), *Human Resources and the Performance of the Firm*, IRRA, Wisconsin.

Knight, K.G., (1989), 'Labour Productivity and Strike Activity in British Manufacturing Industries: Some Quantitative Evidence', *British Journal of Industrial Relations*, 27(3):365-374.

Kniveton, B. and B. **Towers**, (1978), *Training for Negotiating*, Business Books, London.

Knowles, K.G.J.C., (1954), 'Strike-Proneness and its Determinants', *American Journal of Sociology*, 60(3):213-229.

Kochan, T.A. (1980), *Collective Bargaining and Industrial Relations*, Irwin, Harwood Illinois.

Kochan, T.A., H.C. **Katz** and R.B. **McKersie**, (1989), *The Transformation of American Industrial Relations*, (Paperback Edn), Basic Books, New York.

Kochan, T.A., R.B. **McKersie** and P. **Cappelli**, (1984), 'Strategic Choice and Industrial Relations Theory', *Industrial Relations*, 23:16-39.

Kochan, T.A. and A. **Verma**, (1989), 'A Comparative View of United States and Canadian Industrial Relations: A Strategic Choice Perspective', Paper presented at *8th World Congress, IIRA*, Brussels.

Kolaja, J., (1965), *Workers' Councils: The Yugoslav Experience*, Tavistock, London.

Konrad, A.M. and K. **Cannings**, (1994), 'Of Mommy Tracks and Glass Ceilings: A Case Study of Men's and Women's Careers in Management', *Relations Industrielles/Industrial Relations*, 49(2):303-335.

Kornhauser, A., R. **Dubin** and A. **Ross**, (eds), (1954), *Industrial Conflict*, McGraw Hill, New York.

Kressel, K. and D.G. **Pruitt**, (1985), 'Themes in the Mediation of Social Conflict', *Journal of Social Issues*, 41(2):179-198.

Kristol, I., (1973), 'Job Satisfaction: Daydream or Alienation', *American Federationist*, 80(2):11-12.

Kuriloff, A.H. (1963), 'An Experiment in Management – Putting Theory Y to the Test', *Personnel*, 40(6):8-17.

Laffer, K., (1968), 'Industrial Relations, Its Teaching and Scope: An Australian Experience', *Bulletin of the Institute for Labour Studies*, 5:9-26.

Laflamme, G., (1994), 'A Half Century of Industrial Relations at Université Laval', *Relations Industrielles/Industrial Relations*, 49(1):6-8.

Landsberger, H.A., (1985), *Hawthorne Revisited*, Cornell University, Ithaca.

Lawler, J.J., (1990) *Unionisation and Deunionisation*, Columbia, S.C., University of South Carolina Press.

Lawler, E.E., (1994), 'Total Quality Management and Employee Involvement: Are They Compatible?', *Academy of Management Executive*, 8(1):68-76.

Lawler, E.E. and J.L. **Suttle**, (1972), 'A Causal Correlational Test of the Hierarchy Concept', *Organisational Behaviour and Human Performance*, 7:265-287.

Lesieur, F., (ed.), (1968), *The Scanlon Plan – a Frontier in Labour Management Cooperation*, MIT Press, Mass.

Lever-Tracy, C., (1990), 'Fordism Transformed? Employee Involvement and Workplace Industrial Relations at Ford', *Journal of Industrial Relations*, 32(2):179-196.

Lewicki, R.J. and J.A. **Litterer**, (1985), *Negotiation*, Irwin, Homewood, Illinois.

Lewin, D., (1987), 'Industrial Relations as a Strategic Variable', in Kleiner, *et al.* (eds), (1987).

Lewin, D., D.S. **Mitchell** and P.D. **Sherer**, (eds), (1992), *Research Frontiers in Industrial Relations and Human Resources*, IRRA, Madison, Wisconsin.

Lindestad, H. and J. **Norstedt**, (1973), *Autonomous Groups and Paymentless Results*, Swedish Employers' Confederation, Stockholm.

Lipset, S.M. (ed.), (1986), *Unions in Transition: Entering the Second Century*, Institute for Contemporary Studies, San Francisco.

Lipsig-Mumme, C, (1989), 'Canadian and American Unions Respond to Economic Crisis', *Journal of Industrial Relations*, 31(2):229-256.

Livy, B. (1975), *Job Evaluation*, Allen and Unwin, London.

Locke, E.A., (1970), 'Job Satisfaction and Job Performance: A Theoretical Analysis', *Organisational Behaviour and Human Performance*, 5:484-500.

Locke, E. and G. **Latham**, (1990). *A Theory of Goal Setting and Task Performance*, Prentice-Hall, Englewood Cliffs, New Jersey.

Lockwood, D., (1958), *The Blackcoated Worker*, Allen and Unwin, London.

Lumley, R., (1973), *White-Collar Unionism in Britain*, Methuen, London.

Lund, J. and C.L. **Maranto**, (1996), '*Public Sector Law: An Update*' in Belman *et al* (eds).

Lynn, M.L. and J. **Brister**, (1989), 'Trends in Unions Organising Issues and Tactics', *Industrial Relations*, 28(1):104-113.

Mabry, B.D., (1966), *Labour Relations and Collective Bargaining*, Ronald Press, New York.

McAndrew, I., (1992), 'The Structure of Bargaining under the Employment Contracts Act', *New Zealand Journal of Industrial Relations*, 17(3):259-282.

McAndrew, I., J. **Morton**, and A.J **Geare**, (2004), 'The Employment Institutions' in Rasmussen, (ed.), (2004).

McConnell, S., (1990), 'Cyclical Fluctuations in Strike Activity', *Industry and Labour Relations Review*, 44(1):130–143.

McEvoy, S.A., (1992), 'Fat Chance: Employment Discrimination against the Overweight', *Labour Law Journal*, 43(1):3-14.

Macfie, R., (1992), 'Employers' use of Lockouts under the Employment Contracts Act 1991: A New Balance of Power?' *New Zealand Journal of Industrial Relations*, 17(3):319-332.

McGregor, D., (1957), 'An Uneasy Look at Performance Appraisal', *Harvard Business Review*, 35(3):89-94.

McGregor, D., (1960), *The Human Side of Enterprise*, McGraw-Hill, New York.

McHugh, R., (1991), 'Productivity Effects of Strikes in Structural Non-Strike Industries', *Industrial and Labour Relations Review*, 44(4):722-732.

Mankidy, J. *et al*, (1994), 'Disciplinary Rules and Procedures', *Occasional Paper 9*, ILO, Geneva.

March, J.G. and H.A. **Simon**, (1958), *Organisations*, Wiley, New York.

Marchington, M. & I. **Grugulis** (2000), 'Best practice human resource management: perfect opportunity or dangerous illusion?', *International Journal of Human Resource Management*, 11,6:1104-1124.

Marsden, D., (1983), 'Wage Structure', in Bain, (ed.), 1983.

Marsden, R., (1982), 'Industrial Relations: A Critique of Empiricism', *Sociology*, 16(2):232-250.

Martin, R., (1981), 'Power' in Thomson and Warner, (eds), (1981).

Maslow, A., (1943), 'A Theory of Human Motivation', *Psychological Review*, 50:370-396.

Maslow, A., (1954), *Motivation and Personality*, Harper, New York.

Maslow, A., (1965), *Eupsychian Management*, Dorsey, Illinois.

Mason, B. and P. **Bain**, (1991), 'Trade Union Recruitment Strategies: Facing the 1990s', *Industrial Relations Journal*, 22(1):36-45.

Mason, B. and P. **Bain**, (1993), 'The Determinants of Trade Union Membership in Britain: A Survey of the Literature', *Industrial and Labour Relations Review*, 46(2):332-351.

Mathieson, D.L., (1970), *Industrial Law in New Zealand*, Wellington, Sweet and Maxwell.

May, R., **Walsh**, P. & **Otto**, C., (2003), 'Unions and Union Membership in New Zealand; Annual Review for 2003', Victoria University Industrial Relations Centre

Mayo, E., (1933), *The Human Problems of an Industrial Civilisation*, Macmillan, New York.

Mayo, E., (1947), *The Social Problems of an Industrial Civilisation*, Harvard University Press, Boston.

Maxwell, (1953), *Maxwell on Interpretation of Statutes*, Sweet and Maxwell, London, 10th Edition (First Published 1875).

Miliband, R., (1973), *The State in Capitalist Society*, Quartet Books, London.

Mitchnick, M.G., (1993), 'Recent Developments in Compulsory Unionism', *International Labour Review*, 132(4):453-468.

Mulgan, R., (1993), 'A Pluralist Analysis of the New Zealand State', in Roper and Rudd, (eds), (1993).

Musashi, M., (1982), *The Book of Five Rings*, (Translated by Nihon Services Corporation from a seventeenth-century manuscript), Bantam, New York.

Nakano, S., (1999), 'Management Views of European Works Councils: A Preliminary Survey of Japanese Multinationals', *European Journal of Industrial Relations*, 5(3):307-326.

Neumark, D. and W. **Wascher**, (1992), 'Employment Effects of Minimum and sub-minimum Wages: Panel Data on State Minimum Wage Laws', *Industrial and Labour Relations Review*, 46(1):55-81.

New Zealand Business Roundtable, (1986), *A Submission in response to the Green Paper Industrial Relations a Framework for Review*, NZBR, Wellington.

New Zealand Business Roundtable, (1989), *Review of the operation of the Labour Relations Act in the 1988/9 Wage Round*, NZBR, Wellington.

New Zealand Business Roundtable, (1990), *Unemployment: Realities and Illusions*, NZBR, Auckland.

New Zealand Business Roundtable, (1991), *Submission on the Employment Contracts Bill*, NZBR, Wellington.

New Zealand Business Roundtable and New Zealand Employers' Federation, (1992), *A Study of the Labour/Employment Court*, NZBR & NZEF, Wellington.

New Zealand Employers' Federation, (1979), *Redundancy*, NZEF, Wellington.

New Zealand Employers' Federation, (1986), *Response to Government Green Paper or Industrial Relations*, NZEF, Wellington.

New Zealand Employers' Federation, (1990), *The Benefits of Bargaining Reform*, NZEF, Wellington.

New Zealand Employers' Federation, (1991), *Employment Contracts Act 1991: Resource Kit for Employers*, NZEF, Wellington.

New Zealand Employers' Federation, (1992), *Unemployment: Problems and Solutions*, NZEF, Wellington.

New Zealand Employers' Federation, (1994), *Response to the Interim Findings of the ILO*, NZEF, Wellington.

New Zealand Official Yearbook, (1973), Government Printer, Wellington.

O'Keefe, V.A.B and W.L. **Farands**, (1980), *Introduction to New Zealand Law*, Butterworths, Wellington.

Opsahl, R.L. and M.D. **Dunnette**, (1966), 'The Role of Financial Compensation in Industrial Motivation', *Psychological Bulletin*, 66(2):94-119.

Otago Daily Times, 20 April 1974.

Ozaki, M., (1987a), 'Labour Relations in the Public Service 1. Methods of Determining Employment Conditions', *International Labour Review*, 126(3):277-299.

Paish, F.W., (1969), 'Demand and Cost Inflation', in Ball and Doyle, (eds), 1969.

Parkes, K.R., (1987), 'Relative Weight, Smoking, and Mental Health as Predictors of Sickness and Absence from Work', *Journal of Applied Psychology*, 72(2):275-286.

Patten, T.H., (1971), *Manpower Planning and the Development of Human Resources*, Wiley, New York.

Paul, J.T., (1939), *Our Majority: and the After Years 1889–1939*, Dunedin Tailoresses Union, Dunedin.

Payne, S.L. and R.F. **Wayland**, (1999), 'Ethical Obligation and Diverse Values Assumption in HRM', *Manpower*, 20(5):297-315.

Paynter, W., (1972), 'Is there a Future for Conciliation and Arbitration?' *Personnel Management*, December: 18-21.

Pelling, H., (1976), *A History of British Trade Unionism*, Pelican, Harmondsworth.

Perigoe, J.R., (1973), 'Does Final Offer Selection Offer a Strike Alternative?', *Canadian Personnel and Industrial Relations Journal*, 20(1):30-31.

Perline, M.M. and David J. **Poynter**, (1990), 'Union and Management Perceptions of Managerial Prerogatives', *British Journal of Industrial Relations*, 28(2):179-196.

Perlman, S., (1928), *A Theory of the Labour Movement*, Macmillan, New York.

Petty, M.M., G.W. **McGee** and J.W. **Cavendar**, (1984), 'A Meta-Analysis of the Relationships Between Individual Job Satisfaction and Individual Performance', *Academy of Management Review*, 9(4):712-721.

Pfeffer, J., (1992), *Managing with Power*, Harvard Business School Press, Boston.

Phelps Brown, E.H., (1962), *The Economics of Labour*, Yale University, New Haven.

Phillips, A., (1958), 'The Relation between Unemployment and the Rate of Change of Money Wage Rates in the United Kingdom, 1861–1957', *Economica*, 25:283-299.

Phillips, V., (1994), 'Tracking Mediator Behaviour: An Initial Investigation', *New Zealand Journal of Industrial Relations*, 19(1):75-84.

Piore, M.J., (1986), 'Perspectives on Labour Market Flexibility', *Industrial Relations*, 25(2):146-166.

Plowman, D., S. **Deery** and C. **Fisher**, (1980), *Australian Industrial Relations*, McGraw Hill, Sydney.

Podsakoff, P.M. and L.J. **Williams**, (1986), 'The Relationships Between Job Performance and Job Satisfaction', in Locke (ed.), (1986).

Poole, M.J.F. *et al.* (1981), *Managers in Focus*, Gower, Aldershot.

Poole, M.J.F. and R. **Mansfield**, (1993), 'Patterns of Continuity and Change in Managerial Attitudes and Behaviour in Industrial Relations, 1980–1990', *British Journal of Industrial Relations*, 31(1):11-35.

Poole, M.J.F., R. **Mansfield**, P.R. **Blyton** and P.E. **Frost**, (1982), 'Managerial Attitudes and Behaviour in Industrial Relations', *British Journal of Industrial Relations*, 20(3):285-307.

Potter, B., (1891), *The Cooperative Movement in Great Britain*, Scribners, New York.

Purcell, J., (1983), 'The Management of Industrial Relations in the Modern Corporation: Agenda for Research', *British Journal of Industrial Relations*, 21(1):1-16.

Purcell, J., (1987), 'Mapping Management Styles in Employee Relations', *Journal of Management Studies*, 24(5):533-548.

Purcell, J. and K. **Sissons**, (1983), 'Strategies and Practice in the Management of Industrial Relations', in Bain, (ed.), (1983).

Ramsey, H., (1975) Firms and Football Teams, *British Journal of Industrial Relations*, 13(3):395-400.

Ramsey, H., (1977), 'Cycles of Control:Worker Participation in Sociological and Historical Perspective', *Sociology*, 11:481-506.

Ramsey, H., (1993), 'Recycled Waste: Response to Ackers *et al.*', *Industrial Relations Journal*, 24(1):76-80.

Rasmussen, E., (ed.), (2004), *Employment Relationships New Zealand's Employment Relations Act,* Auckland University Press, Auckland

Raven, B.H. and A.W. **Kruglanski**, (1970), 'Conflict and Power', in Swingle, (ed.), (1970).

Reid, J.D. and M.M. **Kurth**, (1984), 'The Contribution of Exclusive Representation to Union Strength', *Journal of Labour Research*, 5(4):391-412.

Roberts, B.C. and S. **Rothwell**, (1972), 'Recent Trends in Collective Bargaining in the United Kingdom', *International Labour Review*, 106(6):543-571.

Robertson, J.F., (1965), 'The Royal Commission on State Services in New Zealand and the State Services Act 1962', *Public Administration*, 43(1):1-14.

Roethlisberger, F.J. and W.J. **Dickson**, (1939), *Management and the Worker*, Harvard University Press, Boston.

Rogow, R., (1973), 'Final Offer Selection: Some Limitations', *Canadian Personnel and Industrial Relations Journal*, 20(1):28.

Roper, B., (1993), 'A Level Playing Field?' in Roper and Rudd, (eds), 1993.

Roper, B. and C. **Rudd**, (eds), (1993), *State and Economy in New Zealand*, Oxford University Press, Auckland.

Rosenstein, E., (1970), 'Histadrut's Search for a Participation Program', *Industrial Relations*, 9(2):170-186.

Roth, B., (1973), *Trade Unions in New Zealand*, A.H & A.W. Reed, Wellington.

Roth, B., (1978), 'Industrial Relations Chronicle', *New Zealand Journal of Industrial Relations*, 3(2):47-51.

Roth, B., (1979), 'Industrial Relations Chronicle', *New Zealand Journal of Industrial Relations*, 4(1):1-7.

Royal Commission on Trade Unions and Employers Associations, (1967), *Research Paper 4: 1) Productivity Bargaining, 2) Restrictive Labour Practices*, HMSO, London.

Royle, T., (1999), 'Where's the Beef?' McDonald's and its European Works Council', *European Journal of Industrial Relations*, 5(3):327-347.

Rudman, R.S., (1974), 'Employer Organisations: Their Development and Role in Industrial Relations', in Howells *et al.* (eds), (1974).

St Antoine, T.J,. (1981), 'The Role of Law', in Stieber *et al.* (eds), (1981).

Sandberg, A., (1993), 'Volvo Human-Centred Work Organisation – the End of the Road?', *New Technology Work and Employment*, 8(2):83-87.

Schmidt, D.E., (1993), 'Public Opinion and Media Coverage of Labour Unions', *Journal of Labour Research*, 14(2):151-164.

Schregle, J., (1993), 'Dismissal Protection in Japan', *International Labour Review*, 132(4):507-520.

Schultz, G.P. and R.B. **McKersie**, (1967), 'Stimulating Productivity: Choices, Problems and Shares', *British Journal of Industrial Relations*, 5(1):1-18.

Screpanti, E., (1987), 'Long Cycles in Strike Activity: An Emperical Investigation', *British Journal of Industrial Relations*, 25(1):99-124.

Singh, R., (1994), 'Equal Pay for Work of Equal Value', *Industrial Relations Journal*, 25(2):150-154

Slater, R., (1971), 'Last-in Third Out', *Personnel Management*, 13(5):32-35.

Sloane, P.J. and H.C. **Jain**, (1990), 'Use of Equal Opportunities Legislation and Earnings Differentials: A Comparative Study', *Industrial Relations Journal*, 21(3):221-229.

Smith, A., (1976 edn) *Inquiry into the Nature and Causes of the Wealth of Nations (Vols 1 and 2)*, Clarendon Press, Oxford. (First Edn published 1776).

Smith, A.E. (1989), 'Industrial Relations in Canada: A Search for Accommodation', *Industrial Relations Journal*, 20(4):299-308.

Smith, D.F., (1987), *White-Collar Unionism in New Zealand*, NZIIR, Wellington.

Smith, G., (1990), 'Union–Employer Bargaining and Product Market Developments: The Black Coal Industry', *Journal of Industrial Relations*, 32(1):19-31.

Smith, P. and G. **Morton**, (1994), 'Union Exclusion – Next Steps', *Industrial Relations Journal*, 25(1):3-14.
Spillane, R., (1973), 'Money and Power Concepts in Industrial Relations', *Journal of Industrial Relations*, 15(2):198-203.
Stettner, N., (1969), *Productivity Bargaining and Industrial Change*, Pergamon Press. London.
Storey, J., (ed.), (1995), *Human Resource Management: A Critical Text*, Routledge, London.
Strauss, G., (1989), 'Industrial Relations as an Academic Field: What's Wrong with it?', in Barbash and Barbash (eds), (1989).
Sutch, W.B., (1966), *The Quest for Security in New Zealand*, Oxford University Press, Wellington.
Swingle, P. (ed.), (1970), *The Structure of Conflict*, Academic Press, New York.
Sykes, A.J.M., (1965), 'Economic Interest and the Hawthorne Researches', *Human Relations*, 18(3):253-263.
Szakats, A., (1975), *Introduction to the law of Employment*, Wellington, Butterworths.
Taylor, B.J. and F. **Witney**, (1987), *Labour Relations Law*, Prentice-Hall, Englewood Cliffs.
Taylor, F.W., (1960), 'Time Study, Piecework and the First-Class Man', in Merill (ed.), (1960).
Thickett, G., P. **Walsh** and R. **Harbridge**, (2004), 'Collective bargaining under the Employment Relations Act', in Rasmussen (ed.), (2004).
Tolliday, S. and J. **Zeitlin**, (eds), (1985), *Shopfloor Bargaining and the State*, Cambridge University Press, Cambridge.
Towers, B., (1989), 'Running the Gauntlet: British Trade Unions Under Thatcher, 1979–1988', *Industrial and Labour Relations Review*, 42(2):163-188.
Treble, J.G., (1986), 'How New is Final Offer Arbitration?', *Industrial Relations*, 25(1):92-94.
Treu, T., (1992), 'Labour Flexibility in Europe', *International Labour Review*, 131(4-5):497–512.
Troy, L., (1990), 'Is the US Unique in the Decline of Private Sector Unionism?', *Journal of Labour Research*, 111(2):111-143.
Turner, H.A., (1969), *Is Britain Really Strike-Prone?*, Cambridge University Press, Cambridge.
Twining, W. and D. **Miers**, (1976), *How to do Things with Rules*, Wiedenfield & Nicholson, London.
Vogel-Polsky, E., (1985), 'Positive Action Programmes for Women', *International Labour Review*, 124(3):253-265.
Walker, K.F., (1977), ' Towards Useful Theorising about Industrial Relations', *British Journal of Industrial Relations*, 15(3):307-316.
Wall, T.D. and J.A. **Lischeron**, (1977), *Worker Participation*, McGraw Hill, London.
Wall, T.D. *et al*, (1986), 'Outcomes of Autonomous Workgroups: A Long Term Field Experiment', *Academy of Management Journal*, 29(2):280-306.
Walsh, J., (1993), 'Internalization v Decentralization: An Analysis of Recent Developments in Pay Bargaining', *British Journal of Industrial Relations*, 31(3):409-432.

Walsh, P., (1989), An Analysis of the Legislative Process: From the State Sector Bill to the State Sector Act, *Public Sector*, 6:1.

Walton, R.E. and R.B. **McKersie**, (1965), *A Behavioural Theory of Labour Negotiations*, McGraw Hill, New York.

Warren, E. and I. **Bernstein**, (1949), 'The Mediation Process', *Southern Economic Journal*, 15:441-457.

Watts, M.J. and W.J. **Mitchell**, (1990), 'The Impact of Incomes Policy on the Male Inter-industry Wage Structure', *Journal of Industrial Relations*, 32(3):353-369.

Webb, B., (ed.), (1901), *The Case for Factory Acts*, Grant Richards, London.

Webb, S. & B., (1896), *A History of Trade Unionism*, Longmans, London.

Webb, S. & B., (1902), *Industrial Democracy*, Longmans, London.

Weber, M., (1947), *The Theory of Social and Economic Organisation*, (Translated by T. Parsons), Oxford University Press, New York.

Wedderburn, K.W., (1971), *The Workers and the Law*, Penguin, Harmondsworth.

Weiler, P.C., (1990), *Governing the Workplace: The Future of Labour and Employment Law*, Harvard University Press, Cambridge.

Weitzman, J. and J.M. **Stochaj**, (1980), 'Attitudes of Arbitrators Toward Final-Offer Arbitration in New Jersey', *Arbitration Journal*, 35:25-34.

Wells, D.L. and B.J. **Kracher**, (1993), 'Justice, Sexual Harassment and the Reasonable Victim Standard', *Journal of Business Ethics*, 12:423-431.

Whatman, R., C. **Armitage** and R. **Dunbar**, (1994), 'Labour Market Adjustment under the Employment Contracts Act', *New Zealand Journal of Industrial Relations*, 19(1):53-74.

Wheeler, H.N., (1977), 'Closed-Offer: Alternative to Final-Offer Selection', *Industrial Relations*, 16(3):298-305.

Wheeler, H.N. and J. **Rojot**, (eds), (1992), *Workplace Justice*, University of South Carolina Press, Columbia, South Carolina.

Whitehouse, G., (1992), Legislation and Labor Market Gender Inequality: An Analysis of OECD Countries, *Work, Employment and Society*, 6(1):65-86.

Whitsett, D.A. and E.K. **Winslow**, (1967), 'An Analysis of Studies Critical of the Motivation-Hygiene Theory', *Personnel Psychology*, 20:391-415.

Williams, C.R. and L. Parrack **Livingstone**, (1994), 'Another Look at the Relationship Between Performance and Voluntary Turnover', *Academy of Management Journal*, 37(2):269-298.

Willman, P., (1989), 'The Logic of `Market-Share' Trade Unionism: is Membership Decline Inevitable?', *Industrial Relations Journal*, 20(4):260-270.

Wilson, N. and M.J. **Peel**, (1991), 'The Impact on Absenteeism and Quits of Profit-Sharing and Other Forms of Employee Participation', *Industrial and Labour Relations Review*, 44(3):454-468.

Wood, S., (1978/79), 'Ideology in Industrial Relations Theory', *Industrial Relations Journal*, 9(4): 42-56.

Wood, S., (1982), 'The Study of Management in British Industrial Relations', *Industrial Relations Journal*, 13(2):51-61.

Woods, N.S., (1963), *Industrial Conciliation and Arbitration in New Zealand*, Government Printer, Wellington.

Zeitlin, J., (1985), 'Shop Floor Bargaining and the State: A Contradictory Relationship', in Tolliday and Zeitlin, (eds), (1985).

TABLE OF CASES

Reference is to paragraph numbers

E

G

H

I

L

M

INDEX

Reference is to paragraph numbers